AMERICAN SLAVERS AND THE FEDERAL LAW

(from *London Illustrated News*, May 1, 1858)

The slaver *Windward* leads H.M.S. *Alecto*
on a moonlight chase off the Congo, November 3/4, 1857

AMERICAN SLAVERS

AND THE

FEDERAL LAW

1837-1862

By Warren S. Howard

GREENWOOD PRESS, PUBLISHERS
WESTPORT, CONNECTICUT

Library of Congress Cataloging in Publication Data

Howard, Warren S
   American slavers and the Federal law, 1837-1862.

   Reprint of the ed. published by University of
California, Berkeley.
   Bibliography: p.
   Includes index.
   1. Slave-trade--United States. 2. Slavery in the
United States--Law. I. Title.
E442.H68 1976   380.1'44'0973   76-5811
ISBN 0-8371-8796-6

Originally published in 1963 by University of California Press,
Berkeley

Reprinted with the permission of University of California Press

Reprinted in 1976 by Greenwood Press,
a division of Williamhouse-Regency Inc.

Library of Congress Catalog Card Number 76-5811

ISBN 0-8371-8796-6

Printed in the United States of America

To my Parents

PREFACE

This book is a study of crime and punishment, or, more precisely, a story of crime that was *not* punished. Federal laws forbade the service of American citizens, vessels, and port facilities in the African slave trade, yet for a quarter century American criminals greatly aided the smuggling of African Negroes into Cuba and Brazil, and at length even brought Africans into the United States itself. Yet the federal government could do little to crush the trade. This study is concerned with the reasons for this impotence.

The help of many persons has made this book possible. Dr. Brainerd Dyer, Professor of History at the University of California, Los Angeles, gave me numberless encouragements during the years when it was taking shape first as seminar papers, then as a doctoral dissertation, and finally in its present form. My thanks here are a feeble recompense for help so freely given. Dr. Malbone W. Graham of UCLA's Department of Political Science spent many tedious hours rescuing me from blunders of composition, and his generous efforts are deeply appreciated. Dr. Clinton N. Howard of the Department of History gave freely of time and encouragement in reading the manuscript, as well as throughout my graduate study; and for their time, instruction, personal advice, and encouragement I likewise am indebted to John S. Galbraith, Yu-Shan Han, George E. Mowry, and the late David K. Bjork, professors in the Department of History, the late Professor Flaud C. Wooton of the Department of Education, and Professor Clifford M. Zierer of the Department of Geography. And I join with the graduate students of the Department of History in thanking Mrs. Helen Braun, department administrative assistant, for her unfailing encouragement of us over the years.

One of the pleasures of research of this kind is to discover the courtesy and interest shown by archivists and librarians to those who use the materials they have so carefully gathered and preserved. The UCLA Library has provided most of the materials used in this study, either from its main collection or from the specialized services of the Department of Special Collections, the Interlibrary Loans, the Law Library, and the Graduate Reading Room. The number of individuals who have helped my work in these various sections is large, and I regret that they must receive my thanks in anonymity. To Miss Mary I. Fry and the staff of the Henry E. Huntington Memorial Library, San Marino, California, I owe many hours of productive research amid surroundings that are a delight to the researcher. In the National Archives I became especially indebted to Messrs. Donald Mosholder, John E. Maddox, F. Hardee Allen, and H. C. Dixon of the Justice and Executive Section, but workers in the Navy, Foreign Affairs, General Reference, and Industrial Records branches were also most helpful. I enjoyed courteous assistance in the Manuscripts Division of the Library of Congress and in the Los Angeles County Law Library. Other librarians, whom I contacted only by mail, were equally helpful; I should like especially to thank John Parker, reference librarian of the Peabody Institute of Baltimore; Margaret L. Chapman of the reference department, University of Florida Library; and Mary C. Frost, chief of the Reference Service Branch, Federal Records Center, East Point, Georgia. The Wisconsin State Historical Society generously loaned microfilm copies of the *Baltimore Sun*.

And finally I wish to thank the people to whom this book is dedicated, my father and mother. My father passed away while I was in junior high school, and never supposed that this book would be written; yet it could never have been produced except for him. My mother, who raised our family during the years that followed, contributed to the writing of this book in so many ways that I could never list them all.

W. S. H.

CONTENTS

- 1 -

THE ILLEGAL SLAVE TRADE

From the outside a slave-smuggling vessel looked very ordinary. She could be rigged in any fashion, as schooner, brig, bark, or ship. A slaver might measure anywhere from less than a hundred to more than a thousand tons, and could be new or old, neat or shabby. Her design was identical with that of hundreds of honest merchant ships whose sails whitened the oceans from Murmansk to Patagonia. Yet the slave vessel was sickeningly different from the honest merchant ship. Lieutenant T. A. Craven, United States Navy, has described the horror concealed within:

The negroes are packed below in as dense a mass as it is possible for human beings to be crowded; the space allotted them being in general about four feet high between decks, there, of course, can be but little ventilation given. These unfortunate creatures are obliged to attend to the calls of nature in this place—tubs being provided for the purpose—and here they pass their days, their nights, amidst the most horribly offensive odors of which the mind can conceive, and this under the scorching heat of the tropical sun, without room enough for sleep; with scarcely space to die in; with daily allowance of food and water barely sufficient to keep them alive. The passage [to the West Indies] varies from forty to sixty days, and when it has much exceeded the shorter time disease has appeared in its most appalling forms, the provisions and water are nearly exhausted, and their sufferings are incredible.[1]

Probably one-fifth, certainly one-sixth, of the Africans herded aboard ship died on the passage from their homeland to the Western Hemisphere.[2] This floating hell is the cause of my story—but it is not the story itself. The horrors of the international slave trade existed throughout the 1840's and the 1850's, and even into the mid-1860's, only because the laws of the civilized world were flagrantly violated. The slave ship was an outlaw, virtually a pirate, yet she continued to roam the oceans in the face of the navies, the legislatures, the magistrates of the world. Frequently the slaver was an American vessel, outraging some of the severest laws upon the federal statute books. How this flagrant violation of the law went on year after year, and what later generations can learn from this, are the subjects of this book.

In the mid-nineteenth century, central Africa was vastly different from what it is today. Instead of republics proudly taking their places on the world's councils, there were scores of tribes and petty kingdoms, chaotic, heathen, and often at war with one another. Instead of plantations and cities, there were unbroken, fever-infested jungles and squalid villages. And instead of freedom there was slavery, not the slavery of European colonization, but slavery self-imposed by Africans upon one another. Almost every tribe held slaves,[3] and some made a profitable business of kidnaping fellow Africans and selling them for the tawdry trappings of civilization: rum, gaudy cotton prints, cheap jewelry, tobacco, and iron hardware. Human flesh was cheap in Africa; 50 dollars would buy a life, while a healthy Negro slave was worth 200 dollars or more to the owner of a Brazilian, a Cuban, or an American plantation.[4]

Scattered along the fringes of the African continent were hundreds of European trading posts, then called "factories." Many merchants were quite satisfied to export the legitimate products of the rain forest, such as palm oil, nuts, ivory, gums, hardwoods. They should have been content, for by systematically cheating their native customers their trading profits were among the highest in the world.[5] But some merchants dealt simultaneously in what they whimsically called "black ivory," an ivory that never came from elephants, an ivory that was shipped out from isolated coves, sometimes at night and always in haste. Why should merchants not export slaves as well as palm oil? The Africans around them treated human labor like any other commodity, the profits were very high, and the risk of punishment was negligible. The only flaw in the trader's paradise was the existence of naval patrols. British, American, French, and Portuguese cruisers prowled the African coast watching out for slavers, and by 1850 slave vessels escaping the coast had also to elude warships patrolling the coasts of Cuba and Brazil.

Why did the civilized world care what the African did with his brother? What forces impelled governments to consign men and ships to the wretched monotony of patrol duty in the sticky heat of an inhospitable coast line? One was the force of human opinion, the awakening of human consciousness to the dreadful concentration of death and misery aboard a slaver. No humane person could view a slaver with indifference. Sometimes, through wise management and good luck, the crew lost very few slaves; but often the vessel was an inferno of disease and starvation, and usually threw a generous share of bodies overboard to the sharks. Despite this brutality, the trade had flourished for centuries while Englishmen, Dutchmen, Spaniards, Portuguese, and Americans scrambled for its profits; but a more humane age had at last risen in wrath against it. In 1794 the United States, in the first action taken against the trade by any nation, prohibited the outfitting of slavers within its ports if they were destined to carry slaves from one foreign country to another. In 1800 American citizens were denied the right to carry Negroes for sale from one foreign country to another, and in 1807, as soon as the federal Constitution permitted,[6] Congress outlawed the trade between Africa and the United States.

In that same year the movement against the African slave trade won its greatest success. The British had been the world's foremost slave traders for generations—some of the finest houses in Liverpool were cemented with human blood—but a determined group of British philanthropists finally attained success in their campaign against the horrors of the trade. In 1807 Parliament legislated British ships, men, and money out of the trade, and from then on the government of Great Britain was the world's leading advocate of slave-trade suppression. Under its prodding other nations outlawed the trade, and often allowed British cruisers to police their shipping. By 1835 the international slave trade had been legislated to death. But the legislation was more idealistic than some of the people who were supposed to obey the laws.

Unfortunately British African policy had overtones that were neither heroic nor humanitarian. Humanitarianism alone could never have sustained the British government's long and costly struggle against the trade. Another mainspring of British action was that slave-trade suppression seemed to be good business. This suggests that some English enemies of the trade were among the world's most brazen hypocrites, attempting to turn purity into profit by using humanitarianism as a cloak for selfish motives. In unguarded moments English officials sometimes admitted that they hoped to protect the wealth of their tropical colonies by choking off the slave trade to the colonies' competitors. If English plantation owners could not import African slaves, why should Brazilians and Cubans be allowed to? Capture their slavers, and they would have no cheap labor to work sugar fields.[7] As an added dividend, the Africans "rescued" from captured slavers could be put to work in British colonies, a partial compensation for the loss of the slave trade. To be sure, the Africans were free men—but free to do what? As the Royal Navy landed them in British colonies rather than near their homes, their choice was either to become contract laborers; strike out for their homes without money, food, clothing, or maps (with reënslavement fairly certain at the end of the journey); or stay where they were landed and starve. English plantation owners, who had little trouble signing them up, were stanch advocates of slave-trade suppression.[8]

English merchants and manufacturers, the most powerful and dynamic group in British society, saw the chance of great profit if the slave trade were put down. England needed sources of raw materials and markets for the flood of textiles and metal goods pouring from her factories. If the Africans raised palm oil instead of hunting slaves, honest merchants could not fail to profit. Everyone agreed that the slave trade severely hampered ordinary trade. It kept the country in turmoil, and even directly competed with honest merchants by dumping cargo on the African market at low prices. Slavers frequently took unneeded cargo to Africa precisely because they would then not look like slavers. It was better to sell such cargo than to throw it overboard. Slave traders could well afford to sell below cost, for the vast profits of black ivory underwrote all losses.[9]

And so the British cruisers patrolling the African coast were there for a variety of reasons. Their guns and engines and hardy tars were simultaneously aiding humanity, helping hard-pressed planters in Jamaica and Mauritius, and increasing the profits of British merchants and manufacturers. Purity and profit truly went hand in hand. Among themselves the British admitted these things. To foreigners, they liked to stress the humanitarian roots of their action. Foreign rivals were likely to emphasize the profit motive. To rivals, Britain's cruisers were fighting a war against their own interests; the self-appointed policeman was using his office as a screen for his own robberies. Britain's chief trade rivals refused to coöperate fully in the suppression of the slave trade. Spain, Portugal, and Brazil had granted to British cruisers the right to arrest their vessels upon very incomplete evidence, and take the cases before mixed courts where the burden of proof was on the accused, not on his accusers.[10] But France and the United States refused to allow British cruisers to touch their merchant vessels, for they feared that the British intended to drive all competing merchants from the African coast. The French and American squadrons patrolling the African coast were intended quite as much to protect their own merchants from the British, as to capture slave traders.

These suspicions seem to have been exaggerated. Sometimes British naval officers did harass honest foreign merchants through mistaken zeal,[11] but most foreign vessels running afoul of British cruisers really were slavers or "auxiliaries" (a term explained below). British cruisers advanced their nation's trade by discouraging the slave trade, by using moral force (with a hint of gunfire behind it) to make African natives keep their contracts with British merchants,[12] and by opening up areas of the African coast to free trade with all nations, not with themselves alone.

The keystone of British African policy after 1840 was negotiation of "slave-trade suppression" treaties with the various chieftains. These treaties really were intended to suppress the slave trade, but each one also included this significant clause:

The subjects of the Queen of England may always trade freely with the people of _____ in every article they may wish to buy and sell in all the places and ports, and rivers, within the territories of the Chiefs of _____ and throughout the whole of their dominions; and the Chiefs of _____ pledge themselves to show no favors and give no privilege to the ships and traders of other countries, which they do not show to those of England.[13]

This was exactly the state of affairs which the British fought two wars to establish in China in these decades. They were equally prepared to fight to maintain it in Africa; once a petty kingdom had admitted British merchants under such a treaty, it could expel them only at great peril.[14] But the system was fair enough to England's competitors, and certainly drove out the slave trade. By 1848 the British had negotiated treaties with forty-two petty kingdoms, and thereby wiped out the slave trade along almost the entire bottom of the great bulge of Africa. Gambia, Nigeria, the Ivory Coast, and the Cameroons were free of it; the only remaining slave-trade center on the west coast of Africa north of the equator was Dahomey, whose savage rulers protected the business for more than a decade longer.[15]

The slave trade from the east coast of Africa had never amounted to much. Though Portuguese officials in Mozambique occasionally winked at it,[16] or were outwitted, conditions there did not favor slave buying, and even slave traders shunned the idea of bringing Africans all the way around the Cape of Good Hope and then across the Atlantic. Dead slaves were sheer loss, too many of them ruined profits, and the transportation costs of bringing them alive were much higher than on the west African run.

Thus by 1848 the African slave trade was principally carried on from the west coast south of the equator. It centered on the Congo

Basin. The British had a treaty covering territory as far south as 2° 24′, but between there and recognized Portuguese territory, in 8° south latitude, were such notorious slave-trading centers as Loango (4° 39′ S.), Kabenda (5° 12′ S.), the Congo River (6° 6′ S., with Punta da Lenha, some 30 miles up river, the chief trading-post center), and Ambriz (7° 50′ S.). Here also were those landmarks whose sinister names figure in so many accounts of the slave trade in later years—Snake's Head, Shark's Point, and Black Point.

Portugal claimed ownership of all the coast between 5° 12′ and 8° south latitude, and thereby gave foreigners yet another reason to suspect British purity. For Britain refused to acknowledge this claim, asserting that Portugal had renounced all territory north of 8° S. under a treaty of 1817.[17] The Portuguese could not risk occupying the territory against British opposition. As the British did not want to go to the expense of occupying it themselves, this long stretch of coast remained in anarchy throughout the 1850's, while the slave traders reaped a bonanza.

The slave trade had very little to do with Britain's refusal to let Portugal take over the area. The British government's overriding interest was to keep Portuguese customhouses out until British naval officers could persuade the natives to sign free-trade treaties. The British did, of course, want to stamp out the slave trade from this coast, for that would further British trading interests, just as keeping the Portuguese out helped British merchants. But the suppression of the slave trade was secondary. When, for example, a Portuguese warship seized a Brazilian slaver near Ambriz in 1846, the British did not rejoice, but sent off a warning that they would not allow Portugal to exercise any sovereignty in the area.[18]

No one can say positively that Portuguese annexation of the disputed territory would have stamped out the slave trade. Although the Portuguese government was sincere in trying to prevent the export of slaves from its African possessions, it was not conspicuously successful. Portugal lacked men and ships, and British help would have been necessary.[19] But the British had no intention of helping Portugal take over a large slice of potentially valuable African trading territory; it was better for anarchy to reign and for the slave trade to continue. Mock humanitarianism had produced an outcome strangely out of tune with the lofty pronouncements of English politicians. And the United States government knew all about it.[20]

There was yet another suspicious circumstance. British merchant vessels were allowed to carry to Africa cargoes that would have caused the confiscation of any Spanish, Portuguese, or Brazilian vessel daring to carry them. The Royal Navy seldom interfered with British vessels; and although the treaties gave reciprocal rights of seizure to Spanish, Brazilian, and Portuguese warships, only Portugal kept cruisers on the African coast. She was not much inclined to use them against the world's greatest naval power.[21] The British defended themselves by saying that British merchant vessels did not turn slaver. Perhaps this was true; but it was also a fact that British vessels were extensively used by slave traders as "auxiliaries." They supplied the goods that enabled trading posts to buy and maintain slaves destined for shipment in vessels of other nationalities. The evidence on this point was so strong that investigating committees of Parliament had to admit it. Again there was a defense: lawful traders and auxiliaries carried out cargoes so similar that any attempt to outlaw one type of trade would necessarily destroy the other.[22] This was not a particularly good defense, as the honest trader usually brought back African produce while the auxiliary came back empty; but it would hamper merchants if they were obliged to bring return cargoes, and plainly the unhampered development of legitimate African trade meant more to the British than the suppression of the slave trade. The two projects usually went hand in hand, each helping the other, but when there was a conflict of interest, humanitarianism bowed before commerce. This, too, was known in the United States.

During the decades preceding the Civil War, Great Britain and the United States lacked friendship and trust in each other. Still fresh in America's national memory was George III, villain of innumerable Fourth of July orations. Tarleton's dragoons, and savage Indians paid by Englishmen to slaughter and pillage, were well remembered. Andrew Jackson bore a scar given him for refusing to blacken the boots of a British officer. When Americans sang "The Star-Spangled Banner," their hearts swelled with patriotic defiance of England, whose rockets had cast their baleful glare over that heroic flag. Great Britain was, in fact, fairly close to being the traditional political enemy of the United States. Some Americans were frankly hostile to the British government, and most could not look upon England as a trusted ally.

Old quarrels were not the only source of friction. Some English aristocrats were still fond of sneering at the "upstart colonists" and their "rabble democracy," while fervent American democrats detested the titles and pomp, the yawning chasm between rich and poor, which still marked English society. The slavery issue produced more tensions. All slaves within the British Empire had been emancipated in 1833, and the British government thereafter had undertaken the task of convincing all other slaveholding nations that they should do likewise. This created bitter feelings in the South. Southerners angrily lashed back at the British, painting dark pictures of the disasters that would follow Negro emancipation, and hinting darkly that the English should mind their own business and take care of their own poor rather than urge abolition on others.[23] Though Southerners detested the inhumanity of the African slave trade, they peered all the more suspiciously at Britain's African policy. Was it somehow designed to be the vanguard of universal abolition?

England's identification with the antislavery movement did win her some friends in the North. Yet the North was also a leading commercial rival. The American merchant marine was pushing toward equality with Britain's, and Yankee merchants were aggressively seeking overseas markets. Here was another source of continuing tension.

Finally, both nations were keenly nationalistic. Many Englishmen looked upon themselves as virtual rulers of the earth after the downfall of Napoleon, and their smug assurance of superiority was galled by the refusal of Americans to admit such superiority. Indeed, Americans were fond of claiming that their nation was the world's finest. These feelings of national pride clashed on many a deck, as British boarding officers clambered onto Yankee merchant vessels. American seamen customarily accused their unwanted English visitors of arrogance and pride, while British naval officers accused American crews of rudeness and insolence. There was undoubtedly a lot of truth in both accounts.[24]

Americans were particularly sensitive about boarding parties, for during the wars of the French Revolution they had had their fill of foreign interference with their shipping. British cruisers, then French, then British again, had halted and boarded thousands of vessels, and confiscated hundreds of them under interpretations of international law which Americans stoutly denounced as false. Even more galling was impressment, the rough-and-ready draft system that allowed English naval officers to seize British-born crew members from American merchantmen. No greater insult to the flag, no greater menace to the personal welfare of American seamen, could be imagined. Through dogged (and vain) protests against these practices, the United States seared indelibly into its foreign policy the doctrine that American vessels on the high seas were immune from any sort of interference by foreign warships—as immune as if they were a piece of American soil. This doctrine, a compound of patriotism and business sense, was very much alive in the 'forties and 'fifties, and applied as much to American vessels trading in African waters as to those trading anywhere else. The fact that British cruisers claimed to be on a humanitarian mission when they halted suspicious Yankee merchantmen did not make the practice a bit more acceptable, especially when many Americans doubted that the basic British motives were really humanitarian. Boston, Salem, and New York were developing a thriving commerce with Africa;[25] Americans as well as Englishmen had high hopes for the future value of African trade;[26] and the United States government was determined that the English should not harass rival merchants under the guise of aiding humanity.

Some rather harsh statements were being made by Americans about British policy. Andrew H. Foote, a vigorous naval officer just back from two years' duty on the African coast, wrote in his widely circulated *Africa and the American Flag* that

It is contrary to national honor and national interests, that the right of capture should be entrusted to the hands of any foreign authority. In a commercial point of view, if this were granted, legal traders would be molested, and American commerce suffer materially from a power which keeps afloat a force of armed vessels, four times the number of the commissioned men-of-war of the United States.[27]

No power but Great Britain kept up such a fleet. Nor was Foote alone in his suspicions. One of the ablest denunciations of Britain's African policy came from the pen of Henry A. Wise, fiery American minister to Brazil in the mid-'forties. Wise was a Virginian, a friend of slavery, and ultimately a secessionist; but he also detested the inhumanity of the slave trade,[28] and the shame that slave traders brought upon the flag of the United States: "To see . . . [our flag] lift its folds, like the bold countenance of a bad woman, over a traffic at once infamous and horrid, is shockingly revolting, and enough to turn its white into its red with shame." [29] Wise acted as vigorously as he talked; he was no insincere observer of British efforts. But in the course of his action against American lawbreakers, he discovered so many Englishmen involved in the trade that he commented acidly,

It is worse than idle for Great Britain to reproach the United States for permitting their flag and their vessels to be common carriers [for the slave traders], as long as British manufacturers, merchants, brokers, and capitalists are allowed to furnish the very pabulum of the slave trade; neither Great Britain nor the United States are exactly in that blameless position to assume the high tone of casting reproach, or of reading moral lectures in respect to the sin of the slave trade.

Wise charged that British-made goods were used in the slave trade, and that British capital financed the shipment of Africans to Brazil. He accused British cruisers of molesting honest American merchants, and of allowing empty slavers to sail past them toward the African coast because their crews got more prize money for capturing laden slavers, and because the British government had ordered them to "rescue" as many Africans as possible for service on British plantations. Wise asserted that British cruisers did not destroy the trading posts through which the trade was conducted because the posts were jammed full of British goods not yet paid for.[30] President John Tyler sent Wise's charges to Congress in a special message, and thus spread them throughout the United States.[31]

At about the same time Commander John H. Bell, another naval officer back from Africa, wrote *The Journal of an African Cruiser,* which flatly asserted that the English could have broken up the trade by destroying the trading posts, had they really wanted to. He further asserted that British merchants on the African coast indiscriminately denounced all Americans as slave traders, while they themselves supplied the trading posts with goods.[32]

It is a steep descent from the level of Foote, Wise, and Bell, who proved their opposition to the slave trade by action, to the level of Nicholas Trist, United States consul at Havana from 1833 to 1841. Trist, as the next chapter will relate, distinguished himself by his inaction toward the trade. But, as his views were widely circulated, his impression of the sincerity of British officials is worth quoting:

This devotion to the extinction of the slave trade is, on the part of these actors, a mere sham; and worse still . . . they are positively averse to the cessation of what, to the minor parties, proves the cause of pleasant official existence, with a snug pension at the end of the vista; and to the more elevated personages affords convenient patronage, in addition to the more important benefit of a sound and not inconsiderable capital to trade on in the House of Commons. . . . The plot upon the peace enacted here, and upon the other theatres under the same management, is very simple, although its effects are very complex. It consists in getting up occasions for crying out "execrable speculation," "nefarious traffic," "dens of infamy"; whereat the worthy zealots in Great Britain are highly edified, and give their votes accordingly.[33]

As there were no public opinion polls in the mid-nineteenth century, there is no way of learning how many Americans read and agreed with the published suspicions of British sincerity. Bits of evidence suggest that at least some of the American people absorbed these ideas,[34] and the fact that part of the charges were true makes it likely that many Americans distrusted British motives.

It is then no wonder that the United States held to a strict policy of maintaining American rights upon the African coast. The African squadron was organized in 1843 as much to prevent British "outrages" upon American merchantmen as to arrest American slavers, and the State Department maintained in note after note that under no circumstances whatever did British warships have the right to interfere with vessels displaying American colors and papers.[35] This was a boon to the slave traders, who could hardly have invented a more useful situation. The American squadron was too small to accomplish its duties properly; it could not police American shipping as well as the British could have. American vessels therefore became favorites in the slave trade, gathering their cargoes from territory kept in turmoil because the British disliked Portuguese customs duties!

The lesson here is that a criminal traffic cutting across international boundaries must be fought by the affected nations with full faith in one another. When they selfishly try to better their own positions, or are consumed by jealousy or suspicion, failure is likely to be their end. This was the story of the last years of the international slave trade.

Arrayed against these quarrelsome nations was a great criminal conspiracy. No one knows what business arrangements bound the international slave traders together. They were plainly associated in a cartel of sympathy, but there is no evidence that the trade was financed as a gigantic cartel. Apparently not many individuals were engaged in it, but rather a number of joint-stock companies.[36] So many slavers were captured [37] that the business was entirely too risky for most individuals. Newcomers also faced the problem that the trade secrets were jealously guarded. There were no guidebooks telling who sold slaves on the African coast and who purchased them in the American continents. There was no way for a newcomer to find crews who knew how to take care of Africans aboard ship, for he could not advertise publicly for men with that sort of training. He had to join an existing company to break into the business.

The prevalence of the slave-trading company creates a difficulty in terminology. It is handy to speak of slavers, meaning the vessels that carried slaves, and slave traders, the men who conducted the business. But slave traders were an astonishingly varied group, comprising men of many occupations. A few of them actually did trade for slaves; they dickered with Africans, or haggled with plantation owners. The remaining members of a slave-trading company supported these vendors of human flesh. There were ships' crews, including captains, mates, seamen, cooks, slave doctors, supercargoes. There were merchants who shipped cargoes of the necessary goods to the African coast, and the dealers in rice and boilers and medicines who supplied the cargoes that the merchants dispatched. There were stevedores who loaded the cargoes aboard ship. There were ship fitters who made alterations in vessels destined for the trade, shipping agents who gathered crews, and customhouse brokers who got a ship's clearance papers through the port authorities. There were fictitious owners and ship captains, whose only duty was to lend their names to voyages managed by others. There were lawyers who came to the defense of slave traders arrested by the law; and more than likely there were government officials well paid to ensure that the trade did not meet effective opposition. Some of these men—and an occasional woman [38]—had no job but slave trading. Most of them dabbled in it as a side line to a regular business, whether that business was sailing ships or shipping cargoes or arguing lawsuits. This suggests that some of the part-time workers in a slave-trading company did not know what business they were assisting. They did their regular jobs in good faith. Even slave ships sometimes put to sea carrying sailors who believed they were on lawful voyages.[39]

The nationalities of those engaged in the slave trade were as diverse as their occupations. A company supplying slaves to Cuba was certain to engage many Spaniards, and Brazilians and Americans dominated the trade to their own countries, but even a single company was likely to include citizens of all these nations, and Portuguese, Frenchmen, Englishmen, Germans, Italians, and other nationalities as well. Seafaring men, like professional criminals, formed a cosmopolitan group.

Although the slave traders possessed both money and organization, they faced formidable obstacles. Even if local officials in Cuba, Brazil, and the United States could not (or did not want to) detect fresh Africans among their neighbors' slaves, the ship itself was painfully vulnerable. Naval officers cruising against slavers had the strongest reasons, moral and financial, for wanting to capture them, and the slaver was defenseless. It did not carry enough weapons to fight off a boarding party,[40] and its illegal business could not be hidden from even the most casual inspection. Several hundred Africans could not be put out of sight somewhere, as if they were smuggled diamonds or narcotics. The only chance for the crew of a laden slaver to escape was to make a run for it, if their ship was fast, or brazen it out with an honest-sounding reply to the warship's hail, if the ship was slow. In reality, therefore, no laden slaver could penetrate naval patrols that were properly handled and had enough fast cruisers and vigilant boarding officers to scour the slave trade's sea lanes.

Unladen slavers headed for a rendezvous with their Africans were very difficult to disguise, for they carried a large amount of equipment which no honest vessel needed. Passenger vessels were so rare in African waters that it was unsafe to use them in the trade; they would be regarded with suspicion from the moment they arrived off the slave coast. But an ordinary freighter had a galley, and bunks, food, water, and medicines for a dozen men, on the average. The slaver had to carry many telltale items of additional equipment: several thousand gallons of fresh water, tons of rice or farina or ship's bread, many kegs or boxes of preserved meat or fish, and quantities of medicines to treat the diseases common among Africans. Medicines were as essential, if not so bulky, as food and water, for epidemics spread with terrifying swiftness among the crowded and weakened Negroes. Slavers often carried a quantity of disinfectants for the same reason. And there had to be boilers, furnaces, firewood or coal, pails, spoons, and other items in the quantities required to cook and serve large amounts of food.

Weapons, such as swords and muskets, were needed to keep the captives in line. Preferably a slaver should have carried shackles to chain slaves to the deck, or at least should have had iron gratings over the hatches to keep them confined below. But this sort of equipment was so incriminating that many slave traders shunned it, trusting to the crew's ability to keep command of the situation. One of the striking facts of the illegal slave trade was the extreme rarity of slave revolts. Two dozen men, working in shifts and having to sail the ship, were able to bring as many as nine hundred Africans across the ocean without serious trouble. Apparently most slaves were so terrified and so weakened by the time they were put aboard ship that they submitted to the most unpleasant conditions with meek resignation.[41] Still, the feeding and the guarding of the Negroes required slavers to carry crews half again or twice as large as usual, and this was another incriminating bit of evidence.

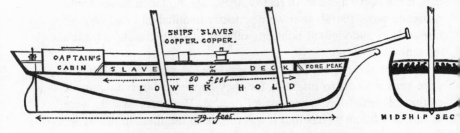

Section of the slaver *Abbot Devereux*
(from *London Illustrated News,* June 20, 1857)

A slaver also needed a slave deck, often considered the most damning of all evidence. The ordinary slaver of this period (averaging perhaps 200 tons) [42] had been built originally for honest trade. Most of its length was occupied by the hold, a large, unbroken compartment measuring 9 or 10 feet from top to bottom. The main deck formed its top. This kind of hold would not do for a slaver. Though some Africans (particularly the women and the children) might make the crossing on the main deck under sheltering tarpaulins, the deck had to support such other activities as working the sails. Most of the slaves had to make the voyage inside the hold. They could not be put in its bottom, like so much cargo; there was no way to ventilate the bottom, and food and water also had to be stored in the hold. And so the slave deck was invented, a middle deck dividing the hold into upper and lower portions, slaves above and provisions below. No ordinary small merchantman needed, or could tolerate, such a division inside its hold. Only by using large vessels of 400 tons and up could slave traders avoid the suspicion aroused by the slave deck, for large vessels had 12- to 15-foot holds

Sleeping position of slaves aboard ship
(from *London Illustrated News*, September 19, 1857)

and occasionally used double decks in ordinary commerce. But large slavers had the disadvantage of concentrating too many financial eggs in one basket, and few of them were operating before 1859.

With all these difficulties, how did slavers continue to roam the oceans? The fundamental answer is that none of the nations trying to suppress the trade was serious enough to employ adequate naval patrols. As naval cruisers were slow and lacked present-day aids like radio, radar, and scouting aircraft, a large number was needed to patrol a coast line effectively. But the much-publicized British African squadron never had half as many cruisers as it needed. England numbered her warships in the hundreds, and yet never sent more than thirty to the slave coast. Four-fifths of this small force were sailing vessels. After the more efficient steamers came into general use, England contented herself with a squadron of twelve to eighteen. With luck, slavers were able to sail to and from the African coast without ever sighting a British cruiser.[43] The French and American navies were much smaller, and their governments were reluctant to contribute a larger proportion than Great Britain. As a result, their African squadrons were still less effective. The Portuguese squadron was no more than a token.[44] Here was the fatal flaw in law enforcement.

But the slave traders *earned* a good part of their success. They did not succeed in running shiploads of slaves through the patrols merely because London and Washington and Paris were apathetic about their operations. They carefully avoided exposing their slavers to meetings with warships while they were full of incriminating evidence. Normally a slaver sailed to the African coast, landed her agents (and sometimes cargo to buy slaves) at a trading post, and then waited, only half-prepared, while the slaves were being gathered and marched to a rendezvous. A ship might wait near the trading post, but often sailed out to sea and passed the prearranged time beyond reach of the regular patrols.[45] Each method had its advantages; the inshore wait permitted a closer watch on the day-by-day movements of the cruisers. In any event, the slave deck and the other fittings might be made ready only a short time before the slaves came aboard. Snatching the Negroes from a flotilla of small boats, the slaver fled immediately, requiring only a day or two to get clear of the patrol zone off the African coast. With similar haste and stealth the surviving slaves were disembarked at the end of the voyage, except when local authorities were complacent about such landings.

While a slaver was waiting for her cargo, a long list of alibis served to explain the equipment she carried. The water casks were invariably passed off as palm-oil casks; if they were full of fresh water, that had no other purpose than to keep the seams tight, or perhaps to ballast the ship. Sometimes water was mislabeled as wine or liquor, legitimate trading articles on the African coast. The lumber was either stacked, as if part of the cargo, or laid out flat with cargo on top and passed off as dunnage. Food was said to be merely for sale, and mess gear, medicines, shackles, and other small items were boxed up, stowed in an inconspicuous place, and mislabeled as hardware or merchandise. Cooking boilers were transformed into "clarifying boilers" for palm oil. Extra crew members were described as passengers. Some of these items, especially the smaller ones, might not be taken aboard at all until the slaver picked up her human cargo.

Mock whaling vessels occasionally entered the trade. Because they had a right to be double-decked, and to have small boats, extra men, casks, furnaces, and bulging larders, dummy whalers were in some ways nicely suited to the trade. Yet not many were used, perhaps because the presence of whalers inshore at any time was suspicious.[46]

The pretense that a vessel was on a lawful trading (or whaling) voyage went back all the way to her outfitting and loading. A slaver's honest appearance was backed up not only by her unreadiness to carry slaves, but by legal papers showing her to be owned by so-and-so (obviously a respectable gentleman) and chartered to some other gentleman for a lawful voyage, et cetera. These subterfuges rarely removed all the taint of suspicion. Some of the "respectable" owners and charterers gradually developed shady reputations, and the cargoes their vessels carried were likely to raise questions. But a taint of suspicion was not enough to stop a voyage. Judges and juries demanded proof for conviction, and often were quite exacting in their notions of what absolute proof really was. The British tried to remove these legal difficulties by treaties that established easy procedures for the confiscation of Brazilian, Spanish, and Portuguese vessels in special courts. But guilty British vessels were still protected by the rigid requirements of proof demanded by their nation's regular courts. The same was true of

American vessels until the summer of 1862. This provided yet another reason that the American flag was a favorite of the slave traders of all nations.

It should have been impossible for anyone but an American slave trader to use the American flag and American registration papers, yet probably 99 per cent of all "American" vessels in the business were actually owned by foreigners. This in itself was a flagrant violation of federal law, which denied registration papers to all vessels except those owned entirely by American citizens. The law decreed confiscation of a ship if foreigners were discovered to hold an interest in it.[47] Thus a vast amount of perjury was committed in American consulates and customhouses. Foreigners swore that they were American citizens, and genuine Americans swore that they were sole owners of vessels that did not belong to them at all. Perjury permitted many an American vessel to be converted into foreign property while sailing under American registry, immune to British seizure.

Or was the vessel immune? The State Department said so, but British naval officers developed some fairly effective tactics to deal with masqueraders. They did not often touch well-disguised slavers, for their crews were not readily frightened; but before the nervous men aboard obvious slavers, British officers acted out a little drama. Scowling at the American registration papers, they pronounced them fraudulent, and declared that if the slaver's crew persisted in claiming their protection, they would be taken with their ship to the nearest American cruiser or to the United States and handed over to American officers for trial. Such a threat frequently resulted in a rapid change of nationality, as the slaver's officers declared that their vessel belonged to no nation. To prove it, they "let the papers swim," throwing them and the American flag overboard. Now under the protection of no nation, their vessel could lawfully be seized by the British. Slavers' crews dreaded capture under the American flag because the United States sometimes punished men serving aboard slavers, whereas the English released their prisoners without trial.[48]

Such threats, however, did not always work. A spunky crew might defy the officer, trusting that the British would not dare carry out the threat because the United States government frowned on seizure of vessels carrying its papers. Sometimes the British did seize slavers and deliver them to American officers; sometimes they backed down. But far more American slavers were disposed of by the British, using threats, than the federal government was able to confiscate using all its apparatus of cruisers and marshals and courts. If the British squadron had been stronger, it undoubtedly could have stripped the slavers of all protection of American papers, for the crews of laden slavers rarely made any effort to use papers to protect themselves.[49] Once Africans were aboard an American vessel, the crew members were literally pirates under American law. They wanted nothing so much as to divest themselves of all connection with the United States. But British cruisers did not meet even half the slavers that succeeded in getting Africans on board. Most of their seizures were of empty slavers at some point prior to the embarkation, as empty slavers spent far more time on the African coast than laden ones. Yet American papers were useful enough to draw many American vessels into the slave trade, and that is the *raison d'être* for this book.

If a soggy flag and papers floating alongside a captured slaver symbolize the weakness of American nationality as a protection to the slave trade, verdicts of "not guilty" returned by judges and juries might be said to symbolize the weakness of the federal government's attempts to enforce the laws against ships and men picked up by American warships and marshals.

Later chapters of this book will go further into this matter, but, in discussing the general means by which the slave trade operated, it must be stressed here that very few slave traders ever admitted responsibility, no matter what the evidence against them. From beginning to end dozens of men were involved in a slaving expedition, some of them certainly guilty, and yet everyone pointed at someone else. "How was I to know?" was the invariable plea. "Everything I did was lawful; how could I have known that others were planning so wicked a scheme?" The registered owner claimed to be merely an agent for the real owner (usually someone out of reach of the law) and, furthermore, had no idea what the charterer had intended to do with his vessel. Did not the charter party guarantee that no illegal cargo would be carried? The captain claimed that he was under the supercargo's orders; the seaman argued that he was under the captain's orders. The supercargo claimed to be merely a passenger. And so the alibis went. If a crew was captured under such circumstances that ignorance was no longer an excuse, its members pleaded compulsion. "Our superiors," or "some Spaniards" who were aboard, "made us turn pirate"; or, "we were merely passengers, and other people were in charge of the vessel." It took proof to destroy alibis like these, and proof was often unobtainable.

And of great value to the slave trade was the fact, too seldom realized, that the slave traders used different kinds of vessels at the same time. These vessels looked alike and carried similar cargoes, yet some of them were honest in the sight of the law, while others were dishonest. Under both British and American law, it was proper to ship goods to Africa for sale even to merchants who dealt in slaves.[50] For lack of a better name, these vessels may be called "auxiliaries," for they were indeed auxiliary to the slave trade, as an essential part of its operations. It was impossible for slavers to carry to Africa enough goods to buy slaves and bring them back alive; a large part of the merchandise had to be carried in other vessels. Part of a slaver's damning assortment of cargo could be shipped out on an auxiliary, and put aboard the slave vessel on the African coast when no cruiser was in the vicinity, and the slaver could carry part of the trading goods needed to buy the slaves. Both vessels would sail with suspicious cargoes, but neither cargo would be suspicious enough to warrant seizure. Sometimes the voyages of a slaver and an auxiliary were not particularly tied to each other, the auxiliary merely landing its cargo at a trading post and its crew never knowing what slaver picked up the goods. But if a particular slaver and a particular auxiliary were teamed together, the auxiliary could be called a tender in recognition of its mothering role. Whether tender or auxiliary, it usually came back in ballast, empty; the main item of return cargo was likely to be seamen put ashore on the African coast after their slavers had been captured by the English.

Apparently not even the slave traders were always sure whether a particular vessel sailing for Africa would turn out to be a slaver or an auxiliary; that would depend on circumstances. If the slaver was captured, the auxiliary might take its place. More than one vessel changed roles from auxiliary to slaver on successive voyages, further confusing any law officer trying to distinguish one from the other. It was extremely difficult, for example, to determine whether a vessel returning to its port of origin with no cargo, or very little cargo, had been an auxiliary or had transported slaves, landed them at some out-of-the-way place, and then been cleaned out so thoroughly that no traces of the illegal voyage remained. Most of the vessels returning from Africa could not have brought back slaves because of the economics of the trade; slaves were high-priced cargo and a shipload of them required a large amount of cargo going the other way in return. But no one could tell which vessels had brought back slaves and which ones had not.

A few vessels could be safely set down as auxiliaries, because they brought back enough stranded seamen to make it plain that they could have carried no slaves on that voyage. For example, the bark *Ceres,* owned by a notorious Brazilian slave trader through an American front man, cleared Rio de Janeiro in November, 1847, and came back in April, 1848, in ballast, with no fewer than 145 white passengers. They could not have shared her 191-ton hull with "black ivory." The 205-ton brig *Oregon,* owned by a reputable Salem shipping firm, went over to Africa in 1848 full of rum, provisions, gunpowder, muskets, and 366 packages manifested in vague terms as "merchandise," and came back with 51 crew members of captured slavers.[51]

But another vessel owned by the same Salem firm typifies the mystery that often surrounded auxiliaries. On March 7, 1846, the 199-ton brig *Vintage* cleared Rio de Janeiro for the port of St. Paul de Loando in the Portuguese province of Angola. Her cargo of brandy, beef, cigars, flour, gunpowder, gold coin, and farina was consigned to a merchant at that port. Her crew was normal, though she carried four Portuguese and Brazilian passengers. Everything was apparently quite lawful. But, in the next report of her activities, Commander Masson of the French brig of war *Le Rossignol* informed the United States cruiser *Marion* that the *Vintage* had carried off more than 400 Africans from the vicinity of Ambriz (a short distance up the coast from Loando) on the night of June 4. Obviously he had not seen her go, but rumors from other sources "corroborated" his report. Yet thirty-two days after the supposed embarkation, the *Vintage* sailed into Rio, flag flying. Her captain reported to the American consulate that he had left Ambriz thirty-four days earlier—that is, on June 2. He reported no return cargo, though the vessel had come back under consignment to Francisco José Pacheco, a Rio merchant who was not above suspicion himself.

So the facts stand, but nothing much can be made of them. The brig could have transported the Africans quickly enough for her crew to have landed them and have scrubbed out the vessel, all in the space of thirty-two days, if the winds had been good. But the *Vintage* continued in the trade between Brazil and Africa, making another voyage in 1846 about which there was no suspicion. The American consul at Rio, who kept a watchful eye on American vessels in that trade, believed her to be honest. Certainly she did not pass into secret Brazilian ownership, but remained in the service of her Salem owners until 1853, when she was lost with all hands on a voyage from the United States to Africa. But her ownership, too, really proves nothing. Probably the rumors about her slaving voyage were false, but there is no proof that they were.[52]

Not only were slavers and auxiliaries often indistinguishable, but undoubtedly honest merchantmen sometimes carried cargoes that made them resemble both. The American brig *Caroline* was detained near Sierra Leone in 1858 on suspicion of being a slaver. The boarding party from H.M.S. *Alecto* found large quantities of rum, tobacco, and gunpowder, well suited for buying slaves; 135 knocked-down casks which could carry water; enough planks and joists for a slave deck; and 40 barrels of bread and 6 of beef. Less suspicious were such items as 40,000 feet of shingles. The *Caroline*'s cargo might well have caused suspicion, yet after her release she traded all of it at Sierra Leone for an innocent cargo of hides, ivory, peanuts, gums, and other tropical products, which she took back to Boston.[53]

On one side there were the executive officers of the United States government, attempting to stamp out the use of American vessels in the slave trade; on the other side were the slave traders, unarmed, but cleverly using every trick that unscrupulous minds could devise. Somewhere between these two forces, the hunters and the hunted, lay that vast abstraction, the law. Law, as embodied in statutes and court decisions, acted as a sort of umpire, determining what acts were punishable, and what rules could be used to determine whether or not a particular individual was guilty.

There were plenty of American laws against the slave trade. Consider, for example, a typical American slaver of 200 tons, brig-rigged, 100 feet long by 25 feet wide by 10 feet deep. As she sailed toward Africa with the wind billowing out the square sails on her two masts, each of the ten or twelve men aboard was violating the act of May 10, 1800. For every man serving voluntarily on board American vessels—as well as every American citizen serving voluntarily on foreign vessels—"engaged in the transportation of slaves from one foreign country to another" was subject upon conviction to whatever imprisonment and fine the trial judge declared, from a minimum of $1 and one day in jail to a maximum of $2,000 and two years.[54] The penalty applied also to men arrested in an American port before they ever got to sea; in fact, the only place where Americans could serve knowingly aboard a slaver without penalty from United States laws was within foreign territorial waters. Once they reached international waters, they had broken the law and were afterward subject to arrest wherever American officials could reach them.

The act of 1800 placed every member of a slaver's crew on the same footing. Two other acts singled out certain individuals for additional punishment, if the voyage had begun in an American port. The pioneer slave-trade statute, the act of March 22, 1794, declared that

No citizen or citizens of the United States, or foreigner, or any other person coming into or residing within the same, shall, for himself or any other person, either as master, factor, or owner, build, fit, equip, load, or otherwise prepare any ship or vessel within any port or place in the United States, nor shall cause any ship or vessel to sail from any port or place within the same, for the purpose of carrying on any traffic in slaves. . . . All and every person so building, fitting out, equipping, loading, or otherwise preparing or sending away, any ship or vessel, knowing or intending that the same shall be employed in such trade, or in any way aiding or abetting therein, shall severally forfeit and pay $2,000. . . .[55]

An act of April 20, 1818, repeated this language, with two significant exceptions. The vessel had to be fitted out with intent "to employ her" in the trade rather than with intent that "she be employed," and the penalty was increased to a statutory minimum of three years' imprisonment and $1,000 fine, with the maximum set at seven years and $5,000. As the "factor" was defined in common usage as the supercargo, both captain and supercargo could receive a far heavier punishment than their mates and seamen, if the expedition was launched from American waters.[56] And if a slaver was deliberately sailed down to Rio or Havana to be outfitted there, in order to avoid the penalty, the act still applied, for the incriminating voyage had in fact begun in an American port.[57]

This was the law as it applied to the men aboard a slaver, up to the moment that Africans were confined aboard. At that moment the dreaded provisions of the act of May 15, 1820, came into operation. This statute, the most severe slave-trade act of any nation, warned:

If any citizen of the United States, being of the crew or ship's company of any foreign ship or vessel engaged in the slave trade, or any person whatever, being of the crew, or ship's company of any ship or vessel, owned in the whole or in part, or navigated for, or in behalf of, any citizen or citizens of the United States, shall . . . seize any negro or mulatto not held to service or labour by the laws of either of the states or territories of the United States, with intent to make such negro or mulatto a slave, or shall decoy, or . . . forcibly confine or detain, or aid and abet in forcibly confining or detaining, on board such ship or vessel, any negro . . . , such citizen or person shall be adjudged a pirate; and . . . shall suffer death.[58]

It is easy to understand why Americans were far more willing to sail empty slavers to Africa than to sail laden slavers away from Africa.

Frequently a slaver's captain was also its owner, and such an owner thus had many penalties to watch out for. The law also provided punishment for owners who stayed at home. The acts of 1794, 1800, and 1818 declared that he should lose his vessel, and the acts of 1794 and 1818 included him within their criminal provisions on the same basis as the captain and the supercargo.[59]

As later pages will reveal, the law in practice was not so clear-cut as it seemed to be on the statute books. Nonetheless, there were enough laws to stop the use of the American flag in the slave trade. But laws do not enforce themselves, and in the 1840's and the 1850's the slave trade flourished, despite the existence of laws against it.

− 2 −

PIRATES AND THE GOVERNMENT

With flaring torches men ran along the decks, here and there touching them to combustibles. As the spots of flame grew into trails, the incendiaries scrambled over the side into small boats. Behind them an inferno broke out. The bark's deck timbers blazed, and tongues of fire ran up the tarred rigging and out on the weather-beaten sails and spars. Foremast, mainmast, mizzenmast came crashing down as a solid mass of fire filled the hold. Months of careful construction and years of diligent repair vanished into heat, light, and smoke, and soon the graceful form that had for ten years advertised America's shipbuilding skill was nothing but a charred hulk, burned to the water's edge. The time was early summer, 1860; the place, an isolated bit of West Indian coast line; the victim of this deliberate holocaust, the American bark *Sultana,* of 452 tons, five months out of New York by way of the Congo River. She was destroyed because she had satisfied the needs of her owners by landing from 850 to 1,300 Africans on the north coast of Cuba, and now it was time to dispose of the evidence.

Dispose of it they did. The *Sultana's* crew, taken into Key West on a fishing boat, claimed to be castaways from another vessel which had burned accidentally. The *Sultana's* hulk was never found, the Africans she landed were never arrested, and not one man faced judge and jury because of her voyage. Indeed, there is no proof that she ever was a slaver, that she ever landed slaves, or that the

Key West castaways were her crew. A reasonable observer must conclude that these things happened, because of a chain of suspicious circumstances: rapid changes of ownership at New York; her sailing to the Congo River under command of the pirate Francis Bowen; the cargo of rice, boilers, lumber, and other suitable items which she carried; the fact that the slave trade from New York was flourishing at this time; and the strong rumors—only gossip, but credible—which began circulating in July, 1860, about her landing of slaves and her destruction.[1] No court would or should have convicted the *Sultana*'s owner on this kind of evidence; but if the *Sultana* may not reasonably be put down as a successful American slaver, then few vessels can be, and no one should attempt to write the history of the illegal slave trade under the American flag.

Yet such a history, speculative as it must be, needs to be written. No study of law enforcement is valid if it concentrates only on the criminals who were caught, or against whom there is full evidence. The criminals who got away must also be taken into account. Such an investigation is difficult in regard to the slave trade, for the victims did not protest to the authorities. Rumors, second- or third-hand testimony, and inferences drawn from a variety of individually unreliable reports are the only sources of information about many voyages. A historian trying to find his way through such sources must be wary lest he become too credulous or, on the other hand, too hardheaded. Anyone who believed all the rumors of slaving voyages would paint a lurid picture of lawbreaking on an incredible scale: of small slavers successfully landing twice as many Africans as they could possibly have carried; of slaving expeditions so numerous that the Africans could hardly have found enough slaves to sell to them, and the plantation owners found work for so many slaves. Unfortunately, this sort of distortion has been committed. On the other hand, satisfactory proof of illegal voyages is so rare that anyone demanding it will close his eyes to most of the lawbreaking that went on. This chapter will attempt to trace, as accurately as possible, the history of American lawbreaking, using the mass of good, bad, and indifferent evidence accumulated by government officials, law courts, and newspaper reporters.

The story begins in 1837, though Americans were old hands at slave trading before that date. Indeed, the trade was so popular that the acts of 1794, 1800, and 1807 had to be supplemented by the more severe acts of 1818 and 1820. The effective action of cruisers and district attorneys finally convinced slave traders that the government meant business, and by 1825 the American flag had vanished from the slave trade.[2]

One lure remained to entice some of Baltimore's keener spirits into a shady business. The trim Baltimore clippers, which had become a specialty of the city's shipbuilders, made very handy slavers. They were fast enough to outrun ordinary British cruisers; as most of them were schooners of less than 200 tons, they could easily be hidden in creeks, and could perform various nautical feats useful in the smuggling of "black ivory." Spanish and Brazilian slave traders paid good prices for Baltimore clippers, and some of the city's businessmen took advantage of this market. They were careful, however, not to violate the law openly. The schooners were publicly sold to foreign owners at Havana or Bahia, and never carried legitimate American papers on their slaving voyages. It was impossible to prosecute the Americans making the sales, for conviction depended on proof that a schooner was knowingly sold into the slave trade. Such proof was never obtainable.[3]

This was the situation until June 28, 1835, when Spain and Great Britain signed a treaty that opened a new epoch in the slave trade. The treaty gave British cruisers authority to arrest suspected Spanish vessels and bring them before mixed commissions at Havana and Sierra Leone. It also included the dreaded "equipment articles"—a list of cargo whose presence aboard a vessel justified its seizure, and made out a prima-facie case that it was a slaver. The prosecution had to prove nothing except that one or more of the items were aboard; if the owner could not prove that his vessel was honest, he lost it. No slaver could avoid carrying such cargo. It included lumber sufficient for a slave deck, more mess gear than the crew needed, foodstuffs not manifested as trading cargo, and empty casks—unless the shipper had posted a heavy bond guaranteeing that they would be used only for palm oil, not for water. The commissioners quickly became skeptical, and owners could seldom talk their property free.[4] Unfortunately, the mixed commissions had no authority to punish owners or crews beyond confiscating their ships; still, slave traders could not afford to lose ship after ship.

As so often occurs, successful law enforcement speedily evoked effective countertactics by the criminals. Spanish slave traders began hiring British vessels to carry hot cargo to Africa, as British cruisers did not interfere with their own merchantmen and the British courts operated under old rules putting the burden of proof on the prosecution rather than on the defendant.[5] And American vessels were soon entering the slave trade to Cuba. Sometimes they served merely as auxiliaries; but many became outright slavers on the African coast, sailing there with legitimate American papers aboard, to the embarrassment of the United States and the vexation of Great Britain.

No one knows how many American vessels were involved. The reports of the British members of the mixed commission at Havana have generally been accepted at face value, a risky procedure. They figured that 16 of the 110 slavers of all nationalities in 1836–1837, 19 of the 71 in 1838, and 23 of the 59 in 1839 were American. But they arrived at these figures by simply counting all American vessels clearing Havana for Africa. They lumped slavers, auxiliaries, and possibly an occasional honest trader together in the indiscriminate fashion so typical of British official reports on the slave trade. They had no substantial evidence against most of these vessels. Yet they may not have been too far off in their calculations, for British cruisers began to encounter numerous American or formerly American slavers, and few American vessels sailing from Havana for Africa ever returned there under the American flag. Vessels in honest trade seldom vanish.[6]

The port of Baltimore, which already had close contacts with Spanish slave traders, naturally supplied most of these American slavers. As before, sharp-eyed merchants sent fast vessels down for sale, but now the price asked was higher,[7] and the sale was kept secret until the vessel was ready to pick up its slaves. At that point the American captain gathered up his register, other official papers, and bill of sale, and turned the ship over to the purchasers; this public sale, which took place out of sight of British cruisers, was enacted merely to satisfy the customs collector at Baltimore that everything had been done legally. But the transaction was as dishonest as it could be. While still navigating under the protection of American papers, the vessel had in fact been engaged in the slave trade, sailing with a Spanish slave cargo, under Spanish orders, and with a Spanish crew. The American captain, later euphemistically styled a "flag captain," had no authority aboard ship, and existed only to give a semblance of American nationality to the vessel. It would not be proper for a Spaniard to show American registration papers to a skeptical British officer; indeed, United States law required that captains of American vessels be citizens.

Many Baltimore owners were reluctant to let ships that formerly belonged to them go off on slaving voyages carrying registration papers showing them as owners, and not every skipper who took a vessel down to Havana for sale was ready to become a flag captain and join the perilous voyage to Africa. As a result, there were many sales and crew changes at Havana, with shadowy Americans hired for the purpose posing as purchasers. They were only front men for the Spanish slave traders, but as citizens they were entitled to own vessels bearing American registration papers. Sometimes the role of new "owner" and that of flag captain were combined in the same man, a most convenient arrangement. These various precautions made the Baltimore shipsellers feel so safe that they enthusiastically pushed forward their get-rich-quick schemes. In 1838 their activity produced a mild boom in Baltimore shipyards, as swift (if flimsy) schooners were nailed together at a faster rate than for many a year. Elsewhere in the United States shipbuilding was in the doldrums, for the nation was in the grip of a general depression; but shipbuilding at Baltimore flourished. Older vessels, too, were withdrawn from legitimate trade and sent south for secret sale; and, in a supreme incongruity, the old federal revenue cutter *Campbell,* sold as surplus by the Treasury Department, joined the procession and ended as a slaver upon the African coast. Along with the schooners (and an occasional brig or larger vessel) went a batch of powers of attorney and other documents needed to facilitate the transfer at Havana or on the African coast.[8]

Set down squarely in the middle of these transactions at Havana was Nicholas Philip Trist, United States consul, a man whose presence in that post at that time was peculiarly unfortunate for the reputation of his nation. Nicholas Trist, who in his less than forty years had studied law and military science, served as a State Department clerk, and in one way or another was closely associated with the most eminent American statesmen of his day, Thomas Jefferson and Andrew Jackson. The question of Trist's guilt or innocence has been disputed ever since.[9] For it was Trist and his vice-consul, John A. Smith, who authenticated the various papers required for secretly selling an American vessel and clearing it out on a slaving voyage in American guise. Every time that the captain and the crew who had brought a vessel to Havana were replaced by the captain and the crew who were to take the vessel to Africa, Trist or Smith placed his signature and the consular seal upon the crew list to give official sanction to the change. Every time a sale was made between an American captain, forearmed with the owner's power of attorney, and the dummy American owner working for a Cuban slave trader, it was Smith or Trist who authenticated the bill of sale and made a notation upon the vessel's official register. It was Trist or Smith who authenticated the manifest of cargo shipped, and delivered up the papers that permitted "American" slavers to sail out of Havana with the authority of the United States protecting them on the high seas, even though the papers were held by fraud. In short, it was Trist and Smith who acted as a cover for the prostitution of the American flag, in defiance of both American and Spanish law. Nor was this all. During 1838 Trist also acted on the side as Portuguese consul, as a "favor" to that government, and the American consulate was thus handling and authenticating the papers of the numerous Portuguese vessels clearing in and out of Havana for Africa. The signatures of Trist and Smith became distressingly familiar to British naval officers and judges, appearing as they did somewhere on the papers of most of the vessels taking part in the Cuban slave trade in 1838–1839. Nor did the British long remain silent about Nicholas Trist; they denounced him as a willful criminal who connived with slave traders.[10]

The story of Trist's life would fill a book; his encounter with the African slave trade, a chapter. Trist does not receive even a chapter in these pages because the evidence about his actions is so ambiguous that his guilt—if such it be—is still clouded by doubt. A few principal facts must therefore suffice. Trist, like most Americans of his time, was a racist; he firmly believed in the inherent inferiority of the Negro, and strongly advocated the slave system dominating his native Virginia. He thought that freeing the Negroes would inevitably lead to racial intermarriage and racial amalgamation. But, although Trist supported slavery, he also detested it. Democracy—"beauteous, lovely, glorious democracy"—could never really thrive in a society with slaves. To Trist the true curse of slavery fell not upon the slave, but upon his master. He felt the same about the African slave trade. It was humane in that it rescued Negroes from the paganism and the cruelty of the Dark Continent; but, by fastening slavery upon the land to which it carried the slaves, it blighted the development of full democracy there.[11]

And what did Trist think of the British? He was fired with nationalistic defiance of them, he despised their mock humanitarianism, he burned with anger against Britain's invasion of the rights of Cubans to import slaves if they wished.[12] He shrugged off the fact that the corrupt Captain General of Cuba received a regular payment, "a princely sum," for each slave he allowed to be landed,[13] for Trist dismissed the laws of Spain against the slave trade as meaningless. They had been imposed upon the Cubans, he felt, only because of British pressure.

These were some of Trist's opinions, and he freely vented them to Englishmen, Cubans, and Americans. He talked glibly, and wrote long, florid, sometimes nearly incomprehensible manifestoes. When acting as Portuguese consul, he apparently had no qualms about giving papers to slave vessels; on the contrary, he derived great satisfaction from so doing, because many of the papers would fall into British hands and would show them the contempt Nicholas Trist felt for their efforts.[14] But, as American consul, Trist had other considerations to weigh, and was not so willing to defy the British. On the contrary, in January, 1839, he urged the administration promptly to suppress the slave trade under the American flag by sending a naval force to Africa, warning that, if the United States did not act, Great Britain would usurp police powers over American vessels. "This is delicate and critical in the extreme," he wrote. Trist also proposed several new legal requirements, aimed at making it more difficult for Americans to sell vessels into the slave trade.[15] Apparently he genuinely wanted his own nation to stay out of the Cuban slave trade, even though he continued to sign papers, change crews, and grant clearances.

Trist did not regard this as duplicity. He did not picture himself as a policeman or a magistrate, passing judgment on the actions of those he met; rather he thought of himself as a notary public, performing certain services for American citizens upon their request. Trist declared that it was a consul's duty to affix his seal and signature to any declaration of any sort which an American chose to make before him; his signature did not mean that he approved of the transaction represented by that piece of paper, or even that he had investigated it, but only that the declaration had been made before him under oath. As he saw it, the law gave him no authority to impound ships' registers, and it was "unethical" for a consul to pry into the contents of cargo manifests. Trist viewed himself as a tool of those who wanted to use him, not as a law enforcement officer. Anyone who reads through the official consular instructions and interprets them strictly must agree with much of Trist's opinion.[16]

But Trist's instructions also ordered him to coöperate with local authorities in preventing American citizens from violating local laws, and to gather witnesses in criminal cases involving violations of American law on the high seas. Perhaps Trist could not have done much along the first line, as the Captain General himself was a criminal, but he should have gathered all the evidence he could against American slavers. Trist did not, arguing that reliable testimony simply could not be had, and that, if it could, he and the witnesses would be assassinated.[17] As other American consuls succeeded in gathering evidence without blood being spilled, the suspicion is strong that Trist simply did not want to betray men who were engaged in a trade he sympathized with.

Trist therefore performed the notarial part of his duties with vigor, gladly pocketing extra fees for the paper work involved in selling American vessels into the slave trade. He almost ignored the duty of gathering information, and made no attempt to establish himself as a law enforcer.[18] Instead he spent his energies carrying on a running feud with the British members of the mixed court at Havana, with the British government, with Alexander H. Everett (sent to Cuba by President Van Buren to try to unravel the truth or falsity of the British charges against him),[19] and with sundry American political enemies.[20] The incoming Whig administration dismissed him in the summer of 1841, with a letter couched in Daniel Webster's most ambiguous language:

The President has felt it his duty, under all the circumstances, to make a change in the Consulate at Havana. He directs me to say that this resolution has been adopted, without his having formed any judgment on the particular charges which have been suggested against you, and to which you have given answers. He desires it to be understood, on the contrary, that this decision has been made upon general grounds of propriety and expediency.[21]

The "general grounds of propriety and expediency" may have been that Trist was a Democrat, and it was time to give patronage to a Whig; or that his honesty was suspected, or that he was incompetent, or that he had become a political liability. President Tyler had not decided about the charges against Trist; that is, he was by no means convinced that the consul at Havana was not guilty of willful connivance with the slave traders. But Trist professed to be gratified with Tyler's letter. He wrote back that he was glad to be leaving his post. He had kept it only for the money, and the worry and the controversy were killing him.[22] Whatever the degree of Trist's guilt, his passing from the scene was no loss to the American consular service.

Meanwhile, the slavers that Trist had helped to spawn, or at least had failed to hinder, had been creating dramatic nautical and legal history. The most remarkable incident occurred in New York harbor. Even the cosmopolitan dwellers of New York were startled on Wednesday, June 12, 1839, when Her Majesty's brig *Buzzard,* commanded by Lieutenant Charles Fitzgerald, came sailing into port escorting two American vessels as prizes. Fitzgerald hoped to have them tried. Not since George III's judges abandoned New York at the close of the Revolution had a British cruiser brought captured American vessels into an American seaport for adjudication. The unlucky pair were the brig *Eagle* and the schooner *Clara,* obviously slavers, and American citizens, their "owner-captains," were held prisoners aboard by Fitzgerald's brawny tars. The prisoners were turned over to the marshal, but the British kept guards aboard the prizes. The excitement increased two weeks later, when the schooner *Wyoming* came into port manned by seamen from H.M. brig *Harlequin.* This time there was no American prisoner, for the slaver's captain had burst a blood vessel and died soon after being told that he would be taken to the United States. Early in the fall of 1839 two more schooners and their captains appeared: the *Butterfly* and the *Catharine,* prizes to H.M. brig *Dolphin.*[23]

These extraordinary arrivals represented what Nicholas Trist had dreaded. The British had simply taken over the policing of American vessels on the coast of Africa. Royal Navy officers, becoming alarmed by the growing number of obviously Spanish slavers masquerading as Americans, had taken several of them into Sierra Leone for trial before the Anglo-Spanish mixed commission. But the judges boggled. It was true that the prizes were full of Spaniards and Spanish documents, but that did not hide the fact that they were navigating under the colors and the papers of the United States. The commission refused to try any of the cases, and the ships were set free. In due course they became frankly Spanish; two were taken full of slaves, and a third was apprehended as it was about to take Negroes aboard.[24]

Thus ended the first act of a little drama in which British naval officers found it easier to capture ostensibly American slavers than to get someone to pass judgment on them afterward. With the mixed commission refusing to act, and no American warships on the African coast to turn slavers over to, the officers decided to take their prizes to the United States and present them for trial before federal courts. Thus came about the little flotilla lying in New York harbor. Some Americans denounced the whole proceeding as an infringement of the "freedom of the seas," [25] but President Van Buren expressed satisfaction at the captures and ordered the district attorney at New York to prosecute the slavers, if he could.[26]

The legal muddle reflected by that qualifying phrase was perplexing enough to make District Attorney Benjamin F. Butler, erstwhile attorney general of the United States, flounder through the cases like a fledgling lawyer. Butler decided that the *Eagle* and the *Clara* could not be confiscated under American law because they were obviously Spanish-owned, and he so informed Lieutenant Fitzgerald, who wearily gathered his men and set sail for Bermuda, where he hoped the British vice-admiralty court might consent to hear the cases. Having let the first cases go, Butler took a second look at his lawbooks and, after sundry courtroom adventures, succeeded in having the similarly circumstanced *Catharine, Butterfly,* and *Wyoming* condemned. The prisoners slipped through his hands by jumping bail. It was all rather ineffective, but the United States had at least put a nick into the slave trade.[27]

Meanwhile more legal trouble was brewing at Baltimore. The British Foreign Office took part by sending a mass of carefully accumulated evidence, which clearly revealed how deeply the city had become involved in the business of supplying slavers. In the fall of 1839 federal officers made several arrests. Robert W. Allen and John Henderson, the *Catharine's* original owners, had neglected to sell her publicly at Havana to an American front man, and the ship's register bore their names when she was captured. Also arrested was Francis T. Montell, owner of the schooner *Elvira,* a successful slaver, and all three men were indicted under the act of 1818. Two schooners being built for the slave trade were seized on the eve of their departure, and the foreign captains supervising the work had to make a hasty departure for safer climates. For the first time, prominent merchants of Baltimore were in trouble.

The trials, keenly followed by the public, turned out badly for the government. Inevitably the defendants pleaded ignorance, and juries of their fellow citizens readily believed them. Chief Justice Roger B. Taney, on circuit court duty, sourly observed the united front of the Baltimore merchants, who eagerly swore to one another's impeccable characters. Shipbuilder John F. Strohm was characterized as a "man of probity," Allen had "good character and high standing," Montell was "a high-minded honorable man." Taney's temper gave way, and when the case of the schooner *Ann* came to him for decision he ripped Strohm's defense to shreds, denounced him as a criminal, observed tartly that public sentiment made it easier to testify for than against the defendants, and blasted the "connivance" at law violations which had brought so much disgrace upon the American flag and the city of Baltimore.[28]

Apparently Taney's lecture made a strong impression upon the Baltimore merchants; or, if it did not, the trials and the confiscation of the *Ann* frightened them out of the business of building slavers. Many Baltimore clippers were used in the slave trade in later years, but only after an honest career in lawful commerce; they had not been built specifically for sale to slave traders. One blot upon the nation's honor was thus removed.[29] This was the federal government's only real success against the slave trade.

While the judicial activity at Baltimore and New York had been gathering momentum, the *Buzzard,* the *Eagle,* and the *Clara* were tossing on the high seas as they sailed to Bermuda. Fitzgerald presented his prizes to the vice-admiralty court there, but the judge decided that he had authority to try only British vessels, foreign vessels arrested in British waters, and vessels claiming no nationality. The *Eagle* and the *Clara* fitted into none of these categories. Fitzgerald set sail toward Sierra Leone, losing the *Eagle* in mid-Atlantic; but the *Clara* survived the winter crossing and dropped anchor at Freetown. The mixed commission there promptly confiscated her, and for good measure decreed that the *Eagle* would also have been confiscated had she still been afloat.[30]

The situation at Sierra Leone had changed. The mixed commission's refusal to try quasi-American slavers had speedily come to the attention of the British government, which sent strong intimations to the British commissioners that they should not hesitate to confiscate "American" vessels if they really seemed to be Spanish-owned. The commissioners accepted the hints, the Spanish members fell in with them, and several "American" slavers were confiscated in short order. Because American papers were now worthless as protection, the secret sales at Havana ceased as soon as word of the commission's new policy reached Cuba. The Royal Navy and the mixed court had practically driven the American flag out of the slave trade.[31]

It did not long stay out, and, ironically, the United States government itself covered its reëntry by the threat of naval force. Though Van Buren had been pleased at the initial British arrests, he and Secretary of State John Forsyth soon realized that they were sanctioning a violation of American sovereignty. The slavers were, after all, navigating with American registration papers. Van Buren and Forsyth lodged complaints with the British. John Tyler's administration took the same position, and Forsyth's successor, Daniel Webster, finally negotiated a settlement with the British. No English cruiser was thereafter to molest any American vessel, even if its papers seemed to be held by fraud. Only American officers were to police American merchantmen. But, to satisfy the British, the United States agreed to station a force of naval vessels, mounting at least eighty guns, on the African coast to take care of American slavers. This squadron would remain for at least five years, and as much longer as the United States wished to keep it there.[32]

These terms did not please supernationalistic Americans, especially if they were Democrats, for Webster and Tyler were Whigs; politicians then, as now, lost no opportunity to criticize their opponents. Typical of the backbiters was James Buchanan, then a senator from Pennsylvania. Buchanan detested the slave trade, as he proved later when he was secretary of state, and still later during his own presidency; but he also disliked the idea that the United States be required to keep a naval force of a certain size on the African coast in order to please the British. He had a disturbing vision of entangling alliances, of tribute money paid to Great

Britain to keep her from seizing American vessels.[33] Tribute or not, the squadron actually had a double purpose. It was there to shoot, if necessary, to keep British cruisers away from American merchantmen.[34]

The African squadron was an unhappy force from the beginning. Until 1859 it never had half, perhaps never a quarter, of the ships it needed properly to accomplish either of its duties. America in the 'forties and 'fifties was a paradise for rugged individualists. It was a paradise where taxes, especially federal taxes, were low, and where opportunities for business ventures were enormous. Its dominant political thinkers fervently believed that the best government was the one that governed least. The results of these circumstances were rather peculiar. There were as many as 6,000 American vessels in foreign trade, sailing on almost every navigable body of water on earth, vessels sent there by the keen business spirit of the nation, while to guard, assist, and police these merchantmen, the federal government normally kept up twenty-five or thirty cruisers, most of them medium-sized sloops of war fit for long voyages but requiring fairly small crews.[35] Only a handful of frigates and no battleships went to sea; they were too expensive for a tax-hating republic. It took hardy men to man warships in those days, for they seldom had shore liberty in American harbors; instead, the fleet's active warships were off on two- and three-year cruises all over the world. Americans hated taxes, but they demanded service. The fleet had to go wherever any substantial number of American merchantmen went, and, as a result, only four or five vessels, barely enough to make up an eighty-gun force, could be spared for the African squadron,[36] which had to patrol 3,000 miles of coast line.

Moreover, the squadron's crews soon discovered that patrol duty on the African coast was extremely uncomfortable. As no one knew that mosquitoes carried fever, no one knew how to prevent it; but everyone knew what fever could do to a ship's crew. If there were any doubts, they were dispelled in December, 1844, when an epidemic carried off ten men on the brig *Truxtun*. The sailors quickly developed a real dread of the coast they were supposed to patrol.[37] The damp heat filled their ships, covered them with rashes, and sapped their energy;[38] perhaps worst of all, there were few places where the men could go ashore, even if they had not been afraid of fever. Men long confined in the crowded little hulls of sailing vessels became desperate. Shipboard song fests and similar jollities helped fill some of the time, but shore leave was what the sailors really wanted. Africa had very little to offer them.

The squadron was based on Porto Praia in the Cape Verde Islands. To the north was the island of Madeira, gem of the Atlantic, beautiful, healthful, full of attractions for tired men in from the sea. Madeira beckoned seductively to the squadron's men; it seduced them from their duty, for no slavers were to be found en route to and from its hospitable shores. Naval officers assured themselves and the Navy Department that it was necessary, for the good of their men, to sail there for relaxation after each cruise on the fever-infested coast line. The argument was unanswerable; and, except during the Mexican War, when austerity was the watchword, the squadron's vessels alternated patrol cruises with pleasure cruises. Undoubtedly these vacations were good for the men of the squadron, who usually kept as healthy as those on other stations, but they did not contribute to efficient performance of the squadron's duty. A cruise to Madeira from Porto Praia took nearly as long as a regular patrol cruise down the slave coast.[39]

The location of the squadron's base at Porto Praia was itself bad. Each summer there was a bad outbreak of fever, and the port was a good month's sail from the Congo Basin. It was not even very close to the remaining slave coast north of the equator. Commodore Matthew C. Perry, the squadron's first commander, chose Porto Praia mainly because it had an American consul who could keep his eye on the depot, and because supplies for the squadron could be landed through the Portuguese customhouse without any special arrangements being required. Perry soon became very discontented with his choice, but could find no better location. He feared that a supply depot on the mainland would kill any unacclimated person in short order, and would spread fever to the ships. Perry wanted to have floating storeships, which would reprovision the cruisers at sea,[40] but the government felt too poor to send such

ships to Africa on permanent duty. As the British treaty system reduced the trade from the north coast, the depot's location at Porto
Praia became more and more absurd. Cruisers patrolling the slave
coast from there spent most of their time simply sailing to and from
the areas where the slavers were.[41]

Thus, of the squadron of four or five vessels, only one or two—
and sometimes none—were actually on the scene of the slave trade
at any particular moment. They could not keep the British from
molesting American vessels, honest or otherwise; all the American
officers could do was gather evidence for the diplomats to argue
about afterward, for the deed had usually been done by the time an
American cruiser arrived on the scene. Neither could the squadron
police American shipping. Half or more of the merchantmen visiting the coast never sighted an American cruiser, and the others
received only the scantiest surveillance. They might be carefully
inspected one day, but if allowed to proceed were soon out of sight
of American officers. The warships could not follow them for long,
as they had many other areas to patrol.[42]

But the presence of the African squadron did effect one change:
no longer could British naval officers simply seize suspected "American" vessels and take them before mixed commissions. Such vessels could now be seized only if they surrendered; that is, if they
yielded to British threats. Slavers' crews often stood on their rights
and defied such threats. By putting the mixed courts out of the
business of trying quasi-American slavers, the settlement between
the United States and Great Britain proved a very bad settlement
indeed. It permitted a revival of the slave trade in American vessels.

Cuban slave traders therefore had an opportunity to use the
American flag in 1844–1845. It was short-lived, partly because the
African squadron picked up three of their schooners, but mainly
because the Spanish government began to take more active measures to stop smuggling into Cuba. As a result, the Cuban trade came
fairly close to disappearing for several years.[43]

The Brazilian trade, however, picked up the slack. As early as
1838 an occasional American vessel had got into the Brazilian
trade; indeed, the *Ann* was being built for it rather than for the

Cuban trade. During the early 'forties an increasing number of American vessels were drawn in, most often as auxiliaries, sometimes as outright slavers; secret sales at Rio de Janeiro and Bahia, and public transfers to Brazilians and Portuguese on the African coast, were the means by which American owners made themselves richer at the expense of humanity. American officials at Rio, notably Consul George W. Slacum and Minister Henry Wise, did what they could to gather witnesses and information about the lawbreaking, managed to get a few Americans and/or their vessels arrested by Brazilian police or American naval officers, and came close to pushing the United States into war with Brazil over the brig *Porpoise*. The *Porpoise* was not only an auxiliary of the most flagrant sort, but also a tender, supplying equipment directly to American slavers, and taking off their American crew members just before the Africans were loaded. The flagship of Uncle Sam's tiny Brazilian squadron arrested the *Porpoise* inside Rio harbor upon her return from Africa, whereupon the Brazilians surrounded her with armed boats and threatened to take her back by force, in order to erase the grave insult to the sovereignty of their country. The United States had no extradition treaty with Brazil, but Wise urged the squadron's commodore to take off the *Porpoise*'s crew by force. Fortunately neither the commodore nor the State Department approved of such heroic (and illegal) measures, and the Brazilians won out. Despite these efforts by American officers in Brazil, and the work of the African squadron, the slave trade was more active at the end of several years of enforcement efforts than it had been at the beginning.[44]

Indeed, in 1847 the traffic in American vessels began to increase sharply, for several reasons. The Brazilian slave trade was reaching boom proportions, as plantation owners got caught up in a mania of expansion. By this time United States naval officers were reluctant to interfere with American vessels. Too many ships and too many men, picked up in earlier years, had been released by the courts. And the American consulate at Rio de Janeiro had received orders that made it easier for American shipowners to turn a dishonest dollar. Consul Gorham Parks, backed up by Minister Wise, had flatly refused to imitate Nicholas Trist and permit the official sale of American vessels to other American citizens at Rio. This meant that slavers secretly sold there had to sail across the ocean still bearing their original registration papers, with their owners still accountable for their actions. No American shipowner wanted to find himself in the position of Allen or Montell, with a judge and jury inquiring into the honesty of his actions; therefore, relatively few American vessels were put up for sale at Rio. But American law gave consuls no right to refuse to recognize changes in owner-ship; protests were made, and the State Department ordered Parks to do his duty.[45]

The result was a marked increase in the number of American vessels offered for sale, and the emergence of a new shipping mag-nate, Joshua Clapp, a twenty-nine-year-old New York ship captain who had only recently been acquitted when put on trial for taking the slaver *Panther* to Africa. Clapp had never had much money, yet within less than three years he became the "owner" of two full-rigged ships, three barks, three brigs, and two schooners. Clapp received a reward from his Brazilian employers for each vessel whose ownership he assumed. It was a perfect scheme. The Yankee shipowner wanting to sell his vessel at a nice profit got out from under any responsibility for its misuse on the voyage to Africa; the Brazilian slave trader got the protection, such as it was, of American registry; and Clapp himself not only enjoyed easy Rio living, but was in no danger of punishment. The law set no penalty for an American shipowner who outfitted his vessel in foreign ter-ritory, except loss of his ship, and Clapp could well afford to lose what was not his to begin with. Other men, too, became dummy owners. Consul Parks did his best to break up the scheme, but to no avail. Clapp and the others had full proof of ownership, which was all the law required. To Parks's searching questions about where their money had come from, they had truthful and unassail-able answers. In advance of purchase, they explained, Brazilians anxious to charter their vessels—"for lawful trade only"—had advanced them enough money on the charter to pay off the original owners. What could be more businesslike? If Clapp later decided to sell "his" vessel to the charterer, that, of course, was merely good business; how could he know what so obliging a gentleman intended to do with it? [46]

During 1848 and 1849 this trade flourished, with seizures by the Brazilian squadron just outside Rio harbor little more than pinpricks against it. David Tod, the new American minister to Brazil, decided that the only way to stop the traffic was to ban all commerce in American vessels between Brazil and Africa; but nothing was done by Congress. In 1848 perhaps one-fifth of all the Africans landed in Brazil came on vessels that had formerly been American; by 1850 the proportion, according to one estimate, was closer to one-half.[47]

And then came the great change. Not a change wrought by American officers, nor British cruisers, but by the Brazilian government itself. It was well known that the Brazilian government had connived at the slave trade, but in 1850 a change of sentiment produced dramatic results. Africans were seized, slave traders were arrested, depots of merchandise were confiscated. By 1851 the Brazilian slave trade was vanishing, never to revive.[48]

The slave traders of course did not give up easily. There was still slavery in Brazil and still a demand for slave labor; prices in local slave markets doubled within a year after the end of imports. Hoping to capitalize on the increased profits, slave traders launched new schemes, centered, apparently, on the use of American vessels. Tod's successor, Robert C. Schenck, wrote the State Department in alarm, urging, as Wise and Tod had urged, that restrictions be placed on the sale of American vessels abroad, that trade with Africa be restricted, that the Brazilian squadron be given a steamer for patrol work, and that other changes be made so that "we can clear our skirts as a nation, and acquit ourselves, as we better might, of the obligations we owe to God and the cause of humanity." Nothing, of course, was done by Congress to implement any of these suggestions.

But the Brazilians themselves took care of the last Americans who participated in the slave trade to their country. Seemingly the last successful landing of slaves was from the brig *Camargo,* which carried 500 Negroes from East Africa to Brazil in the fall of 1852. "Successful" is hardly the word; the brig had to be burned, as there was no place she could be refitted safely, and some of the crew and the Africans were arrested.[49]

There was one final attempt to bring Negroes into Brazil. It was made by the schooner *Mary E. Smith,* which left Boston on August 25, 1855, under circumstances to be described in a later chapter. On the coast her managers packed upward of 400 Africans into her 122-ton hull, and she set sail for the great eastward bulge of Brazil. Ten years earlier her arrival would have caused delight, but times had changed. Wherever the schooner's crew tried to land the Africans, they met hostility. There was nothing more hopeless than trying to force several hundred slaves upon a population that did not want them, and the schooner sailed along the coast, her crew frantically looking for a landing place. Food and water gave out, and the Africans began to die. The ordeal was ended only when a Brazilian warship intercepted the *Mary E. Smith* and took her into Bahia, where her arrival was no cause for celebration. The "moving skeletons" carried off the ship would have outraged even the hardiest supporter of the slave trade. The principal American involved died in prison, other guilty parties were punished, and the debacle proved that the Brazilian slave trade had indeed ended.[50]

It is a striking fact that neither the British navy nor the American government, with all its judges, naval officers, consuls, ministers, marshals, and district attorneys, had been able to break up this traffic. Only the people to whom the Africans were being sold had been able to do so, not by capturing ships and prosecuting crews, but by preventing the sale or the holding of smuggled Africans. At the time few people gave much thought to the lesson to be learned, that Anglo-American efforts were unlikely to succeed by themselves, for the developments in Brazil had made many believe that the international slave trade was on the verge of extinction. The Cuban trade remained, but it was measured in thousands, not in tens of thousands. The British relaxed, and pulled out some of their war-ships; by 1855 only 15 of the 303 vessels in the Royal Navy were assigned to the west coast of Africa.[51]

Relaxation was also evident within the United States. Successive squadron commanders had asked for a steamer to supplement their sailing vessels, and for a supply depot located closer to the Congo Basin. In November, 1851, Commodore Elie A. F. Lavallette wrote a strong denunciation of Porto Praia:

It is quite as unhealthy as any part of the African coast, its anchorage is unsafe, it furnishes very indifferent supplies of beef and vegetables, the water is bad. The climate so much so, as to cause great loss in our pro-visions, and the moth is very destructive to clothing. The island itself has a very inconvenient position as regards our cruising, being in a region subject to tornadoes, almost constant rains, calms, and currents, which present more obstacles to the navigation in making passages from thence to Monrovia and back, than are encountered on any other point on the entire coast.

Lavallette suggested St. Helena as the best location, and went to the trouble of obtaining estimates on the cost of purchasing and storing provisions there.[52]

Even before Lavallette wrote his letter, the complaints about Porto Praia had made some impression on the Navy Department. During 1851 plans were afoot to move the supply depot to the port of Loando, in Portuguese Angola, or somewhere else south of the equator. But the trade was so clearly on the wane that Sec-retary W. A. Graham began to talk of abolishing the squadron in-stead. It would make more sense, he argued, to put vessels into the home and Brazilian squadrons and send them out to cruise along the tracks of the remaining slavers, than to keep a squadron on the unhealthy African coast. Graham's idea attracted substantial support, both in and out of Congress. The agitation for abolition of the African squadron became serious enough to make Com-mander (later Rear Admiral) Andrew H. Foote write the widely circulated *Africa and the American Flag*. In this earnest appeal to the American people he stressed the squadron's aid to humanity, and to American commerce. By the time the book was published in 1854 Foote had powerful support. The election of 1852 brought a new administration into office, and Navy Secretary James C. Dobbin came out in favor of the squadron.[53]

So the squadron remained. But the Navy Department did nothing about relocating its depot or reinforcing it with a steamer, and did not even keep it up to treaty strength. The African squadron continued its desultory cruises from Porto Praia to Loando and back, with frequent diversions to Madeira. It showed the flag, but maintained nothing remotely resembling a tight patrol of the coast.

The official optimism about the slave trade was misplaced, for sometime in 1852 a new business began operations in New York City. This in itself was not unusual. Manhattan Island fairly teemed with activity that spilled over into its rapidly growing suburb of Brooklyn. A hundred thousand people a year moved into the area; shipping lines, banks, insurance companies, factories, newspapers multiplied swiftly in this largest and fastest-growing of all North American cities. Three thousand ships a year set sail to all corners of the earth, in eloquent testimony of the city's economic prowess.

The business established in New York in 1852 was nonetheless highly unusual. It had no name, at least no name that anyone saw fit to reveal; some called it the Portuguese Company, but that was only a nickname, and not all its members were Portuguese. Nor did it have a single office, though in the aggregate its business facilities were fairly impressive. Its very existence was concealed as well as could be; for this company, unlike any other in New York, specialized in the business of transporting black ivory from Africa to Cuba.

The company had members active in the territories of at least three nations: Spain, Portugal, and the United States. On the African side, the business of shipping slaves was managed from Portuguese Angola, though the Africans were usually bought and loaded in the no man's land between the equator and the northernmost limits of Angola. They were Congo Africans; by 1852 the slave trade from the Bight of Benin north of the equator was very much on the decline, thanks to the encroachments of civilization in that area. Before the extinction of the Brazilian trade, these same merchants had probably been active in it rather than in the Cuban trade; but, with their livelihood at stake, they turned to the business of sending Africans to Cuba, and caused a distinct increase in that trade.

New York figured in their schemes as a base for slavers and auxiliaries. They chose New York because that port, unlike Havana, had an honest trade with west Africa, a trade that could be used to mask the illegal schemes of the Portuguese Company. There were also fewer British officials stationed there, and American vessels could be purchased at New York without suspicion. When an American vessel changed hands at Havana, everyone, remembering the late 'thirties, was suspicious. But hundreds of vessels changed owners in New York every year, in the course of ordinary business; an occasional dummy owner could easily be introduced.[54]

The New York offices of the Portuguese Company were concentrated on the lower end of Manhattan Island. One belonged to José da Costa Lima Viana, an old hand well known on the African coast. He could be found at 158 Pearl Street, hard at work dispatching trading vessels of one kind or another to his agents at Punta da Lenha and Banana Point in the Congo River. A more distinguished office of the company was located at 81 Front Street under the name Figaniere, Reis & Co., genuine wine importers who dabbled in black ivory on the side. The senior member was the eminent C. H. S. de la Figaniere, Portuguese consul general in New York and son of Portugal's minister to the United States. His brother William, a naturalized American (and hence able to own vessels), was his principal partner. Their chief manager of slaving expeditions seems to have been Manoel Basilio da Cunha Reis, another long-time resident on the African coast.

A third office was just down the street from Viana's—the office of John Albert Machado, 165 Pearl Street. Machado was a native of the Azores who came to the United States in the later 'forties, became a naturalized citizen in 1853, and commenced directing an extensive legitimate and illegitimate trade with west Africa.

Machado "owned" some vessels, chartered others, and distributed funds to his subsidiary firms and individuals as needed. Viana and the Figanieres and Machado kept their own names out of their transactions. The slavers they prepared were usually registered in the names of their puppets, such as the firm of Benjamin Wenburg and John P. Weeks, or, more commonly, in the names of their captains or of obscure New Yorkers. Obscurity, indeed, was the hallmark of most of the men engaged in the equipping of slavers. Whether they were ship fitters, suppliers of cargoes, or recruiters of crews, or bribed deputy marshals, assistant district attorneys, or customs men, they managed to keep out of the public eye. Perhaps the most conspicuous workers for the Portuguese Company were those indispensable tools, the attorneys who became expert in defending slave traders when they ran afoul of the act of 1818 or other federal laws. The most frequent pleaders for accused vessels and men came from the firm of Beebe, Dean, & Donohue, leading admiralty lawyers whose offices at 76 Wall Street welcomed many a worried criminal describing a new arrest. Beebe's mentor, Erastus Benedict, also handled a few slave-trade cases, and Charles N. Black, a relatively obscure Brooklyn attorney, frequently pocketed good fees financed by slave sales in Cuba. To these men, and a few others, belong much of the credit for the successful New York operations of the slave trade.[55]

First of the known slavers to depart from New York was the appropriately named *Advance,* which sailed on September 18, 1852. She and another schooner, the *Rachel P. Brown,* while en route to the Congo, made the mistake of putting in at Porto Praia, which lay on the normal shipping route between those places. The Portuguese officials did not like slavers, and the entire African squadron was at anchor in the harbor waiting for an overdue store-ship. After assorted adventures both slavers were seized and sent to Norfolk. But other slavers—the *Silenus* from New York and the *General Kalb* from Baltimore—got safely to the Congo by avoiding Porto Praia, and together carried off perhaps 900 Africans.[56] They were the first American slavers known to arrive off the southern slave coast since the latter part of 1850, but not the last; in succeeding years driblets of evidence revealed that the United States in general, and New York in particular, had indeed become the principal base for the African slave trade. Through capture, the testimony of informers, or the finding of abandoned derelicts, some of their names became known: *Mary Reed, Peerless, C. F. A. Cole, William Lewis, Oregon, Julia Eliza Ridgway, Jasper.* No one knows precisely how many slavers were sent out. The *New York Tribune,* always inclined to credit rumors, claimed in 1854 that a slaver was fitted out in that port every two weeks, or twenty-six a year. By 1856 it had boosted its estimate to thirty a year, and in mid-1857 it guessed that the number might reach even forty. The paper gave no details. More reasonable was the figure twelve, accepted by the State Department in 1857. Equally unreliable are the guesses at the total size of the Cuban trade. In 1853, for example, the rumor-gathering British commissioner at Havana believed that 12,500 Africans had arrived, while his counterparts at Sierra Leone believed that only four or six vessels had escaped from west Africa all year. As schooners and small brigs were still the mainstay of the slave trade, this number of ships could hardly have carried a fourth of 12,500 Negroes.[57]

Neither the British, the American, nor the Spanish government seemed able to do anything very effective against the enlarged Cuban trade. Bad as their failure was when measured against the human misery created by the traffic in slaves, the failure became intolerable when, in 1857, the slave trade suddenly revived and became big business. Slaves were still cheap in Africa. In February, 1857, the British commissioner at Loando reported that they could be purchased for $15 to $20 each, but later the price apparently went up as the demand increased. One 1860 report placed the Congo price at $40–$45 for men, $40 for girls, and $30–$35 for boys, while another less reliable source gave prices in the Bight of Benin at $34 for men, $17 for women, and $10 for boys. Whatever the prices, they were trifling compared with the prices on the other side of the Atlantic. An agricultural boom in Cuba and the United States sent the price of smuggled slaves up to $400–$500, the lowest rumored prices, or even as high as $1,000–

$1,200, according to the wildest rumors. A slaving expedition was, of course, expensive and risky, and the delivered cost of a slave probably exceeded $300. Even so, the profits were high enough to make a slave trader's eyes gleam, and to make him expand his schemes.[58] As for several years past, this enlarged trade used mainly American vessels.[59] And, for the first time in many years, part of the international slave trade ran to the United States. This development deepened the sectional animosities, born of slavery, which were already threatening to tear the Union apart.

Only rumor supplied details of the trade's business organization. In 1857 rumors of the formation of a great new slave-trading company in Havana began to circulate. According to one report its shares were openly sold at $1,000 each, but this is hardly likely. In 1859 British Consul General Joseph T. Crawford reported that the company was capitalized at $600,000, and the following year he added more details. It owned thirty-seven vessels, but plans were under way to increase its capital to $1,250,000 and its fleet to eighty. One of its slavers would be sent off every two weeks or oftener, and the company expected to land 150,000 to 200,000 Africans despite heavy losses. To get men for the hazardous job of running the patrols, it would pay captains $10,000, chief mates $2,000, other mates and carpenters $1,500, and seamen $1,000 for each voyage, whether successful or not. This was what Crawford had heard.[60] At least one flaw in the story was that eighty slavers could not have transported as many as half of 150,000 Africans, even without any losses. As more than half of the slavers sent to sea in this period were actually being captured, a fleet of eighty of the largest slavers could scarcely have brought 40,000 Negroes to Cuba.[61]

Although such estimates are palpably false, it is fairly certain that a large slave-trading venture was indeed launched in 1857. For lack of a better name, it might be called the "Spanish Company." Apparently it absorbed the old Portuguese Company, for Machado, Viana, and the Figanieres remained active; to them were added a few new names, such as Abranches, Almeida, & Co., whose senior member, Innocencio A. de Abranches, chose to carry on his mixture of legal and illegal business from an office at 158 Pearl Street, conveniently located in the same building with Viana and just down the street from Machado. John P. Weeks discreetly dropped out of the business after the capture of his bark *Petrel,* full of slaves, by a Spanish cruiser; but Pierre Lepage Pearce, a ship chandler already well established at 27 South Street, was chief among a number of new persons employed to further the business.[62]

Even more shadowy is the company that specialized in supplying slaves for the United States. This "American Company" may have included nothing more than a few zealots under the leadership of C. A. L. Lamar of Savannah, Georgia, or it may have been a large, well-organized firm. It is impossible to know without data on how many Africans were smuggled into the South. But, whether large, small, or nearly nonexistent, the American Company must have worked in close coöperation with the Spanish Company. No doubt the established slave traders welcomed the newcomer, for it promised to open a rich new market for the sale of slaves.

The new boom in the slave trade was first felt in Africa in mid-April, 1857, in the Bight of Benin. After four hours of hard steaming, Her Britannic Majesty's steamer *Prometheus* overtook the American brig *Adams Gray,* a fully equipped slaver with $20,000 in cash aboard, including American $10 gold pieces, British gold sovereigns, Spanish doubloons, Mexican silver dollars, and other coins. The *Adams Gray* was one of the richest prizes ever taken, but her capture was memorable for more than the coin. She had sailed directly from New Orleans to the slave coast, and her seizure marked the beginning of intense activity by the British squadron. In all of 1855 and 1856 only seven slavers had been captured, and not a single one in the ten months preceding April, 1857; yet in the next ten months the British seized twenty-one slavers, while the American and Portuguese squadrons each accounted for one more. It was strongly rumored that other vessels had escaped with slaves, and Spanish cruisers soon furnished proof of the truth of this rumor. They captured four slavers, carrying almost 1,600 Africans, off Cuba in September and October, 1857.[63]

Such was the beginning of the last great surge in the west African slave trade. The operations of this trade make an extremely confusing narrative. For the first time, a large-scale slave trade was conducted with no secure base. During the 'thirties in Cuba and the 'forties in Brazil, slavers sailed for Africa by the dozens and neither Spanish nor Brazilian officials attempted to stop them. Now it was different, and the trade shifted from port to port with bewildering swiftness. The Spanish Company was like an octopus, thrusting its tentacles into several ports simultaneously. Where officials were not vigilant, or where they were hampered in performance of their duties, the tentacles took hold firmly; if seizures were made in those ports, the tentacles recoiled or even withdrew entirely for a time until quiet was restored. As one tentacle recoiled, others increased their pressure so that the desired three or four slavers left for Africa every month. Many nations had their ports quietly invaded by the trade: the United States, Spain, Mexico, Venezuela, Portugal, Great Britain, Denmark, and Haiti. Vessels were purchased at New York and New Orleans for the trade and fitted out in Havana, or were purchased at New Orleans and fitted out in New York; vessels were fitted out partly in New Orleans and partly in Cuba, or partly in New York and partly in Charleston, or partly in Havana and partly in the Spanish Canaries. Sometimes successful slavers were burned, scuttled, or set adrift; or they might be refitted in obscure ports in Yucatan.[64]

Adding further confusion was the fact that slavers and auxiliaries were not the only vessels owned by slave traders and roaming the seas. Crawford had mentioned that the Spanish Company owned many vessels, but dispatched one only every two weeks or so; the remaining vessels were employed in lawful trade until it was their turn to go to Africa. A well-documented example is offered by the brig *Nancy*. Purchased at New Orleans in the spring of 1857 and registered in her captain's name, she immediately went slaving, brought over a cargo of Africans, and reëntered lawful trade after being refitted in Yucatan. A few months and a few genuine cargo voyages later, her owners tried to fit her out again for the slave trade. This time she was seized. After her release she went back to lawful trading. Her owner "sold" her, and two owners and fifteen months later she returned to the slave trade, landed a full cargo of Africans, and found an end to her wanderings in the same kind of holocaust that had claimed the *Sultana*.[65]

The slave traders, of course, wanted to use American vessels for greater safety, and they were aided by the chance that the upsurge in the slave trade coincided with a severe depression in the American shipping industry. So many Yankee sailing vessels had been put afloat in the late 'forties and the early 'fifties that the market was glutted by 1856. The commercial depression of 1857 worsened the situation, and by 1859 the merchant marine was in very poor condition. New shipbuilding sharply declined, while hundreds of old vessels swung idly at anchor. Many owners who sold their ships did not care who bought them, and thus slave traders were able to pick up good bargains. This ushered in what might be called the "romantic period" of the African slave trade, when the graceful forms of barks and full-rigged ships of 250 tons or more became predominant. But within their slender hulls and beneath their towering tiers of square sails were the same horrors of human misery that had defiled the smaller schooners. Now for the first time slave traders could afford to use large vessels: they cost no more than the small slavers had cost earlier; they were no more vulnerable, especially when they had American papers; and they brought over twice as many Africans.[66]

Not all the slavers of this period were American. Some were still Spanish, and a few vessels flying the flags of Mexico, Chile, and France entered the business. As in earlier years, most slavers went to the Congo region, where Kabenda, Punta da Lenha, and other trading centers continued their mixture of legal and illegal business. Perhaps one-fourth of the total trade was still carried on from north of the equator, in the Bight of Benin, and an occasional slaver rounded the Cape of Good Hope and brought slaves from east Africa.[67]

It is difficult to determine the size of the slave trade. Contemporary estimates were so erratic that little trust can be put in them. In 1857, for example, British Consul General Crawford could account for reports or rumors of only 5,200 Africans successfully smuggled into Cuba. Fully 2,700 others had been captured by the authorities. Crawford seems to have accepted rumors very easily, yet the British Foreign Office set the total of smuggled Africans at 10,000, for reasons it did not reveal. Nicholas Trist would have concluded that a sinister purpose, such as justification for British interference with American slavers, underlay this apparent over-estimate. Later on, Crawford himself made his estimates much higher; in 1859 he believed that 11,100 Africans had been landed within four months, But his conclusion must have been based on shaky evidence, for he singled out the report of only one landing as coming from sources "on which I could thoroughly rely." The Captain General gave credence to only three of Crawford's seven-teen reported landings. British official estimates of the total trade to Cuba in 1859 varied from 12,000 to 30,000, with no explana-tion of the wide range. Equally unreliable estimates appeared for 1860, whereupon the Spanish government, accusing Crawford of gullibility, protested that only 5,000 or 6,000 Negroes had been smuggled.[68]

On the other hand, the British government never charged that any Africans were being imported into the United States. The re-ports of large-scale landings in the United States all emanated from American sources, and the government denied them. From calcu-lations based upon the number of known slavers and their carry-ing capacities (set forth in detail in Appendix C), it seems that most of the estimates of slaves smuggled were badly exaggerated. The total number imported into the United States and Cuba could have been little more than 6,000 a year in 1857 and 1858, and 11,000 a year in 1859 and 1860. The increase resulted more from an increase in the size of slavers than in their total number; the 1859–1860 slavers averaged about 100 tons heavier than the 1857–1858 slavers. Most of the Africans must have gone to Cuba.[69]

Why was the traffic no larger? Perhaps planters were not anxious to have too many fresh imports on their hands, fearing discovery and possible unsettlement of their domestic slaves. And Africa may not have had the inexhaustible supply of slaves assumed by many writers. It is known that slavers sometimes had to wait weeks for their cargoes to be assembled,[70] which suggests that there was not a superabundance of Africans in the slave markets. It is likely that the international slave trade carried off just about as many Africans as could be bought and sold. Whatever the truth, there were plenty of slavers roaming the seas and plenty of slaves being packed into them during these last years of the trade. Whether only forty American vessels were used each year, or twice that number, and whether they carried 6,000, 10,000, or 30,000 men, women, and children into bondage, the fact remains that humanity was outraged and the American flag was prostituted on a shameful scale.

As details of the voyages of many of the American slavers may be found in the appendixes, only the barest sketch need be given here. New Orleans was the chief base for American slavers during the spring of 1857, the first time that port had contributed substantially to the trade. In the summer of 1857 the outfitting of American slavers was transferred to Havana, apparently because one of the New Orleans slavers had been seized and her captain and supercargo put on trial. Although they were acquitted,[71] the experience suggested that Havana would be a better base. And so it was, until the spring of 1858. The Captain General of Cuba believed that the Spanish law against the outfitting of slavers applied only to Spanish vessels, that is, to vessels whose ownership by Spaniards could be proved. "American" slavers outfitting in the harbor were outside Spanish jurisdiction, he claimed.[72] As the American consulate had no authority to stop them, two or three slavers a month were sent off until the British navy and a heroic American vice-consul stepped in and with forceful (and illegal) actions gave the slave traders a severe fright. Thereafter the trade migrated from port to port. New York, Havana, New Orleans, and other ports received vessels at irregular intervals for outfitting, but New York and Havana remained the principal centers. During most of 1859 and the first half of 1860 New York was the chief center, with two or three slavers a month fitting out, but after several seizures by federal officers, the slave traders moved elsewhere. They used American whaling ports and such harbors as Liverpool, England, and Wilmington,

North Carolina, but most of all Havana, where the American consulate had formally renounced authority to interfere with suspected vessels.[73]

The governments of Spain, Great Britain, and the United States did little. Spanish cruisers did not effectively guard the Cuban coast line; the British did not substantially reinforce their squadron; the American squadron was almost criminally inefficient for the first two and a half years. In the latter part of 1859, however, the Buchanan administration built up a formidable naval force. In 1858 Congress had voted generous appropriations for the now-forgotten punitive expedition against Paraguay, and five private steamers chartered by the Navy Department for that enterprise were afterward purchased, giving the navy for the first time in its history a substantial number of small steam-driven cruisers. Adding a few other warships to supplement the steamers, Buchanan not only brought the African squadron up to a fairly strong force of seven or eight vessels, but placed four American steamers off the Cuban coast to watch for slavers that had escaped the squadron on the African coast. Moreover, the African squadron's depot was moved from Porto Praia to Loando—ten years late—and for the first time the American navy began to capture slavers filled with Africans.[74] Between 1839, when American cruisers began patrolling the African coast, and 1859, only two laden slavers had been seized by the United States Navy; in 1860 it captured seven, carrying a total of 4,300 Africans.

This did not terminate the slave trade under the American flag; but the Lincoln administration, coming into power in March, 1861, found it in a genuinely harassed condition.[75] The new government officials, antislavery Republicans who detested the African traffic, were determined to obliterate the slave trade. But the outbreak of the Civil War, creating a need for warships even more pressing than the need to help the afflicted humanity of Africa, forced withdrawal of the naval patrols off Africa and Cuba. The African squadron was called home, the Cuban patrol was diverted to the shores of the Confederacy, and the high seas were left open to any American vessel that wished to carry slaves.[76]

President Lincoln and Secretary of State Seward had no more intention of letting the British police American shipping than had their Whig and Democratic predecessors. They counted on vigorous criminal prosecutions to frighten American citizens out of the traffic. But the Republicans soon discovered, as their predecessors had, that it was extremely difficult to convict either men or vessels; half a year of trying produced no results, except for the conviction of the only man ever to be hanged for taking African slaves aboard his vessel. His execution early in 1862 did not frighten Americans out of the trade, and ominous reports began to come in from Havana and New York. With no American cruisers to interfere, the outfitting of American slavers was on the increase. From the African coast, too, came disturbing news. The withdrawal of American cruisers had emboldened slavers' crews, who now defied British naval officers attempting to frighten them into surrender.[77]

The government's dilemma was serious. No end to the Civil War was in sight. To let the slave trade revive under the American flag was unthinkable; but to allow Great Britain, America's maritime rival, to police American shipping was a bitter pill no American statesman wanted to swallow. Lincoln and Seward tried to find a middle ground. They instructed Charles Francis Adams, American minister at London, to find out whether or not the British would send a force of cruisers into Cuban waters to intercept incoming slavers. Lord John Russell, British foreign secretary, gently rebuffed the suggestion, pushing forward the alternative that his government had so long desired. Sending cruisers to Cuba, he argued, would probably prove useless unless the United States would allow British warships to search and seize American vessels. The overtone to his answer was clear. If the Republicans wanted British help, they would have to sign a treaty of the same sort that Spain, Portugal, and Brazil had long since granted.

Russell's argument was a feeble one. Slavers approaching the Cuban coast did not use the American flag for protection. As a practical matter, any cruiser of any nationality could pick up laden slavers, with or without treaty rights. But Russell's position left Lincoln and Seward no choice; they would have to capitulate, or allow the trade to revive. To their honor, they capitulated. Within a few days Seward and Lord Lyons, British minister at Washington, had agreed on the text of a treaty allowing the Royal Navy to arrest suspected American vessels and present them to mixed commissions for trial. Lyons wanted to make the treaty perpetual, but Seward cannily refused, and it was set to expire in ten years. On May 20 formal ratifications were exchanged at London, and the treaty was declared in effect on June 7, 1862. Lincoln asked Congress for money to implement the agreement three days later, and on July 11 he signed the appropriation bill.

This radical departure from American foreign policy of seven decades was kept secret from the American people until it had become firmly entrenched as part of the "supreme law of the land." As required by the Constitution, the Senate considered the treaty, but it did so in executive session, behind locked doors. No mention of the treaty appeared in the newspapers, or even in the *Congressional Globe*. Reputedly the vote for its approval was unanimous; but four Democratic senators subsequently voted against the appropriation bill. Their spokesman, Senator Saulsbury of Delaware, denounced the courts it supplied money for as "unconstitutional." At any rate, the Senate was overwhelmingly in favor of the treaty, and the appropriation bill was hurried through the House without debate, by a voice vote.[78]

The treaty introduced novel features into the legal system of the United States. It gave the warships of each nation the right to search the other's vessels in the Atlantic Ocean, below 32° north latitude. A later protocol extended the area to cover the east African slave coast. If any one of the items specified in Article VI was found, the vessel could be taken by her captor to a mixed court at New York, Capetown, or Sierra Leone. There could be no damages for false arrest. The presence of such an item would establish a prima-facie case of slave trading, and the burden of proof was on the vessel's owner. He had to satisfy the judges that his vessel was not a slaver, or lose her. The decision would be made jointly by a British judge and an American judge; if they could not agree, American and British arbitrators would be called in. One of them, chosen by lot, would cast the deciding vote. There was no appeal from the verdict of a mixed court.

The items listed in Article VI were varied enough to incriminate most of the vessels that had sailed from New York to Africa in earlier years: spare planks fitted as a second deck, more water than the crew needed, a boiler or other cooking apparatus in excess of normal needs, extra bulkheads, grated hatches, and shackles. It was permissible to ship provisions if they were manifested, and knocked-down casks if they were bonded with the customhouse, but a vessel intended as a slaver could pass muster under the equipment articles only at a very early stage of preparation.[79]

The treaty offered a brilliant solution for the problem created earlier by federal judges who persistently refused to see slavers for what they were. The new courts simply bypassed the regular courts. To make certain that no objections could be raised, the appropriation bill repealed all conflicting legislation. To be sure, the treaty did not work a thorough reformation of the slave-trade laws. It did not apply to vessels fitting out in American ports; they could load as much incriminating equipment as the regular courts would allow, and yet could not be arrested until they were intercepted, if at all, on the African coast or in the West Indies. Nor did the treaty facilitate the conviction of officers and men. Property could easily be taken, but prisoners turned over to the mixed courts would be sent home to stand trial in regular courts. It was possible, therefore, that evidence sufficient to condemn a vessel before a mixed court would fail to obtain even an indictment of the owner and the crew. And the treaty made it no easier for consuls to detain suspected vessels, or for vessels seized in American waters to be denied release on bond.

Perhaps the most obnoxious aspect of the treaty was its tacit admission that the United States could not police its own shipping, that it had to turn law enforcement over to its principal rival. This humiliation doubtless did more moral than economic damage. It is true that American commerce with Africa declined sharply after the treaty went into effect, but not because the British abused their new-found power by haling vessels indiscriminately into court. The traffic fell off because slave traders had taken warning by the time the judges took their posts in the spring of 1863.

Only one mixed court for the suppression of the African slave trade was ever established on American soil. It was held in a rented room in the Union Building in New York, certainly one of the most modest courts on the North American continent. Judge Truman Smith had no clerk, and his furnishings were limited to a carpet, one table, a washstand, one lounge, a secretary, six chairs, and three volumes of the *United States Statutes at Large*. Yet this humble establishment was more than equal to the demands placed upon it, for not one case ever came before Judge Smith's court. Until the mixed courts were abandoned in the fall of 1870, Smith had a perfect sinecure. Benjamin Pringle and William L. Avery, judge and arbitrator at Capetown, likewise drew a regular salary for several years for doing exactly nothing.[80]

Sierra Leone was expected to be a different proposition, for English cruisers had frequently sent prizes there. The American arbitrator of the court at Sierra Leone was Timothy R. Hibbard, a physician with a genuine missionary zeal for uplifting the Africans. He prepared for a full calendar, beseeching Secretary of the Interior J. P. Usher for a supply of lawbooks and stationery, and medicines, tents, and firearms to deal with the prisoners he expected the court to receive into custody. Hibbard even asked to have a fast, well-armed, flat-bottomed steamer put under the court's orders, and he assured Usher that it could do more damage to the slave trade than half a dozen regular warships. But that sort of steamer was precisely what the Union navy needed at home, and Hibbard did not get one. As it turned out, he needed neither lawbooks, nor medicines, nor firearms, nor tents. Shortly before he and Judge Charles V. Dyer arrived, the *Sultana*'s old skipper, Captain Bowen, and the schooner *Mariquita* had been taken with 471 Africans by H.M.S. *Zebra*, but the prize was taken into St. Helena for confiscation. Bowen had not insisted upon his American nationality. In 1864 H.M.S. *Dart* captured what everyone thought was a Yankee brig, but the crew destroyed their papers and flag and claimed to be of no nationality. The Anglo-American mixed court at Sierra Leone did not hear the case; in fact, not a single vessel was ever tried before it.

But it would hardly be fair to say that Hibbard and Dyer had a sinecure. Sierra Leone was infested with fever, and Hibbard suffered a severe attack before he had been there a year. A second attack in the summer of 1864 sent him to Europe for a year's recuperation, and he and Dyer resigned in 1867. The Department of the Interior did not bother to send out a new arbitrator, but it did send George W. Palmer as judge. He stayed for only two years, fleeing to Europe in the spring of 1869 to avoid a fever outbreak, and then resigning. He pointed out that the court heard no cases, that cruisers no longer were operating on the coast, and that there were no slavers to be captured in any event. His resignation put an end to the court at Sierra Leone.[81]

In fact, the slave trade died out rapidly after 1862. One reason was that participants were frightened out of using the American flag, as good proof as any of the treaty's effectiveness. For a time slave traders turned to the French flag. Napoleon III refused to concede rights of seizure to the British squadron, though his own squadron was relatively small.[82] But the business was plainly on the decline. As early as September, 1862, a visiting naval officer found the trading centers on the Congo River in a very depressed condition. Slave prices had fallen to one-third or one-fourth of the 1860 levels. A year later British Commodore A. P. E. Wilmot found the fifteen "factories" at Punta da Lenha on the verge of collapse. The slave traders were living comfortably enough, with roomy houses and prolific back-yard vegetable gardens, but they were at their wits' end for business. Slaves had been their business, and few vessels were coming for them.[83]

But factors other than a shortage of shipping were mainly responsible for the decline of the slave trade. The smuggling of slaves into the United States, which had earlier helped to sustain the trade, was a thing of the past by 1864 because of the strict Union blockade and the growing likelihood that all slaves in the South would soon be freed. No plantation owner wanted to spend money for Africans whom federal troops might emancipate within a year or two. And Spanish officials in Cuba began, or intensified, their efforts to stop smuggling (the choice of verb depends on one's views of their earlier sincerity in this matter). By 1865 British officials were agreed that slave landings were being effectively combated, and the substantial trade may have ended much earlier. Consul General Crawford, to be sure, was still sending in accounts of large-scale landings, declaring that 6,807 slaves had been smuggled in during 1864. When his published report got back to Cuba, the Captain General wrote an angry retort:

To judge from the manner in which it is drawn up . . . the number might have been increased according to his fancy, even to 20,000. . . . Your Honour's predecessor frequently failed to reply when the incorrectness of his intelligence was shown and proved to him; and as a consequence of this conduct, probably with a view of convincing his government of his unwearying activity, he was not very scrupulous in furnishing information of a doubtful character.

Crawford had arrived at the figure of 6,807 by counting among slave imports the 2,980 Africans liberated by Spanish cruisers from captured slavers and subsequently landed, adding the figures from two fictitious reports of large-scale landings, and then increasing the known landings by one-third in order to compensate for unreported landings. The Spanish government declared that not one slave had been smuggled in in 1864, and the British Foreign Office admitted that Crawford had been guilty of exaggeration.[84]

This is the end of the story of the African slave trade under the American flag. Though filling many pages, it has in reality only skimmed the surface of the hundreds of criminal schemes, the thousands of perjuries, which made up that story. It has slighted the horrors suffered by fifty thousand or more human beings crowded into American slavers, and the wanton waste of perhaps ten thousand lives, snuffed out aboard vessels whose criminal purpose had been aided by the flag and the papers of the first nation in all the world to outlaw the African slave trade. To the dismal catalogue of the horrors of the trade itself is added the shameful blot that it left upon the honor of the American people. No sensitive person can escape a feeling of shock that such iniquities could be perpetrated under the American flag.

Some partisan writers, not content to record this national disgrace, have claimed that it was deliberately permitted by the United States government. The argument, apparently first concocted by abolitionist crusaders in the mid-1840's, seized upon eagerly by Republican campaigners in the late 1850's, and finally given an aura of scholarly soundness by a well-known historical work of the 1890's,[85] has a simple, almost irresistible logic. The United States government, it claims, was controlled by Southern slaveowners before the Civil War. These slaveowners disliked the laws against the African slave trade, either because they implied a slur upon domestic slavery or because they impeded the import of fresh Negro labor to the United States. Therefore the slaveowners saw to it that the government made no sincere attempt to enforce the laws, but rather assisted the slave trade by refusing to permit British vessels to police American shipping. But the antislavery Republican party promptly wiped out the traffic after getting control of the government in March, 1861, proving that their Democratic and Whig predecessors could have done the same if they had wanted to.

The trouble with this argument is that the facts do not support it. No one has ever demonstrated how a minority of slaveholders in a minority section of the nation were able to control the entire federal government. Republicans used to write of a great "slaveowners' conspiracy," a formidable "slave power," but in fact the national government did not shape its policies exclusively to aid the South. In carrying out the terms of the compact by which free and slave states had been united in one federal system, the national government did attempt to return runaway slaves to their masters; but federal expenditures, tariff and land policies, and foreign policy by no means reflected exclusively Southern interests in the decades preceding the Civil War. This, indeed, was the frequent complaint of Southern political leaders, whose image of themselves was far different from the all-powerful image concocted by ardent antislavery men in the North. Those who still believe that the South controlled the federal government should subject their belief to a thorough scrutiny. In many of its actions the government did try to please the South; in many others, it tried to please the North.

Even if Southern slaveowners had controlled the national government, they could still have opposed the African slave trade. Some of them made good profits by raising slaves for sale to other Southerners, and they had strong economic motives to oppose the trade in Africans because it might diminish the value of domestic slaves. Humane Southern slaveowners (and there were many such) detested the cruelty of the international slave trade quite as much as Northerners, not because the trade was in slaves, but because it inflicted severe suffering upon human beings. It is true that Nicholas Trist, a Virginian, viewed the international trade as humane, but Henry A. Wise, another Virginian, saw it as an abomination. There are no statistics to prove whether the Trists outnumbered the Wises in the South, or vice versa, but there is ample evidence that Southern judges, Southern naval officers, and Southern juries were as active against the slave trade as their Northern counterparts. It was only in the very last years of the trade, when slave smuggling into the United States was resumed, that there was substantial evidence of Southern hostility to the laws.[86]

Well-documented facts demolish the arguments that Democrats and Whigs made no sincere efforts to enforce the laws and that Republicans found the task easy. Appendixes A and B list numerous arrests, prosecutions, and convictions under Democratic and Whig administrations, and relatively few under the Republicans. This does not mean, of course, that the Republicans were any less sincere; they found themselves in different circumstances. They had no cruisers to make arrests; they had a relatively short-lived trade to combat. But it does seem clear that Democrats and Whigs had also been trying to do their duty.

As to whether or not the Republicans deserve special credit for allowing the British to take over a duty properly their own, opinions may well differ. Certainly the signing of the treaty with Great

Britain was courageous proof of their sincerity. But they had not signed the treaty willingly; they had done their best to avoid it by attempting to uphold the traditional policy of the United States that American vessels be immune from foreign control. No doubt the Whigs and the Democrats could have driven the American flag out of the trade by signing a treaty with Great Britain; indeed, they could have done so by simply allowing the British to hale American vessels before the mixed courts at Sierra Leone. But Whigs and Democrats were as attached to the traditional policy as the Republicans were, and, moreover, they were never in the position of being unable to police the American flag with American warships. They lacked the cruisers to police it properly; even Buchanan's unprecedented naval effort of 1860 was only partially successful. But the manner in which the slave trade fluctuated excused their determination to use cruisers, and to spurn British help.

There were three principal periods of American lawbreaking. The first came in 1838–1839, and British cruisers had brought the situation under control even before the United States government became fully aware of what had been happening. Slave traders had not voluntarily reported their activities, Nicholas Trist had chosen to remain silent, and there was not an American warship assigned to the entire African coast to gather information. During the early 1840's there was not enough lawbreaking for the government to consider renouncing its traditional policy to suppress it. The second great outbreak of criminal activity under the American flag, in 1848–1849, likewise ended before the cruisers had a chance to show what they could or could not do. In the early 'fifties the lawbreaking was again on too small a scale to warrant surrender of national sovereignty to suppress it, and during part of that period the British squadron was itself too small to lend really effective help. When American slavers became prominent in 1857–1860, the Buchanan administration put a large naval force to sea, and had enough success so that once again there was no impelling reason to surrender sovereignty. It was only the Republicans who found themselves in the painful position of having a slave trade to suppress, and no warships to use.

Except for the lack of naval action, the Republican experience against the slave trade was much like that of their predecessors. It was still difficult to confiscate vessels upon circumstantial evidence. It was still very difficult to convict men. Consuls and marshals and attorneys encountered the same troubles as always. Congress passed no legislation to lessen the difficulties. It has sometimes been asserted that the Lincoln administration revitalized the suppression of the slave trade by concentrating all activities under control of the Department of the Interior, but careful investigation reveals that the department never effectively controlled them, and merely followed policies already established by the Buchanan administration.[87]

The cause of the government's ineffectiveness lies elsewhere than in a sinister plot concocted by Southern slaveowners. The shameful debacle stemmed from a variety of causes, some of which have instructive value even today. The following chapters, highlighting incidents from the government's effort against the slave trade, point up these causes and direct attention toward the basic reason that American laws were violated year after year with near impunity.

— 3 —

HOW TO CATCH A SLAVER

The drummer's arms rose and fell, as with stirring beat he summoned the crew of the United States steam sloop *San Jacinto* to another day of duty patrolling a 60-mile square of ocean west of the Congo River. It was October 10, 1860; a quiet day, cloudy and warm, with a faint breeze barely giving the vessel steerageway as it puffed out the canvas set by the night watch. Soon the engineers were trooping into the deserted firerooms, lighting furnaces and beginning the weary transfer of 2,000 pounds of coal an hour, shovelful by shovelful, from the bunkers to the insatiable flames. It would be a hot business before the day was over, for the tropical waters encompassing the *San Jacinto* kept her lower compartments warm even when the furnaces and boilers were cold. As the smoke curled up through her stack, the watch officer topside prepared to give the orders that would bring her canvas down and start her on a leisurely 5-knot sweep across the patrol sector. Aloft, the fresh lookouts, truly the eyes and ears of the ship in a day when radio and radar were unknown, began to scan the horizon for other vessels sharing that calm patch of ocean. Who knew what exciting discovery might be made at any moment?

The *San Jacinto*'s cruise had been a full and varied one for all hands ever since leaving New York in the summer of 1859. On her way across to the Cape Verde Islands, pieces of the propeller-shaft bearing began to work out of the casing, and a double injection of tallow, water, and graphite lubricant was of no avail. Twelve pounds of chippings had accumulated by the time the *San Jacinto* reached the islands, eloquent testimony to the mechanical weakness that plagued early naval steamers. Irritable old Flag Officer Inman had decided that the bearings would last a good while longer, but the ship's captain disagreed; one quarrel led to another, and finally Inman had removed him from command. But that did not repair the bearings, and Inman at length agreed that the sloop had to go into dry dock. There was no other way to reach the bearings. Her 1,567 tons made her far too heavy for dry-docking anywhere short of Cadiz, Spain, and there the *San Jacinto* had gone, her first year of duty in the African squadron netting only two or three weeks of anchored patrol at Shark's Point in the mouth of the Congo River. But on the way back from Cadiz in early August, 1860, the sloop had run into the slaver *Storm King,* bound for Cuba with 619 Africans aboard, and caught her in a dead calm. And on October 8, in erratic sweeps off the Congo, the *San Jacinto* had caught up with the bark *Splendide,* with 300 Africans aboard, bound from Loango for the Congo to pick up 700 more. Because the Africans were intended to work as contract laborers in the French West Indies, in a scheme sanctioned by the French government, the *Splendide* was set free.

At nine o'clock on the morning of October 10, as the lookouts peered toward the invisible coast line of Africa, some flecks of white caught their attention. It was a hermaphrodite brig, square sails on her foremast and triangular studding and mainsails all set, heading to seaward. No sail went unchallenged in these waters, and the *San Jacinto* swung around to close with the stranger. It quickly became apparent that the visit would not be welcome, as the brig alternately swung northeast to put the wind behind her for greatest speed, and made desperate tacks to the westward to gain sea room. The wind freshened into a strong breeze, and whitecaps played around the ships as they raced out the drama. At noon the brig was still five miles ahead but the *San Jacinto,* sails set and engines pounding, had worked up to 9 knots and was steadily closing the range. By 12:30 she had pulled within shot of the long-barreled pivot gun and a team of brawny men cast loose its lashings, rammed home powder and shot, and heaved it up to the starboard bulwarks. The gun captain carefully pushed a wire into the firing vent, pricking a hole in the flannel bag enclosing the powder, and then inserted a percussion cap and cocked his firing pin. Squinting over the bar sights as the target slowly rose and fell, he gave the quick jerk on his lanyard that ignited the charge, and sent the shot screaming out across the water to plummet just beyond the brig's stern. Still she did not heave to. The recoil had rumbled the gun back across the deck and its crew applied damp sponge, rammer, and tackle to reload and run out again. A second shot followed the first, and that was enough. The brig shortened sail while the *San Jacinto* hurtled down upon her, and so ended the longest successful chase of a laden slaver ever made by an American cruiser. The boarders found that the captive was the *Bonito,* which had bolted New York without a clearance on the preceding July 16 and was carrying 750 Africans packed into her 277-ton hull.[1]

The capture of the *Bonito* illustrates a number of facts about the capturing of undisguised slavers. The *San Jacinto* had, first of all, to be in the right place at the right time, and this meant not only the right time to be within eyeshot of the *Bonito,* but within eyeshot during daylight. Although a cruiser's lookouts could scan several hundred square miles at a time on a clear day, they could see very little indeed on a dark night; searchlights were unknown aboard the warships of 1860. To be at the right place at the right time required luck. It also required that cruisers searching for slavers have a fairly convenient supply base so that they could spend as much time as possible in the areas where slavers were likely to be found. The patrol area had to be well chosen. Alertness was an essential; alertness and dogged determination to approach and board every vessel met at sea in that area. One final point, beyond the control of the men who took cruisers to sea, was that the designers had to have put enough speed into them, for slavers were usually chosen from among the fastest ships of the merchant marine.

Over a period of eighteen years, American cruisers took upward of fifty real or suspected slavers, but only nine times did a fortunate conjunction of circumstances allow them to capture laden slavers. The arrest of so many vessels, whether laden or unladen, resulted from a great variety of particular circumstances. Dramatic chases at sea were not always the means. Sometimes slavers simply dropped into the hands of naval officers by sailing into ports where warships were at anchor—as did the *Advance* and the *Rachel P. Brown.* In other instances British naval officers pointed out suspected slavers, or even, at some risk to the harmony of Anglo-American relations, took possession of them and surrendered their catch to the first American cruiser that happened along. Or American cruisers came upon slavers while they were anchored off trading posts. None of these arrests required American naval officers to do more than their minimum duty, and seamanship played no part.

But seamanship, nonetheless, did play a part in the suppression of the slave trade. It sometimes seemed as if naval officers needed most of all to be walking lawbooks, full of precedents and wise in the ways of jurists; but they also had to be good sailors. They did not need to be fighters, for slavers never resisted; but they had to make opportunities to meet slavers, and to be skillful in capitalizing on such meetings. In the following pages are a few of the most striking examples of the usefulness of seamanship in the suppression of the slave trade.

Rising amid the smell of fresh wood and pitch and paint upon the building ways of American shipyards in 1843 were two sleek-lined brigs destined to have a fateful confrontation eleven years later. One was the *Perry,* built for the navy and serving fairly continuously against the slave trade from late 1848 until 1855, a fruitful period in which she arrested six suspicious American vessels, four of which were confiscated by the courts. The other brig was the *Glamorgan,* built at Baltimore for private owners, and finally sold as a slaver toward the end of the *Perry's* tour on the African coast. Sailing from New York in October, 1853, she landed slave goods in the Congo and at Ambriz, and then stood out to sea to await the gathering of her return cargo. The rendezvous had been set for March 11, 1854, and the *Glamorgan* was headed in toward it when her crew sighted the *Perry* inshore of them.

These two vessels were as closely matched as any that ever played the game of hunter and hunted. *Perry* was the larger, measuring 280 tons against *Glamorgan*'s 191; but they carried the same rakish press of sails and were almost identically slender. The *Perry*'s maximum beam was 24.2 per cent of her length; the *Glamorgan*'s, 24.6 per cent. Observation through telescopes could not reveal these precise figures, but it was evident aboard the *Glamorgan* that the *Perry* was fast and dangerous, and the men on the *Perry* knew that the *Glamorgan* could lead them on a long and lively chase out to sea which might never end if she doubled about under cover of dark. Therefore Lieutenant Richard Page, commanding the *Perry,* craftily ordered a British flag hoisted on the *Perry*'s mainmast. Shrewd American officers kept such a flag handy to deceive slavers into hoisting American colors (for an American slaver was more likely to show French or Spanish or Brazilian colors to one of her own cruisers); at a distance an American man-of-war was indistinguishable from an English warship. The trick worked, and the *Glamorgan*'s captain, Charles Kehrman, a seagoing vagabond with a dubious past, hoisted American colors to discourage a visit from the "British" cruiser.

Page then boldly steered his vessel away from the slaver, utterly disinterested, it seemed, because she was an American, and Kehrman, his mate, and the Portuguese supercargo were all deceived by the ruse. They continued their approach to the shore and to their waiting cargo of slaves, unaware that under cover of night Page was following at a distance, using his night glass to keep in sight the faint blob of his quarry. When daybreak came it was the *Glamorgan* that was inshore and the *Perry* that was to seaward, and Lieutenant Page had no trouble following up his carefully earned advantage. The slave trade was soon poorer by one expedition.

Yet Page, though a skillful seaman, blundered when he got into the realm of the law. According to the federal laws authorizing naval vessels to arrest slavers, he was to send home for trial every-one "being of· the officers and crew thereof." Page, reasoning that the supercargo was not a crew member, put him ashore, but sent Kehrman, his mate, and the prize into Boston. This action drew a blast from the Boston grand jurors, who pointed out that under the act of 1818 the supercargo was as guilty as Kehrman, and that "his release by Lieut. Page has left him at liberty to pursue his atrocious traffic, and to take off, by some other vessel, the very cargo of human beings he had prepared for the *Glamorgan.*" That was Page's thanks from the grand jury for apprehending a slaver.[2]

Similarly shrewd were the tactics of Commander John Taylor of the sloop of war *Saratoga,* as he watched the suspicious clipper *Nightingale* near Kabenda in April, 1861. Days had passed with the clipper showing no signs of going to sea. Taylor, reasoning that it was his presence which kept the *Nightingale* immobile, believed that the slaves were to come aboard right in Kabenda Harbor. One afternoon he ostentatiously set sail, while cunning eyes aboard the clipper and on shore rejoiced at the billows of canvas appearing on the *Saratoga*'s masts. As darkness settled a flotilla of small boats emerged from its hiding places and converged on the *Nightingale,* thrusting Africans into her capacious upper hold as rapidly as pos-sible. Nine hundred and sixty-one had been loaded before the *Saratoga* intervened. Taylor had sailed back inshore after dark, and sent his own· flotilla of well-armed boats to reëxamine the quarry. His men were not surprised at what they found.

Again there were problems with the prisoners, several of whom escaped ashore the night before the *Nightingale* sailed under guard from Kabenda. Among them was Captain Francis Bowen, the *Sultana*'s late master; he was a pirate who managed to elude Re-publican officers and roam the seas for years afterward. Three years later British Commodore Wilmot met at Loango a "most shrewd and intelligent person, very gentlemanly, and with a perfect knowledge of everybody and everything connected with this part of the coast and the slave trade." Wilmot learned later that this gentleman was Bowen, who had just been released by the British after their capture of his schooner, the *Mariquita.* At that moment

Bowen was living comfortably in the house of the agent recruiting contract laborers for the French West Indies.[3]

Shrewdness resulted in captures, but so at times did sheer persistence. During the latter part of April, 1860, the steamer *Mohawk* was patrolling off the northern coast of Cuba in waters that were crossed and crisscrossed by many honest merchant vessels. Boarding parties had to go through a wearying routine—lowering a boat, rowing over, clambering up to inspect papers, getting off, rowing back, and rehoisting the boat—several times a day, day after day. That was what they were paid for, but any hint of laziness on the commander's part would have opened the way for the simpler process of steaming nearby, shouting across for the name and the destination of an innocent-looking vessel, and going on. And the *Wildfire* looked innocent—fast and slender, to be sure, but apparently quite ready to be boarded. She made no suspicious movements (which tipped off many a commander that the vessel he was approaching was no honest merchant), while her crew hoisted American colors promptly upon request and in a remarkable display of coolness went about their duties as if they had nothing to fear from the most painstaking search. As the *Mohawk* pulled alongside, seamen were visible at work in the bark's rigging, while her officers leaned calmly on their rail and placidly gazed at their visitor. But Lieutenant T. A. Craven, commanding the *Mohawk,* with the persistence that had become habit, ordered away a boat, and the boarding lieutenant scrambled up the side of the *Wildfire* and saw the telltale sign of gratings over her hatches. He waved his sword as a signal, his boat's crew let out a whoop (as well they might, for they were now richer by a good many dollars each), and the Africans, peering through the gratings and realizing what was happening, joyfully started singing and clapping their hands. They had been rescued from slavery in Cuba, and Craven's persistence had made it possible.[4]

But persistence did not always win out, and even the best officers were sometimes unable to meet up with slavers. In 1860 Lieutenant John N. Maffitt, later famous as commander of the

Confederate raider *Florida,* wrote home to his daughters from his station off north Cuba:

My Dear Florie and Mary:

We are cruising off the east mouth of the Old Bahama Channel, looking out for slavers; if our engine had not broken down on the 30th of April we would no doubt have had a slaver by this time; but as I caught the first [the *Putnam,* while commanding the brig *Dolphin* in August, 1858] it is but reasonable to expect that Captain Craven and Captain Stanly should have the next. If the *Crusader*'s engine will only stand, I think we will catch the next; but the truth is I am in constant dread of an accident. The cylinder, the *lungs* of the engine, is broken and only patched up.

Maffitt's slaver did indeed come, only two days later. It was the *Bogota,* whose 400 Africans burst open their hatches with a great shout and poured out on deck, dancing and singing in a wild and discordant symphony. But breakdowns plagued the steamers.[5]

Shrewd tactics were used against the cruisers as well as by them. Slavers tried to sail where there were no warships, and even devised a direct method to remove unwanted cruisers from a particular place at a particular time. The plan was simple, and almost foolproof if properly worked out: a decoy was used to draw an intercepting cruiser off on a long and vain chase while the slaver slipped through. As the naval patrols were always dangerously thin, getting one cruiser out of the way could leave a comfortably large gap.

Lieutenant Maffitt and the broken-lunged *Crusader* were the victims of such a scheme. The decoy and the slaver came inshore together, and the decoy stood out to sea as soon as the steamer was sighted. During the three hours it took Maffitt to catch the decoy, determine its innocence, and return to the place from whence it had come, the slaver was emptied. The red-faced Americans found a derelict. Three African boys left behind in the rush to disembark were the only human life aboard. The *Wyandotte,* Lieutenant Fabius Stanly, had suffered even greater chagrin three weeks earlier, while watching out for an American slaver rumored due in at Trinidad, Cuba. The local slave traders, knowing that Stanly had picked up the rumor, sent a Spanish brig to sea at the appropriate moment and, the wind being good and Stanly's steamer slow, got him to chase the decoy all the way to Cienfuegos, fifty miles down the coast. As the *Wyandotte* went, the thick smoke belching from her stack signaled the end of an already depleted coal supply. Stanly had to put into Cienfuegos to recoal, and after that it was too late to return to Trinidad in time to intercept the expected slaver. Some days later Stanly learned that the slaver had in fact arrived and landed its Africans while he was on his wild-goose chase. Stanly relieved his feelings in an angry tirade at the local grandee of Trinidad, but that did not recover the Africans or capture the vessel they had come from.[6]

Not only did the navy's seamanship sometimes fail, but occasionally officers were unfit for their posts. On the whole, however, they did a good job with what they had. Lack of numbers and adverse court decisions, rather than clumsy ship handling, crippled their efforts. There were not enough cruisers, and they had far too much coast line to patrol and too many merchantmen to watch. Normally naval officers were not able to shadow suspected vessels long enough to get absolute evidence of guilt, for slavers merely delayed completing their outfits until the cruiser had moved on. If a cruiser did seize a slaver, the evidence was likely to be circumstantial rather than absolute. Circumstantial evidence often failed to win convictions, which discouraged further arrests. Thus lack of numbers and adverse court decisions made a combination devastating to effective law enforcement. But naval officers could do nothing about these things.

The navy does not deserve exclusive credit for smart seamanship in arresting slavers. Even inside American harbors there was sometimes lively action, carried out by marshals and revenue cutter officers. The arrests they made were usually routine: papers served, guards placed aboard, cargo unloaded for inventory, prisoners taken peaceably before a United States commissioner, and so forth. Essential as this activity was, it called for nothing more than routine attention to duty. But exciting adventures did sometimes occur, as on the night of March 18, 1856, in New York harbor.

A visitor to New York's water front along the East River during the days preceding that night would have seen a pretty little schooner, the *Falmouth,* 105 tons, lying moored to a pier at the foot of Clinton Street. Many visitors did, in fact, see her; but two of them, Deputy Marshals Lorenzo de Angelis and George Nevins, had more than casual interest in the cargo. They were therefore keenly interested when, on the morning of March 18, a steam tug pulled alongside, picked up the *Falmouth's* hawser, and towed her up river to Hellgate, where the schooner dropped anchor. The deputies had good reason to be suspicious. Early in 1856 both the American and the British squadrons on the African coast were weak, and the *Falmouth's* managers had decided to send her to sea, without clearance or papers, as an outright pirate, and trust to luck and her speed to elude the cruisers. By leaving without a clearance she would avoid all difficulties with the customhouse. After darkness dropped its protecting shadow over the anchored *Falmouth,* another schooner, her tender, was moored alongside and a hasty transfer of cargo began. Rice, meal, lumber, boilers, spoons, tubs, buckets, empty casks, medicines were heaved onto the *Falmouth's* deck and into her hold. About midnight the tug *Ajax* took up the *Falmouth's* hawser, and the two set off down river. At the foot of Sixty-first Street they stopped at the wharf long enough to open the hydrant and steal fifty-six caskfuls of fresh water. Then they headed on toward the harbor and the open sea beyond.

De Angelis and Nevins were waiting for them. A few hours earlier they had hurried to District Attorney John McKeon and told him what they expected would happen. He authorized them to charter an intercepting steam tug and to get help from the Brooklyn Navy Yard. At midnight Commodore Bigelow was roused from his bed by the deputies, who already had the tug *Only Son* and wanted United States marines to give her teeth. The commodore quickly sent a file of sleepy leathernecks aboard the *Only Son,* and ordered the steamer *Despatch* to get up steam. In the small hours of the morning the *Falmouth* and the *Ajax* passed the darkened navy yard on their way to the sea. If those on board noticed the smoke rising from the *Despatch,* they paid too little attention to it. For the *Falmouth* was headed into a trap. The *Only Son* was hove to off Fort Diamond in mid-harbor, while the *Despatch* had orders to follow the *Falmouth* down harbor an hour after she passed the navy yard. Surprise was essential so that no evidence could be destroyed.

The hours dragged by, and the men aboard the *Only Son* began to fear that the schooner had taken another route. But the light of dawn revealed her coming out, still towed by the *Ajax.* As the pair passed Fort Diamond, the *Only Son* surged forward and pulled alongside. Marines scrambled aboard, muskets at the ready, but the sullen-faced men aboard the *Falmouth* dared not resist and were herded together. The *Ajax* was still towing, and one of the marines seized an axe and cut the hawser. The schooner went dead in the water then, while her tug hurried back to New York. A piratical expedition had been foiled on the very doorstep of New York City.[7]

This good night's work had a salutary effect in inhibiting the unscheduled sailing of slavers from New York; the *Bonito* is the only vessel known to have left port afterward without a clearance. But, for reasons to be related below, slavers still sailed from New York, and expert ship handling was still sometimes necessary. A merchantman leaving the harbor publicly was easy to stop, but slave traders sometimes had tenders put aboard embarrassing items of crew or equipment outside the harbor, after clearing. Thus, in March, 1857, the bark *Paez* took aboard her Spanish captain (a replacement for the unsuspecting American captain who cleared her), a boxed boiler and furnace, and four cases of medicines from a tug about two miles outside the Narrows, well beyond ordinary customhouse observation.[8] Apparently a rumor of this exploit got back to the officials, however, for they were more alert when dealing with the next suspicious vessel on their list.

This was the schooner *Merchant,* lately a Richmond coaster but more recently the subject of two fast sales arranged by John P. Weeks, a disreputable go-between. As her loading went on at the same pier whence the *Falmouth* had started her voyage, Marshal Isiah Rynders and his nephew Theodore watched her by turns night and day. They saw 140 water-filled casks, stacks of lumber, and barrels of flour, codfish, bread, and rice vanish into her hold. The marshal, dressing himself like a country bumpkin, visited a nearby vessel to learn what he could about the *Merchant*. When the sailors told him that the *Merchant* was a "blackbird," "Farmer" Rynders retorted: "Sho, you can't come that over me, you know. I know blackbirds too well for that—have plenty whar I come from." The sailors then explained the meaning of "blackbird" in waterfront language, and regaled him with tales about this and other slavers. Rynders left, well satisfied as to what should be done.

On the morning of April 23 the *Merchant* got under way behind the steam tug *George Birkbeck,* her announced destination Corsica. As they slid down the channel they passed close by the revenue cutter *Washington*. Scrutinizing glances swept over the cutter, but she was neatly secured and seemingly no obstacle to their departure. Down to Sandy Hook the *Birkbeck* and the *Merchant* went. Meanwhile the *Washington*'s commander, Captain John Faunce of the Revenue Cutter Service, was giving orders to the captain of the chartered tug *Satellite*. Not wanting to reveal his presence too soon lest the suspected tender be frightened off, Faunce got under way half an hour behind the *Merchant,* passed her at a distance in the outer harbor, steamed into the swells outside Sandy Hook, and swung in toward the shore. Out came the *George Birkbeck,* still towing the *Merchant;* a couple of miles out to sea the tug cast off the schooner. It was the moment for seizure—or was it? Another tug, the *John Birkbeck,* was steaming toward the schooner. Making a circle around the *Merchant,* the tug took up the hawser and steered farther out to sea. Faunce pulled alongside an anchored merchantman and went aboard to get a better view from its loftier deck. He watched the receding *Merchant* for awhile, then returned to the *Satellite* and ordered full steam ahead. The crew of the *John Birkbeck* saw Faunce's tug coming, suspected she was full of officers, and heaved the schooner's hawser overboard as the engineer opened his throttle. But it was in vain, and federal officers were soon striding the decks of both slaver and tender.

It was a neat capture. The only possible blunder was in overlooking several objects floating in the water as the *Satellite* pursued the *Merchant* and her tug. Afterward the *Satellite's* captain recalled that he had seen something that looked like a bed go overboard from the schooner, and his lieutenant later noticed a few bundles of cotton and letter paper, perhaps the contents of a slit mattress, floating on the water. In the excitement no one connected the two events; Faunce knew nothing of either, and the letters were not picked up. No one will ever know whether or not the letters were instructions to the slaver's captain.

But some interesting items were discovered when the *John Birkbeck* was searched back in the harbor. Crowded behind a couple of chests underneath a berth was Andreas Castro, a Spaniard who had no explanation for choosing to ride in so strange a place. Hiding half-submerged inside the water tank was José Santos, who was similarly uncommunicative; a memorandum book extracted from his soggy clothing revealed that he had helped to outfit the *Merchant*. Aboard the schooner was found Casper Mauricio Cunha, who had been the *Falmouth's* supercargo. Indictments were soon returned in circuit court against Santos, Cunha, owner Thomas Carlin, and shipper Vincent Beiro for fitting out a slaver. McKeon filed libels against not only the *Merchant,* but also the *John Birkbeck,* making her the only tugboat ever tried for being engaged in the transportation of slaves.

But the prosecutions so promisingly begun crumbled into nothing. The *Merchant's* cargo was not incriminating by the standards of the federal courts at New York. It was easy to guess what connection the tug's passengers had with the schooner, but it was not so easy to prove it. McKeon wanted more time to prepare his case, but District Judge Betts had little patience with government delays. A year earlier he had refused to confiscate the slaver *Braman* when the normal period of time for a claimant to begin his defense had passed, arguing that he should have more time to appear. But now the judge hurried to dispose of the *Merchant's* case. Declaring petulantly, and inaccurately, that the case had been on the calendar for two or three court terms, he ordered McKeon to try it immediately. When the district attorney was unable to do so, Betts dismissed the libels. The criminal prosecutions, requiring even more rigorous evidence for success, were finally abandoned. But Captain Faunce had at least demonstrated that skill was useful in catching slavers inside harbors as well as on the African coast or off Cuba.[9]

Faunce had one more opportunity to use his skill. In July, 1860, the bark *Kate* made ready to put to sea, with Henrico da Costa, alias José Hernandez, alias Antonio Henriques, intending to skipper her to Africa. Because da Costa had been indicted four years earlier for his part in the preparation of the *Braman,* he decided to be prudent and join her outside the harbor, in the event that the bribe offered to clearance clerk James L. De Graw for not warning his superiors about her cargo should fail. Therefore, on the afternoon of July 3, four vessels headed for a rendezvous off Sandy Hook. One was the *Kate,* the second was her tug, and the third was the tug *Magnolia.* No one aboard these three expected to see the fourth vessel: *Harriet Lane,* New York's steam revenue cutter. The attempted bribery had not worked. Captain Faunce did not expect to see da Costa, but guessing why the second tug had come along, he quickly captured both craft. When the prisoners were brought back from the *Magnolia,* there was an electric moment of recognition when da Costa was prodded before Captain Faunce. The next morning New York was startled at the news that a man fugitive for nearly four years had been retaken.

The lawyers hurried down to undo Faunce's work. Beebe, Dean, & Donohue started an ineffective damage suit against Faunce for alleged losses of an unspecified nature suffered by the *Kate*'s crew members because their vessel had been arrested. The lawyers also had the prisoners released on bail, and that "golden key" (in the sarcastic words of the *New York Tribune*) allowed da Costa to resume his role as a fugitive. But the *Kate* was confiscated, and da Costa's narrow escape so unnerved the slave traders that, after sending *Bonito* out without a clearance, they shunned New York in favor of other bases.[10]

Thus it was not only sleek sailing brigs and sloops and smoke-belching naval steamers that fought against the slave trade. Steam tugs and revenue cutters also did their part. Whether at home or on the shores of Africa and Cuba, American officers displayed considerable skill in capturing their elusive quarry. Their problems were more legal than nautical, as the following chapters will show.

- 4 -

HOW TO RECOGNIZE A SLAVER

Churning paddle wheels slashed a streak of white foam into the South Atlantic Ocean as the United States steamer *Alleghany* headed seaward from Rio de Janeiro on the morning of May 28, 1848. She had come out in such haste that her men had not had time to rehoist her foremast and yards, which had been taken down for repairs. Her lubberly appearance belied the historic nature of her mission. This was the first assignment of an American steamship in the fight against the slave trade. But Lieutenant-Commanding William W. Hunter, peering intently at a small bark ahead, had little time for reflecting on the potentialities of steamers as seagoing police. A few weeks earlier, when he had brought the *Alleghany* into Rio, the American minister, David Tod, had written enthusiastically: "She is exactly what we wanted. . . . Our ability to seize will make seizure unnecessary." [1] But Tod was a bad prophet, and Hunter had orders to search the bark *Louisa* and seize her if she seemed to be a slaver.

The train of circumstances leading up to Lieutenant Hunter's problem went back to mid-April, when Joseph Souder appeared at the American consulate in Rio. Souder, a Philadelphia sea captain already notorious for taking the schooner *Van Buren* to Ambriz and selling her to slave traders, claimed he had just purchased the *Louisa*. He had chartered her for lawful African voyages, he said, to a Brazilian named Miranda,[2] and demanded that Consul Gorham Parks issue him a temporary register. It was done, and the consul, making a mental note to watch out for the *Louisa*'s clearance, sent a warning note to Commodore Daniel Storer aboard the *Brandywine*. Within a few hours Hunter had received written orders to follow Souder out to sea and halt him as soon as they were in international waters. If the *Louisa* indeed looked like a slaver, Hunter was to send her and every soul aboard under strong guard to Norfolk or Baltimore. If she did not look guilty, he would let her go on, and hope that if he was wrong someone on the other side of the ocean would terminate her voyage.

The *Louisa* was certainly not fully prepared to take slaves aboard. Four months earlier Lieutenant O. H. Berryman and the *Onkahye*, halting the *Laurens* just outside Brazilian waters, had found her first mate quite ready to talk about the criminal schemes of the supercargo, who had in glowing terms described the slave trade as a profitable business for a young man.[3] That kind of testimony was certain proof against a vessel, just as a slave deck and extra mess gear were; but perhaps Hunter would not find so ready a source of information. What if everyone stoutly protested innocence, pointing to the charter party and the clearance papers as proof of their honesty? Hunter read in his copy of the Navy Department instructions the cheerful assertion that "there are a variety of signs and indications by which . . . [the] true character [of slavers] may, at all times, be conjectured," and noted a list of five such signs: double sets of papers or logbooks, high wages promised to the crew, forged consular seals, an unusual number of water casks or provisions, and special fittings. But the instructions ended with a more chilling observation:

These are a few of the devices to which the slave trader resorts. In calling your attention to them, I have in view only to impress you with a deep sense of the artful character of the adversaries with whom you have to deal, and of the reckless disregard of all truth and honor as well as of all law and humanity. Nothing but the utmost vigilance and caution will enable you to detect them. I have no doubt that your own observations and sagacity will soon discover other contrivances for deceiving and escaping you.[4]

Hunter must have wondered whether his sagacity would be equal to the task, and whether an unknown judge and jury at Norfolk or Baltimore would agree with his conjectures. He would soon have to decide, for they were now pulling near the *Louisa,* well outside the limits of Brazilian sovereignty. One of the *Alleghany*'s gun crews rammed home a blank cartridge and fired it, the universal signal to "Heave to!" Souder's men backed their main topsail, and the *Louisa* lost headway. Lieutenant Hunter bade his boarding party good luck, and watched as they rowed over to seek the information he wanted.

The drama now centered on the *Alleghany*'s second-in-command. Clambering up *Louisa*'s sloping side, he found Souder in a coöperative mood. The shipping list was produced and the crew were lined up on deck, answering promptly enough as their names were called. The two mates seemed to be Americans, but the remaining eleven were Spaniards, Brazilians, and Portuguese—precisely the nationalities one would expect to find aboard a slaver. This was not an unusually large crew—or was it? Eleven other men were on board, likewise Spaniards, Brazilians, and Portuguese. Four bunked aft with the officers and seven shared quarters with the seamen in the forecastle. They were explained as passengers. Hunter's deputy noted that the wages set down on paper for the admitted crew members were not especially high, and no one from among the motley crowd of foreigners on deck said that the crew and the passengers had been promised anything extra.

The *Alleghany*'s sailors started the laborious task of searching the hold for hidden or suspicious cargo. This was a difficult job, even under the favorable circumstance of a calm sea. It was easy enough to open the three hatches on the main deck, but beneath them was a bewildering maze of boxes, bales, and barrels. It had taken days for this cargo to be loaded, and the searchers could hardly hoist it all out on the deck. Even that would not be enough, for boxes and bales and barrels did not always contain what their labels claimed. They had to compromise, then, probing here and there, opening an occasional package, and, to speed the work, carefully taking down the bulkhead separating the forecastle from the hold, piece by piece. At the end, the cargo seemed to agree with the manifest: 320 barrels of gunpowder; 161 barrels of farina; 27 dozen planks; good quantities of rum, rice, beans, and dried beef; some wine; cases of muskets and other ironware; and forty casks filled with salt water. Souder explained that he needed the water for ballast because the cargo was too light for his 267-ton vessel. As slaves could not exist on salt water, the casks were harmless unless the water was changed.

The planks and the farina and the casks may have seemed suspicious, but nowhere in sight was any extra mess gear to cook and serve food for slaves. There were no medicines, no disinfectants, no shackles, unless they were hidden below. The charts and the logbook and the papers were normal—they could hardly be otherwise, when the *Louisa* had just lawfully cleared Rio for Africa—and the charter party looked businesslike enough. The passengers were suspicious, but there was no proof that they were extra hands to manage Africans on the return voyage. It was indeed difficult to decide whether or not a judge and jury would be impressed by this kind of circumstantial evidence.

And that was precisely Lieutenant Hunter's problem. Many officers in the same circumstances would have reached the same conclusions he did, and would have given the same orders that he gave his men. He decided not to apprehend the *Louisa* for lack of sufficient evidence. Late in the afternoon, after the boarding party returned to the *Alleghany,* the two vessels parted company, and by nightfall were miles apart, the *Louisa* headed for Africa, the *Alleghany* returning to her moorings in Rio harbor. The first cruise of an American steamship against the slave trade had ended.

Eleven days later Commodore Storer had further orders for Lieutenant Hunter. Consul Parks had just written a letter denouncing the *Juliet,* a 138-ton schooner hailing from Portland, Maine. On the surface the *Juliet* seemed more honest than the *Louisa.* She had not changed her registry at Rio, and Captain Nathaniel Gordon, son of a respected seagoing family, had no record of delivering ships to Brazilians at Ambriz or anywhere else. But Parks, carefully gathering Rio gossip, believed that the *Juliet* was carrying shackles, and that the cook would point out their hiding place if the vessel was stopped at sea, away from the possible vengeance of Rio's slave traders.

A little game of cat-and-mouse followed, with the mouse resigned to what it expected would be a harmless visit from the cat. In the late afternoon of June 9, 1848, a steam tug pulled the *Juliet* away from her pier to the mouth of the harbor, where Gordon anchored, presumably to await a better wind or tide. Hunter and the *Alleghany* followed, and spent the night to seaward of their quarry. At eight the next morning Gordon's men hauled up their anchor and hoisted sail, and the steamer followed the schooner out. Five miles offshore the *Alleghany,* her 1,000-ton iron hull dwarfing the *Juliet,* pulled close alongside. Hunter shouted across that he was sending a boarding party. The steamer's first and second lieutenants and master conducted one of the most rigorous searches ever made of a suspected slaver at sea; it lasted eleven hours and thirty minutes. The cook was a disappointment, for he knew nothing of any shackles. In the search for such evidence, both hatches were opened and the cargo was shifted out to the hull planking at several places. But the incriminating hardware did not appear, nor did anything else that was not on the manifest. There were, to be sure, such suspicious items as twelve dozen planks, a fair amount of biscuit and farina, and a few copper basins that could be used in a slaver's culinary department. But there were also many articles of little or no value in transporting slaves (though some of them could buy slaves): bundles of cotton prints; 1,200 bars of iron; nine cases of knives; some wine; quantities of paint, oakum, tar, tacks, and leather; and that most unlikely of all items aboard a slaver, a barrel of china dolls. The only water aboard was the 1,100 of 1,200 gallons needed by the crew. There was no extra mess gear, the papers were normal, and the crew numbered only seven men, none of whom was Spanish, Portuguese, or Brazilian. There were no passengers of any nationality.

This time few would disagree with Lieutenant Hunter's decision that Parks was the victim of malicious gossip, or perhaps had an overactive imagination as a result of hearing constant rumors about slaving expeditions. Hunter gave his permission for the *Juliet* to go on her way.

The affair was ended, but only for the moment. The *Juliet,* vanishing into the darkness that night of June 10, never returned to Rio de Janeiro. A few weeks later rumors began to circulate that she had crossed the Atlantic safely, had come under the direct management of Brazilians, and had returned to Brazil with a cargo of slaves. Fourteen years later her captain, Nathaniel Gordon, unsuspected as a slave trader in 1848, ended his days on the gallows. He was the only American ever to die for transporting slaves, but then his ship was the *Erie,* not the *Juliet.* On the basis of these facts it is very likely that the *Juliet,* accepted as clean by Lieutenant Hunter, was indeed a slaver.

And what of the *Louisa,* "owned" by a dishonest sea captain and carrying foreign seamen and doubtful "passengers" and extra water casks? Lieutenant Hunter had allowed her to proceed only because he feared that the case against her would not stand up in court. Her voyage to Africa was seemingly guiltless; on October 1 she returned to Rio harbor, thirty-three days out of the Congo, in ballast, with Souder still in charge and his crew intact. If the *Louisa* brought back slaves, the Rio rumormongers did not pick up the story. She may have been merely an auxiliary on that trip, possibly tied in with the *Juliet.* Her passengers and water casks and food would have been useful to Gordon's crew.

These two stories point up a serious problem, which was encountered by other naval commanders, and by marshals and customs collectors and district attorneys in the United States. How could one distinguish a slaver in the early stages of its preparation and voyage? How could one then convince judge and jury that property should be confiscated and men sent to prison because a web of suspicious circumstances had gathered around a particular voyage?

Lieutenant Hunter had been very cautious. Any naval officer looking for slavers in the year 1848 had to be equally careful, for reasons to be explained later. Other officers doing their duty at other times were more daring, and occasionally even bold. Sometimes their boldness in seizing suspicious vessels paid off, and sometimes it did not; but on the whole discouragement was the reward of officers who acted upon circumstantial evidence alone. The reason for this is the subject of the next chapter.[5]

= 5 =

CONFUSION ON THE BENCH

Five days before Christmas, 1860, as the Union was crumbling to pieces, the United States steamer *Mohawk,* Lieutenant T. Augustus Craven, steamed into Havana harbor. Craven was a doubly worried man, concerned both with his duty to suppress rebellion and with the warning of Thomas Savage, an alert American consular officer. Two New Orleans vessels had just cleared the Havana consulate for Africa, and were probably slavers. Craven steamed out to sea and waited for them to come out, and by the next morning both were sailing toward Key West in charge of prize crews. On the Florida mainland secessionists were in control, menacing the Florida keys and forcing the handful of small steamers operating out of Key West to maintain a wary lookout astern lest their base be seized in a sudden coup; but Judge William Marvin of the South Florida district was still holding court amid the tensions and the rebellious sentiment of his own town. Deciding that both prizes, the bark *Mary J. Kimball* and the brig *Toccoa,* were indeed slavers, he ordered them confiscated. The threat of the *Toccoa's* owner to appeal his case to the Supreme Court [1] turned out to be a bluff, and Judge Marvin's decision stood. It was an extremely informative decision.

The brig *Toccoa,* built of timbers hewn from the forests of northern New England, first tasted salt water at Camden, Maine, in 1854. Measuring 105 feet, 1 inch, from bow to stern, with a 26-

foot beam and a 9-foot hold, she carried about 227 tons, and was large enough to transport upward of 550 slaves to Cuba in reasonable safety.[2] But it was not until November, 1858, that she became the property of Anthony Horta, an agent for African slave traders.[3] Horta did not immediately send the *Toccoa* into the trade. Using her to carry ordinary cargo in honest commerce, he kept her in readiness until her real owners needed her as a slaver. Early in December, 1860, the *Toccoa*'s turn came, and Messrs. Galdiz & Nenninger of Havana, commission merchants, arranged for her to bring over a cargo from New Orleans. Additional items were put aboard at Havana, and a charter party was drawn up for a voyage to England or the United States via the Congo River. It was in good form, promising Horta $600 a month for the use of his vessel. Along with it went a letter to Don Luis Juveneido, the merchants' agent in the Congo, instructing him to sell the cargo brought out by the *Toccoa* and purchase palm oil for delivery either to England or to the United States, depending on prices in the two countries. Nothing, seemingly, could have been more businesslike; no fuller arrangements for an honest voyage could have been made.

The trading cargo that *Toccoa* took out of Havana was not particularly well designed for a slaver. Three thousand gallons of fresh water was not nearly enough, and the hundred knocked-down casks were a logical preparation for a homeward voyage with palm oil. Sixty-three barrels of rice, forty-one of bread, twenty-six of beef, and twelve of pork would take care of slaves well enough, but there was no cooking equipment to prepare the food and only a dozen buckets (with no spoons) to serve it in. There was, moreover, no lumber with which to build a slave deck. A large supply of calico prints and some liquor and cigars could be used to buy slaves, but they could also be traded for palm oil. A case of preserves, seven barrels of flour, fifteen kegs of lard, and a variety of other minor items added nothing to the *Toccoa*'s criminal appearance. One suspicious sign was that the cargo was altogether too small to make a long voyage profitable; others were the presence of fifty bundles of hoop iron, twenty pounds of rivets, extra medicines, and a new French flag, all unmanifested. Still, the crew of twelve was not unusually large, and its members swore that to their knowledge the *Toccoa*'s voyage was nothing more than an honest palm-oil speculation. Indeed, she looked as clean as any vessel that was ever condemned as a slaver.

At this point one might question Judge Marvin's decision that the *Toccoa* was a slaver. Apparently he reached his decision on the basis of both history and intuition. The slave trade between Cuba and Africa was notorious, and its existence needed no proof: "I say it is impossible without wilful blindness to ignore these facts, for they are notorious and part of the history of the day." Furthermore, no honest trade between the two places was known to exist. Theoretically it could exist, but Marvin trenchantly declared that it was up to Horta to prove that the *Toccoa* was on honest business; it was not the government's responsibility to disprove it. Having taken this position, the judge proceeded to interpret the various pieces of circumstantial evidence to fit his conviction that the *Toccoa* was not on legitimate business. The French flag was intended to keep off American or British boarding parties, and not merely for "occasions of courtesy or ceremony," as Horta's attorney had argued. The smallness of the cargo, which only half filled the hold, was not simply bad judgment, but proved that the vessel was a slaver, for only slave traders could undertake so long a voyage for so meager profits. Everything in the cargo could buy or feed slaves, and the absence of lumber and mess gear meant nothing because they could have been put aboard on the slave coast. The careful business arrangements Marvin dismissed as sheer subterfuge.

The fundamental reasoning behind Marvin's decision was that the *Toccoa* had been arrested while in a trade that was notoriously suspicious; that the total circumstances of the voyage suggested a dishonest purpose; and that, because she looked like a slaver, he could interpret each individual piece of evidence on the way it fitted into an over-all pattern of guilt. Though Marvin would not have admitted it, his reasoning came close to maintaining that any vessel trading between Cuba and Africa was automatically presumed guilty until her owners proved her otherwise, even though it was theoretically possible for lawful trade to exist between those places.

This viewpoint reversed the traditional concept that the accused is to be presumed innocent until proven guilty; that was why Horta's attorney talked of appealing to the Supreme Court. What untoward event caused him to drop his plans? While the case was hanging fire, Horta got his vessel back to sea by a process to be described later, and in September, 1861, the Spanish cruiser *Neptuno* confronted her off the Cuban coast. This event was fatally embarrassing, for the Spanish sailors discovered aboard no fewer than 627 "bozals," illegal African "immigrants" whose transportation to the Cuban cane fields was being charitably assisted by Horta's brig. The *Toccoa* was supplying the Africans with free passage, food and water, and the prospects of lifelong employment in a Christian country, though the recipients of these blessings seemed singularly unappreciative. Neither did the Spanish government appreciate the services of the *Toccoa,* and thus ended the troubled career of Horta's slaver.[4]

At this point the reader may well ask why there was any serious trouble in suppressing the slave trade. Even if juries were unwilling to send men to prison on circumstantial evidence, the trade could easily have been stamped out, or at least severely harassed, if American vessels sailing to Africa from notorious slave-trade centers like Rio and Havana were automatically confiscated unless their owners could prove they were on honest voyages. Why, for example, should Lieutenant Hunter have hesitated to seize the *Louisa,* which was surely as suspicious as the *Toccoa?* The answer may be found in the case of the ketch *Brothers,* owned by Saul Street of Charleston, South Carolina, and sent into that port for confiscation by Commander Thomas W. Brent and the sloop of war *Marion.*

The case against the *Brothers* was as damning as it could be, short of catching her fully prepared to load slaves or with a crew member willing to testify that he knew she was a slaver because Captain James Gage had told him so. The *Brothers'* registered owner had already sold the brig *St. Andrew* into the trade, and Captain Gage himself held official title to the slaver *Lyra,* seized and condemned at Key West at the same time that the *Brothers* was sailing to Africa. The ketch had been chartered by a Havana merchant for lawful trade with Africa, but the legality was dubious because the cargo included nearly everything needed to buy, confine, and feed a group of Africans. The list was remarkable for its completeness: two tons of rice, a hundred barrels of bread, some preserved fish and dried beef, stacks of empty water casks, enough lumber (thoughtfully unmanifested) to build a slave deck, two iron cooking boilers, bricks enough to build furnaces for them, five hundred wooden spoons, five cases of drugs, five kegs of vinegar, a large quantity of rum, and $8,416 in hard cash. The seamen, though few in number, were all Spaniards hired at high wages; the only items the *Brothers* lacked were extra men, weapons, firewood, and water in her casks. All of them could easily have been supplied at the embarkation point. Captain Gage, realizing that his vessel looked like a slaver, tried to avoid arrest and hove to only when the *Marion,* after a three-hour chase, pulled close enough to send the contents of a loaded 32-pounder whistling across the ketch's bows.

The arrival of the *Brothers* at Charleston on November 11, 1858, created considerable dissatisfaction among certain circles in that city. The editors of the *Mercury,* who had been agitating since 1854 for legalization of the African slave trade, declared that the seizure of vessels upon "mere" suspicion was an atrocious affront to the law. It was better, they argued, that ninety-nine criminals go free than that one innocent man be condemned. In scornful words they decried the efforts of the federal government against the slave trade:

We are glad, however, that the law is bearing such brilliant fruits! While England imports her coolies and France her African emigrants, our fleets are engaged in the brilliant and peculiarly American crusade of playing police, and interfering against Americans engaged in trade between foreign countries.

Politicians, too, beat their breasts, while a grand jury had little trouble in deciding not to indict Gage. Some of the same spirit evidently animated District Judge Alexander G. Magrath, who declared: "I cannot discover what there is in this cargo which of itself leads to a conclusion of a criminal purpose or excludes the fact

of such articles having been intended for a lawful purpose." The
Brothers had been chartered lawfully, and lawfully cleared from
Havana, and had lawfully hired her foreign seamen. "If it is as-
sumed," Judge Magrath argued

that the voyage was unlawful, then these circumstances . . . appear
as so many agencies employed in the execution of that purpose. But if
regarded as the circumstances out of which the proof of an illegal purpose is to be derived, I do not perceive how . . . they can aid the
conclusion sought to be derived from them.

Magrath's opinion was obviously based on exactly the opposite
principle from Judge Marvin's. Magrath started out by assuming
the vessel innocent, and then interpreted each piece of evidence to
fit that assumption. He found, inevitably, that not a single piece
would stand on its own feet. He ignored, or was unable to perceive,
the damning pattern formed by the various pieces of evidence when
fitted together.[5]

It may easily be argued that Magrath was a secret supporter of
the slave trade, or that at least he was influenced by South Carolina hostility toward the *Brothers'* arrest, and used perverted logic
in reaching his verdict. But his logic was not perverted, as is proven
by these words spoken by another judge in a different slave-trade
case:

Most, if not all, of the articles of merchandise which are employed for
the purposes of the slave trade are also capable of being employed for
the purposes of lawful commerce, and in these cases, therefore, it is
not sufficient to consider merely what are the cargoes of the vessels accused . . . but all the circumstances.

This judge went on to decree the release of a vessel captured after
sailing from Havana under command of a mariner who had just
purchased it from a notorious slave trader. The vessel had extra
hatches, beams spanning the hold, planks, bricks, charts of Africa,
and a large quantity of fresh water. But this judge was no advocate
of slavery; he was Lord Justice George James Turner, of the Judicial Committee of Her Majesty's Privy Council, reviewing the
case of the British brig *Laura* which had been condemned at An-

tigua.[6] Magrath's opinion was based on the same idea, that over-all patterns of circumstantial evidence should be ignored; that each specific item of evidence should be weighed individually to determine whether it was incompatible with an honest purpose. A particular judge might choose this method of interpreting circumstantial evidence on the basis of his personal philosophy, his prior legal training, prejudice born of local sentiments, or a conscious wish to have the case turn out in a certain way.

Uncertainty concerning the views of the judge who would try a case was bound to have some effect on the officers who arrested slavers and their crews, and particularly on lieutenants and commanders in the navy, who were unfamiliar with the vagaries of individual federal judges but could be called upon to send prizes into any port or any judicial district. The law specified that arrested vessels be sent to their home ports; [7] although the law was often violated (as in the *Toccoa*'s case), a conscientious officer was likely to obey if he possibly could. We may imagine cautious exchanges of advice between old and new officers: "Capture all the Key West vessels you want, but don't touch one from Charleston"; "Judge Sprague at Boston is all right, but watch out for Judge Betts at New York"; "Try to get your prizes into Norfolk, because Judge Hallyburton gives good decisions"; and so on. No one can ever know whether or not such advice really did circulate, but it easily could have, for Marvin and Magrath were by no means the only judges to differ on circumstantial evidence.

Another pair of contrasting decisions illustrates the perplexity that vexed naval officers. The *Panther* and the *Chancellor* were arrested off the slave coast in the mid-'forties, after American and English naval officers alike had become convinced of their guilty intentions. Both were commanded by dubious characters. Both vessels were large and costly to maintain; both had loitered for months doing little visible trading, apparently waiting for an opportunity to slip out with a cargo of slaves. Both were fairly well outfitted for carrying slaves, and the few essential items that were lacking could have been put aboard in a few hours of hard work on a secluded bit of coast. But the *Panther* went into Charleston, where its case was heard by Magrath's predecessor, Judge Robert Gilcrist, and the *Chancellor* was tried in New York, before Judge Betts. Juries acquitted the captains of both vessels, but Gilcrist declared the *Panther* forfeit while Betts released the *Chancellor*. The *Panther*'s owner protested the decision and, after losing a circuit court battle, threatened to take the matter to the Supreme Court; later he had a change of heart and dropped the suit. Thus both decisions stood, and one or the other was plainly a mockery of justice.[8]

Another example is found in the cases of the whalers *Laurens* and *Augusta*. Both had been purchased by newcomers to the whaling business, both were fitted out adequately with food and mess gear, and both proposed to go to sea so ill equipped with whaling gear that they could not have taken a single whale. This was merely bad judgment, their owners' lawyers argued. Trying the *Laurens* case, Judge Charles H. Ingersoll of the Connecticut district decided that no convincing proof of guilt had been offered; that, on the contrary, the evidence against the vessel was weak. This opinion so unnerved the prosecuting attorney, William D. Shipman, that he wrote to Washington: "I am in great doubt whether to appeal this case. The Judge's opinion is so decided, not to say fervid, in vindication of the ship, that it is calculated to inspire me with distrust of my own opinion, which may be biased." In the end he did not appeal, but, when raised to the bench after Ingersoll's death, Shipman delivered an opposite verdict in the *Augusta* case. Deciding that she looked like a slaver, from all the circumstances, he wrote an opinion permeated with the prosecutor's viewpoint; he interpreted the various pieces of evidence, not as separate items, but as components of a guilty pattern.[9]

These judicial differences created problems for naval officers, but they were much harder on land-based officers who were located permanently in a district, under the complete control of the local judge. Judge Betts laid down a rule that no cargo of any kind was incriminating;[10] the result was that the port of New York became a haven for the outfitting of slavers, as no one dared raise a hand against them unless some other evidence, such as testimony from a crew member or an illegal departure, was available. Yet Betts himself seemed to deal in subtleties, and to shift ground slightly from time to time; and an interim judge once gave a verdict utterly in conflict with Betts's usual views.[11] This was hardly calculated to ensure a strict and even administration of justice.

It is difficult to know where to place the blame for this confusing pattern of contradictory decisions, or to decide which method of interpreting evidence most closely conformed to real justice. Some people thought that Congress should have spelled out the method of construing circumstantial evidence, or should have named certain items as incriminating cargo whose presence would require automatic confiscation, unless adequately explained. The British, in their treaties with Brazil, Spain, and finally the United States, used the latter method, but never on their own vessels, as witnessed by the Privy Council decision referred to above. Apparently the British government viewed Englishmen as a more privileged group than Brazilians, Spaniards, and Americans, though it is only fair to add that Englishmen were much less likely to engage in the slave trade, because of the dangerous Royal Navy patrols. The question was whether or not Congress, which did not operate enough cruisers to frighten Americans similarly, should have established stricter rules for Americans than Parliament established for Englishmen.

Perhaps the federal courts themselves were to blame. There is no certainty that the judges themselves were fully aware of what was going on, for their decisions in slave-trade cases often vanished into courthouse archives without ever being printed. The decisions that were published usually appeared only in local newspapers. Exactly who was to blame for this is almost impossible to say. The judges had no money to print and circulate decisions themselves, unless they wanted to dip into their own pockets. Lawyers' associations and publishers of legal books seldom bothered to sponsor volumes of decisions, and rarely published all the decisions of a court. Only a handful of Americans had much to do with federal law; very few indeed had any personal involvement with slave-trade cases, which were fairly rare exceptions to the usual run of admiralty suits and criminal prosecutions.

The Supreme Court could have done much by ruling on a few

cases based on circumstantial evidence, but then, as now, it acted only on decisions appealed to it. If the government won a lawsuit, the only appellant would be the vessel's owner; and no owner appealed before 1864, when the slave trade was vanishing. If the *Panther's* claimant had carried through his appeal, the Supreme Court might have gone on record as favoring a liberal interpretation of circumstantial evidence; he may have failed to do so precisely because of this possibility.

It could be argued that the government's attorneys should have been more vigorous in appealing cases that the government lost. They did appeal from district courts to circuit courts on a number of occasions, but in all the years when the slave trade was being suppressed not one district attorney—Democrat, Whig, or Republican—ever pushed a suit into the Supreme Court. Here, again, it is difficult to pin down the blame. The attorney himself might have been convinced by the judge's arguments, as Shipman, most assuredly no slacker, was convinced. The *Brothers'* prosecutor wrote to Washington that he was satisfied with Magrath's reasoning; in fact, he was so well satisfied that he did not even bother to send along any details for his superiors to ponder.[12] The superiors themselves were too shorthanded to take a keen interest in the matter. There was no centralized law enforcement agency in Washington; normally each attorney decided for himself what he ought to do, though he could call upon the solicitor of the treasury for help if necessary.[13] Only Congress had the power to create and support a central law enforcement agency, and congressmen were under pressure from their constituents to save money and avoid the creation of a possibly dangerous bureaucracy. In the final analysis, then, the blame might be laid on the public, except that the public had never heard of such incongruities in the law, and, indeed, would have had difficulty in discovering that they existed.

– 6 –

BURNED FINGERS

It was night, and aboard the United States brig of war *Boxer* seamen hurried to and fro securing tackle and rigging as the ship dropped anchor in the placid waters of Kabenda Bay. The date was Sunday, April 12, 1846. Suddenly across the dark waters came the sound of rowing, and alongside the *Boxer* appeared the dark form of a small boat which came from Her Majesty's frigate *Action,* lying at anchor nearby. The English officer explained to Lieutenant John E. Bispham of the *Boxer* that an American brig, the *Malaga,* full of slave-trade merchandise and under charter to the notorious Brazilian slave trader Manoel Pinto da Fonseca, was in Kabenda Bay. Bispham thanked his visitor and promised to take a look at the *Malaga.* At daylight the next morning two American boats and thirty men were on their way to board the brig. They found her indeed full of slave goods: brandy, muskets, dry goods, tobacco, farina, rice, biscuits, salt beef. They probably did not know that the brandy, the farina, and the rice had been sent over by the same Rio merchants who had supplied the notorious *Pons,* lately captured full of slaves; but Lieutenant Bispham correctly concluded that the *Malaga* was aiding and abetting the slave trade as an auxiliary, if nothing more. Such activity was presumably in violation of the act of May 10, 1800, which stated: "It shall be unlawful for any citizen directly or indirectly to hold or have any right or property in any vessel employed or made use of in the transportation or carrying of slaves from one foreign country to another." Bispham ignored the protests of Captain Charles Lovett, and the *Malaga* was soon recrossing the Atlantic with nine navy men in charge. The *Boxer* continued down the slave coast on patrol.[1]

At the time this incident at Kabenda seemed unimportant. It paled into insignificance, so far as excitement was concerned, alongside the *Boxer*'s unsuccessful chase of a half-laden Brazilian slaver a few months later. This chase gave the *Boxer*'s crew the rare opportunity to see an actual slave embarkation. They passed so close to the beach that through telescopes they could see several hundred slaves left behind in the hasty departure of the slaver; a large contingent of disappointed Africans guarding them; the boats, with black oarsmen, which were used to put the slaves on board; and, supervising the work, several men in European dress who were looking at the sailors with spyglasses.[2] The unopposed seizure of an anchored brig loaded with cloth, liquor, and food was a minor event in comparison, yet in the long run the capture of the *Malaga* was far more significant than the seizure of that Brazilian slaver would have been.

Back in Massachusetts, learned gentlemen of the law were considering the *Malaga*'s case. Justice Charles L. Woodbury, presiding over the New England circuit courts, had recently decided in parallel cases that it was no crime to ship goods to Africa and sell them to slave traders, unless the men sailing the auxiliary had a personal financial stake in the slaves that could be purchased with the goods.[3] Ten years later another justice on that circuit, Benjamin R. Curtis, modified Woodbury's ruling to some extent,[4] but as the law stood in mid-July, 1846, a craft like the *Malaga* violated no law. Her captain and owners had no demonstrable link with the slave trade, beyond the hiring out of their services in a profitable, if questionable, freight business. On July 17 the lawsuit against the *Malaga* was therefore abandoned, and the Secretary of the Navy warned the African squadron to be more cautious in seizing vessels. His warning was reinforced a few months later when the brig *Casket,* seized by Commander Lewis E. Simonds of the *Marion,* was libeled and tried under circumstances similar to the *Malaga*'s; Judge Peleg Sprague ordered the release of the vessel, and did not even award Simonds a certificate of probable cause, that prized document certifying that the arrest had been well justified by the evidence and that therefore the owners had no right to bring damage suits for false arrest.[5]

Thus, according to the law, no one could arrest a vessel merely for aiding and abetting the slave trade. Strict construction of the act of 1800 had triumphed. It was a potent construction; how potent became tragically apparent on the slave coast a few months later. Lieutenant Bispham released the suspicious brig *Senator* because the evidence against her was no stronger than that against the *Malaga* had been, and the *Senator* went on to pick up more equipment, to take 900 slaves aboard, and to land 600 survivors in Brazil. Seventy-four suffocated the first night, and more than 200 others died of thirst during the remainder of the three-week ordeal.[6] But stench and death agonies and bodies thrown overboard to the sharks did not disturb the orderly processes of lawyers and judges in the United States. When Bispham broke down and returned home an invalid in the summer of 1847, he received the rudest jolt that a naval officer could experience in line of duty, short of a court-martial: a summons to appear as defendant in a damage suit, filed by the *Malaga*'s owners and captain, which charged him with false arrest.

As commander of the *Boxer*, Lieutenant Bispham had received $2,500 a year. The plaintiffs presented him with a bill for $10,380. The fact that the *Malaga* had been detained only three months (plus the time it took her to get back to Kabenda) did not deter co-owners Josiah Lovett, Elliott Woodbury, and Seward Lee from demanding excessive damages. Neither did they seem embarrassed by the fact that, before the suit came to trial, they "sold" the *Malaga* to Captain Lovett, who proceeded to take her on an outright slaving voyage. The *Casket*'s owners, eager to get in on a good thing, started two lawsuits against Commander Simonds. The Navy Department bestirred itself to find good lawyers to defend Bispham and Simonds, but there was no certainty that either one would win his case, or that Congress would show much speed in repaying their fines.[7] The same thing could happen to any other officer who took the responsibility of seizing a vessel which a remote judge, whose reasoning could not be divined in advance, might decide was an honest trader unreasonably harassed by the law.

At this point fear—cold, well-justified fear—gripped the officers of the African squadron. Thus far they had done their best against the slave trade, but now things looked different. Commodore George C. Read wrote the Navy Department that officers "dread the trouble and expense to which they are liable to be put, and they will hereafter be so very cautious as to what they seize that I have reason to doubt the probability of your hearing of a capture." [8] Read had predicted that if even an indubitable slaver like the *Chancellor* could escape condemnation, "it will be time to give up all cruising on the coast of Africa." [9] His words were almost prophetic, and presaged one of the most inglorious episodes in American naval history: a mass shirking of assigned duties, carefully concealed from the American public.

Until the blow descended upon Bispham and Simonds, American naval vessels had patrolled the entire slave coast, both north and south of the equator. The patrols south of the equator were slender, as there were few cruisers and the supply depot was far away, but the cruisers had gone to Kabenda and the Congo and Ambriz and along the rest of the coast as often as they could. Most of the captures they had made had been south of the equator, and in the future almost all of them would have to be there, for during 1847–1848 the slave trade shifted southward as the British extended their treaty system along the underside of the great African bulge. If the squadron had followed a logical course, it would therefore have increased its patrols off the Congo Basin after 1847. Instead, it abandoned them entirely for more than two years. Not until March, 1850, did an American cruiser ply the waters south of the equator, and this at a time when American slavers were reaching the height of their participation in the Brazilian trade, a trade conducted entirely from the Congo Basin.[10]

Naval officers knew where the slave trade was, for they frequently met well-informed British cruisers. Moreover, it is not likely that they suddenly turned indifferent, for the same type of men had been there a year or two earlier. Though not a hint of their motive was released to the public, and they may not even have formally notified the Navy Department of it, the only possible explanation for the sudden disappearance of vital patrols is fear.[11] The United States had entered a solemn compact to patrol the African coast, and the squadron was under orders to carry out that compact, but the treaty did not specify what part of the coast was to be patrolled. If the cruisers carefully patrolled only those portions where slavers were rare, no naval officer would have to make the difficult choice between doing his duty by arresting a suspicious vessel, and protecting his pocketbook by letting the vessel go.

The Brazilian squadron was infected by the same fear,[12] and that is why Lieutenant Hunter was so cautious with the *Louisa*. It could not, however, shirk its duty so successfully as the African squadron did, and that is why the only arrests made at the height of Amercan participation in the Brazilian trade came on the near side of the Atlantic. If Consul Parks sent a specific warning about a suspected vessel, the Brazilian squadron could not afford to ignore it. Parks could write home if they did, and his more influential superior, David Tod, was as anxious to have such vessels searched as Parks was. On the African coast, however, duty could easily be shirked, and nobody but Englishmen and slave traders would be the wiser. There was not a single American consul on the west coast of Africa south of the equator, or anyone else likely to reveal the news. For two years the African squadron carried on its sham patrol, while its officers awaited developments.

Then, in 1849, came cheering news. Both damage suits had failed, and Judge John K. Kane of the Eastern Pennsylvania district placed on record a decision that did much to lessen the fears of officers. He rebuked the *Malaga*'s owners for bringing suit, telling them bluntly: "I can only say that I am by no means satisfied of the innocence of this vessel, and that I think the owners may be well content with her release without asking more." Judge Kane pointed out technical deficiencies in their suit, such as their failure to make a protest at the time the brig was released to them. But the heart of his argument was that courts should always be lenient about holding naval officers responsible for mistakes made in arresting vessels. He agreed that if the arrest was unreasonable—that is, if the evidence was flimsy—they would have to pay for their unreasonableness; but naval officers, he argued, operated under grave difficulties not found, for example, when arrests were made in American ports. An officer at sea could not thoroughly investigate the background of a suspicious vessel whose voyage had begun thousands of miles away. In this case, the judge found that the *Malaga*'s chartering to a notorious slave trader, and her cargo, were ample evidence to justify arrest, because an outright slaver looked much as she had. Kane gave no opinion on whether the *Malaga* had violated the law by serving as an auxiliary.[13]

Kane's decision was picked up by the law journals and widely circulated. In effect, it deterred naval officers from arresting vessels for aiding and abetting, for the evidence had to be sufficient to convince a judge that there was reasonable ground for suspecting them of being slavers. Reasonable evidence was whatever the judge might decide was reasonable; but Judge Kane, at least, and any other judge who agreed with him, would be liberal in his interpretation of reasonableness. This was not all that officers could wish for, but it was at least encouraging. And soon African slaves who had never heard of the *Malaga* or of Judge Kane had reason to be encouraged, for the African squadron resumed active patrolling. Three cruisers sailing south of the equator captured three American slavers;[14] the crisis in law enforcement was past. From the spring of 1850 until the withdrawal of the squadron in the summer of 1861, patrolling continued south of the equator, and really suspicious vessels were arrested.

Some residue of the old fear remained, however. There was always the danger that another judge might not be so understanding as Kane, and the contradictory and sometimes absurd decisions coming from the federal courts made it difficult to tell what evidence would seem reasonable. One naval officer who pursued his duties with a keen regard for his pocketbook was Isaac Mayo, commander of the squadron in 1853–1854. His flagship, the *Constitution,* ran down and captured the schooner *H. N. Gambrill* when she was nearly ready to ship slaves and thus had incriminating evidence aboard, yet Mayo released all her crew except for two men who were willing to testify against her. When the district attorney at New York complained about this, Mayo in a burst of honesty wrote the Navy Department: "I freely admit I was unwilling to send these miscreants home to give the harpies who infest the purlieus of our courts an opportunity to bring vexatious suits during my absence and seize upon my property which is tangible and open to their reclamations." Mayo was afraid that the *Gambrill's* case might drag on for a long time, or that she might even escape confiscation if she were vigorously defended. But if her crew was allowed to abandon ship, that in itself would prove their guilt so convincingly that no one would dare bring suit for false arrest.[15]

Secretary of the Navy Dobbin did not approve of Mayo's reasoning, and apparently there were no more cases of this kind until 1860. This time the arresting officer was Lieutenant William E. LeRoy, commanding the steamer *Mystic.* Having seized a suspicious New York brig, he wrote an almost pleading letter to the district attorney of that city: "Should my expectations not be realized, I most earnestly hope the Court will find the cause of suspicion sufficiently strong to relieve me from all claims for damage, &c., that terror of all our naval officers who strive for conscientious discharge of their duties on this station." The brig was in fact released, but the certificate of probable cause granted at the same time saved LeRoy from a possible damage suit. His fear, however, is the best explanation for his action a few days later when, having captured the fully equipped slaver *Triton,* he put the entire crew ashore at their request.[16]

Such fears were well known outside the service, and early in 1860 Senator Henry Wilson of Massachusetts proposed that Congress pass an act explicitly prohibiting damage suits against naval officers. As neither Democrats nor Republicans showed any interest in this rather radical proposal, the problem was finally solved only when the slave trade ceased.[17]

The last claim for damages filed against an American naval officer had a curious twist. Thus far we have been interested in domestic damage suits, operating within the framework of United States law. But there were other laws that could be invoked by wily criminals.

Early on the morning of August 14, 1860, off the northern coast of Cuba, a boarding party from the *Crusader* clambered onto the deck of a 190-ton brig. They found no slaves, but that seemed to be the only thing missing. A slave deck had been laid, and cooking boilers were ready. There were sixteen or eighteen men—twice as many as in an ordinary crew—and a small arsenal of muskets and cutlasses. There were even two 6-pounder cannon, unusual equipment for an 1860 slaver. The crew members declared that they belonged to no nation, and apparently the brig was in the same situation. When Lieutenant Maffitt pressed the captain for an explanation, he admitted that he had been to Africa for slaves. The expedition had gone afoul when the supercargo absconded with the money, and an inquisitive war steamer had made it expedient for the brig to leave the coast. Maffitt sent the brig into Key West with a prize crew in charge.

District Attorney John L. Tatum libeled the brig under the act of 1800, charging that it was the property of an unknown American citizen, and managed to bring it under the act of 1794 by alleging that some unknown person had dispatched it from Boston for the slave trade. The latter libel was sheer imagination, but Tatum expected no trouble. As owners rarely put in a claim for vessels taken under circumstances so incriminating, there would be no one to dispute the accuracy of the statements in his libel. Judge Marvin could confiscate the vessel without qualms.

This neat scheme fell apart when José Colon, a resident of Cárdenas, Cuba, came forward to claim the brig. Colon's attorney offered convincing proof that the vessel was the *Joven Antonio*, Spanish-built, Spanish-owned, and sent from a Spanish port into the slave trade. She had violated no American law. But the attorney did not stop there. It was a grievous breach of international law for Lieutenant Maffitt to have interfered with a Spanish vessel, he declared, and the lieutenant should be made to pay for this wrong.

At this moment a minor case about an obscure vessel suddenly became of great importance. If Maffitt had to pay damages for seizing a vessel showing no colors or papers because she later turned out to be Spanish, the effect on naval patrols would be disastrous. It was usual for crews caught with undeniable evidence of guilt on board to renounce nationality, yet no naval officer could safely interfere with them in the future. Judge Marvin did not let Maffitt down, but blasted Colon's brazen claim:

The persons on board, by their own showing, had abjured the protection and the law of every nation. They had piratically assumed the supposed rights of men in a state of nature. A state of nature is supposed, by many philosophers, to be a state of war, where the law of the strongest governs. If they discarded the obligation to observe any law but the law of the strongest, how can they complain if others did the same thing? . . . They were liable to punishment by the laws of their own country, and international law cannot be invoked in their favor, for this law is made for the benefit of nations and for individuals living in society and subject to its laws.[18]

The courts sympathized with naval officers, even if they did not always agree with them as to what evidence proved a vessel's guilt. Nevertheless, the threat of damage suits was an additional impediment to effective action by American naval officers.

= 7 =

UNSUNG HERO

The island of Cuba was deep in slave-smuggling plots. During the 1830's the trade was so open that Her Majesty's commissioners at Havana were able to keep track of slaves landed by going to a store in the Government Plaza which displayed a tally of them.[1] Nicholas Trist described Cuban sentiment on the subject:

The truth of the existing state of things here, in relation to the slave-trade, can be condensed into one sentence. It is a pursuit denounced in every possible way by the LAW—by law FOREIGN *made* and FOREIGN *imposed*—and supported by an overwhelming PUBLIC OPINION. . . . Is it not in the nature of man that such an effect should follow from such a cause? Thank God! it is. . . . *The trade is made no secret of, except towards the authorities,* and towards them *only* when acting in their official capacity. On all other occasions, it is spoken of with as little reserve as any other pursuit; . . . a pursuit in regard to which the people consider themselves *at war*. . . . Every capture of a slaver is a wrong: to be talked of, to become known to all, to be stored up in the memory of each. Every arrival is an exploit—a victory over the common enemy: the news of which (that would be proclaimed by the church bells, but that the Government does not dare) runs like wildfire, to arouse exultation in every breast, and to kindle anew both the spirit of cupidity and the flames of defiance. . . .[2]

As the years went by, Spanish officials apparently became more willing to do their duty, but strong sentiment still persisted among

Cuban plantation owners. As Lieutenant Stanly reported in July, 1860,

The whole population of Cuba appears to be warmly in favor of the slave trade. It is currently believed that the Spanish authorities are also favorable to it, and receive large bribes for every cargo landed; that the estates require more slaves; that the cultivation of the island is behind the demand for its products; that our cruising on this coast to suppress that trade is regarded with general hatred. . . . The feelings of the people are turning against us, and those who still like us tell me it is dangerous for them to show it. . . .

Stanly added that the residents of Cuba, Spaniards and foreigners alike, believed that anyone could be bribed, and to back up his point reported that he himself had been approached "in every way, with open offers and by insinuations amidst pleasant attentions." Three separate parties had each offered to give him $25,000 if he would not cruise in certain locations at certain times, both to be revealed to him upon acceptance of the offer. As a result, the *Wyandotte*'s frequent breakdowns placed him in an embarrassing position: "That which mortifies and frightens me is that the repairs of the engine of this vessel are so often demanded while it requires so many days to make them, that I am apt to be subject to the suspicion from some, that I have accepted bribes from others to lay in port." [3]

Abraham Lincoln's consul at Trinidad, where Stanly had had so much trouble, reported in some terror that

Situated as I am, a single unprotected individual, amidst the very people who carry . . . [the trade] on, and constrained to transact most of my official business with the Spanish officials who, if not engaged in it, for large bribes connive at it, what can I do to arrest it? If it were known to those unfeeling monsters engaged in it . . . my life would not be worth a brass pin if I was considered a spy or an informer. I do not consider it prudent to send this communication by Havana for fear of espionage upon the mail, and I therefore send it in a sail vessel bound direct to New York. [4]

Rumors of official corruption were numerous; those concerning the Havana customhouse were proven true, for in 1857 and early 1858 it permitted vessels to load cargoes almost entirely different from their manifests.[5] The American consulate saw only the manifest, not the cargo, and therefore could more easily be kept from interfering.

Cuban sentiment, and Spanish official actions concerning the slave trade, must be understood properly to appreciate the unsung hero of this chapter. Thomas Savage, United States vice–consul general at Havana, was a young man who had grown up as a member of the little American colony in that city. Vigorous and honest, well acquainted with the Spanish language and with affairs of the city generally, he was a natural assistant for the procession of Americans sent to the island as consul general under the haphazard operations of the Jacksonian spoils system. Successive newcomers chose him as an assistant, paying him $2,000 a year from the income of the consulate for his services.[6]

Savage hated the slave trade, though, so far as we know, he was no abolitionist. But he detested the cruelty of the trade and determined to do what he could to root out American assistance to it.[7] Normally he did not have much power, beyond turning up facts and rumors and witnesses for the consideration of his chief; he did not even have the right to furnish information to the State Department except in the occasional intervals when the consul general was out of Havana. Savage could not inaugurate new policies, even when he was temporarily in charge, for the consul general, upon his return, could reverse anything the vice-consul had done, and might even dismiss him. Until the summer of 1858, therefore, Savage had done nothing more than gather information about the slave trade for Consul General Andrew K. Blythe, and write several detailed dispatches about lawbreakers to the State Department. Secretary of State Lewis Cass had thought them so valuable that he had them copied and sent to key district attorneys.[8] Blythe, too, disliked the slave trade, but he was unwilling to do more than ask for increased personal authority to stop transfers of vessels between American citizens at Havana and to search suspected vessels.[9] The State Department could not grant such authority, and Blythe remained helpless.

During the months that Savage was gathering facts about slavers and Blythe was becoming more and more vexed at the problems of his post (which included sky-high living costs as well as slavers), an increasing number of American slavers had been leaving the island. Between the spring of 1857 and the middle of April, 1858, upward of twenty of them had cleared Havana. The British finally took action, seizing the *Cortez* just after she had sailed out, and began to harass American shipping in Cuban waters. The United States threatened war, and toward the end of June came word that the British were withdrawing their cruisers. There were celebrations in Havana that night, for the threat of British seizure had badly disrupted the normal flow of slavers out of the port. By the beginning of July three American slavers were ready to sail.[10]

At this time Thomas Savage, not Andrew Blythe, was in charge. Early in June Blythe had finally resigned his post, complaining that the pay was "mean, contemptible, and unworthy of our government." [11] He departed for his home in Mississippi in a huff, leaving Thomas Savage in full charge, with no superior below Secretary of State Cass. Savage, lacking political influence in Washington, had no hopes of succeeding Blythe; but a new consul could not arrive for several months, and, as Washington's control was remote, he could meanwhile act as he wished against the new crop of American slavers. For four months Savage fought the good fight at Havana; and it is this period of intense activity which earned him the title of "hero." He was prepared to do what no American consul had dared to do before: ignore his official instructions and the statute law, flatly refuse to clear suspicious vessels, and thus prevent them from going to Africa with the vital registration papers that discouraged British boarding parties.[12] Savage also continued vigorously to gather evidence against both intended and successful slavers. He performed these services in addition to his ordinary duties, which constituted a full-time job in themselves. But the voluminous paper work required of a consul in a major seaport gradually overcame him, so that his successor found a mass of poorly kept records; Savage had worked to the limits of human endurance.[13]

James Gage, master of the *Brothers,* was deeply involved in the first rush of American slavers from the reopened port. Not only did he take her out with a damning cargo, but he also purchased the bark *Lyra,* and chartered her to Havana merchants for a voyage to Africa. Everything was legal on the surface, but the transaction nevertheless seemed incriminating. The *Lyra* had come down from New York under mortgage to Don Ramon Guerediaga, who had previously owned at least one "American" slaver; [14] Gage got possession of the bark by paying off this known criminal. Where the money had come from was not clear. Another known cat's-paw of the Havana slave traders, Antonio Cabarga, put $7,000 aboard the *Lyra* as well as $8,000 on the *Brothers,* claiming that the money was to purchase palm oil. Savage decided that the best way to take care of both vessels was to let them clear, but to make certain they were searched as soon as they left port. American warships, thanks to British provocations, were now more numerous in gulf waters than they had been for years, and Savage tried to arrange a rendezvous between the *Brothers* and the *Macedonian.* But Gage remained in port until the warship left, and then sailed off undisturbed on July 3 for his meeting with the *Marion* off Africa.

Savage had better luck with the *Lyra,* for he had necessarily issued her a temporary register and wrote into its orders that she should go directly to Key West for a permanent register, and an inspection. He suggested to Commander Henry J. Hartstene of the steamer *Arctic* that he put aboard the *Lyra* what would have amounted to a prize crew. Hartstene shrank from that responsibility, but agreed to follow the bark. The *Lyra* sailed on July 7 and, encouraged by the trailing *Arctic,* did go to Key West. There Collector John P. Baldwin, as soon as he heard of Savage's suspicions, sent officers aboard who discovered that the wine listed on the *Lyra*'s manifest was mostly water, and that there was a remarkable assortment of unmanifested cargo: swords, rifles, an iron boiler, extra provisions, wooden spoons, and other items of a similar character. Captain William C. Dickey seemed overcome with astonishment as the search proceeded, declaring that he had been ill when the cargo was taken aboard and knew nothing about it. As soon as the officers left to report their findings, Dickey recovered from his astonishment, snatched Cabarga's money, and fled. Even with this loss it was a profitable day for the Key West customs, for the bark was condemned the following November and brought them $3,500 in prize money.[15] Thomas Savage, who received not a penny of it, deserved the credit; he had disposed of his first slaver.

Events soon became even more dramatic for the vice–consul. On July 3, the same Saturday that the *Brothers* left for Africa, Savage was investigating the honesty of the brig *C. Perkins,* just getting ready to follow Captain Gage. Savage searched the streets of Havana for sailors from the brig who might know something of her affairs. Finding one, he learned more than he had expected to. The sailor, recently discharged by the brig's captain, swore that the *C. Perkins* was a slaver, and not merely an intended slaver. She had landed slaves in Cuba a few months earlier, when he had been aboard. Upon hearing this story, Savage had to decide whether or not the sailor was lying in order to get even for being discharged. Looking into his records, Savage discovered that the *C. Perkins* had cleared Havana for St. Thomas with an alleged cargo of rum on November 27, 1857. She had been in Yucatan in May, 1858, but he had no further information.

A little later the brig's captain came to Savage's office, displayed his customhouse clearance, and asked for his papers. Savage told him that he would not turn the papers over until the story was cleared up, and returned to his search for witnesses. By Monday, July 5, he had found two other seamen who admitted that they had been aboard when the *C. Perkins* was carrying slaves.

On Sunday night a visitor at Savage's home, a stranger, had claimed to be connected with Don Joaquin Lequerica, the brig's current charterer. The stranger, declaring that the new voyage was honest, asked Savage to clear the brig. Savage replied that he first intended to find out about her previous voyage from Havana. The stranger withdrew. The next morning he appeared at the consulate, bowed, silently handed Savage a sealed envelope, wheeled about, and bolted down the stairs into the street. In the envelope Savage found a brief but eloquent message: a $1,000 bank note, wrapped in a sheet of blank paper.

That was proof enough for Savage. Confronting Lequerica, the vice-consul declared that he would not let the brig go to sea. He then sent a note to the Captain General, telling him he intended to seize the brig and send her to the United States if that would not offend Spanish sovereignty. In the meantime news that the bribe had not worked had reached the brig's real owner, Don Francisco Duranon, a merchant in the Plaza San Francisco. After darkness settled over Havana on Monday night, Duranon and his men began to unload the *C. Perkins,* probably to destroy evidence of the slaving voyage the brig was about to make. In the midst of their work the harbor police appeared and Duranon's men fled, leaving behind a boat partly filled with sacks of beans and rice and drums of codfish. Thus frustrated, Duranon obtained a large drill, returned to the brig, and bored a series of holes in her bows below the water line. As the night passed the warm gulf waters surged into her hold, until she lost buoyancy and settled heavily to the bottom sometime in the early morning hours.

In the dawn of July 6 harbor officers discovered the *C. Perkins* sinking, and official cogs began to turn as the Spanish authorities and Savage probed the matter. Duranon's guilt was uncovered, but he and the brig's officers had fled Havana. Using the bribe money, Savage had the brig raised, and abundant proof of customhouse negligence appeared when her cargo was inventoried. None of the rum supposed to be on board was there, and most of the provisions were missing. Instead, the searchers found lumber for a slave deck, plenty of fresh water, a boiler, and mess gear. After lengthy proceedings the Spanish turned the *C. Perkins* over to the United States, and Savage had accounted for his second slaver. The Ladies' Benevolent Association of Havana was the richer by $297, the remainder of the bribe money.[16]

The sinking of the *C. Perkins* evidently aroused the Havana port officials to greater vigilance. She was still being pumped out when they took the unprecedented action of seizing an American vessel, the notorious *Nancy* of New Orleans. Already a successful slaver, the brig had sailed into Havana on July 4 and was promptly hired for an African voyage by Ramon Guerediaga. A new crew was surreptitiously signed on. Rumors were soon flying, and customs officers, more alert than usual, discovered the *Nancy* with two lighters alongside with cargo not cleared through the customhouse. The men loading the illegal cargo warned the officers not to interfere, telling them that the governor, the chief of police, and the commandant of the revenue guards all had shares in this "slaving expedition." When the commandant heard this story he had the vessel seized and the crew put into Tacon prison.

Savage had been keeping a close watch on the *Nancy,* but thus far had played no part in these events. Now he was drawn into the affair in the difficult dual role of prosecutor and defender. It was his duty to expose the crew if they were criminals, and to defend them if they were not. The next few days Savage was busy carrying on investigations and writing letters, his task made more disagreeable by the increasing insolence of the *Nancy*'s captain, John Williams. This erring son of Boston denounced Savage in a series of letters for not protecting American citizens, and insulted him to his face when released from prison to watch the *Nancy*'s inventory. The inventory proved beyond reasonable doubt that the brig was a slaver. The illegally embarked cargo included 1,300 feet of pine scantling and 4,000 feet of boards, 7,500 gallons of fresh water, a variety of mess gear, some medicines and vinegar, and firewood. Much of the cargo supposed to be there was missing. Williams' defense alternated between a charge that the Spanish authorities had planted the supplies aboard in order to incriminate him, and the claim that a captain does not know if his cargo is mislabeled because it comes in sealed packages. The second proposition was as silly as the first, for neither lumber nor liquids were mentioned on the customhouse permits.

After the second day of taking inventory in the oppressive heat, Savage was incapacitated for a few hours. He recovered in time to write a note to the Captain General that evening, and to begin a dispatch that, with its twenty-eight enclosures, filled twenty pages of small print when it was later published. In order to get the report aboard the next mail steamer for Washington, he worked on it all day on July 24 and on into the night, finishing at 3 A.M. on July 25. Exhausted from the work, and discouraged by the constant complaints of those around him, Savage wrote an almost plaintive justification of his activities:

My efforts in detecting and putting a stop, in this place, to the prostitution of the American flag for purposes of slave trading, have created a considerable excitement and hostility to me among a certain class of persons here. I understand that some abusive letters have been sent on to be published in certain journals of the United States, with the view of raising a clamor against me. This cannot and will not deter me from performing my whole duty without fear or favor. I trust the President, the department, and the respectable portion of the community, who hold their country's interest and honor at heart, will believe in the rectitude of my purpose. I have acted according to the best of my judgment, and trust that the department will give me instructions; that if my course should not entirely meet its approval, it will inform me where I have erred, in order to rectify, if possible, any mistakes I may have made.[17]

Secretary of State Cass had already written a note praising Savage's "industry and efficiency," but the vice-consul had to wait for this encouragement until August 8.[18] Don Antonio Cabarga, as he questioned crew members, decided that the nosy vice-consul who could not be bribed might be put out of the way by slander. He therefore persuaded some of the crew to sign a prepared letter of protest accusing Savage of "third-degree" tactics. But nothing was settled in the case while Savage was in charge of the consulate.[19]

This troublesome interlude did not prevent Savage from continuing his efforts to gather and forward detailed information on American slavers. On August 29 he closed a dispatch with this ominous remark: "There are two or three vessels under American colors now lying in this port that appear under rather suspicious circumstances. I understand it is their intention to fit out, whether in this port or in some out-of-the-way place, for a slaving voyage. I have my eye on them." [20] Two of the vessels under Savage's searching eye were the schooner *Enterprise* and the bark *Ardennes.* The owner of the *Enterprise,* who came from Brunswick, Georgia, had chartered her to Antonio Pelletier, an American sea captain, for voyages between Havana and Savannah. This seemingly innocent act became suspicious when John W. Disney was put in command, for he had taken the slaver *Niagara* to Africa the year before. Upon making careful inquiries, Savage learned that Pelletier had an unsavory reputation, and that the *Enterprise* had been secretly sold to slave trader Gregorio Tejedor. The charter party was a blind. But, as always, there was no legal proof of the sale, and Savage plainly went beyond the letter of his instructions when he wrote the State Department: "I suppose there is not sufficient evidence to justify me in seizing the *Enterprise* and sending her to the United States; but I will, unless instructed to the contrary by the department, refuse to allow her to proceed to sea under American colors." [21] By sending no reply, Washington gave Savage carte blanche to refuse to give the *Enterprise* her papers.

Meanwhile most of the crew of the *Ardennes* had been changed, and her Spanish charterer began loading her for the Congo River. Antonio Pelletier, though he had no formal connection with the vessel, seemed to be in charge of the preparations, while nominal captain Thomas Marsh was very vague about his own plans. Savage made it his business to encounter Marsh nearly every day, and ask him if he was going to take the *Ardennes* to Africa. Marsh never gave a definite answer. When Savage warned him to stay clear of slave traders, Marsh gave him a peculiar look and exclaimed, "Oh, I am ruined!" On October 12 Savage held a frank discussion about the *Ardennes* with Brigadier José Echevarria, the governor of Havana. Echevarria told him that the Captain General was suspicious about her, but had no evidence to justify seizure. There were credible reports, but no proof, that Gregorio Tejedor had secretly purchased the vessel. Her loading had been carefully watched, and all the cargo aboard was manifested. But it included ample plank and scantling, a large number of knocked-down casks, plenty of liquor and cigars, and an abundance of bread, rice, beef, pork, and other provisions.

Savage returned to the consulate more suspicious than before. Late the same afternoon Pelletier and Marsh came to his office to get papers for the *Ardennes*. Marsh said he had suddenly become too ill to go, and they wanted Pelletier installed as captain. Savage examined the charter party, and found that it gave Don José Hernandez full control over the vessel for three years, with power to change her captain at will. Savage flatly refused to turn over the papers unless Pelletier and Marsh would agree to take the *Ardennes* to Key West, and receive aboard enough men from an American warship to make sure the agreement was kept. The two men objected. They said they would go to New Orleans, if Savage insisted, but not to Key West, even though Key West was on the route to Africa and New Orleans was not. Savage refused. The argument ended as Marsh entered a formal protest against the detention of the papers, and Savage telegraphed to Cardenas for the war steamer *Despatch*.

The *Despatch* arrived at Havana on October 15, and her skipper, Lieutenant Enoch G. Parrott, joined the dispute. Marsh and Pelletier wrote him a violent letter denouncing Savage's "tyranny" and "malice," saying that he had "made himself blockade master for the coast of Africa," and declaring that "the evil can be no longer tolerated." Pelletier persuaded eight American captains to sign a memorial denouncing Savage, but Parrott also dismissed this and backed up the vice-consul. In the midst of their protests, Marsh and Pelletier offered to post heavy bonds that they would go to New Orleans, while Savage remained obdurate in insisting that they leave—if they left at all—only for Key West. No one openly said what was probably at the root of the argument, that Judge Marvin was more likely to confiscate the *Ardennes* than was Judge Theodore McCaleb at New Orleans.[22] Finally Pelletier threatened to unload the bark and abandon her into Savage's hands, and Savage retorted that he would take care of her.

Captain Disney now joined the argument, for the *Enterprise* was ready for sea. As Savage told it, Disney "seems to have adopted a different course from the others. He uses no threats, has not even noted a protest against me; he on the contrary, humbly prays that

I will let him go to sea. But prayers have the same effect with me." [23] At this point the affair reached an impasse. Savage would not let the *Ardennes* and the *Enterprise* clear except on his own terms, and Pelletier would send them to sea only on *his* terms. Meanwhile the vessels remained idle in port, their owners denied the legal right either to use them or to have their cases decided in a port of law. Savage was thus committing what, under other circumstances, would be considered a tyrannical abuse of his position.[24]

And this is the main lesson of Savage's story. No consul, not even the most dedicated, brave, and skillful, could stop the sailing of slavers by any method consistent with American law or, indeed, consistent with justice. If he could act as the eyes and the ears of an American cruiser—that is, if such a cruiser could wait outside a harbor for suspected vessels to come out—then a consul might be able to do real harm to the slave trade. Otherwise he was powerless.

Savage had got himself into a hopeless impasse. The duty of getting him out fell to Charles J. Helm, transferred from the consulate at St. Thomas, Virgin Islands. Helm, who later achieved notoriety as the Confederacy's chief purchasing agent in Cuba,[25] brought to the Havana consulate a distressing naïveté about the cunning of slave traders (which was gradually educated out of him), and an abiding determination to pull the consulate out of the business of stopping slavers. "These cases give much trouble and great vexation," he wrote home.[26] This was true, but it was also an accurate expression of Helm's basic attitude. Savage had not considered the cases vexing enough to complain about.

Helm's efforts to divorce himself from any responsibility toward slavers can be disposed of quickly. He allowed the *Ardennes* and the *Enterprise* to sail for Jacksonville, Florida, after taking some curious but effective precautions to make sure they went there. As Jacksonville was outside Judge Marvin's district, Pelletier was not afraid to put into that port for permanent registers; his confidence was borne out by events. The district attorney had Pelletier arrested, and libeled the *Ardennes* as a slaver, but Judge McQueen McIntosh of the North Florida district, finding little merit in the evidence, quashed the prosecution.[27] The subsequent career of Pelletier and the *Ardennes* was a lurid one, but at least Helm had got rid of one burdensome legacy from Savage's policies.

Helm soon found a chance to inform the Captain General that he had no authority to detain vessels that had been cleared by the port authorities; [28] and he finally undertook to persuade the State Department to serve formal notice upon Spain that the consulate would never interfere with an American vessel that had been allowed to clear the customs. This would shift the onus of responsibility to Spain for allowing the outfitting of slavers within Spanish territory.[29] Helm's suggestion received sympathetic attention at Washington; good politician that he was, he had fitted it to the current administration line that the United States should acquire Cuba in order to stamp out the African slave trade.[30] The blame for further sailings of slavers would be on Spain, a reinforcement of the administration's argument. Of course, slavers going to sea from Havana caused trouble elsewhere, and Secretary Cass had qualms about accepting Helm's idea; but when the Attorney General assured him that consuls had no authority to detain American vessels anyway, Helm was granted his request. The consulate formally renounced interference with American slavers.[31]

The advent of the Republicans to power in 1861 made no change in this policy. Although they had neither the wish to acquire Cuba, nor schemes to place the onus for slave trading on Spain, the legal argument still remained. The consulate continued to stand aloof in self-proclaimed impotency so long as the trade lasted.[32] In the end Thomas Savage's efforts came to nought, his achievement only the derangement for a few months of the slave trade from Havana. Heroes do not always succeed.

— 8 —

MEN WITH CLAY FEET

The afternoon of August 24, 1855, was long remembered by John
H. Riley. History has forgotten Riley, for he was only a deputy
working for the United States marshal of the Massachusetts district.
But that afternoon he had a part in the making of history, as he
was handed warrants for the arrest of Vincent D. Cranotick and
Charles Martin, supposed to be in charge of the schooner *Mary E.
Smith* loading for sea at a dock in East Boston. Primarily, Riley
regarded the mission as a way of earning a little money; for each
warrant he served, he and the marshal shared the fee of two dollars.
Like all marshals and deputies, they received little or no regular
salary, but were paid in fees for work actually performed. Congress
used this device widely to make sure that federal workers were on
their toes, and to prevent its tax-hating constituents from having
to pay money to men who did nothing. Of course deputies were
likely to be underpaid under this system, and they were discouraged from carrying out long, difficult investigations because they
received not a penny unless an arrest followed. But presumably
Congress was more interested in saving money than in creating an
efficient law enforcement body. Riley of course had no tenure of
office. The marshal was likely to leave office the next time the
Democrats lost a national election, and the new marshal might
have his own friends to please with jobs. But did not politics count
for more than *esprit* among government workers?

The *Mary E. Smith,* which Cranotick had recently purchased, was on the verge of sailing as Riley hurried toward his rendezvous. Coming onto the dock, and seeing her already being pulled away by a tug, he hastily persuaded four men with a small boat to row him out. In mid-harbor they caught up with the slowly moving schooner, and Riley scrambled aboard and headed for the quarter-deck, where the pilot, Jacob Lunt, was shouting orders to the tug-boat captain up ahead. Also on the quarter-deck was Lieutenant John L. Prouty, second-in-command of the revenue cutter *Morris,* with a handful of his men; they had been ordered over to help Riley should he have trouble making the arrests. Riley ordered Lunt to stop the vessel, and went below with Prouty to search out Cranotick. Picking their way through a large crew of tough-looking fellows, and a clutter of lumber, water casks, provisions, and other cargo, they finally found the vessel's owner, Vincent D. Cranotick himself.

In observance of the proper formalities, Prouty introduced Riley to Cranotick, and Riley read the warrant, charging Cranotick with being engaged in the slave trade. At these words the *Smith*'s owner interrupted Riley with the seemingly irrelevant question, "Are you a Mason?" and then asked a more obvious one, "How much will it cost me to secure you?" Riley replied that he was not to be secured, and that Cranotick would have to go back and explain his business to the authorities. Leaving him then, the deputy found his way back to the quarter-deck, where, to his astonishment, he saw the tug still pulling seaward. Pilot Lunt had been arguing violently with Prouty as to whether the latter had the authority to stop the schooner; Lunt said that he was hired to take the *Smith* to sea, and that he intended to do it. The tug's captain shouted across to see what the trouble was, and Lunt shouted back that the officers had come to stop the vessel but had no lawful authority.

The argument on the quarter-deck continued. Prouty said he would go to sea with the *Smith* if necessary, and Lunt retorted that he would put Prouty and his men in irons and drop them off in their boat. Riley, meanwhile, had found Cranotick again, and had taken him firmly by the arm; he called on Prouty for help. But the lieutenant answered that he was helpless, and that he feared resistance. And then came the call: "Everyone to the tug who is going ashore!" The *Mary E. Smith*'s sails were hoisted, and her crew made ready to cast off the tug.

Riley had three choices: he could stay with Cranotick, whom he had under arrest, and go to Africa with him; he could try to take him off, without help from Prouty or his men; or he could release him and return safely to Boston. No hero would take the last alternative; but Riley was not a hero, and soon he, Prouty, and Lunt were aboard the tug heading back to Boston, while the *Smith* vanished over the horizon.

Cranotick died in a Brazilian prison, the *Smith's* supercargo was convicted, and the other parties connected with the schooner went free. Pilot Lunt managed to win an acquittal when put on trial for resisting a United States officer. The affair was shocking from beginning to end, and left the federal officers at Boston covered with disgrace: District Attorney B. F. Hallett, for getting out his warrants too late and neglecting to libel the schooner herself; the customs collector and the commander of the revenue cutter, for not getting the government vessel into position, or at least not sending a large enough detachment, to seize the schooner; Lieutenant Prouty, for acting like a coward; Riley, for not risking his life—to earn two dollars! The only satisfactory aspect of the episode was that Boston was demonstrated to be an unsafe place to fit out slavers; so far as anyone knows, not one was ever prepared there again. But that did not halt the slave trade or the violation of the laws of the United States.[1]

The escape of the *Mary E. Smith* strikingly illustrates another reason that the slave trade in American vessels was not suppressed. Most of the officers discussed in these pages were reasonably conscientious and skillful, and a few of them possessed great ability and determination. Their failures came not from themselves, but from the impossible situations they were placed in. But occasionally officers with clay feet, or clay minds, or clay integrity, were thrown by chance into important positions in the battle against slave traders, and by their failure contributed to the government's failure.

This chapter is concerned with the most striking of the known cases of incompetence or corruption, the exceptions to the general rule of official competence.

In the fall of 1854 sinister events in New York raised a suspicion that the slave-trading interest had gained a foothold inside the United States customhouse. Early in October the British consul general at Havana had warned that Don José Egea, a Spaniard with piratical schemes on his mind, was headed for New York. Consul Crawford's information was so complete that he was able to pinpoint the business house through which Egea would operate: Rudolph Lasala's, at No. 6 Broadway. But the warning letter traveled less swiftly than Egea did, and on the very day that District Attorney McKeon received it Lasala appeared at the customhouse to swear that he had just purchased the brig *Horatio*. He began fitting her out for sea.

McKeon spread the alarm, and the port's collector and surveyor watched the brig's movements. As the preparations neared completion the *Horatio* changed ownership again; this time she was "sold" to her supercargo. On November 2 Joseph H. Porter, one of the surveyor's men, went out to search the vessel, but he was not able to find her. Apparently she had slipped off without her papers. Registry clerk Sidney P. Ingraham was ordered not to deliver the papers without further instructions. Despite his orders, Ingraham turned over the register on November 4, for the *Horatio* had not left harbor at all. Ingraham also failed to demand a copy of the master's oath of citizenship, though he afterward maintained that he had administered it. He warned no one; his superiors forgot the matter; and the *Horatio* was well out on a successful slaving voyage before McKeon learned what had happened. Obviously Porter had not searched very thoroughly, Ingraham had not taken his orders very seriously, and their superiors had not been greatly interested —if the failure was not bought. McKeon reported the affair to Secretary of State Marcy with the rueful observation, "I have not been able to accomplish the purpose desired." Was it because of corruption, apathy, or carelessness? No one ever found out.[2]

But there was no doubt as to which of these qualities was responsible for the events at New York which got the *Storm King* out at sea so that the *San Jacinto* could capture her full of slaves. On May 1, 1860, the *Storm King* was libeled on the eve of sailing for Africa, and the attachment papers ended up in the hands of two deputies, Theodore Rynders, the marshal's nephew, and John H. Munn. Up to this point young Rynders had shown no signs of moral collapse; indeed, he had acted with considerable energy and effectiveness in the fall of 1858 while the marshal was looking for the crew of the successful slaver *Haidee*. But this time things were different, for Rynders had learned how to make good money in New York; his friend Munn was in full agreement. Not attempting to get help from the revenue cutter, they hired a tug and went out alone to the *Storm King*, anchored in the Narrows. They climbed aboard, spent fifteen minutes (out of sight of the tug captain), and returned telling him that their trip was a mistake. Rynders went back to the marshal's office, where chief deputy Joseph Thompson asked him about the *Storm King*'s location. Rynders' reply left Thompson gaping. He baldly admitted that he had failed to arrest her. When he boarded, the man in charge offered him $1,000 to let her leave. Rynders assured Thompson that he had not fallen for any such offer. No; he had demanded $1,500 instead. The money was promised, and he and Munn left the vessel.

When Thompson recovered from his shock he informed Marshal Rynders, and District Attorney J. J. Roosevelt was called in. Almost as soon as they had been discharged from the marshal's force, Theodore Rynders and Munn were examined on charges of aiding a slaver to escape. The circuit court's grand jury indicted them under the act of 1818; defense counsel argued (as we will see later) that only owners, masters, and factors were liable under that act; and the grand jury of necessity indicted the ex-deputies for "willfully and unlawfully obstructing the due administration of justice." Apparently Congress had never deemed this a serious offense, for the act carried only the penalty of six months in jail and a $500 fine.

The strange episode continued its curious course. Rynders, released on bail, began showing "fits of gloomy foreboding." He went over to Newark, and drove his horse through the streets so recklessly that he was arrested for speeding and locked up. In jail his mind snapped. After he was removed to New York's lunatic asylum, his malady was diagnosed as "softening of the brain," and he was placed in a private asylum where he raved almost incessantly. An insane man cannot be tried, Munn was only his accomplice, and the whole affair was so embarrassing to the ruling Democratic politicians that it was quietly shelved. Nor did the Republicans later reopen the case.[3]

The *Storm King* episode set rumors flying, and by the end of the month New York newspapers were carrying this startling item:

We have received information . . . to the effect that the price for the clearance of a slaver is as well-known to those in the trade as the price of a barrel of pork. It is said that a certain amount of gold is placed in the locker of the cabin; the officers board the ship and commence a search for materials, arguing the intention of the vessel to carry slaves. They search all the lockers especially, and suddenly find the particular one in which the gold—commonly ranging from $2,500 to $4,000, according to the size of the vessel—is concealed. This, the inference being that it is at least part of a sum designed to purchase negroes from the King of Dahomey, the officers at once proceed to confiscate; but, failing to find any other evidence of a slave-trading purpose on board, they merely remove the treasure, and offer no further resistance to the departure of the ship.[4]

But no one except Rynders ever admitted taking a bribe. The most reasonable conclusion, in view of all the circumstances, is that the *Storm King's* escape was unusual, and that the rumors of widespread bribery were based upon this one instance. Eighteen months later, when the whaler *Augusta* slipped out of port under suspicious circumstances, there were charges that Republican officeholders, too, were being bought off; but an official investigation cleared the implicated parties, though not everyone was satisfied that the truth had been uncovered.[5] Suspicions of corruption sometimes extended to American consuls: Nicholas Trist, Alexander H. Tyler (consul at Bahia during the 1840's),[6] and Ebenezer Eggleston (Lincoln's consul at Cadiz).[7] But the evidence against any of these men is not conclusive.

The role of official corruption as a cause of the slave trade's success under the American flag is a very difficult subject. Unquestionably bribes were offered; Stanly and Savage and Riley and De Graaw reported them, and it was generally accepted that slave traders used gold freely to lubricate their activities. But not all officials will take bribes. Furthermore, prize money often dangled as an alternative to the bribe; a poorer alternative, to be sure, but much safer.[8] And officers willing to sell out may sometimes have been reluctant to do so for fear of exposure. If, for example, an officer in charge of a boarding party was bought off, his own men would know about it. They could hardly all be bribed, too, and a ruined career was not worth a few thousand dollars. The slave traders themselves had to use caution, for a bribe offered to the wrong man increased the likelihood of conviction. A pile of farina in the bottom of a hold was not conclusive evidence, but a bribe offered to the officer looking at it certainly was. The only fair conclusion is that bribes had something to do with the success of the slave trade, but that they were a minor factor compared to the serious problems that handicapped law enforcement.

But men could fail in other ways besides dishonesty. They could fail in determination; they could value their own comfort above their duty. And some of them did, disgracing the uniform of the United States Navy. The island of Madeira, gem of the Atlantic, was the lure that brought their weakness into the open.

In chapter 2 we noticed that the African squadron spent a great deal of time sailing to and from Madeira, or enjoying the scenic, climatic, and social attractions which the island offered to men just in from monotonous cruises in the fever-ridden tropics aboard crowded little vessels. These controversial pleasure cruises certainly did help the squadron's health and morale; and though they may have cost too much in lost patrol time to be fully justifiable, they at least were honorably managed by most commanders. Cruises to Madeira and cruises on the slave coast alternated, with the patrol cruises lasting somewhat longer than the pleasure cruises. Leaving the question of whether naval commanders might not have demanded more of themselves and their men, we come to two flagrant cases where there was not even a reasonable pretense of activity. They revealed the weak links in the navy's command structure: the officers who commanded squadrons.

By the 1850's the navy's officer corps was in a precarious position. Promotion was, and had long been, by seniority alone. There was no enforced retirement at an early age; an officer living long enough and avoiding misconduct so flagrant as to call for a court-martial could look forward, ultimately, to the rank of captain, the highest regular rank authorized by Congress. He might, furthermore, hope to become a captain commanding a squadron, which entitled him to a bonus in pay and the honorary title of commodore or, after 1857, flag officer. As soon as his tour of duty as squadron commander ended, he reverted to his regular rank and pay, though courteous friends would ever after address him by his temporary title. This was the utmost to which a naval officer could aspire: command of the handful of ships making up a single squadron.

To achieve such a command, an officer had to be both long-lived and patient. The navy expanded very little from decade to decade, and, as there were few vacancies for captains compared to the number of junior officers, a career man had to wait until resignation or retirement or death had removed those who outranked him. An officer had little chance of commanding even a small warship—a brig or a third-class steamer—until he had upwards of twenty-five years of service. It took more than thirty years' service to become commander of a sloop of war, still more to be put in charge of a frigate, and close to forty years to become a squadron commander. Men rarely served long enough to command more than one squadron for one tour of two or three years.

This slow promotion system dampened the ardor of officers of all ranks. Time, not brilliant achievement, was the key to success, a key that could bring complete fulfillment only when the officer was too old to enjoy life at sea any longer. The system did at least have the advantage of ensuring that even the smallest cruiser went to sea under the command of experienced officers, and this was no small advantage in an age when vessels at sea were completely isolated and their commanders cut off from the advice of superiors. But the system also ensured that no squadron commander could ever be an expert in his job, and that only old men ready for permanent shore duty would take squadrons to sea. In 1855 Congress at last took action, and authorized forced retirement of some of the less effective officers. The reduction does not seem to have been particularly effective, as two of the worst misfits in the service survived it.[9]

One of these misfits was Flag Officer Thomas J. Conover, who boarded the sloop of war *Cumberland* at Boston in 1857. Conover was a native of New Jersey who had spent forty-five years in the navy; he had never before been a squadron commander. Though some questioned the suitability of his flagship because of her 1,700 tons, heavy armament, and draft of 21 feet, she was fast and by no means unfit for African duty. But not so the man whose flag she flew.

They sailed from Boston in June to relieve Commodore Thomas J. Crabbe, and by the fall of 1857 were on their first cruise to the slave coast. It was not a very profitable cruise. Conover reached the southern limits of the African station by cruising far out to sea, and he did not tarry long off the Congo on his way back to Porto Praia. He evidently did not like what he saw in his brief look at the slave coast. By mid-February, 1858, the *Cumberland* was anchored at Funchal, Madeira, and amid these pleasant surroundings Conover passed the remainder of the winter and the early spring. The end of his first year found him at Porto Praia, with no more than two weeks of duty on the actual scene of the slave trade to his credit.

But duty finally beckoned, and in mid-August, 1858, the *Cumberland* once more put to sea with her aging flag officer. Carefully remaining far out at sea, away from the unhealthy shore line (and from lurking slavers), the vessel called briefly at Loando, southern limit of the station. After some relaxation in this old, rather Italian-looking place, Conover and his crew retraced their track of the previous year, making good time up the coast and getting back to Porto Praia by the start of winter. They spent some time here (the monotony of life at Porto Praia broken by a pleasant cruise up to Gorée to see the French admiral), but they were again in the harbor of Funchal by April 30. Here they remained until August, waiting, Conover explained, for their relief. On August 31, 1859, the *Cumberland* dropped anchor at Portsmouth, New Hampshire; in twenty-six months of "sea" duty she had patrolled the active slave coast for no more than twenty-six days.

There was no excuse for such dereliction. It is true that African duty was disagreeable, so disagreeable that most commodores begged to come home early; but naval officers, even flag officers, cannot always expect pleasant duty only. And Conover had reduced his squadron by one-fourth, for all practical purposes. Admittedly his flagship was a little large for African duty, but she needed only two more feet of water to float her than did the *Constellation,* the sloop that replaced her as the flagship and captured three slavers. The fact that *Cumberland* drew a few more feet than the average African squadron cruiser did not doom her to remain so far out at sea that Conover could not have sent his boats after small slavers trapped inshore. He found that her hull fitted very handily into the waters near the pleasant island of Madeira. The flag officer might even have resupplied his smaller vessels from the flagship, allowing them to remain on patrol longer, as at least two of his predecessors had done. Conover was not even a competent administrator. Usually several thousand miles away from the rest of his squadron, which he ordered to follow the usual cruising routine, he knew so little of what they were doing that he once cited the newspapers in writing a report on their activities. He was never given another assignment, either afloat or ashore, but that did not undo the damage he had caused. He had been in command of the squadron at a time when the most vigorous exertions by its officers would have been little enough to meet the demands placed upon them by unprecedented lawbreaking in American vessels.[10]

Conover's replacement was William Inman, another New Jerseyite whose service dated back to the War of 1812. As flag officer, his responsibilities were even heavier than Conover's. Not only was his mission exacting, but he also had to administer one of the largest peacetime squadrons of American warships. As late as 1858, Inman's chances of commanding the largest squadron seemed as slight as those of the lowliest seaman aboard any of its warships. His rank, if distinguished, was damning: he was twenty-first on the list of captains not recommended for further employment on active duty. In the 1855 reduction of the number of naval officers he had been declared unfit for duty in the rank of captain, and an appeal board decided that his irritability outweighed his qualities of character, intelligence, and good health. Blackballed by two boards, Inman refused to give up and went to the expense of publishing a pamphlet to appeal his case to the President.[11] His earnest argument that the testimony against him had been faulty and biased struck home; when the time came to select Conover's replacement, Secretary of the Navy Isaac Toucey decided that Inman was the most likely man for the job. An officer with two strikes against him, desperately wanting to redeem his reputation, was not likely to slumber away his tour at the end of an anchor rope.

Whether or not Toucey's logic was sound is another matter. Inman, like most of his contemporaries, had never commanded a squadron, and his zeal became suspect after he was a few months out from the United States. Reaching Madeira and relieving Conover on August 8, 1859, he kept the *Constellation* riding in Funchal Harbor until September 3, explaining to Toucey that he was waiting for the *San Jacinto* to arrive so that he could give her orders to fill up with supplies at Porto Praia and thenceforth operate out of Loando. But the *San Jacinto* did not appear, for the sound reason that her captain had headed directly for the Cape Verde Islands; Inman discovered this when he reached one of the islands of that group on September 10. Inman ordered the *San Jacinto* to go on, and then decided to wait for more letters from home and for the *Mystic* and the *Sumpter*. All had come and gone by October 1, but Inman still could not get to sea until October 5. He detained the *Constellation* at Monrovia for a week as he sailed down the coast toward Loando, and it was not until mid-November that the flagship reached the Congo and began to patrol the slave coast. Inman cruised there long enough to capture the *Delicia,* and then put into the harbor of Loando for several weeks of shore duty. The long stay may have been required by the problem of setting up a new supply depot there, but up to this point Inman's eagerness to command a large squadron seemed to exceed his zest for active cruising in disagreeable localities. Inman hoisted his true colors when he informed Secretary Toucey that he would sail from Loando about February 20, pick up supplies at Porto Praia, and then begin a vacation at Madeira. He explained that his arduous cruising (mostly at anchor) since leaving Madeira the preceding September had "enfeebled" his men, and it would be good for them to get away from Loando during the rainy season. Inman also proposed to allow the sloop *Portsmouth* the same vacation, though he ordered the vessels that had reached the coast at the same time as he had to wait for their vacations.[12]

Although Conover had been allowed to get away with much more than this, the administration was now thoroughly alarmed about the slave trade and Toucey was bearing down on his cruisers. When Inman's letter reached Washington in mid-March, Toucey sent him curt orders to return to his post, and soon afterward informed the flag officer that no vessel was to leave the African coast for any point beyond 20° north latitude without departmental permission. As Funchal lies at 32° 38′ N., Madeira was put off limits to Inman and his warships. The orders reached Inman while he was at Madeira.[13] The *Constellation* and the *Portsmouth* did not return to active duty until the summer of 1860. As the *San Jacinto*'s bearings had gone bad, this subtraction of two more cruisers reduced the squadron to three steamers.

Other reasons besides the flag officer's dislike of the slave coast crippled the squadron during its first year of operations. The *San Jacinto*'s bearings were one; Inman's cruising plans were another. Before abandoning his command for the pleasures of Madeira, Inman had drawn up orders to control the cruising of the three remaining steamers. Dividing the slave coast into three sectors, he ordered the steamer on the northernmost station (Number One) to coal and reprovision at the island of Fernando Po; the others, at Loando. Number One would make connections with the monthly mail steamer from England, and pick up and deliver the mail to Number Two at a specified rendezvous. Number Two would do the same for Number Three. The steamers would change stations every three months to equalize the duty, and were allowed no more than five days at a time for reprovisioning.[14]

This neat, simple plan took care of the problem of keeping the cruisers in frequent contact with home via the post office, no small matter on so remote a station as central Africa. But it was not so skillfully calculated to do maximum damage to the slave trade. Only Station Three covered the Congo and the adjacent coast line, the most active part of the slave coast. Number One was not likely to meet any slavers. As Inman had made no arrangements for patrols north of the equator, in the Bight of Benin, an occasional American slaver going there was in absolutely no danger from United States cruisers. Furthermore, anyone making it his business to learn the cruising pattern of the steamers would soon discover the best times for running slavers clear of the south coast. On the fifth of each month Numbers Two and Three met at Loango Bay to exchange southbound mails, and they met again on the eighteenth to transfer northbound mails. Because Loango is more than a hundred miles north of the Congo and twice as far from Ambriz, Number Three would be away from the heart of its station for two or three days at a time. It is small wonder that American slavers in good numbers were still reaching the Cuban coast during the spring and summer of 1860.

Nor did Inman show sufficient energy in following suspected slavers. Most embarrassing was the escape of the *Orion,* recognized as a slaver from her first boarding by the *Mystic* off the Congo in November, 1859. In the ensuing days she was boarded at various times by the *San Jacinto,* the *Portsmouth,* and the flagship. For good reason, the *Orion* was not seized in that state of preparations, but the squadron's failure to follow her when she left the Congo for an unspecified "southward" destination can hardly be excused. For all Inman had done, she could easily have got clear of the coast;

fortunately, H.M.S. *Pluto* caught her full of slaves. Inman was active enough afterward, sending to St. Helena for the prisoners and shipping the three not yet released by the British home for trial as pirates, but that did not gloss over her outwitting of his squadron, which he conveniently ignored in his dispatches.[15]

Inman's time in the Navy Department's good graces had thoroughly run out by May, 1860, when the capture of three laden slavers off Cuba offered tangible proof that his squadron was not accomplishing its duty. Toucey sent a rebuke to Inman, politely worded, but bearing the ominous suggestion that he "renew his exertions." Inman, knowing well what such language meant, replied with a letter that earnestly set forth his squadron's achievements while ignoring its failures.[16] By that time he had something to brag about, for on August 8, 1860, fortune smiled upon his cruisers.

As the sun's rays slanted through the warm air about 6 A.M. that morning, they threw the shadows of four vessels across the placid sea west of Kabenda. In the northwest corner, 5° 8′ S. and 10° 4′ E., of a 100-mile square was the *San Jacinto,* fresh from repairs at Cadiz and steaming south-southeast at 6 knots to rejoin the squadron. Along the eastern edge of the square, at 5° 30′ S. and 11° 19′ E., was the *Mohican,* which had picked up the mails at Fernando Po and was now headed for Loando to replace the *Mystic* on Station Three. Along the bottom edge two vessels were headed in the opposite direction, their canvas drawing listlessly under a light southeasterly breeze. They were the *Erie* and the *Storm King*.

There was no particular reason that these four vessels should have been in this place at this moment. None was aware of the presence of the others, and their meeting was owing to the kind of chance that makes history. At 7:30 the *Mohican*'s lookouts shouted to the watch officer, "Full-rigged ship off the port bow," and a few minutes later the sloop was full of activity as the helmsman swung his heavy wheel, deck hands unlashed and hoisted sails, and engineers opened wider the valves through which hot steam poured to work the cylinders. By 8:30 the steamer was drawing near her quarry, the *Erie,* and other hands loaded and fired a blank cartridge as a signal to the *Erie* to show her colors. An American flag ascended the ship's mizzenmast, she shortened sail, and fifteen minutes later the *Mohican*'s armed boat pulled alongside. So far the chase had been routine, but the boarders scrambling unopposed to the *Erie*'s deck discovered 900 Africans aboard, a fine beginning for the greatest rescue ever accomplished in a single day. For later the same day the *San Jacinto* found 130 women, 68 girls, 164 men, and 261 boys aboard the *Storm King*. Inman did not really have much to do with planning this mass rescue of African slaves, but he made the most of it in his dispatches.[17]

And at last the flag officer himself accomplished something. Chastened by Toucey's rebukes, he cruised actively with the *Constellation*. At dusk on September 26 her lookouts sighted an unknown bark. More than one slaver had eluded a pursuer under cover of darkness, but that night a brilliant harvest moon allowed the flagship to press unerringly toward her quarry. Soon the slaver was littering the sea with spars, casks, a hatch and a boat, and other jetsam in a vain attempt to lighten herself for greater speed. As the range closed blank shots were fired, and ignored. Captain Nicholas ordered shot loaded, and the peaceful night was rent with gun flashes and fountains kicked up by 8-inch balls splashing near the bark. The sloop's gunners carefully missed their target, but the threat was enough. At 11 o'clock the bark hove to. The prize was the *Cora,* arrested at New York on May 19, bonded and cleared out again on June 27, and two days out from Mangua Grande with 705 Africans riding in relative comfort on her permanent middle deck.[18]

Inman had no other similar successes, but during the remainder of his tour he exerted himself with enough energy to win the praise of his British counterpart.[19] He did not, however, redeem his reputation sufficiently to remove the stigma of being found unfit for command by two navy boards; despite the demands of the Civil War, the Navy Department never again assigned him to duty, afloat or ashore. His name went back onto the list of captains "not recommended for further employment," and there it remained.

Who was to blame for Conover and Inman? Was it the Navy

Department, for not choosing its commanders more carefully? Or was it a disinterested Congress, for carelessly creating a system that ground down the ambitions and wore out the bodies of capable men before they could get to the top? At any rate, squadron commanders with clay feet had something to do with the failure of American efforts to suppress the slave trade.

Benjamin J. Totten, commander of the U.S.S. *Vincennes,* was angry. A marine private who had misbehaved had been court-martialed, and Totten's officers had had the temerity to acquit him. Totten nevertheless ordered that the private be put in irons. When the marine officer came to protest, Totten suspended him from duty. The officer retired abashed, and Totten retired well satisfied that he had restored his position as master of an 18-gun sloop and 150 men.

The rights and wrongs of this little fracas need not detain us. They were typical of an age full of shipboard disputes over fancied (or real) slights to authority. This forgotten incident is of interest because it is also typical of Commander Totten. Some months earlier, he and his gunnery officer had argued about the proper use of the high-explosive shells allotted for training purposes, and Totten had suspended the officer. Later on the same cruise he suspended two more lieutenants for "insubordination." When Flag Officer Inman, himself no easy person to get along with, heard about these incidents, he rebuked Totten for his oversensitivity. Although Totten was a petty tyrant on his quarter-deck, he was also a lax commander. When the *Vincennes* was inspected in the summer of 1858, her crew was found to be so badly trained in gunnery that she could not have fought effectively.[20]

Totten showed the same unfortunate traits in dealing with the slave trade, and this is why he has the unenviable distinction of being the only American naval officer ever formally denounced by the British government for negligence in suppressing the slave trade. The situation that caused this denunciation was an unusual glut of slavers off the Congo. Slave traders had just begun to use large vessels, which were difficult to fill. In the spring of 1859 they were so successful in getting large slavers out of port that by August several of them were in the vicinity of the slave coast waiting for cargoes. At this critical moment the *Vincennes* was anchored at Loando, while Totten was enjoying shore leave. The British commodore wrote to Totten, urging him to take immediate action to intercept four vessels cruising near Ambriz. Totten sent out two boats, which an English steamer transported to the area. The British commissioner at Loando tried to prod Totten into going after the suspicious vessels himself, but received only a curt note in reply: "The Commanders of The United States' vessels on this coast need no other advice or inducements than are contained in the instructions received from their own government. . . ."

Having thus asserted his independence, Totten retrieved the two boats (which, as it developed, had been on a wild-goose chase), and set sail for Porto Praia. As he passed up the coast on August 26 he fell in with H.M.S. *Triton*, Lieutenant Richard Burton commanding. Burton came aboard the *Vincennes* and, pointing out one of the suspicious vessels cruising in the distance, offered to tow the *Vincennes*' boats out to board her, but Totten declined the offer and said he could overtake the vessel himself. Burton left, and soon observed that Totten did not even try to get under way. Another of the suspicious vessels had actually been taken into custody by the British, a grave breach of etiquette, and Totten promised to look into the matter, as his instructions required him to do. But he ignored his promise, flouted his duty, and sailed off for Porto Praia. This was the conduct that made the British lodge a formal complaint against Totten with the State Department.

It is true that Totten was in a hurry to get back to Porto Praia; even so, he arrived well behind the schedule set for him by Flag Officer Conover. It is also true that Totten had occasionally done his duty against the slave trade earlier. And he had given the British halfhearted coöperation; the fact that his boats were taken on a wild-goose chase could not have improved his temper. Nevertheless, Totten was a pretty sorry specimen; something was quite wrong with the navy's selection system, for Totten, like Conover, had survived the purge of 1855. When he came back from Africa he was permanently "beached"; but that did not make the *Vincennes* effective when she was so badly needed.[21] With Totten and Conover serving by chance in the same four-ship squadron—a squadron whose utmost exertions would have been little enough against the unprecedented surge of American slavers in 1857–1858—circumstances had indeed combined to make a sad day for the navy's reputation. It was even sadder for the African carried across the seas because the navy's personnel system could not ensure reasonably competent men in key posts.

Conover and Totten were, of course, exceptions. Their own squadron was blessed with two vigorous ship commanders, the *Dale*'s William McBlair and the *Marion*'s Thomas W. Brent. It should be noted in passing, by those who profess to see a sectional bias in the suppression of the slave trade, that both McBlair and Brent were Southerners, whereas Conover and Totten were Northerners. British Commodore Charles Wise, an outspoken critic of the squadron, admitted that its officers usually acted with "considerable energy," and he once praised Brent for "very cordial" cooperation. The commissioner at Loando was all the more astonished at Totten's rudeness because of his experience with the "enlightened spirit" of American naval officers in suppressing the slave trade.[22] But incompetent naval officers did indeed play a significant role in the failure of the federal government.

= 9 =

THE ELUSIVE SMUGGLED SLAVE

On September 14, 1859, United States Secretary of the Interior Jacob Thompson admitted a visitor to his office in Washington. Thompson's visitor had come to help the department solve a new and vexing problem suddenly thrust upon it by the lawless schemes of a group of men in the South. Apparently these men were smuggling African slaves into the United States, though no one in authority was sure of it. There was no Federal Bureau of Investigation to turn to in 1859, nor a Secret Service, and so the task of obtaining information about the suspected slave smuggling was being entrusted to one temporary special agent. Benjamin F. Slocumb, Thompson's visitor, had been selected for the job because he was honest and courageous, and because he spoke with a Mississippi drawl that would allow him to pose as a slaveowner wanting to buy cheap smuggled Africans. There was no guarantee that Slocumb would come back alive from his mission. Slave traders usually avoided violence, but there was always the danger that one of them would resort to a pistol shot or a dagger thrust to preserve the secrets of his business.

Rumors of slave landings had already harried the administration for eighteen months. In the spring of 1858 three revenue cutters and the naval steamer *Despatch* had been ordered out on patrols in the Gulf of Mexico to apprehend the bark *E. A. Rawlins,* which was rumored to be headed for Texas or southwestern Louisiana with slaves aboard. They had searched up and down the coast, and their small boats had hunted in rivers and bayous, without finding anything. Early in August the *Rawlins* had sailed into Savannah for a reunion with her owner, the notorious slave-trade advocate C. A. L. Lamar. Her arrival caused much speculation. According to various rumors, she had landed slaves in Texas, or in Louisiana, or in Florida; Thomas Savage, at Havana, heard that she had landed them in Cuba. In New York, Nathan Trowbridge, one of Lamar's associates, had privately admitted that the *Rawlins* was engaged in the slave trade; he would say no more, and she might have been only an auxiliary.[1]

This was only one set of rumors. Others had come flooding in: that a suspicious vessel was seen hovering off the north Florida coast in December, 1858;[2] that another vessel going aground had possibly landed slaves;[3] that the sloop *Fairy* was expected to lighter slaves to Louisiana from a larger slaver at sea (though a careful watch had not surprised her).[4] Latest of the rumors, and apparently the strongest, had come in from central Florida, where Deputy George J. Zehnbauer had heard (but had no proof) of a landing of slaves at Jupiter Inlet in the spring of 1859; Marshal E. E. Blackburn had afterward positively reported a secret landing of 600 Africans near New Smyrna, 120 miles north of Jupiter.[5] But he, too, lacked evidence. No one knew whether these rumors referred to two landings, or to the same landing, or to no landing at all.

And there was more than rumor. Federal officers in the lower South were sending in alarming reports of adverse public sentiment. In March, 1858, the collector at New Orleans reported:

In our community there are many whose sympathies are elicited in favor of the revival of the African slave trade, and others who are reluctant to punish offenders on suspicions, be they ever so strong and well sustained, for which reasons it is exceedingly difficult to obtain a verdict before a jury.[6]

In December, 1858, the assistant district attorney at Jacksonville made this startling observation:

This community is strongly opposed to the execution of the laws prohibiting the slave trade, and every obstacle is thrown in the way of the officers who are endeavoring to discharge their duty. I have good reason to believe that many persons in this vicinity seriously thought of engaging in the slave trade. . . .[7]

That same month the United States attorney at Savannah reported a "heavy tide of public opinion" flowing against his efforts to enforce the laws; soon afterward the attorney at Charleston spoke of his prosecutions as "unpopular" and "perilous"; [8] and in June, 1859, the attorney for the Alabama district related that

There is a very strong disposition manifested there [in Montgomery] to defeat the execution of the law—and in fact open declarations of hostility to the law, and of a determination to nullify it, are made by many. Two of the defendants are wealthy, and all are influential, and an impression prevails there, that a jury cannot be found that will find a verdict of guilty against them.[9]

Certain verdicts of Southern judges and juries seemed to support these reports. Most celebrated of these involved the captain and the crew of the *Putnam,* captured off Cuba in August, 1858, with 318 starving, diseased Africans confined below. The brig bore the false name *Echo,* and the so-called *Echo* trials became a touchstone of Southern sentiment in the eyes of hostile Northerners. The crew had been taken into Charleston with their vessel and thrust into jail awaiting grand jury action. To the amazement of the nation, the jury refused to indict them as pirates. Already voices had been raised in South Carolina denouncing the act of 1820 as unconstitutional, and the legal proceedings after the grand jury's action produced a spirited debate on this issue. Justice James M. Wayne, presiding over the court, declared the act constitutional and forced the grand jury to return indictments. When the trials were held the nation was shocked once more, for the crew was acquitted to a man despite the most damning evidence. Many Southern papers hailed the action as a slap at the North and a vindication of the system of slavery.[10]

Even Judge Marvin had become suspect, for when the *Putnam*'s captain was put on trial at Key West for piracy, the judge ordered the jury to acquit him upon a mere technicality.[11] And everyone knew that there was a noisy crowd of zealots who for several years had been pouring forth manifestoes demanding a reopening of the trade to the United States. The North had its European "wage slaves"; why should not the South have its own supply of cheap labor? Slaves were becoming so expensive that only the rich could afford them. These slave-trade advocates had violent opponents, who obviously spoke for a fair segment of public opinion—but was it a large enough segment? [12]

More conclusive than rumors and reports of hostile public sentiment was the capture of two slavers just off the Florida coast early in 1859. The *Tryant,* a New York brig and an obviously successful slaver, had piled up on the Marquesas Key only twenty-five miles west of Key West, where a revenue cutter found her. She could have been the vessel supposed to have landed 367 Africans east of Cárdenas, Cuba, in the latter part of February, but her black ivory could have gone to the mainland instead.[13] At about the same time the *E. A. Rawlins,* out on a second voyage, had put into Apalachicola Bay, west Florida, with a slave cargo below deck and blood topside where her Spanish supercargo had been murdered by the ship's officers. The steamer *Vixen,* coming upon her at anchor, had taken her into custody while rumors that she had landed slaves again flew across the nation. The rumors were false, for the *Rawlins* was just out of Havana bound for Africa; but her unexplained presence in American coastal waters was not reassuring.[14]

Even more distressing to the administration was the notorious and indisputable fact that a very neat coup had been carried out on the coast of Georgia late in November, 1858. The yacht *Wanderer,* ostensibly owned by Captain William C. Corrie of Charleston but suspected to be the property of a syndicate led by Lamar, had left New York after escaping slave-trade charges, cleared Charleston for "Trinidad," and gone to the African coast instead. On October 12, when she was taking on slaves just north af Ambrizete Bay, Commander Totten and the *Vincennes* cut short the operation by appearing on the southern horizon, pushed along on patrol at 3 knots by a feeble breeze. The *Wanderer* went out to sea, apparently taking an African slave merchant with her. Totten ordered his men to set more canvas and to roll the starboard 32-pounders inboard to give the sloop better trim; he then sent the crew forward to add its weight to the trimming. By means of these expedients, the *Vincennes* worked up to 7 knots, but that was not enough to close the gap. Nor did Totten succeed in catching the small boat cut loose from the *Wanderer* to take her unintended passengers ashore, and by nightfall the yacht was well clear of the African coast. About November 28 she slipped quietly into St. Andrew's Sound, anchored off the south end of Jekyll Island, and put perhaps 300 or 400 surviving Africans ashore on the Dubignon plantation. As late as December 10 some of the slaves were still there; yet the entire affair had been engineered so perfectly that the fact of the landing became known only when Corrie foolishly took the *Wanderer* into Brunswick, Georgia, for supplies, instead of scuttling her. This maneuver, too, almost succeeded, so carefully had the yacht been cleaned out; only the alert detective work of Collector Woodford Mabry, and the hairbreadth capture of the last three crew members minutes before they shipped out of Georgia for New York, enabled officials to verify the story.

Not only had slaves been landed without the federal government's knowledge, but the government was unable to do anything about it afterward. The *Wanderer* had been confiscated, it is true, and resold at auction to Lamar himself (at half her value), but not one African had been rescued. A ten- or twelve-year-old boy, sick, was found early, but he was soon recovered by a group of unknown but well-armed men. The marshal resigned in mortification. The chase had gone on, and when two Negroes, supposedly Africans, were found in Lamar's possession, he brought a countersuit for theft and obtained a court order for their release. Thirty-three Africans were captured near Hawkinsville, Georgia, but they, too, were spirited away from the marshal, and more lawsuits were started against him. Rumors of other Africans kept the officials busy, but after six months all the government had for its efforts was a dozen indictments, likely unprovable, against men in Georgia, Alabama, and Louisiana for holding Africans. Though a number of witnesses believed that they had seen Africans, all the imported Negroes had vanished into the general mass of slaves in the lower South.[15]

Conservative slaveowners and law-abiding men were shocked by this gross defiance of federal law, and by the fact that the government could do nothing to punish it. Even more dangerous to the Buchanan administration were the gibes of the rapidly rising Republican party, whose antislavery members professed to see in all this the lesson that Democrats were not to be entrusted with enforcing the slave-trade laws. They had already issued a pamphlet which boldly asserted:

If the African slave trade, now opened, is to be closed again . . . the whole *animus* of the government at Washington must be changed. Interpreting the past by the light of present events, it is now evident that the real object of certain preposterous pretensions as to the sacredness of mere flags, without reference to the real nationality of vessels, was to facilitate the carrying on of the slave trade. . . . He must be charitable and confiding indeed, who believes that administrations at Washington, controlled by the Gulf states, will ever do anything effective towards shutting up the African slave trade. Not such aid, nor such defenders, do the times demand. If our laws are to be executed, there must be different executive agents. What is wanted, in short, to put down this infamous traffic, is a Republican President, and that would suffice to accomplish the object. The election of such a President would be felt in every slave barracoon in Africa. . . .[16]

Ever since 1800 the party of Jefferson and Jackson had dominated the American political scene, but its opponents had always been strong and were rapidly growing stronger. An accusation like this posed a real political threat to the Democrats. Politics, sentiment, and duty alike demanded that something be done to quash the slave-importing business (if the *Wanderer* landing was indeed no isolated example). Benjamin Slocumb played an important part in this determination. In mid-September, 1859, he headed south from Washington carrying a heavy burden of responsibility, for he was going to the region whence all the manifestations of danger had come.

As Slocumb rode toward North Carolina, he could well have

filled his time with gloomy reflections upon the weakness of federal authority. For decades Democratic politicians had been speaking of the United States as a confederation. The United States "are," they said, not "is"; and that almost unconscious use of the plural bespoke the states'-rights sentiments so dominant before Appomattox. Political theory had been translated into political action. Americans were as military-minded as most peoples, yet throughout the eastern half of the nation federal garrisons were nonexistent. Fortress Monroe, guarding the water approaches to Washington, had the largest concentration of bluecoats along the entire Atlantic seaboard—362 artillerymen tied down to fortifications. Between Fortress Monroe and Fort Moultrie at Charleston not a single federal soldier was stationed, and over the lower South there was only a handful of tiny garrisons: Key West, Pensacola, Baton Rouge. On the western frontier there were 14,000 soldiers; but in the East the militia alone defended the country, and these citizen-soldiers were under the absolute control of the separate states. Federal marshals in the South had no mounted troopers to help them look for smuggled slaves. United States naval cruisers were everywhere but at home—unless they were in dockyard for repairs—and there were hardly fifteen revenue cutters to guard the entire coast line of the United States. Marshal Blackburn complained bitterly that he had no cutter to help him; the *Dobbin,* operating out of Savannah, and the *Appleton,* cruising from Key West, were the only cutters available to patrol the vast east coast of Florida. There were innumerable inlets, but there was no one to guard them.

It was true that a slaver running into shore could encounter one of the two or three surveying ships at work, just as the *Rawlins* had; but her descent into Apalachicola Bay was apparently unplanned, and anyone making it his business should have been able to avoid the surveyors, who were not only few but tied down to specific and well-known localities. The same applied to the army triangulation teams ashore, and to the lighthouse keepers maintaining their vigil along the coasts.[17] It is difficult to see what any of these people could have done to oppose a landing. If a community was determined to import slaves, federal officials could place few hindrances in its way.

Furthermore, once arrests had been made, the jury system could defeat an unpopular prosecution, as the citizens of Charleston had already demonstrated. Attempts to move prisoners from a law-defying to a law-abiding area for trial were obnoxious to the spirit of the Sixth Amendment, and were certain to fail if the federal court in the rebellious area refused to grant the change of venue. Attorney General J. S. Black engaged in a long, and ultimately unsuccessful, effort to get Captain Corrie of the *Wanderer* removed from the South Carolina district to the Georgia district for trial as a pirate. Judge Magrath not only refused to let the case be moved, but obligingly released Corrie on bail so that he could mingle freely with his fellow Charlestonians.[18] All this was a bulwark against tyranny by the federal government, but a bulwark that could destroy the Union if local communities abused the liberty it had given them.

Slocumb's first stop of his fact-finding mission was Wilmington, North Carolina. The Tarheel State, as Slocumb soon discovered, was clean. Three days of diligent inquiry turned up not a trace of Africans for sale; on the contrary, no one had heard that any of them had been in the state for many years. Continuing his mission, the special agent went on to South Carolina, and soon was looking over at the little federal garrison in Fort Moultrie, and walking the streets of Charleston, where the Civil War would soon begin. Pretending to be a Mississippian anxious to buy slaves, Slocumb sought out a local resident best known for public advocacy of the African slave trade, and listened attentively to reports that Charleston had indeed been active in the trade.

Slocumb's informant assured him that some Charlestonians had been interested in importing Africans. About the beginning of September, 1859, a New Yorker had appeared in Charleston and had confidentially told some enterprising merchants that his father was about to land 400 Negroes at Beaufort. When he asked them for financial help, they chartered a small vessel to assist in the transfer of the Africans from the slaver to dry land. But something went awry, and the New Yorker's backers discovered that the whole story was a hoax, a swindle intended to line his own pockets. The irate Charlestonians had rewarded their Yankee deceiver with a cold bath, and no Africans had been landed. According to Slocumb's informant, all the reports of landings had been sheer fabrications, except for the *Wanderer*'s. No Africans from that vessel had ever been on sale in Charleston. Other residents told Slocumb much the same story, and he left after two days satisfied that the law had not been violated—although there were men quite ready to break the law if they thought they could escape punishment.

Slocumb traveled to Jacksonville, the community to whose sympathies Antonio Pelletier had thought he could trust himself and the *Ardennes*. There Slocumb fell in with an out-of-towner who said that two months earlier he had heard of Africans being landed at the mouth of the Indian River, near New Smyrna. This information coincided with the report Marshal Blackburn had sent in. Rumor had it that the vessel had been burned, and that the Spanish captain had later been seen in a Florida hotel. The informant did not know more. Slocumb hurried south to St. Augustine, and there found several men ready to give information. The editor of the *St. Augustine Examiner* said he believed there had been a landing at Jupiter Inlet, though he knew nothing of a landing at New Smyrna. An army surveyor to whom Slocumb revealed his true identity also accepted the fact of the Jupiter landing, and referred Slocumb to an individual whom, he suspected, had been financially concerned in the affair. Posing again as a slave buyer, Slocumb talked to an Ocala (Fla.) lawyer who told him that he had been offered Africans at a low price. The lawyer named several Ocala residents as the agents of slave traders. He estimated that 380 Negroes had recently been landed in Florida.

Surely where there was so much smoke there was fire—or was there? Not one of Slocumb's informants had actually seen any Africans, not even the lawyer to whom some had been offered; and those Africans could have come from the *Wanderer* rather than from a later landing. No one had any idea where the recent imports, if they existed, were being hidden. But the trail was getting warm, and Slocumb lost no time in heading for Ocala. On the way he stopped for the night at the Pulaski House in Pilatka, and there he found what seemed to be a real clue. Another guest at the hostel was "Colonel" John H. Newman, a sixty-year-old slave trader from Louisiana who was currently buying and selling domestic Negroes in the northern part of Florida. Slocumb, sensing that Newman might know a great deal, invited him to go for a walk. The detective, pretending that he wanted to buy Africans, drew out of Newman a startling story of slave smuggling.

There was indeed an organized company of African traders. Newman was in close correspondence with Hiram T. Mann of Ocala, though they wrote in terms so obscure than an intercepted letter would be meaningless to anyone else. Newman had a contract with the company which gave him first choice on all shipments, and he had agencies at Nashville, New Orleans, and Mobile to dispose of the Africans. The landing at Jupiter Inlet was real; 300 to 400 Africans had been added to those brought in by the *Wanderer*. The Africans had been widely spread over the South; most of them were in Florida, but some had been sent to Alabama, Tennessee, Mississippi, and Louisiana. Only forty of the *Wanderer*'s cargo were still up for sale in Georgia. Newman himself had taken thirty-four Africans to Nashville, twenty-seven to his own property on the Tuckapaw River in Louisiana, and fifteen to New Orleans. He had sold fifteen more near Pilatka only ten days before, and twenty had been sold near St. Augustine. But most of the smuggled Africans were still in hiding, learning English and agriculture. A modicum of training raised the value of Negroes from the $350–$400 obtainable for fresh imports to the $700 planters were willing to pay for "educated" Africans. Most of the schooling was going on in Florida, and the company was now using the sparsely populated coast between St. Augustine and Lake Worth for its landings. Newman, however, assured the detective that the newspaper reports of slave landings were greatly exaggerated. The cargo landed at Jupiter was the first since the *Wanderer* had come in, and no other slavers had yet arrived. But this was expected to change within the next few weeks. One slaver was due in ten or fifteen days, nine others were at sea, and the trade was soon to be expanded by large-scale smuggling from Cuba and by the kidnaping of free Negroes from the Bahamas.

Slocumb was shaken. As quickly as he could, he dashed off an excited letter to Secretary Thompson. The cabinet was alarmed, and orders were soon going out in several directions. The *Harriet Lane* was loaded with new percussion-cap rifles and sent off to cruise along the coasts of Georgia and South Carolina, while the *Dobbin* and the *Appleton,* less needful of frequent coaling, put to sea along the eastern Florida coast. As the men on these vessels cruised wearily up and down the coast, looking for something they never found, they little realized that it was the chance conversation of a gossipy old man that put them on their chase.[19]

Meanwhile Slocumb, continuing his quest, first went to Savannah, then took the train to Montgomery, Alabama (where he heard nothing except the latest vague rumors about the movements of the *Wanderer*'s Africans), and went on to Mobile. His prime target there was John McClusky, a trader in domestic slaves and one of Newman's agents for smuggled Africans. Up to this point Slocumb had not suspected Newman's truthfulness, but now he began to wonder. McClusky admitted that he was acquainted with Newman, but added that he would not trust him, even under oath. Four months earlier he had gone to Florida to get some Africans that Newman had promised were about to be landed. But the ship never arrived, and he returned to Mobile in disgust. Slocumb asked McClusky about buying Africans, and was told that none had ever been for sale in Mobile, though two small parties of *Wanderer* Africans had passed through on their way to other places. He had briefly put up twenty-three of them himself, but they had been taken on to Louisiana. He knew of no other landings of Africans.

Slocumb now had a great deal of thinking to do. Newman, according to his "agent," was a liar who spun yarns that were as unsubstantial as the smuggled slaves Slocumb was looking for. McClusky himself seemed honest—as honest, that is, as a man could be who admitted to being a frustrated dealer in smuggled slaves and an accomplice in the *Wanderer* crime. Slocumb's belief was further shaken as he traveled on, still posing as a slave buyer. A hundred or more of the *Wanderer's* Africans had actually been in New Orleans, but they all seemed to have gone somewhere else, and no later shipments had arrived. At Galveston, Indianola, and Port Lavaca, Texas, there were no rumors of landings, though there was a rumor about the location of a small number of the *Wanderer's* Africans. Forest & Company, Vicksburg slave traders, had sold thirty Negroes from that importation, and had received none since. Only seven of the *Wanderer's* Africans had changed ownership at Memphis. Adding up the credible reports he had heard about Africans, Slocumb was able to account for only 338 who had been seen at various places in the South, and this was no more than the 225-ton *Wanderer* could easily have brought. He finally reported to Secretary Thompson that he believed there had been no landing at Jupiter Inlet, and none anywhere else except for the *Wanderer's*.

But there remained the rumors to account for. It was puzzling that one cargo of Africans could raise so many rumors of separate landings. It did not seem possible that rumors so widespread, which had plagued the authorities for eighteen months, could have had no basis in fact. Slocumb decided he knew how so colossal a misconception had grown up. Many people had seen, or had heard credible reports of, Africans in their vicinity. The *Wanderer* Negroes, split up into numerous small parties scattered all over the lower South, had provided the basis for many true reports. Deliberate hoaxes could account for the reported large-scale landings.

There were many people who would not hesitate to start a lie: politicians looking for a way to discredit the administration; newspapermen wanting to fill a column; pranksters simply having fun. Slocumb had encountered one such man on his travels, the editor of the *St. Augustine Examiner*. He had published the text of a legal agreement disposing of a cargo of slaves, and Northern newspapers had written strong editorials denouncing this brazen violation of the law. When Slocumb asked to see the original agreement, he was shown an old document dated 1804. The typesetter had blurred the date in order "to bamboozle the Northern abolitionists." Yankees taunted Southerners for holding slaves; Southerners could taunt Yankees by fabricating reports of slave landings. Thus intersectional tension helped to create rumors of a large-scale African slave trade where none existed.[20]

Slocumb decided that despite the existence of many advocates of a reopened slave trade, there was in fact no important public sentiment in favor of smuggling. On the contrary, most Southerners were hostile to a revival of the trade. Whether or not Slocumb's conclusions were valid, the rumors of landings continued, month after month, and, month after month, the officials found no evidence. Lucien Peyton, a clerk in the Pension Office who was sent south to gather evidence against the *Wanderer*'s supercargo (who was finally arrested early in 1860), became convinced that

The slave trade is carried on to a large extent by citizens of the United States, who have an organization for that purpose extending along the Atlantic coast from Maine to Florida; that they have a very large amount of capital invested in the business, most of which is owned in the city of New York, in which part the larger part of the vessels used in the traffic are equipped for the voyage.

But Peyton admitted that he had no legal proof of the existence of a slave-trading company; there were only numerous bits of hearsay and inference.[21] Also, he found no Africans in the flesh; nor, for that matter, did the Census Bureau, which after the Civil War tabulated the number of American Negroes who admitted being born abroad. The smuggled slave remains so elusive that one may wonder whether in fact he ever existed in very large numbers.[22]

Whatever the truth, the United States government finally gave official sanction to the idea that the *Wanderer* landing was the only one. President Buchanan readily accepted it because it removed blame from his administration; but so did Abraham Lincoln, who had no reason to conceal any frauds carried on despite, or by, his predecessor.[23] With the end of slavery in the United States came the end of the problem of finding smuggled slaves, but not before federal officers had suffered a good deal of harassment.

_ 10 _

LASALA, MORRIS, AND
JUDGE BETTS

In June, 1856, twelve men selected to discharge the heaviest responsibility falling upon ordinary citizens of a free nation sat in the jury room of the United States Circuit Court, earnestly considering the case of Rudolph E. Lasala. If they found him guilty, the court was bound to send him to prison for at least three years and to fine him $1,000; if they found him not guilty, enforcement of the act of 1818 would receive a sharp setback and hundreds of Africans would continue to cross the Atlantic aboard vessels outfitted in New York City. The decision of these twelve jurors was made even more difficult by the interpretation placed upon the law by His Honor, Judge Samuel R. Betts, presiding over the court in the absence of Justice Samuel Nelson.

Rudolph Lasala was the registered owner of the brig *Horatio* when she was being fitted out for the slave trade. That in itself deeply implicated him, but District Attorney John McKeon had substantial evidence besides Lasala's oath of ownership. Lasala had not been a passive owner, but had actively assisted in getting the brig ready to go to sea. It was he, not the charterer, who had paid the stevedore's bill for stowing water casks, firewoood, and other useful equipment aboard the vessel. McKeon also had a note in Lasala's own hand, an ambiguous but damning note proving that

Lasala had remained in charge of the brig up to the time the loading was finished. The note, signed by Lasala, read: "Everything is now on board, except, &c. It is desirable to haul out and anchor in the stream, and as soon as the weather permits we will clear at the Custom-House. We should like to see you about noon today." Waiting until the weather cleared at the customhouse meant waiting until it was safe to get the *Horatio*'s papers from clearance clerk Sidney Ingraham. The note had been sent to the brig's captain, who was under joint indictment with Lasala; in order to obtain the note to use as evidence, McKeon had to abandon his case against the captain. But the evidence was worth the price, for it seemed to promise that, for the first time in many years, an American shipowner would suffer for sending his vessel into the slave trade. Captains and mates had sometimes been sent to prison, but never owners.

Lasala's lawyer, James W. Gerard, had not tried to dispute these embarrassing facts. The story he wove out of the testimony of an assortment of Lasala's business acquaintances centered rather on the mysterious Don José Egea, the tall, red-bearded Spaniard whose journey from Havana to New York set the *Horatio*'s voyage in motion. Egea (now safely in Cuba) had, it developed, brought certain bills of exchange to New York, and deposited them at Lasala's establishment. Because he was unfamiliar with the English language, Egea needed an agent and interpreter, and Lasala had undertaken the job at 2½ per cent commission on all money spent. He had never owned a penny's worth of either vessel or cargo, but acted throughout merely as an agent. His agency ceased when the vessel's title was formally transferred to her supercargo, shortly before sailing. Lasala claimed that he had no idea that the *Horatio* was a slaver, for many vessels sailed to Africa with similar cargoes. He also protested ignorance of the fact that Egea was a scoundrel.

The jurors could hardly have believed such flimsy defense, but Judge Betts's charge left them sorely puzzled. The act of 1818 seemed to say that anyone who knowingly helped to fit out a slaver was guilty:

No citizen or citizens of the United States, or any other person or persons, shall, after the passing of this act, as aforesaid, for himself, them-

selves, or any other person or persons whatsoever, either as master, factor, or owner, build, fit, equip, load, or otherwise prepare, any ship or
vessel, in any port or place within the jurisdiction of the United States,
nor cause any such ship or vessel to sail from any port or place whatsoever, within the jurisdiction of the same, for the purpose of procuring
any negro . . . to be held, sold, or otherwise disposed of, as slaves.
. . . Every person or persons so building, fitting out, equipping, loading, or otherwise preparing, or sending away, or causing any of the
acts aforesaid to be done, with intent to employ such ship or vessel in
such trade . . . or who shall, in any wise, be aiding or abetting therein,
shall severally, on conviction . . .

But Judge Betts had read the law otherwise. Before the jurors retired, he told them that Lasala was guilty only if he had held actual
control over the voyage; that is, only if he could have managed it
as he saw fit. If he did not have full power, he had not violated the
act of 1818. And yet the law stated that anyone "aiding and abetting" the preparation of a slaver was guilty. Certainly Lasala had
been aiding and abetting. It was true that part of the act singled out
for punishment persons who fitted out vessels for their own use, but
the next phrase, mentioning their accomplices, was separated from
it by that unambiguous word "or." Any person sending away a
vessel under his own control, *or* anyone helping him to do it, was
guilty. Nothing could be plainer.

Jurors do not question the law as it is laid down by a judge. But
the jurors in the Lasala case, after arguing for two hours over Judge
Betts's obvious mischarge, filed back into the courtroom to ask for
clarification. The foreman had his question ready: "If the defendant was aware, at the time of fitting out the vessel, that she was to
be engaged in the slave trade, does he come under the section of the
law under which he is indicted?" The judge replied: "Not unless he
acted in preparing or fitting her out or aiding in doing so in the
capacity of master, owner, or factor, with intent to employ her in
the slave trade, under his own power or control." The jurors withdrew for further discussion. If Betts was right, no one could ever be
guilty of "aiding and abetting" in fitting out a vessel, for no one
assisting someone else to prepare a slaver would have personal con-

trol over it. It was a contradiction in terms. But the judge had left no doubt as to what he thought about the case, and no doubt that the jury would have to obey. If the jurors decided that Lasala was guilty, on the basis of their own reading of the act of 1818, Betts would declare a mistrial and get another jury. And so they reached their verdict, and again filed into the courtroom to declare Lasala innocent of wrongdoing.[1]

It was an important verdict, involving an important interpretation of the law. One of the peculiarities of the slave trade was that nearly everyone could plausibly claim to be an agent of someone else, except, perhaps, the captain of a slaver. Under the law as Judge Betts interpreted it, men could do almost anything they pleased to aid the equipping of slavers, and ignore the act of 1818. That is, they could flout the law so long as Betts and Justice Nelson were controlling the courts of the Southern New York district; Nelson agreed with Betts, and any jury instructed by them could do nothing but find defendants not guilty. The district attorney could not appeal their mischarge to the Supreme Court, because the review of such a case would constitute double jeopardy. The system was foolproof for slave traders.

In other cases coming before them in 1856, Betts and Nelson decided that the act of 1818 applied only to captains, owners, and supercargoes, and not to any other person who might be connected with a slaver.[2] This point was unimportant when set alongside the Lasala ruling, as no one outside those categories was likely to have control over a voyage anyway, but the judges also applied the same principle to the act of 1794, the pioneer slave-trading statute. Its wording, they decided, permitted persons to be fined, though not imprisoned, if they knowingly assisted in the outfitting of slavers, regardless of the degree of their personal control. Under this interpretation anyone helping to outfit a slaver might have been fined $2,000, but by limiting the act's scope to the owner, the captain, and the supercargo, the financial liability of slave traders was limited to $6,000 for each vessel found to be a slaver. Even so, as a practical matter, they stood to lose very little money; apparently the only collection ever made was $4,000 from the owner and the captain of the schooner *Falmouth*. The supercargo denied being such, and the jury believed him.[3]

To sum up this complicated set of rulings, the law as practiced without possibility of appeal in the Southern New York district provided that: (1) No one could be convicted for helping to outfit a slaver, unless he were owner, captain, or supercargo. Men could furnish supplies, ship crews, take bribes, clear papers through the customhouse, and so on, with absolute impunity. (2) An owner, a captain, or a supercargo could not be sent to prison for helping to outfit a slaver, unless he had full control over the voyage, which could be proved in court.

This does not seem consistent with the wording of the laws. Justice Nelson never put his reasoning on record, but Judge Betts, who apparently was the brains of the pair on this subject, did give the public an explanation of his rulings. The first section of each act stated that it was illegal for owners, captains, and supercargoes to fit out slavers. It said nothing about carpenters, bribed deputies, or anyone else who might be involved; neither did it fix any penalty for such act, except confiscation of the vessel. According to Judge Betts, the first section was related to the second section, which set a penalty for persons fitting out or aiding in the fitting out of vessels, in that it fixed the quality of the crime. The word "so" in the second section—"every person *so* building . . ."—attached the second section to the first, and the first named only captains, owners, and supercargoes as liable. In brief, Betts made the second section subordinate to the first section, rather than equal to it in weight.[4] This may be plausible logic, but it is a very narrow interpretation. One could easily find reasons for making the two sections independent: one provided only for confiscation of the vessel while the other provided only for punishment of the men involved. Perhaps Congress meant that a vessel should be confiscated only if the owner or one of his agents—and not someone who seized control of it—was responsible for its guilty use, whereas the second section was written to punish anyone, owner, agent, or some other party, who was involved in the vessel's guilt. No debates were recorded on this subject, and therefore no one will ever know what Congress intended to do. Certainly Judge Betts upheld the most stultifying interpretation of the law.

But this explains only the limitation of the law to owner, captain, and supercargo. Betts ruled that personal control must have existed, even though the statute obviously provided for punishing persons who did not have and could not have had personal control. To twist this meaning out of the law, Betts had recourse to an act long since repealed: the act of March 2, 1807, which the act of 1818 had supplanted. The act of 1807 had stated that persons preparing slavers should be fined $20,000 each, or ten times the penalty provided by the act of 1794. Both these acts included the phrase, "with intent that the vessel shall be employed [in the slave trade]"; in other words, the guilty party had to have the intent that the vessel become a slaver. But the act of 1818 was worded differently. It outlawed the preparation of vessels "with intent to employ" them in the trade, and provided for a prison term as well as a fine. Betts reasoned that the penalty specified by the act of 1818 was the more severe, and that Congress had therefore intended to limit the crimes to which this severe penalty could be applied. Anyone (so long as he was owner, master, or factor) could have been fined $20,000 under the act of 1807 for helping to outfit a slaver, but only those in personal charge could be sent to jail under the act of 1818. Judge Betts declared that the Supreme Court had upheld this interpretation.[5]

The core of Betts's reasoning apparently was that (1) the act of 1807 stipulated a milder penalty than the act of 1818; (2) the act of 1818 used different language in describing the crime of the principal parties; and therefore (3) the clause of the act of 1818 dealing with accomplices of the principal parties could be dropped out. The absurdity of such logic is obvious. It is equally obvious that Betts credited Congress with very little sense by holding that it had narrowed the definition of the crime at the same time that it had increased the penalty—for the act of 1818 *repealed*[6] the act of 1807, and thus left a large category of crime prohibited only by the act of 1794 and its mild penalty. The act of 1818 was (as Betts stated) intended to make the law more severe; yet, according to his reasoning, all it did was to increase the penalty for some crimes while sharply reducing the penalty for others. A more sensible explanation would be that Congress intended to make more severe the penalty for all the crimes described in the act of 1807, and expressed its intent in language easily understandable by anyone who used common sense in reading the law.

Betts had also invoked the Supreme Court as his support. This is not the place to consider the intricacies and the ambiguities of *United States v. Gooding,* an 1827 case. It is enough to say that the decision in that case does not, upon careful reading, support Judge Betts's reasoning. Indeed, the case dealt with an entirely different question. Betts and Nelson were not, in fact, following the Supreme Court. Rather, they were faultily construing acts of Congress, under such circumstances that the Supreme Court could never intervene. Thus New York became a haunt of pirates and their backers, and so remained until well into 1862, when the slave trade vanished.[7]

Samuel Rossiter Betts was at this time one of the oldest men on the federal bench. Appointed when John Quincy Adams was president, he had already served thirty years as district judge; he would see Andrew Johnson in the White House before retiring a decade after his vital decisions in these slave-trade cases. As judge of the district court in by far the busiest judicial district of the United States, he had accumulated enough prestige to be called "the father of American admiralty law." [8] History has charitably forgotten most of his decisions against the slave trade; has forgotten how he could lean over backward to ignore what was obvious to anyone with a less prejudiced mind.

Before Justice Nelson came onto the Second Circuit, the mischief that Betts could accomplish was checked by Justice Smith Thompson, a vigorous proponent of practical law. In the fall of 1839 Betts heard his first slave-trade cases, against Captain Isaac Morris of the *Butterfly* and Captain Frederick Peterson of the *Catharine.* At their examination, Betts publicly expressed his doubt that the eminent Justice Joseph Story of Massachusetts had been right in ruling some years earlier that the act of 1800 outlawed not only the transportation of slaves, but also voyages made with the intent to transport slaves later.[9] To Betts, it was perfectly legal for a captain to sail his fully equipped slaver up to the beach and his waiting Africans; only after they came aboard could the captain be punished under the act of 1800. Judge Betts did not explain why the act of 1800 had not been repealed by the act of 1820; he simply reasoned that a vessel could not be "engaged in the transportation of slaves" until it was actually carrying them. To reason thus, he not only had to impugn Justice Story's logic, but he also had to ignore a whole series of Supreme Court decisions.[10] Perhaps his public statement was what induced Morris and Peterson to await their trials instead of jumping bail; at any rate, Morris did stand trial. His attorneys raised the question of whether or not the act of 1800 covered his case. Betts and Thompson, sitting jointly in circuit court, clashed over the question; they could agree on nothing except to send the matter to the Supreme Court. Both trials were postponed, and a certificate of division was made out. Thompson traveled to Washington for a meeting of the Supreme Court, whose justices affirmed that crew members did violate the act of 1800 by willfully doing anything to advance a slaving voyage, at any stage of the proceedings. Learning of this, Morris and Peterson took advantage of their bail and departed for friendlier climates.[11]

The Supreme Court had rebuked Betts's pettifoggery, but the rebuke failed to alter his habit of compressing the law within its narrowest terms. When the suit for confiscation of the *Butterfly* came before him, he declared her forfeit after pointedly asking why Captain Morris did not appear to explain her business. But in passing judgment he laid down the rule that no cargo in itself could induce him to confiscate a vessel. Even if no legal sale for it on the African coast could be demonstrated, the presumption would be that it was intended for lawful trade. It was not the schooner's cargo of lumber, a large boiler, and knocked-down water casks that made Betts confiscate her, but these items plus twenty-three Spanish and Portuguese passengers and seamen and some odd business arrangements.[12] Slavers could avoid carrying over the extra seamen, or could have perfectly plausible business arrangements to explain their presence, but that possibility did not deter Betts from laying down his ruling that no cargo was incriminating.

Everyone expected Betts to confiscate the *Catharine* as well. Her cargo was even more suspicious: a large boiler, 1,500 feet of plank and some joists, enough casks for 7,000 gallons of water, 570 wooden spoons, 36 tin dishes, and a large quantity of brandy and tobacco. The captors found twenty or twenty-five Spaniards and Portuguese aboard, along with a handful of Americans, and a paper in Spanish listing the duties of the "passengers" when they took over the vessel under the supercargo's direction. The supercargo had committed suicide when the vessel reached New York. The logbook had been kept in Spanish, and there were other assorted documents in that language. Most interesting of all was a letter taken from Captain Peterson while several English seamen held him. This document told him what to do with the *Catharine*'s register when she was sold, and also advised him to be "careful that, in any cross questions, you do not commit yourself; but always stick to the same story," and, if boarded, to "take all command with your American sailors, according to your roll; and all the others are to be passengers."

Betts, well aware of these discoveries, agreed that the *Catharine* was more suspect than the *Butterfly,* yet he found that the business arrangements for her voyage put her entirely outside the law. The *Butterfly* had been chartered for a voyage to Africa, with no obvious preparations for selling her on the coast. But "public" arrangements for the sale of the *Catharine* had been completed at Havana, and an agreement drawn that she was to be delivered to her Spanish purchaser on the African coast on October 1, 1839. According to this legal fiction, her voyage to that coast was partly to deliver a cargo that she had been chartered to carry, and partly to deliver her to the purchaser. Betts therefore decided that because the *Catharine* was to change nationality before shipping slaves, her voyage was not in violation of American law. He still did not grasp the essential point of the Supreme Court's rulings: a vessel was engaged in the slave trade as soon as she was destined for it, regardless of changes in ownership and fittings before the deed was consummated. To the astonishment of those watching the case, Betts dismissed the libel.[13]

The decision was appealed to Justice Thompson. Meanwhile, two large sacks of handcuffs had been found hidden near the bottom of the schooner's hold. But it was not this conclusive proof of her criminality that aroused the justice; it was the stupidity of Betts's reasoning. Thompson pointed out that the laws could be violated with great ease if Betts's views were permitted to stand. He agreed that American vessels could be lawfully sold and delivered on the African coast, but only for legitimate purposes, not to become slavers. He reversed the verdict and ordered the *Catharine* confiscated.[14]

Because Betts had ruled that no cargo in itself warranted confiscation of a vessel, some rather brazen actions went on at New York in later years. For example, the bark *Emily* took to sea in the summer of 1859 with all the equipment of a slaver: 15,000 feet of lumber, 103 casks of fresh water, 100 barrels of rice, 25 barrels of codfish, 20 barrels of pork, 50 barrels of bread, 150 boxes of herring, 2 boilers with furnaces, 10 dozen pails, and 2 cases of drugs. In a shrewd display of skill, found in other slavers as well, the water casks had been stowed to fill the bottom of the hold, and the planks laid on top so that their surface formed a perfect slave deck. As the *Emily* manifested nearly everything that a slaver needed, the authorities did not bother to search her but only mustered the crew; neither did they detain her. But Commander John Calhoun and the *Portsmouth* intercepted her and sent her home under guard; after prolonged litigation, however, the libel was dismissed with a certificate of probable cause. The *Emily* was not the only example; there were so many fully equipped counterparts that the British commodore wrote in some heat of a nation that allowed undisguised slavers to clear its ports. But the voyages of such vessels were legitimate in the eyes of the court; American merchants had the right to carry on whatever kind of business they wished.[15]

Ultimately Betts softened his views. The *Kate,* captured with

Henrico da Costa, was confiscated on grounds that the vessel's business, and da Costa's connection with it, had not been satisfactorily explained. The *Weather Gage,* a fully equipped slaver, was confiscated on grounds that her cargo was not suitable for the announced purposes of her trading voyage. Betts did not reverse his position on cargoes, but his evident softening did introduce enough hazard into the outfitting of slavers at New York to make slave traders begin to look elsewhere for places to fit them out. In the meantime, however, New York had served as a pirates' lair, with the United States courts their surest defense.[16]

Between the double-jeopardy injunction in the Constitution, and the legal niceties that covered Betts's decisions, only once was a federal attorney able to appeal a decision to the Supreme Court. In the spring of 1857 the brig *Ellen* had been purchased by John P. Weeks, and loaded with a mixed cargo of rum, shooks, gunpowder, and dry goods. Her supercargo was José de Aranga, who carried $1,200 in gold inside his trunk. The captain was Philip S. Van Vechten, by occupation a "rover." Van Vechten openly told his brother, a customhouse clerk, that he was taking the *Ellen* to Africa for slaves. The clerk reproached him, and, moreover, warned the authorities. Just before the *Ellen* sailed the talkative Van Vechten also admitted to Captain Faunce of the revenue cutter that his vessel was a slaver. Her seizure a short time later was an anticlimax.

Betts's clerk, acting as a United States commissioner, discharged Van Vechten and Aranga from custody, but his chief placed more credence in the confessions. Indeed, Betts stated in court that Van Vechten's later retractions of his statements had not convinced him at all. The judge then went on to demonstrate how law can sometimes outrage justice:

This expurgating testimony of his [Van Vechten's] would have no weight with me in displacing the effect of his declaration, solemnly made and repeated, if his relation to the vessel was such in law as to subject her to be chargeable with his statements. Although my mind was brought to some hesitation upon this point, still I think not only the rule of evidence deducible from the general laws of agency, limits the effects of acknowledgments or statements by an agent as against the interests of the principal to matters relating directly to the business of his trust, within the plain purview of his powers, and made in and about the performance of his agency, but that in respect to this specific question the Supreme Court of the United States has so explained and limited the character of this proof as to exclude it, where the declarations are not part of the *res gestae,* employed in aid or furtherance of the object of the agency, and plainly within the scope of the master's powers (12 Wheat. 460. The United States vs. Gooding). The conversations and declarations of the master had no relation to the prosecution or furtherance of the voyage, either in employing men or means to aid it, or removing impediments from its prosecution. Nor can the Court find authority in the proofs before it, to justify the presumption that the admissions or assertions of Van Vechten were made with the knowledge or approval of the owner.

With that Betts dismissed the libel, but he did award a certificate of probable cause.

There was only one fault with this opinion: the Supreme Court did not say what Betts claimed it said. Volume 12 of Wheaton's *Reports,* page 470, reads as follows:

Our opinion of the admissibility of this evidence proceeds upon the ground that these were not the naked declarations of the master, unaccompanied with his acts in that capacity, but declarations coupled with proceedings for the objects of the voyage, and while it was in progress. We give no opinion upon the point whether mere declarations, under other circumstances, would have been admissible.

District Attorney McKeon, despite the attempts of Beebe, Dean, & Donohue to dissuade him, appealed the matter to Justice Nelson. This was in vain, for Nelson invariably supported Betts. Still unsatisfied, McKeon asked the Solicitor of the Treasury (his nominal superior in such cases) for permission to appeal to the Supreme Court. It was granted, but the case got in too late to be docketed for the court session in the winter of 1857–58. McKeon left office soon after, and his successor decided that the case was too rare to be worth pushing. The matter quietly expired, and the *Ellen* was released. Weeks sold her to José Santos, Santos sold her to one

Augiolo Dello Astrologo, and she went off to Africa for a cargo of slaves.[17]

By the late summer of 1857 the list of adverse legal decisions at New York was formidable:

1) No one could be prosecuted for fitting out a slaver unless he was acting as owner, captain, or supercargo.

2) The owner, the captain, and the supercargo had to have control over the vessel if they were to be subject to the fines and imprisonment specified by the act of 1818. If they were working as agents of someone else, they were subject only to the moderate fine specified by the act of 1794.

3) No cargo in itself was incriminating; if properly manifested, it was presumed legal.

4) Confessions given to law officers or others were not admissible evidence, unless they had been made as part of the arrangements for prosecuting the voyage.

5) Evidence that a vessel was sailing for Africa with a cargo and a crew well adapted to the slave trade, and with papers enabling a quick sale on the coast to the charterer (papers he had attempted to destroy when arrested), was inconclusive.[18]

6) Papers proving an individual to be a slave trader were not admissible as evidence, unless they related to the adventure in which he was currently engaged.[19]

An accused party could also benefit from any legal procedures and loopholes his attorneys might think of.

Several years later, when the Republican *New York Tribune* was trying to make political capital out of the slave trade, it denounced Marshal Isiah Rynders, a prominent Tammany Democrat, as a tool of the slave traders.[20] But this was not its opinion in 1857; in an editorial on July 10, it specifically exonerated Rynders, McKeon, and their assistants from blame:

All the persons connected with these offices have, we believe, done their best for some time past to put a stop to . . . [the slave trade]. The whole difficulty has arisen—the impunity we were about to say with which the slave trade is carried on from this port of New-York—has arisen from the construction which Judges Betts and Nelson have seen fit to put upon the laws for the suppression of the slave trade. There is a singular but very natural contrast between the spirit of good will with which these two learned Judges apply themselves to the enforcement of the Fugitive Slave Act, and the severe spirit of strict construction with which they seem to be seized whenever the slave trade suppression acts are before them. . . . Property—such is the substance of their decisions upon this [fugitive slave] act—is a much greater thing than the the freedom or personal rights of any number of niggers. But this same maxim, which appears to be about the beginning and end of the law with these two learned Judges, when applied to the slave-trade suppression acts, leads to a totally different system of construction. The utmost rigor is required in bringing the case within the strictest letter of the law. Property is not to be interfered with on slight grounds, and though invented for the purpose of the slave-trade, it still remains highly sacred. . . .

The editorial went on to say that Betts and Nelson "strain every nerve" to nullify the slave-trade laws. Some rewording of those laws might be useful, but "with a court really disposed to suppress the slave-trade, we are inclined to think that the existing laws could be made to answer every purpose." [21]

This is a remarkable pronouncement, distinguished more by zeal than by fairness. The abolitionist *Tribune* detested the fugitive slave act, and anyone who did his duty under that act was likely to raise its wrath. Judges were not placed on the bench so that they could suppress the slave trade, or suppress any other crime. Their job was to see justice done, to ensure that cases brought before the courts were decided in strict accordance with law, evidence, and Anglo-American legal concepts. A judge who determined to suppress a crime might wreak havoc on the guilty, but he would also be false to the very reason for his existence. He might as well be replaced by the district attorney.

But there was some justification for the *Tribune*'s attack. No one has ever suggested that Betts and Nelson were being bribed by Viana or the Figanieres or Machado, or that they secretly approved of the slave trade, rejoiced in its successes, and contributed consciously to its advancement. Nevertheless, they did greatly assist the trade by their extreme concern that every possible opportunity be given to the accused. Certainly concern for the accused is basic to American liberties, but society also has rights, and is entitled to protection from criminals who prey upon it. It may well be questioned whether or not the judges of the Southern New York district discharged their duties toward their nation, as well as toward the accused individuals who came before them.

There was a remedy at hand for the situation. Judges cannot be impeached merely for giving unpopular or controversial decisions, but laws can be changed. In October, 1856, the *Tribune* had itself suggested that possibility:

One fact, which was pretty well ascertained before this last seizure, appears now to be established. The parties engaged in the business are few and of foreign extraction; mostly Portuguese. . . . All of these are old customers, who have been tried and acquitted under the statutes, as construed by the Court, though no doubt could exist that they were morally guilty. No sooner are they out of the hands of the law, than they go at the business again. . . . What a commentary on the legislation of Congress in this regard! Let us have a penal statute at the next session, which, however strictly construed, shall hold these Portuguese rats, in spite of their utmost efforts to nibble themselves free.[22]

But nothing was ever done. Neither Republican nor Democratic congresses ever showed much interest in rewording the laws to make their meanings unmistakable.[23] Only with the end of the slave trade did the decisions of the Southern New York district cease to harass law enforcement officers.

– 11 –

THE VANISHING SLAVERS

In October, 1859, the judge of the Southern New York district court declared the American bark *Orion* forfeited as an obvious slaver. And yet, only a month later, the *Orion* was in the vicinity of the Congo River looking for slaves. On November 30 she was captured with 888 men, women, and children confined aboard by Her Majesty's steamer *Pluto*. These contradictory facts point to one of the strangest loopholes of American law exploited by slave traders.

The *Orion*'s career as a slaver began ordinarily enough, with her sailing from New York on January 20, 1859. She was a handsome, 450-ton vessel, one of the first of the large slavers. Her cargo generally resembled that which the *Emily* would take out a few months later: lumber, empty casks, bread, rice, rum, beef, pork, boilers with furnaces, muskets, buckets, and the rest. The *Orion* differed from the *Emily* in that the lumber did not rest upon the water casks to form an improvised middle deck, but it did not need to. *Orion* was registered as a double-decked vessel, and had permanent beams spanning the hold to support the extra deck. She was perhaps an undisguised slaver, but no one interfered. Had not the judges decided that no cargo was incriminating? Otherwise her voyage looked proper. She had changed crews shortly before sailing, but that was legitimate. Her owner, Harrison S. Vining, was undoubtedly a genuine merchant (who dabbled in the slave trade as a side line); supercargo Tristas P. Canhao professed to have lawful use for her cargo on the far side of the Atlantic. The *Orion* therefore went to sea with the blessing of the lawful authorities, the power of the United States government standing behind her papers and her immunity from British molestation.

Unfortunately for the band of pirates aboard the *Orion,* at that time the power of the United States government was not very substantial off the Congo. Only an occasional American cruiser patrolled the coast, whereas Her Majesty's steamer *Triton,* Lieutenant R. H. Burton, had control over all the shipping that came and went around the river's mouth. Burton's men boarded the *Orion* to see her papers and verify her American registration, a procedure to which the United States government did not object. The *Triton* boarding party, however, investigated further and discovered that the *Orion* was on a slave-trading voyage. There is much dispute as to what happened next. The *Orion*'s men swore that Burton, by using threats, tried to force them to renounce their nationality and surrender to him; Burton, who had no right to make such threats, denied that he intended to do anything but keep the *Orion* in custody until he could turn her over to an American cruiser. Whatever the truth, the *Orion* remained under British guard for several days, until Commander T. W. Brent and the *Marion* arrived at the anchorage. Brent did not officially approve of the detention, but after looking over the *Orion* he put her crew in irons and started her off for New York in charge of a prize crew.

The voyage home was a melodramatic one. Captain John E. Hanna became deathly ill with what the naval officer in charge unscientifically diagnosed as "a broken heart." As Hanna lay dying he confessed that the *Orion* was a slaver, and committed his last perjury by swearing that his mate, Thomas Morgan, was not in on the secret. International storm clouds began to gather. The State Department, learning of Burton's action, roundly denounced him for infringing on American sovereignty, and later blamed him for Hanna's death, disregarding the possibility that going home to face trial as an American prisoner was a more likely cause of his broken heart than the harassment he had suffered from the *Triton*'s men. But diplomatic arguments had no effect on the federal officers who took care of the *Orion* when she arrived at New York in June, 1859. The marshal's deputies picked up the prisoners and took them to jail, and the prize commander swore an affidavit for their arrest; other deputies guarded the vessel, and the district attorney prepared a libel requesting the court to confiscate the vessel for violation of the acts of 1794 and 1818.

The law firm of Beebe, Dean, & Donohue joined forces with Charles N. Black to get the charges against the *Orion*'s crew dismissed; the slave-trading interest also took the precaution of sending Jesse Braddick to bail out the crew. Braddick, an obscure New Yorker who made sails for slavers and bailed out their crews when necessary, posted the small amounts of money demanded by Commissioner Joseph Bridgham for their release. But the precaution was unneeded as the commissioner decided that the evidence did not warrant prosecution. The district attorney acceded to his judgment, and did not take the cases to the grand jury; the owner, Vining, was not even arrested. This was rather meager encouragement for naval officers trying to rid the seas of slavers.

The *Orion*, however, remained in custody, with the libel hanging over her future. Although attorneys Donohue and Black wanted the case disposed of quickly, Judge Betts said that he could not hear it until September. The *Orion*'s lawyers next looked into the possibility of having Judge Charles Ingersoll of the Connecticut district hear the case when he came to New York to help out the overworked Betts. Ingersoll and Betts shared the same outlook; Ingersoll had lately released the whaler *Laurens*, and had earlier proven himself reliable, from the point of view of slave traders, when he ignored or ruled out of order all the evidence damning the owner and the officers of the slaver *Panchita*. But Ingersoll, too, had other duties to perform, and meanwhile the *Orion* remained under guard.

The villain of this story is the act of March 3, 1847, a piece of legislation struck off in haste by a preoccupied Congress which, as its title said, was intended to "Reduce Expenses of Proceedings in

Admiralty." That act seemed thoroughly sound. It provided that whenever a vessel was libeled, the owner could regain custody by posting a bond for its value. Two appraisers, one appointed by each side, would decide what the ship was worth. The cargo, too, could be bonded. If the decision of the court ultimately went against the owner, he could either surrender the vessel or forfeit the bonds. Ordinarily vessels were libeled in federal court for some specific sum of money, such as wages due a seaman, damages due a shipper of injured cargo, or damages inflicted upon another vessel in collision. By bonding his vessel the shipowner could keep it in service; the person making the claim against the owner could avoid the heavy costs of guarding the vessel, and money to satisfy the claim (if the court approved it) would be readily forthcoming.

But Congress had made no distinction between ordinary libels and the libels lodged against vessels accused of being used for criminal purposes. The same law applied to both. A slaver's owner could therefore post a bond for the ship's value and send it back to sea, while the lawyers were arguing over who should possess the bond. The profits of a successful slaving voyage dwarfed the value of the ship. Slave traders had seen this possibility, and two slavers had already gone to sea while under bond. The *Orion*'s backers decided to do the same thing.

On August 6, 1859, the *Orion* passed from the custody of Marshal Rynders, who had no choice under the law but to surrender her to Vining. Perhaps Judge Betts's clerk had not been very cautious in accepting the bond, which amounted to $17,923, a large sum of money in 1859. As Rudolph Blumenberg, the bondsman, had no property, the *Orion*'s bond was worthless. But Blumenberg's oath that he had the money had satisfied the district court. The slave traders had therefore taken back a fully equipped slaver in exchange for a piece of paper and an oath.

The next step was for Vining to get rid of his title to the *Orion*. As he was already suspect, it was better for him not to have anything to do with the vessel's second voyage to Africa. On August 18 a properly sworn bill of sale was passed through the customhouse to transfer the bark's registered ownership from Vining to Thomas

Morgan, who had been Captain Hanna's second-in-command. Morgan wrote Secretary of State Cass for reassurance that the British had no right to interfere with American-registered vessels, gathered a crew, and applied at the customhouse for clearance to Africa.

The *Orion* was as flagrant a slaver as she had been the preceding January, when the district attorney and the customs collector had let her go without protest. The libel against her was practically dead. Morgan could take the vessel anywhere he wanted to, so far as the district court was concerned. She could, of course, be libeled again for the guilty voyage Morgan was about to take her upon, but it was doubtful that such a libel would stand up in court. The commissioner who released her crew had not thought the evidence strong, and Betts's words in an earlier case might have given the officials pause:

It is to be assumed, on entering upon the subject, that it is lawful for an American vessel to trade to the coast of Africa, and to carry for such purposes all the articles found on board this schooner, and also that every article of her lading was proper for and adapted to a lawful trade there; for although there is no particular evidence that the large boiler, or the bundles of shooks, or the loose lumber found on board this vessel could be advantageously disposed of on the coast, or had any of them been before used in the trade there, yet without express testimony to the contrary the presumption would be in favor of their being proper articles for that market, of if they possessed no known value there at least, they might be carried, and offered in such trade without subjecting the vessel to any injurious imputation. Considering, then, that all the lading of this vessel might be lawfully employed in trade on that coast, and that she was directed to districts where an innocent commerce may be carried on, it will not be sufficient for the prosecution to show that these facts are equally compatible with an engagement in the illicit trade. Such a state of the case would entitle the claimant to an acquittal of the vessel; for The United States must show by preponderating evidence that the vessel had violated the Act, and when the testimony as well applies to an innocent as an illicit enterprise, the law will not regard it as creating a presumption of guilt.[1]

There was no better evidence now than before, and if the *Orion* was libeled again, Morgan could have her bonded again. The officials gave in, and Morgan put to sea. He now had command of an invulnerable ship, the dream of all slave traders. Behind him at New York the officials were hopelessly mired in the law, while ahead of him on the slave coast not a cruiser would dare oppose him. As the State Department's protests over the *Orion*'s detention by the *Triton* had won a grudging admission from the British that they had been wrong, British cruisers would not accost the *Orion,* and no American officers would dare interfere after Morgan told them that the court at New York had dismissed the charges against his vessel. No one on the African coast knew that the *Orion* had been bonded, for, even if the newspapers had reached them, it is doubtful that naval officers would read the legal columns.

Slipping away from the American squadron in African waters, Morgan succeeded in getting his slaves aboard. This proved to be his undoing. The *Orion*'s invulnerability ended at that point, for Morgan had no wish to claim the protection of the American flag after becoming a pirate under American laws. When found by H.M.S. *Pluto,* Morgan meekly surrendered. Taken "without colors or papers," as the British phrased it, the *Orion* was subject to the decree of the vice-admiralty court at St. Helena, where she was declared forfeit and sentenced to be broken up. Piece by piece the *Orion* disappeared, and thus ended the astonishing career of a vessel that sailed in the slave trade in one place while she was being declared forfeit for that crime in another.

The *Orion* was declared forfeit at New York. By chance her case came not before Judge Betts or Judge Ingersoll, but before Judge Nathan K. Hall of the Northern New York district. Judge Hall normally did business at Albany, but Congress had authorized him, as well as the judge of the Connecticut district, to come into Southern New York district to help out Judge Betts when he had time. Hall had not come down very often, and he had never before presided over a slave-trade case; the result was that he approached the evidence in the *Orion* case with the same blunt practicality that he had shown when he served President Millard Fillmore as postmaster general. As the *Orion* was an undisguised slaver, Hall ordered her forfeited. Hanna's deathbed confession was not legal evidence, according to Betts and Nelson, but the *Orion*'s damning cargo was proof enough for Hall.

Vining's lawyers announced that they would appeal the case to Justice Nelson. It would have been interesting to see what he would have done with Hall's verdict, but this never happened. Before the case came up in circuit court the news of the *Orion*'s capture reached New York. One condition of her bond had been that she not be used in the slave trade while the case was pending, and Blumenberg was called on for his money. He had none, and was tried for perjury. Two trials ended with hung juries, but at a third trial in May, 1861, he was convicted. Justice Nelson sentenced him to five years at Sing Sing as a warning to others. Blumenberg won pardon after serving a little more than two years by telling Lincoln's marshal at New York what he knew about the slave trade. From beginning to end the *Orion* affair had shown the United States government to be almost impotent to deal with one of the most heinous crimes against mankind.[2]

The *Orion*'s career was unique in its melodrama, but other slavers used the same gap in the laws. *Ardennes, Isla de Cuba, Cora, William Clark, Lewis McLain, Augusta*—all these and probably more went off on slaving voyages while their bonds gathered dust somewhere in a clerk's desk.[3] The loophole was never plugged up; Congress never amended the act of 1847 so as to exclude criminal libels from its benefits.

Slave traders as well as slavers escaped from the law's feeble grasp. In a barroom in Rio de Janeiro, Brazil, in February, 1845, Cornelius E. Driscoll, erstwhile captain of the brig *Hope,* boasted to his cronies:

Well, boys, you don't have to worry about facing trial in New York City. Let the cruisers take you, if they will; I can get any man off in New York for $1,000. All you have to do is get some straw bail, and you'll be free as the birds. Look at me. I went to Africa, sold the *Hope* at Kabenda, and took my men over to the *Porpoise* while the Dagoes put 600 niggers aboard. But we saw what we thought was an English cruiser coming, so I went back with my papers to keep her away from the *Hope*. Made myself a pirate, they say. Some of my scurvy seamen informed on me afterwards, and the marshal caught up with me in New York and put me in jail. Pretty soon they had me up before old Betts and were talking of hanging me. But here I am, and I'll never go back.

There was nothing that Henry Wise, American minister to Brazil, could do about this kind of talk. The United States had no extradition treaty with Brazil, and indeed the two countries were on bad terms precisely because American pirates were being sheltered in Brazilian territory. Driscoll's talk may not all have been drunken boasting; whether or not $1,000 bought his freedom, the record of Judge Betts's dealings with him is damning. The court records of his case have vanished, but newspaper accounts and Wise's dispatches reveal that Driscoll was arrested in the spring of 1844 and released on $10,000 bail by the commissioner who examined him. This procedure was legal, but risky; Congress had stipulated that prisoners did not have to be released on bail if they were charged with a crime for which the death penalty was prescribed, but they could be if the commissioner or judge so ruled. The grand jury indicted Driscoll for piracy, and the captain appeared for arraignment. Betts looked into the amount of bail and decided that Driscoll was still free to roam on the $10,000 bond; but he also discovered that the original bondsman was not worth a tenth of that sum. The commissioner had released Driscoll on straw bail. Betts ordered the prisoner jailed until he found a better bondsman, and for five weeks Driscoll languished in prison.

Finally a new bondsman was produced. George W. Morton, Betts's clerk, accepted the bond and announced to the press that it was "good and sufficient" to ensure Driscoll's appearance for trial. Driscoll then obtained from Judge Betts a commission to take evidence in his own defense, which gave him authority to travel to Rio de Janeiro with the blessing of the court! Driscoll carried out the first part of the commission with zeal, promptly heading south to Brizilian territory. But once in Rio he showed little interest in gathering evidence for his own defense. Slipping out of town, he was last heard of aboard the slaver *Calhoun,* which was beached on the African coast after mistaking one of the rare steam slavers for an English cruiser. Driscoll never returned to New York to present his case to a jury.[4]

This incredible story overshadows even Betts's leniency with Manoel Basilio da Cunha Reis, who had been indicted at Boston for plotting the escape of the *Mary E. Smith.* Reis was repeatedly arrested at his office in New York, and each time Betts released him on bail with orders to go to Boston and face the court there. Each time Reis ignored the orders. Betts refused to grant an order for removal so that Reis could be forcibly taken to stand trial in Boston, and thus prevented the Massachusetts court from laying hands upon him.[5]

These were extraordinary cases; but the fact that they could happen in New York suggests the ineffectiveness of the ordinary bail system there. Congress had required that all prisoners be bailed out, except in capital cases, and the Eighth Amendment stipulated that the amount of bail should not be "excessive." This meant, presumably, that criminals were not expected to linger long as government boarders. These provisions were wise when applied to ordinary criminals, but most unwise when applied to participants in the slave trade, who could well afford to forfeit bail money. If a man was a genuine New York resident, as Lasala was, and thought he could beat the charges pending against him, he would not jump bail; otherwise, he was almost certain to clear out unless he was held on a capital charge, when bail was refused him. Because of the chaotic condition of the records, it is not known how many men jumped bail in New York City, but the number included the captains of the *Catharine,* the *Butterfly,* the *Eagle,* the *Martha,* the *Emily,* the *Josephine,* and the *Kate,* as well as slave-trade managers John A. Machado, M. B. da Cunha Reis, and Pierre Pearce. Perhaps fewer men jumped bail in other cities, because the courts were less ready to accept unknown bondsmen.[6]

Nothing was ever done to correct this abuse. Republican and Democratic marshals alike saw their prisoners vanish in the crowded city, but they had neither men nor money to pursue bailed prisoners, nor authority to rearrest them until their cases were called up in court. In an era lacking centralized law enforcement, when photographs, fingerprints, identification cards, and passports were not used in police work, it was nearly impossible to find and rearrest fugitives from justice. This was another reason that men seldom stood trial in American courts for slave trading. Even more rarely were they convicted.

12

"EVERYTHING I DID WAS LAWFUL"

In 1845 a new boarder arrived at the jail in Salem, Massachusetts. The United States would pay for his five years of confinement, for at the time the federal government did not maintain its own penitentiaries. The prisoner had been convicted of slave trading upon circumstantial evidence. His name, Peter Flowery, was as ill-suited to his character as the names of such vessels as the *Pilgrim*,[1] the *Nightingale*, and the *Reindeer* were inappropriate to the slave trade in which they engaged.

The circumstances that brought Flowery to the Salem jail went back to 1843, and centered on the *Caballero*, a Baltimore clipper. Purchased for the slave trade in Maryland, the *Caballero* had actually set sail for Africa from New York, and, after touching at the Cape Verde Islands, arrived in the Pongas River, before the trading post of Peter Faber. Like other African merchants, Faber dealt mainly in slaves, but he also handled any other products of the country his customers wanted to buy. After taking on 346 Africans, ferried out to the ship in canoes, the *Caballero* left Africa. As she measured only 96 tons, she was jammed to capacity, but, through good management and good luck, nearly all her passengers survived to be landed near Matanzas, Cuba.

Peter Flowery's association with the *Caballero* began later, at Havana. The vessel's crew, after putting the Africans ashore, jettisoned the incriminating equipment and scrubbed out the hold, so that the *Caballero* sailed into Havana as if from an honest trading voyage. Apparently Spanish officials did not investigate the background of such mysterious arrivals, for the *Caballero*'s officers were not questioned. By this time the vessel's name had been changed to *Spitfire*. Her American register had been removed in the Pongas River, and she was now navigating with Spanish papers. It is curious that she had a Spanish name while American-owned, and an American name while Spanish-owned. Flowery was signed on to take her on a second African voyage. He sailed her over to Key West, where he "purchased" her for $7,500 from Edwin A. Faulkner, a merchant of that city. How Faulkner obtained paper title to her, and why, was never brought out. Flowery would have liked to obtain an American register for the *Spitfire* on the strength of his Key West purchase, but he could not; the law forbade collectors to register as American any vessels that had ever been owned by foreigners. Probably this purchase before a notary public was enacted to give the color of American nationality to the schooner. Flowery could exhibit his bill of sale to British boarding officers, and possibly discourage them from seizing the *Spitfire* as a Spanish slaver.[2]

And now appeared on the scene a Spaniard named Don Juan Scorsur, "Long John," who owned a plantation near Matanzas and extensive property in Brooklyn, New York. Flowery made out a note to Scorsur for the sum of $7,500, exactly what he had "paid" for the *Spitfire*. Flowery owed Scorsur the entire value of the schooner, a convenient device if a fast change of ownership should become necessary. This formality completed, Flowery weighed anchor and sailed for New Orleans, where five days later Scorsur chartered the *Spitfire* for an African voyage. Apparently he expected the profits to be high, for he promised Flowery $5,000 for the use of his vessel, yet put aboard merchandise worth only $4,000. The charter party, however, stipulated that no contraband was to be included in the return cargo. The cargo, incidentally, was not shipped by Scorsur himself, but by a front man. Flowery set sail from New Orleans late in November, 1844, Scorsur going along to oversee his property.

Off Havana the *Spitfire* conveniently sprang her bowsprit, and put into port. More cargo and crew members were added, bringing the *Spitfire* up to slavers' requirements. The most important additions were Don Francisco Ruiz, Spanish, and Don Adolphe Fleuret, French, described as mates on their Spanish passports. Aboard the *Spitfire* they were supposed to be merely "passengers," albeit very useful passengers who stood watch for Flowery and kept their own log of the crossing. Scorsur left the vessel at Havana and settled down to wait for its return. The *Spitfire* put to sea, her destination in doubt. The official manifest (which the American consul saw) gave her destination as the Cape Verde Islands, and her consignee as Charles Keirn. But the bills of lading, which were not public information, designated part of the cargo for Peter Faber in the Pongas River, Africa, and the remainder for a Madame Liceburn, who kept a neighboring establishment on the slave coast.

As the *Spitfire* sailed toward Africa, some of her crew—Frederick Enners, German; Ebenezer Jackson, American Negro; Antonio del Mejo, Spanish—became suspicious about the voyage. They had thought that the *Spitfire* was an honest trading vessel, but little things began to reveal the truth: overheard snatches of conversation among Flowery, Ruiz, and Fleuret about slaves; discussions as to who was to take the schooner back; furtive actions by the "passengers." Near the African coast, when an English steamer was sighted, Enners saw Fleuret take out a French flag he had carried aboard and throw it overboard. Fleuret explained that he did not want the English to find it. As the *Spitfire* was sailing under American colors, why should there have been a French flag, and why should Fleuret have considered it incriminating? One day when Jackson, the cook, was digging into the lard barrel, he uncovered a broad, thin, tin case buried in the fat. Ruiz had taken it, carefully washed it, and hidden it somewhere else. When the first English boarding party came to puzzle over the *Spitfire*'s nationality, carpenter Del Mejo saw Ruiz hide four sacks of Spanish doubloons under a pile of casks, and strap some papers to his leg beneath his trousers. When the vessel arrived at Peter Faber's establishment, the truth became inescapable, but there was nothing the honest crew members could do. Seamen in the midst of a hostile wilderness do not rise up against heavy odds to escape being drawn into a slaving voyage. So they waited, while Ruiz and Fleuret dickered with Faber over slave prices and hoped that the English steamer at the mouth of the river would run out of supplies.

Now appeared the third principal figure in this drama, Thomas Turner. He had been aboard the *Spitfire* when she was still the *Caballero,* shipping out, he claimed, for what he thought was a lawful voyage. He had remained with her after her real mission was revealed, had traveled back to Cuba with her, and had found his way from Matanzas to Boston. Turner soon shipped out again on the schooner *Manchester,* commanded by the *Caballero*'s former American captain. The Boston port authorities did not know these things, but were suspicious enough of the *Manchester* to search her thoroughly; they finally let her go for lack of evidence. She was totally wrecked in a disaster off Cape Mount, where she piled up on the shore. African natives came down and plundered the crew as they came ashore; Turner and his captain struggled overland to Peter Faber's, where the captain died of fever. Faber refused to pay Turner the wages owing for the *Manchester*'s outbound voyage, and returned to his dickering with the *Spitfire*'s managers. Turner plunged off into the jungle, reached the mouth of the Pongas, found the United States brig of war *Truxtun,* and denounced the *Spitfire* to Lieutenant Henry Bruce. Armed boats were soon being rowed up the river, and the schooner and her crew were taken into custody. Ruiz and Fleuret were ashore, and, because the United States had no authority to raid African territory, they were left there; but the schooner was soon on her way to Boston. She had not been found ready to take slaves aboard, but the testimony of Turner and of her crewmen seemed to be enough evidence.

On June 2, 1845, Peter Flowery was brought to trial in the circuit court for the Massachusetts district. As Justice Story, who normally presided over the court, was busy on another case, Judge Peleg Sprague of the district court was in charge. The indictment, framed under the act of 1818, accused Flowery of launching—or of aiding and abetting in the launching of—a slaving expedition from New Orleans. It was necessary to show that his intent to aid the slave trade went back to that point. If his willful service aboard the slaver began only at Havana, or on the high seas or the African coast when he discovered the schemes of Ruiz and Fleuret, he had violated only the act of 1800. District Attorney Robert Rantoul therefore prepared an impressive case, with three days of testimony, to set forth the facts already related here. On June 5 it was the turn of the defense attorney, J. P. Rogers, who hoped to clear Flowery of any guilt whatever, or at least save him from conviction under the act of 1818.

The defense followed a familiar pattern in prosecutions under the slave-trade acts. There was a procession of merchants and sea captains, mostly long-time friends of Flowery's, who testified that the *Spitfire* was an ordinary schooner like hundreds of others, and was certainly not so radical in design or fittings that Flowery could have known she was a slaver. One witness remarked that the *Spitfire* would not make a good slaver because "slaves could [not] be very comfortably brought on boards laid over the water casks," to which Rantoul made the dry comment, "So the slaves think too, I presume." Defense witnesses also testified that passengers did sometimes stand watch aboard vessels, if they happened to be seamen, and also kept logbooks. Many vessels carried Spanish navigational charts because they frequently were better than American charts. The outbound cargo was similar to many lawful cargoes; the Treasury Department's own statistics showed that lawful African trade did exist. One captain testified that the vessel's entry into Havana in false distress was just good business, as certain port fees were waived for such entries. A painter testified that the name *Caballero* had been so thoroughly painted out that Flowery could never have seen it on the schooner.

Flowery did not take the stand in his own defense, in accordance with the custom of the time; his attorney did all the talking for him. Flowery was not the loser for this, as Rogers skillfully brought the weight of his powerful personality to bear on the jurors. First he appealed to them to shut out public prejudice, to keep their dislike of slave trading and the general impression of Flowery's guilt from influencing their deliberations. Then he proceeded to the law, carefully stressing that Flowery could not be found guilty unless the circumstantial evidence against him admitted no other conclusion than his guilt, and, in an indictment under the act of 1818, only if he had a fixed intention of using the *Spitfire* in the slave trade when he left New Orleans. If he merely intended to sell her on the African coast after delivering Scorsur's freight, or, failing that, to make the best of the situation and get his money out by turning her into a slaver, he was not guilty. His purpose had to be immutable, from the time he left American soil.

So much for the law. But Rogers obviously did not want the jury to think that even fleeting thoughts of slave trading had entered Flowery's mind. His client, he said, had kept aloof from actions that would warrant his conviction. Everything that Flowery did was lawful. The *Spitfire* cleared New Orleans lawfully; she cleared Havana lawfully. Her cargo could be used in lawful trade; Peter Faber conducted some lawful business; the schooner's build was consistent with lawful voyages; and Flowery knew nothing of her criminal history. Scorsur may really have loaned Flowery $7,500, and evidently Flowery had paid back the money before leaving Havana, for Scorsur had returned the note to him. The purchase at Key West, therefore, was not necessarily a sham. If Flowery had passengers who stood watch and used foreign charts, that was merely a coincidence; if these passengers chose to hide their money or sink their flags when English cruisers approached, that was their affair, not Flowery's. He had no control over his passengers' personal quirks.

Rogers also denounced the government's key witnesses as unreliable, and sought to find inconsistencies in their statements. He dismissed Rantoul's case as no more than a tissue of innocent, irrelevant, disconnected, and inconsequential circumstances, slightly leavened with a few incidents that were equally consistent with innocence or guilt. Flowery was the victim of circumstances, of Rantoul's excessive zeal, and of Judge Sprague's refusal to allow him to be transferred to New Orleans for trial. Rogers had earlier argued this point with Sprague, and now took his complaint to the jurors. "My client," he said in effect, "could quickly clear up all the suspicions against him if he had witnesses from New Orleans to testify to the honesty of his voyage. Judge Sprague has said that we could subpoena them to come here, but that would keep him in jail several months longer. He is the victim of persecution by the government."

The defense rested. Rogers had spoken for nearly three hours without referring to a single note; he had spoken with power, dignity, impact. Some of the spectators thought his summation was the most forceful they had heard in many years. Slave traders' gold could command fine legal talent.

But the government, too, had talent. Under the spoils system federal district attorneys were chosen from among the party faithful, but chosen, nonetheless, with an eye to their ability. Robert Rantoul was not only a good Democrat, but an able lawyer. Rogers had used most of the fifth day of Flowery's trial for his argument; Rantoul consumed the sixth day in a spirited reply. For three hours and forty-five minutes he hammered away on the theme, "How strange that this lawful trader should have had such a conjunction of unhappy circumstances befall him!" How strange that he should have paid more for the *Spitfire* than she was worth, and that Scorsur happened to be on the scene to lend him the money and then immediately charter her. How strange that Flowery should have hired eleven men, twice as many as he needed for a lawful voyage, and yet should have had no mates to help him navigate the ship. What an odd coincidence that he should have found two passengers who happened to be navigators and who would stand watch for him simply to "amuse" themselves. Why so small a cargo, why a lack of visible trading in the Pongas River, why so many provisions on board? Occasionally Rantoul's style sagged, but his logic had an irresistible appeal. After a brief charge from Judge Sprague the jurors retired, deliberated for an hour, and returned with the verdict of guilty. They recommended that Flowery be shown mercy in the court's sentence.

Rogers immediately moved for a new trial. He had several complaints: no evidence about the *Spitfire*'s misdeeds before Flowery came aboard should have been admitted; Rantoul had no right to argue that Scorsur was a slave trader, and the schooner's real owner; Flowery had been tried before an illegal court because, while Judge Sprague was holding the trial, Justice Story had been hearing another case in another room. Hence there had been two United States circuit courts meeting simultaneously in the Massachusetts district. The law established only one circuit court in each district.

All these ingenious arguments were beaten down by Story and Sprague, and Peter Flowery came before his trial judge for sentencing. Peleg Sprague had bad eyesight—so bad that his courtroom was kept dimly lighted, while he relied upon a keen memory of the spoken word when reviewing cases—but Flowery may well have trembled as the judge fixed his gaze upon him. In passing sentence, Sprague said:

> You have been convicted of aiding the fitting out of a vessel for the slave trade. No intelligent jury could have found you otherwise. And the slave trade is, to any normal person, a mass of horrors. There was no excuse for participating in it. Men steal, assault, lie under the sudden impulse of passion; commit crime before they have time to reflect upon what they are doing. It was not so with you. The criminal voyage was first planned at Havana and steadily pursued, through various stages, from Havana to Key West, thence to New Orleans, then back to Havana, and from there to the River Pongas; if you had gone one step further, and taken slaves on board, your life would have been forfeited by the laws of your country. Your offense originated in a cold, deliberate calculation of monetary gain; there was hardly a mitigating circumstance in the whole transaction. You deserve the severest punishment; but since the jury recommended mercy and is entitled to respect, I will give you only a medium punishment. I sentence you to five years' imprisonment, and $2,000 fine.

Flowery went to the Salem jail to serve his sentence because his attorney argued that it was more healthful than Boston's city jail.[3]

But this is not the end of Peter Flowery's story. Salem jail was not, after all, a very healthy place, and after twenty-one months Flowery's physical condition had so deteriorated that Sprague, the jailer, and a physician petitioned President James K. Polk for a pardon. It was granted, and Flowery left prison a free man.

Flowery apparently still dreamed of the money to be made on the African coast, and upon his release went to New York. There he approached the right parties, and soon was at sea in the schooner *Mary Ann,* bound for the notorious Gallinas River. His men, who had signed on for an honest voyage, were distrustful of ex-convict Flowery. At Gallinas their worst fears seemed to be realized. Flowery went ashore and began consorting with Brazilians. Coming back periodically to the schooner, he ordered his men to make some changes in the interior arrangements, explaining that he had chartered the *Mary Ann* to carry passengers to Bahia.

He may have meant just that. There is no proof that he intended to use his vessel as worse than a common auxiliary in the slave trade—perhaps to take back some of the castaways left on the African coast from the numerous slavers captured by the British. Flowery's men, however, came to the conclusion that the passengers would be colored and slave, not white and free. The crew waited until Flowery had gone back on shore, and then hoisted sails and anchors and fled from the anchorage. The captain rushed back and persuaded the British cruiser guarding the port to send an armed cutter in pursuit; but the *Mary Ann* was swifter, and soon had left cutter and captain far astern. She cruised along the coast, her seamen hoping to fall in with an American cruiser. Finding none, they set course back to New York. Flowery took passage in a trading vessel to follow them, but he never again trod on American soil. He had ignored the ill health that had won him a pardon, and died of asthma on his return voyage.

The *Mary Ann's* crew themselves got into trouble. The district attorney was happy to take their story and libel the schooner as a slaver; but Judge Betts dismissed the libel. The seamen had also libeled the *Mary Ann* for their wages, and Betts dismissed that too, using the occasion to denounce their action and to expand his own views on the sacredness of commerce:

The interference with merchant vessels . . . by public officers of high intelligence and responsibility, and free from personal bias or apprehension in the matter, is a most delicate power, the exercise of which is, by all free governments, placed under careful supervision. . . . Seamen are not a class of men whose prudence or discretion could be trusted with the exercise of such delicate and extraordinary powers. . . . It can never be expected that the right of a crew to interfere at their discretion, and take forcible possession of a vessel on mere circumstances of suspicion against the master, can be countenanced by the Courts.

Betts conceded that seamen had the right to arrest a superior officer who committed an open and flagrant crime in their presence; but there had to be "no room for doubt." Agreeing that the suspicions of the *Mary Ann*'s crew members were reasonable, he denounced their seizure of the vessel before their suspicions were confirmed as "a naked aggression upon the rights of the owner." If such things were not checked by the courts, commerce would be exposed to the "most appalling" uncertainties and perils. This was the position of Judge Betts on the suppression of the slave trade.[4]

Peter Flowery was not the only man ever to be convicted under the act of 1818. At least six others went to prison at various times (see Appendix B), and a few more men were jailed for violation of the act of 1800. With two exceptions, they were all ship's officers. Albert Horn, owner of the steam slaver *City of Norfolk,* was convicted at New York City in October, 1862, but he was pardoned within seven months by Abraham Lincoln on grounds of ill health.[5] Appleton Oaksmith, owner of the mock whaler *Margaret Scott,* was convicted at Boston in the spring of 1863, but escaped from jail within three months, leaving behind a long note "exonerating" himself and assuring his captors that he had taken this drastic step only as a last resort to obtain justice. The grand jury found the jailer negligent.[6]

This meager record was made yet more meager by the fact that, except for Horn and Oaksmith (who probably were only agents), none of the few men sent to prison were leading figures in slave trading. Certainly captains and mates played an important part, but they were nonetheless well down in the hierarchy; they followed orders and used money and vessels provided by others. So long as the others remained unscathed by the law (except for the occasional confiscation of a slave vessel), the slave trade was likely to continue. Apparently a century ago there were a substantial number of men who were willing to turn a dishonest dollar if they thought they could get away with it. Captains and mates could be hired, so long as the risks they ran were not extreme. Surely the risks were small. Relatively few men were arrested, fewer still brought to trial, fewer yet proven guilty; prosecutions on the basis of circumstantial evidence are always difficult. And when, occasionally, a ship's officer did go to jail, he could almost invariably obtain executive clemency. Usually his fine was remitted if he pleaded poverty; frequently his sentence was reduced by many months; sometimes he received both benefits. No one was ever pardoned outright; but a fairly strong sentence was often reduced to a mild one. And judges themselves did not always decree the maximum penalty provided by the law.

This executive lenience with slave traders has been explained as part of the slaveowners' conspiracy against the law, but this can hardly be true, as there was no such conspiracy. But there were various reasons for such generosity. Men who received nothing except remission of their fines were being saved from imprisonment for debt, a relic from a less enlightened age, which was generally being abolished in the United States in this period. A convicted slave trader would remain in jail until his fine was paid, unless he had the money or the president gave him a pardon; probably slave traders preferred to let their imprisoned compatriots plead poverty so that a presidential pardon would be forthcoming, removing any civil disabilities resulting from conviction. As for shortening jail terms, public pressure or ill health were sometimes brought forward, but then, as now, it was common practice to reduce sentences. Anyone leafing through the fat volumes of pardon records in the National Archives must be struck by the fact that mail robbers, counterfeiters, shipboard brawlers, and other sorts of culprits were also generously treated by presidents.[7] Slave traders were no exception, especially when those whose cases came to the presidents were almost invariably the less important figures in the trade, men whose guilt consisted of coöperating in the commission of crime rather than in the planning of it.

So much for prosecutions under the acts of 1800 and 1818. There remained yet another class of prosecutions: the dreaded piracy prosecutions under the act of May 15, 1820. Seafaring men were genuinely afraid of that act. Piracy prisoners did not have to be bailed out, and ordinarily could not escape justice by flight; the evidence of their guilt was palpable, not merely circumstantial; the penalty of their crime was death. It was true that presidents were wont to commute death sentences to life imprisonment; but no one could depend on that, and at the least a convicted pirate had to serve many years in prison. The act of 1820 was potentially one of the strongest bulwarks against lawbreaking. Why it did not meet the expectations of the congressmen who framed it is the subject of the next chapter.

13

PIRATES WHO WERE NOT HANGED

On November 8, 1854, District Attorney John McKeon brought to trial James Smith, erstwhile master of the brig *Julia Moulton*. Smith was a pirate who had helped to kill one hundred and fifty Africans on a voyage from Ambrizete to Trinidad, Cuba, in the summer of 1854; he had not been a dummy captain, but had remained in command of the *Julia Moulton* from the time she left New York until she was burned on the coast of Cuba. He had even bought a little Negro boy, five years old, for $7.50, as his own personal speculation. McKeon had witnesses to verify all these facts, and his opponent, Charles O'Conor (who years later was selected to defend Jefferson Davis against treason charges), made not the slightest effort to defend Smith on the merits of his case. There was no attempt to show that Smith was a young man misled by wicked deceivers into thinking the slave trade a humane business; no attempt to excuse his actions as forced by necessity. Instead, O'Conor relied upon a technicality in the law for his defense.

The act of Congress declaring the slave trade to be piracy had been worded as follows:

If any citizen of the United States, being of the crew or ship's company of any foreign ship or vessel engaged in the slave trade, or any person whatever, being of the crew or ship's company of any ship or vessel, owned in the whole or in part, or navigated for, or in behalf of, any citizen or citizens of the United States, shall . . . seize any negro or mulatto not held to service or labour by the laws of either of the states or territories of the United States, with intent to make such negro or mulatto a slave, or shall decoy, or . . . forcibly confine or detain, or aid and abet in forcibly confining or detaining, on board such ship or vessel, any negro . . . , such citizen or person shall be adjudged a pirate; and . . . shall suffer death.[1]

The law applied, then, only to American citizens serving aboard any vessel or to foreigners serving aboard American-owned vessels, for the United States had no right to hang foreign pirates serving aboard foreign vessels. No other nation had declared the slave trade piracy. Even if the American courts had power to execute culprits under the shadowy authority of international law (which was doubtful), Smith was immune to punishment except under American law.

Was Smith an American? He had sworn that he was a citizen when he took out the *Julia Moulton*'s register, and she went to sea with flag and papers certifying her as an American vessel. The evidence certainly indicated that Smith was liable under the act of 1820. But O'Conor brought forth a parade of friends and relatives who testified that Smith was a German, and that his name was really Julius Schmidt. Reared in Bederkesa, Hanover, he had attended navigation school at Hamburg, and had first shipped out to the United States in the fall of 1849. He had never been naturalized (nor could have, legally, with less than five years' residence); he had simply passed himself off as an American when signing aboard various merchant vessels, and when joining up with the *Julia Moulton*. As he was a foreigner, his vessel (if he owned it) was also foreign, though O'Conor carefully brought into the picture a Cuban named Lamos, who had stayed in the background when the *Julia Moulton* was being fitted out and was probably the real owner.

The question of citizenship was what most angered John McKeon. To him it was particularly repugnant that a cold-blooded pirate had passed himself off as an American, sailed to Africa with the protection of the United States government, and had then blithely renounced his claim to American citizenship when it had become a liability rather than an asset. McKeon faced the jurors and demanded of them whether such an outrage should be allowed. He reminded them that 664 human beings had been packed together like sardines in a can—lying on their right sides, to be sure, so their heart action would be as easy as possible. He pointed out that oaths should be binding on those who made them. Seizing upon O'Conor's remark that he was groping in the dark with a dagger to find persons to prosecute, McKeon stirred the jurors to bold action with the declaration that "there are real daggers in the hands of the persons engaged in this traffic in this city, and any man's life is in danger who attempts to expose them. But for myself, even if I should lose my life, I will fearlessly do my duty."

The jurors retired deeply impressed, and returned an hour later with the verdict of guilty as charged. Smith was the first man ever convicted as a slave-trading pirate under American law, and one of only two men ever to be found guilty in such a case. It was a historic moment in the American courts, though Smith did not seem much affected by it. He knew that his friends would not abandon him, and that the keenest legal minds available would be searching for a way out.

Smith was right; as a result, his name has been virtually forgotten. While Justice Nelson was charging the jury, McKeon and O'Conor had broken in to argue about the jury's rights in the case. Could they decide only the question of Smith's citizenship, or could they also decide whether or not the *Julia Moulton*'s former owners had kept an interest in her after transferring title to Smith? If they had, the vessel would have had partial American ownership while on the slaving voyage. As Nelson had ruled that the jury could look into the ownership question, O'Conor now claimed a mischarge. Throughout the trial, he argued, he had assumed that everyone agreed that Smith (or Lamos) owned the brig. If he had known that at the last moment her former American owners would be brought into the picture, he would have offered evidence to show that they had really severed their connection with the vessel. He asserted that the jury had brought a verdict against his client because they had been confused by the charge. The truth of this proposition was doubtful, but Nelson finally agreed to declare a mistrial. Smith had been convicted, but the conviction was now no good and McKeon would have to try again.

The district attorney had a difficult choice. He could prosecute Smith again as a pirate, probably unsuccessfully. He might prosecute him for perjury. But Smith had the testimony of Henry C. Smith, the broker who had assisted him in his dealings with the customhouse, that he had not understood the papers before him. James Smith's attorney had argued: "Everyone knows what is a custom-house oath. The mariner looks upon it as mere form; it is taken to satisfy the custom-house, and is never read to him, as it has been shown was not done in this case; and not one shipmaster in fifty knows what he is swearing to." Or McKeon might prosecute Smith under the act of 1818 for taking a vessel to sea from an American port. But, if he did, another technicality might arise. There was no doubt that Smith had "caused the *Julia Moulton* to sail from" New York, but Justice Story had ruled long before that this particular crime was necessarily committed on the high seas, at the instant the vessel left the territorial waters of the United States off the port. If Smith had been on the high seas when he "caused her to sail from," would he not be a foreigner in a foreign vessel in international waters, and hence outside United States jurisdiction? If he was to be prosecuted for his actions in fitting out the brig, rather than in causing her to sail, it would be difficult to prove what part he had played.

It can only be conjectured that these considerations made Mc-Keon decide to strike a bargain with Smith: if Smith would plead guilty to violating the act of 1800, McKeon would let him off with that. As a foreigner in a foreign vessel Smith was invulnerable to that act also, but he and O'Conor decided to take the bargain. Nelson sentenced Smith to two years in jail and a fine of $1,000. Smith went into King's County jail and served his term. In the spring of 1857 he applied to President Buchanan for a remission of the fine, and the President granted him a full pardon on May 22, 1857. The *Tribune,* ever quick to gibe its political opponents, editorially surmised that Buchanan "thinks it a pity, we suppose, now that the slave-trade is so brisk, that Captain Smith should not have an opportunity to reengage in his favorite employment." There was irony in the comment, as the *Tribune* ordinarily was a firm opponent of imprisonment for debt; but, whatever Buchanan's motives, Smith's punishment ended on a very flat note. The first man ever convicted as a slave-trading pirate went free after thirty-two months in jail, counting the time he was held as an unbailed suspect.[2]

The trial of James Smith is a good illustration of why the act of 1820 was a dead letter for almost forty-two years, and why only one of the hundreds of men who deserved death under it ever suffered the penalty. For the execution of a slave-trading pirate could come about only if a chain of five circumstances existed.

First, the pirate had to be arrested by American officers. No requirement was more difficult to meet than this one. As men became pirates only after they had loaded slaves aboard their vessels, they came directly into the hands of federal officers only when their vessels were captured at sea, full of Africans. This happened rarely, and only once before 1858. The cruisers patrolled so thinly that they seldom picked up loaded slavers. If a laden American slaver was captured by the British (a fairly frequent occurrence), the crew was let go; if it was captured in Cuban or Brazilian waters by officers of those nations, the seamen were punished, if at all, under the laws of Spain or Brazil. Once the Africans were landed, the chances were slim that American officers would arrest the crew (who often debarked at the same time), unless the Africans and the crew came ashore in the United States. Five pirates fell into federal hands as a result of the *Wanderer* importation, but slave landings in the deep South were usually so shadowy, if indeed they existed, that no other crew members involved were ever arrested. Also, the law applied only to seafaring men, not to ships' owners or anyone else who remained at home.

Smith came into the hands of the law not by direct, but by indirect, arrest. The *Julia Moulton*'s voyage was completed in so great secrecy and with so good luck that Smith would almost certainly have got away without suspicion, had not his chief mate, believing himself cheated on his pay, talked about the voyage, thus revealing Smith's crime. His arrest was due in part to good work by the authorities, but more particularly to Smith's own rashness in coming back to New York. He had not expected to be informed on; if he had, and had changed names and sailed out of another port, he might never have been found. The federal law enforcement machinery was too disorganized, and there was apparently no co-operation between it and the police of any other nation.

Piracy prisoners thus were few and far between. Yet apprehending a pirate, with enough witnesses against him to make out a reasonable case for a grand jury, was only the beginning of the difficulties. The second link in the chain leading to his execution was the obvious one that he had to be held for trial. Cornelius Driscoll, boasting in Rio of his exploits, escaped justice even though informers had talked, and he had been arrested, indicted, and arraigned. John B. Macomber, first mate of the slaver *Haidee,* was arrested in New York City in October, 1858, upon testimony from fellow seamen, indicted, and lodged, like other federal prisoners, in a county jail. Within three weeks the jailer let Macomber out into the jailyard alone, after dark. Someone was waiting on the other side of the fence with a rope, the jailer was slow in discovering his guest's departure and informing the marshal of it, and Macomber was never seen again.[3] And still other arrested pirates slipped through the hands of federal officers.[4] Perhaps the arrested pirate was hard to hold onto because his friends used gold to grease the palms of the men in charge of him; perhaps merely because he was a desperate character with the best of reasons for wanting to get out of jail.

The third circumstance was that the prisoner had to be brought to trial in a community that was willing to convict him. Some observers felt that the act of 1820 was too severe; that, by imposing a mandatory death sentence, it went beyond public sentiment. The men presented to juries for conviction were, after all, the tools of others rather than the prime movers behind the ventures they were arrested for. The big operators were quite safe. A hired thug deserves punishment; but when his employer invariably went free, when many shared in the commission of the crime, and when there was no malice in his actions, the sentiment for hanging him was weakened. A jury's sentiments might be swayed by the fact that men arrested for slave-trading piracy had not harmed Americans, but rather foreign Negroes who had been enslaved by their own people. Good juries are not supposed to consider any of these factors, but only the law and the evidence, yet even a good jury is likely to let its verdict be influenced by its own sentiments when the evidence presented to it is contradictory and uncertain.

Southerners, who felt their domestic institutions more and more menaced by the North, became highly sensitive to anything that seemed like a slur upon slavery. They might despise the cruelty of the African trade, and dread the effect of African imports upon the domestic slaves; but they might also shun the epithet "pirate" and the severe penalty that went with it. They might hesitate to hang men for enslaving others, lest all Southern slaveowners be considered pirates. Abolitionists were boldly proclaiming that slaveowners were indeed almost the same as pirates. Death, to the Southerner, might be too severe a penalty merely for the inhumane treatment of Africans, because such treatment was not the fault of the ship's crew, but rather of the men who ordered them to take aboard more slaves than they could safely transport. Attitudes such as these probably led to the acquittals of the *Putnam*'s crew at Charleston, of the *Wanderer*'s supercargo and seamen in Georgia, and of Captain Weston of the *William* at Key West; they caused the government to despair of convicting Captain Corrie at Charleston.[5]

A pirate who was not aided by any of these circumstances, like Captain Smith, might still escape on the technicality that he was outside the law's jurisdiction. Any slaver could be "proven" foreign-owned in a pinch; if the vessel really was American, witnesses could readily be found to swear that mysterious Spaniards or Portuguese were the real owners. But perjury was not usually necessary; most slavers undoubtedly were not "owned in whole or in part by, or navigated in behalf of," American citizens. For all practical purposes, then, only American citizens whose citizenship could be proven were in danger of conviction. But slave traders often recruited their crews from among the foreign-born. Thus Smith, as

well as several other men, went free. This same technicality sometimes defeated prosecutions under the act of 1800.[6]

A pirate who could be proved American, who was arrested, and
who was brought to trial before a jury willing to convict him had
yet a fifth resource. Unlike Smith, but like many others, he could
plead nonresponsibility. He could argue that when the slaves came
aboard, he was only a passenger; that he had turned control of
the ship over to its foreign purchasers, and was merely riding along
because there was no other way to come home. Or he might claim
compulsion. He could blame his superiors, or, if he was the captain, "some Spaniards who were aboard." He could claim that he
had signed on for a lawful voyage and then, realizing the truth,
had been threatened by those in control with death or with abandonment on the African coast.[7] It was extremely difficult to prove
that such statements were falsehoods. If he had been arrested at
sea, all the naval officers knew was that he had been found on board
a vessel loaded with Africans. Only his fellow seamen could tell
whether his role had been active or passive, willing or unwilling,
and they might not talk. Thomas Morgan, the *Orion*'s commander,
and his mates got free of piracy charges precisely because the British
had released all the seamen; no one could testify as to what part the
officers had played in the enslavement of Africans. Morgan and his
mates were finally punished for only a misdemeanor.[8] Judges disagreed over how much personal control a man had to have over
a voyage before he could be held accountable as a pirate; but it was
painfully difficult to get over this last hurdle to conviction and execution. James Smith was one of the two men to be pushed even
briefly across it; the other was Nathaniel Gordon.

Gordon and his mates William Warren and David Hale had been
brought into New York in the late summer of 1860, and their cases
came before the circuit court in October. They had been indicted
under the act of 1800 as well as under the piracy act, and their
attorney had them ready to plead guilty to a misdemeanor in order
to avoid a capital trial. To their dismay, District Attorney J. J.
Roosevelt announced that the government would not promise to
accept their confession, but might prosecute them under the piracy

act in any event. The three men then pleaded not guilty to both charges, and the lawyers settled down to prepare their cases. Through the winter of 1860–61 little was done. Roosevelt's Republican successor, a political opponent, reported that by the time he came into office in April, 1861, no preparations had been made to try Gordon. That may have been an exaggeration.[9] At any rate, the new district attorney vigorously pushed ahead, and Gordon was brought to trial in circuit court on June 18, 1861. The judge was William D. Shipman, hearing his first slave-trade case.

The prosecuting attorney was E. Delafield Smith, chairman of the New York Republican Central Committee and a protégé of Secretary of State Seward. The *Tribune* commented that Smith "is still one of the younger members of his profession, and has not achieved its highest distinctions; but he has talents and a spotless reputation." This rising young lawyer presented a forceful case to the jury. He traced the history of the *Erie*, stressed the inhumane way in which the slaves had been packed into her, and pointed out that when naval officers had been unable to repack the Africans into their places, Gordon had shown how to arrange them. But Smith's case was weak on some important points. Gordon claimed to have sold the *Erie* to Spaniards in the Congo River, and that he was merely a passenger when the slaves were shipped; a Spaniard, released by the *Mohican,* was in charge of the *Erie* at that point. Gordon's mates readily confirmed his statements, and there was no one to disprove them. Judge Shipman gave a stern charge, full of references to the inhumanity of the voyage, and warning the jurors to be wary of accepting this defense story, but he also insisted that Gordon be shown as the "master spirit" in the confinement of the Africans. The jury was out all night, and returned on the morning of June 21 hopelessly deadlocked. A majority favored conviction.[10]

Smith began the arduous task of finding more witnesses. He obtained a copy of the *Erie*'s crew list, and sent out detectives to watch vessels arriving at Boston and New York. His persistence was rewarded when four *Erie* seamen were picked up at Boston. Examined separately by Smith, they told the same story: Gordon had remained in command after the Negroes had been taken aboard, and had offered the seamen a dollar a head for every African landed in Cuba.

On November 6, 1861, Gordon was again brought to trial. This time Judge Shipman was joined on the bench by Justice Nelson. One of the partners in the firm of Beebe, Dean, & Donohue assisted in the defense, but it was a lost cause. The two mates still testified that Gordon was a passenger, but, as they were under the same indictment, they were untrustworthy witnesses. The lawyers turned to technicalities. Gordon was a foreigner in a foreign vessel, they argued. The *Erie* had been sold at Havana, as her former New York owners had been paid off, and was therefore not an American vessel even before the transfer in the Congo. Although it was true that Gordon's parents were long-time residents of Portland, Maine, Mrs. Gordon had occasionally gone to sea with her captain-husband and their son might have been born in foreign territory! But the lawyers could not demonstrate that he had. Justice Nelson quashed this ingenious argument by ruling that any person born of American parents while on such a voyage was an American citizen. He also pointed out that the defense had not demonstrated to whom the *Erie* was sold at Havana, or that the purchasers were foreigners. He sent the jury out to decide on the conflicting testimony of the mates and the seamen, and it returned twenty minutes later with a verdict of guilty.

The attorneys for the defense raised every conceivable objection to the conviction. Most remarkable was the claim that the crime had been committed at the mouth of the Congo, in Portuguese waters, and hence outside American jurisdiction. But Justice Nelson ruled that the river's wide mouth was clearly in international waters, and observed that the *Erie* had afterward sailed out many miles into the Atlantic before capture. All the other objections were similarly beaten down, and on November 30 Judge Shipman, speaking for the absent Nelson, pronounced the sentence of death upon Gordon. In a stern lecture on the wickedness of the slave trade, he declared: "Do not imagine that because others shared in the guilt of this enterprise yours is thereby diminished; but remember the awful admonition of your Bible, 'Though hand join in hand, the wicked shall not go unpunished.' " Shipman advised Gordon to make his peace with God. Frantic appeals to President Lincoln brought no pardon, and on February 21, 1862, the convicted pirate was hanged. A large crowd followed the coffin on its way to Cypress Hills Cemetery, where Gordon was laid to rest.[11]

Some writers have claimed that Gordon's execution proved that government policy toward the slave trade was radically altered after the Republicans had come into office, and that Democrats and Whigs had not been sincere in fighting the trade. Certainly the execution was a convincing demonstration of Republican sincerity and efficiency. It reflected particular credit upon District Attorney Smith for his relentless prosecution, and upon Abraham Lincoln for refusing to grant a pardon. But Democrats had contributed heavily to the conviction. Gordon had been arrested by a warship assigned to the Congo by Democrats for the purpose of capturing such pirates. He went to his death under an indictment obtained by a Democratic district attorney. Perhaps the attorney had been slow in bringing Gordon to trial, but it had been Democratic policy to prosecute pirates to the end, as several cases proved. One of those prosecutions had resulted in a conviction, though it was overturned by Justice Nelson. Nelson, a Democrat, presided over Gordon's second trial, and his party therefore deserves as much credit for his actions there as it does blame for his release of Smith. Judge Shipman, too, was a Democrat, and it is hardly likely that the jury that found Gordon guilty included only Republicans.

In fact, Gordon's conviction was a fluke, coming from the chance conjunction of all the circumstances necessary to hang a pirate. Those who object to the word "fluke" should ponder the record of subsequent piracy prosecutions at New York. By the summer of 1861 a small number of pirates had been apprehended, brought in mostly by the Democratic cruisers but in part picked up by Republicans. Of all these men, only Gordon paid the penalty. Unnoticed amidst the jubilation the day after Gordon's conviction, District Attorney Smith quietly nol-prossed the indictments against half a dozen or more prisoners from the *Bonito*. Apparently they were all foreigners, and he despaired of convicting any of them. He allowed

Gordon's mates and the second and third mates of the slaver *Cora* to plead guilty to the misdemeanor, and they received jail sentences of eight to ten months each, and fines of $1 to $500. The *Cora*'s first mate escaped and was never recaptured. Henry C. Crawford, captain of the steam slaver *City of Norfolk,* agreed to turn state's evidence against his vessel's owner.[12]

Thus, within a few months, the number of pirates awaiting prosecution at New York shrank to three mates of the *Nightingale* and Captain Erastus H. Booth of the bark *Buckeye.* District Attorney Smith wanted to move first against Samuel Haynes, the *Nightingale*'s first mate, for he had treated the Negroes brutally during the short time he had power over them. A jury could be more easily aroused against him than against the others. But Marshal Robert Murray of the Southern New York district kept breaking his promise to obtain proof of Haynes's American citizenship, and Smith passed on to the others. He believed second mate Winslow to be a foreigner, practically immune to the law. And that left Minthorne Westervelt, third mate and scion of a well-known Staten Island family. Smith was not very optimistic about convicting him, for Westervelt had little more authority aboard the *Nightingale* than an ordinary seaman, had been sick during much of the voyage, and had not been guilty of brutality.

When Westervelt came to trial a few days after Gordon's conviction, his attorneys pleaded ignorance and compulsion. They argued that he knew nothing of the voyage when he signed on, that he had no choice but to obey once he found out, and that men who had no control over the shipment of Negroes could not be convicted under the act of 1820. Justice Nelson disagreed with this last point, ruling that anyone who willingly helped confine Negroes was guilty; but the remainder of his charge was decidedly favorable to Westervelt. Nelson said that he did not wish to sanction the obeying of unlawful orders, but he urged that "circumstances" could require a man to commit unlawful acts. He told the jury that it had to decide if Westervelt was to be hanged for his failure to escape from the *Nightingale* after he discovered her destination. Nelson also permitted testimony about Westervelt's former good reputation. On the other side, Smith demonstrated that Westervelt had actively helped to take the Africans aboard. The result of these crosscurrents was a hopelessly deadlocked jury, with a strong majority for conviction.

Whether because of sympathy for this young prisoner, or because of Westervelt's family connections, Justice Nelson continued his preferential treatment. On November 23, 1861, Westervelt was released on $5,000 bail with the remark that he was too good a man to be kept in confinement with criminals. At this point Smith gave up all hope for a second trial. Westervelt offered to join the army in expiation of his crimes, and Smith closed the bargain after also requiring his help in tracking down Haynes's birth record.[13]

The latter requirement was based on Marshal Murray's failure to send a detective for the evidence. With Westervelt's help, the district attorney finally learned that Haynes had been born at Dresden, Maine. The trial started in May, 1862. Haynes's attorneys did a fine job, for after twenty hours the jury returned with the news that it was deadlocked. Reporters questioning them discovered that eight were for acquittal and that four favored conviction with a recommendation of mercy. Haynes went back to prison, where he idled away the hot summer of 1862. In October Smith again brought him to trial. An enthusiastic *Tribune* reporter characterized James T. Brady's summation for the defense as "eloquent, clear, and logical," Smith's final argument as "an elaborate and forcible appeal" which had commanded "the closest attention of the throng in the courtroom," and Shipman's charge as "lucid," but, despite all this brilliance, the jury was unable to agree on a verdict after nineteen hours of deliberation. The judge complained openly that they should be able to decide one way or the other, but two jurors retorted that they would not agree if they were kept together a whole week. Shipman dismissed the jury, and soon afterward released Haynes and Winslow on $2,500 bail each. Nothing more was ever done in their cases.[14]

Nor did the last piracy trial held under the Lincoln administration turn out to be any less a fiasco. Erastus Booth was finally brought to trial before Judge Shipman on October 30, 1862. He had been arrested a year earlier, upon testimony from crew members of the *Buckeye,* but nothing was done about indicting him until February, 1862. He was almost immediately released on bail; this was an unusual procedure at New York after the Driscoll fiasco, and indicated a weak case. Booth did not jump bail, perhaps because the chief witness against him had left town. The result was a case so weakened that District Attorney Smith announced, when the trial began, that he was abandoning the capital prosecution and would try Booth under the act of 1800 instead. His testimony was so inconclusive that Judge Shipman told the jury it was its duty to declare Booth not guilty. Some of the jurors seemed reluctant, whereupon Shipman warned he would dispose of the case in another, equally decisive, manner if they did not agree. This suggestion was enough and Booth walked free, "acquitted by a jury of his peers." [15]

This debacle was a fitting end to American prosecutions of slave-trading pirates. As in everything else, only the disappearance of the slave trade brought an end to the government's inability to enforce its laws. Nor is there any danger that Nathaniel Gordon will lose his unique position among American criminals, for in 1948 Congress decided that it was not a capital crime to enslave Negroes, and reduced the maximum penalty to the same as that provided by the act of 1818—seven years' imprisonment and $5,000 fine.[16] Thus the law stands today.

– 14 –

RETROSPECT

Only a few of the most striking episodes of the vain effort to enforce the laws against the slave trade have appeared in these pages. A vast amount of human energy was expended in patrols, chases, arrests, and prosecutions. Some idea of the multitude of events connected with the slave trade and the efforts to suppress it can be gathered from the lists of crimes and prosecutions in the appendixes of this book. But the incidents described in the preceding chapters illustrate the diverse reasons for the lawbreaking that went on year after year.

At first glance it seems impossible to find beneath these incidents a common denominator that explains the debacle in law enforcement. The slave trade flourished in part because the United States did not have enough cruisers; in part because federal lawmen did not always act vigorously or intelligently; in part because some judges handed down blind decisions; in part because some Southerners finally sympathized with the trade; in part because Congress passed *An Act To Reduce Expenses of Proceedings in Admiralty*. The list could be extended to great length, ultimately reaching such fine details as the rate at which early steam engines consumed their own parts, or the haphazard manner in which decisions of one federal court were published for other judges and lawyers to read.

The men involved thought of each event in such concrete terms.

Deputy Riley saw the distant and immobile form of Boston's revenue cutter, and the weak-kneed lieutenant at his side, as the reasons for his failure. Consul Parks blamed his instructions to issue temporary registers for the gross lawbreaking that went on before his eyes. The New York slave traders must have prized Judge Betts's legal doctrines as a major safeguard of their operations. Probably no one on either side of the law spent much time pondering the fundamental weaknesses of American society which permitted the slave trade to continue.

Yet some social weakness was plainly at work. The American people (as their politicians loved to tell them) were sovereign. They were not ruled over by a king, or a church, or an aristocracy. Nearly all white adult males counted for something in the political life of the country. Through their lawmakers they had sovereign power to determine what things should not be done by American citizens, or upon American soil, or under cover of the American flag. They had sternly forbidden the African slave traders to use either citizens or soil or flag. If the laws embodying their wishes were truly unenforceable, then the American people were not capable of effective self-government. If this conclusion is rejected—and few could bear to accept it—an alternative explanation has to be found.

Did the fault lie in the representatives of the American people? Were the people deceived and betrayed by unworthy officials? Occasionally, yes. Flag Officer Conover did not earn his pay; Deputy Marshal Rynders outraged his trust; other men fell short of their duty. Yet such instances are conspicuous precisely because they were unusual. Most officers attempted to do their duty, and were at least as skillful as the public had a right to expect them to be. Should naval officers be blamed for being very careful of the health and the morale of their men—and of themselves? Their operations against the slave trade were carried on in peacetime. Are judges to be blamed for demanding full proof? It is a heavy responsibility to punish unless the evidence is unequivocal. Are presidents to be blamed for pardoning the few slave traders who were convicted? Pardons were given freely to all sorts of criminals, and so few slave traders were convicted that the pardons certainly did little to stimulate the trade.

Inevitably the finger of guilt points away from the officers charged with enforcing the laws, toward those who made the laws. For Congress had power to correct nearly every deficiency of enforcement. It is true that the House and the Senate had no constitutional authority to prevent the president from letting men out of prison a year or two early. As a practical matter, Congress could not accompany every Lieutenant Prouty and every Flag Officer Conover to see that their duties were properly done (though it might have taken better measures to insure that only good men remained in office). But Congress had ample authority to correct all other shortcomings. Were the penalties of the law too light? Congress could increase them, even over a presidential veto. Was the act of 1818 turned into a hollow shell by Judges Betts and Nelson? A newer act, bluntly worded, could not have been twisted out of shape by overstrict constructionists. Did the law enforcement effort require more cruisers, or a department of justice, or new rules of evidence, or increased powers for consuls, or tighter restrictions on bail and bonding? Congress could have provided all these things. Yet it did not, and few individual congressmen attempted to make it act. The only piece of corrective legislation ever passed was the treaty with Great Britain, pushed through only when the government was reduced to utter impotence.

What was wrong with Congress? Surely it could not imitate the slave traders and plead ignorance of the true state of affairs. Periodically a senator or a representative put forward a motion asking the president to furnish information about the slave trade under the American flag. As resolutions cost nothing, his colleagues agreed, and the information was supplied as soon as clerks in the executive departments could copy off the pertinent dispatches. Such information was voluminous and frank. It is true that Congress was never given any information on the misinterpretation of the act of 1818, or on the details of other unsuccessful prosecutions, for the ample reason that no official in Washington possessed much information on these subjects. But a great deal of information came from the

State Department, and much from the Navy Department. Anyone carefully studying the documents that were supplied should have been shocked into further researches. Apparently not many congressmen bothered to read them. Furthermore, the law courts did not operate in secret. Anyone who carefully read the *New York Tribune* during 1856–1857 should have become aware of the rulings handed down by Judges Betts and Nelson. The facts of the situation were certainly not concealed from Congress. Apparently the people's representatives, whether Northerners or Southerners, Whigs, Democrats, Free Soilers, or Republicans, were really not much interested in the African slave trade. It meant little in comparison with the absorbing business of allocating the federal pork barrel, and arguing interminably about the true extent of the federal government's powers, and finding occasions to embarrass the opposition party.

But Congress reflected the attitudes of the voters behind it. Obviously the American people were not sufficiently interested in slave-trade suppression to send their representatives a clear call for action. There were various reasons for this apathy. Though many Americans of that generation were public-spirited, most of them—like most people of most generations everywhere—were chiefly absorbed in their personal activities. There was no economic motive to draw them from their disinterest, for enforcement of the slave-trade laws promised no greater wealth to anyone, except perhaps to a few merchants engaged in African trade. On the contrary, enforcement threatened higher taxes and expansion of the federal bureaucracy. Neither did enforcement find a place alongside temperance, abolition, public education, and other reform movements then sweeping the nation. An occasional dishonest sea captain selling his vessel to foreigners at Ambriz or up the Congo did not create an evil that could compete in the public consciousness with the social problems existing at home.

This was the more true because even well-informed Americans were not likely to read a great deal about the slave trade until the late 'fifties. The surges of lawbreaking in 1838–1839 and 1848–1849 were ended by British and Brazilian action before the American people had heard enough about the crimes to become deeply aroused. Immediately after each of these crime waves, the trade declined so sharply that corrective action seemed unimportant. As federal officers were obviously attempting to do their duty against a shrewd group of criminals, a casual observer might decide that little could be done to improve matters. Even if large numbers of people had felt the need for better law enforcement, the strenuous measures necessary would have been unpalatable to a generation of Americans reared upon the doctrines of rigid governmental economy, no interference with private enterprise, suspicion of the British, and legal procedures designed to protect the accused at all costs, including the cost of effective law enforcement. Ironically, the result of these public attitudes was the intrusion of a foreign power into American law enforcement, and the creation of a system of courts whose guiding principles were utterly foreign to the spirit of American legal institutions.

If there is any lesson to be drawn from American efforts to suppress the slave trade, it is that the citizens of a democracy must be ever alert to crime in their midst. They must be forthright in their insistence upon adequate legislation and full enforcement. If they are not, one of two results will inevitably follow. Lawlessness will reign, thriving upon their apathy and indeed upon the guarantees of individual liberty written into their institutions; or, when the abuse has become too great, rough hands will take over and curb lawlessness and liberty at the same time. To be free, a society must behave with the self-discipline that goes with freedom. Eternal vigilance is the price of liberty at home, as well as abroad.

APPENDIXES

APPENDIX A

VESSELS ARRESTED BY AMERICAN OFFICERS FOR VIOLATION OF THE SLAVE-TRADE ACTS, 1837–1862

This list does not include all the vessels that were arrested, but only those that were libeled in United States district courts or made naval prizes. No arresting authority is specified for vessels seized in American waters, because such arrests were usually coöperative actions involving the local marshal, the revenue collector, and the district attorney. A few vessels seized by British naval officers or by their own crew members have been included because they were subsequently surrendered to federal officers and prosecuted. Vessels were usually libeled under the acts of 1794, 1800, or 1818 (and frequently all three) for being engaged in the slave trade between foreign countries. Notes are attached to various special cases. The sources listed are by no means exhaustive, but merely document the arrest and the results of the judicial proceedings. The letter "C" under the heading *Results* indicates that the vessel was confiscated; "D," that the libel was dismissed; "NT," that the legal proceedings were abandoned before a judicial decision was delivered; "U," that the disposition of the case is unknown. Source abbreviations in addition to those used in notes to the text include A.D. (Admiralty Docket, U.S. District Court, Southern New York district); and S.L. (Solicitor's Letters).

Ship	Rig	Place of arrest	Arresting authority	Date of arrest	Court	Re-sults	Source
Emperor	Schr.	Florida		5-26-37	W. Fla.	D[a]	HED 7, 36-2, p. 630
Wyoming	Brig	Gallinas	H.M.S. Harlequin	5-17-39	S.N.Y.	C[b]	H. Rep. 283, 27-3, pp. 657–661
Euphrates	Schr.	African coast	H.M.S. Harlequin	1839	E. Pa.	U	Balt. Sun, 10-1-39
Catharine	Schr.	South Atlantic	H.M.S. Dolphin	8-13-39	S.N.Y.	C	Fed. Cas. #14,755
Butterfly	Schr.	5° 25' N., 30° W.	H.M.S. Dolphin	8-26-39	S.N.Y.	C	39 U.S. 464; Balt. Sun, 4-9-40
Ann	Schr.	Baltimore		11-27-39	Md.	C	Balt. Sun, 5-20-40
Sarah Anne	Schr.	Pongas R.	U.S.S. Grampus	3- 3-40	S.N.Y.	C	H. Rep. 283, 27-3, p. 664; A.D., II, p. 171
Independence	Schr.	Louisiana		9- 4-41	E. La.	C	HED 7, 36-2, p. 627
Uncas	Brig	Gallinas	U.S.S. Porpoise	3- 1-44	E. La.	NT[c]	SED 150, 28-2, pp. 110–112, 145
Seminole	Schr.	Louisiana		5-16-44	E. La.	C	HED 7, 36-2, p. 627
Porpoise	Brig	Rio de Janeiro	U.S.S. Raritan	1-23-45	Mass.	C	Fed. Cas. #11,284
Spitfire	Schr.	Pongas R.	U.S.S. Truxtun	3-24-45	Mass.	C	HED 104, 35-2, pp. 31–32

Albert	Brig	Bahia	U.S.S. Bainbridge	6-45	E. Pa.	D [d]	HED 61, 30-2, pp. 181–209; *Phila. Public Ledger*, 11-1-45, 2-25-46
Patuxent	Schr.	Off Cape Mount	U.S.S. Yorktown	9-27-45	S. N.Y.	D	HED 7, 36-2, p. 628
Merchant	Schr.	Sierra Leone	U.S.S. Jamestown	12- 3-45	S. Car.	C	HED 104, 35-2, p. 32; case of Capt. Larkin, App. B
Pons	Bark	Off Kabenda	U.S.S. Yorktown	12-45	E. Pa.	C°	HED 73, 31-1, p. 2; *Phila. Public Ledger*, 4-9-46
Panther	Ship	Kabenda	U.S.S. Yorktown	12-15-45	S. Car.	C	HED 7, 36-2, p. 627; Supreme Ct. Case File 3,150 (NA)
Robert Wilson	Schr.	Porto Praia	U.S.S. Jamestown	1-15-46	S. Car.	C	HED 104, 35-2, p. 32; HED 7, 36-2, p. 628
Malaga	Brig	Kabenda	U.S.S. Boxer	4-13-46	Mass.	NT	Fed. Cas. #8,985
Casket	Brig	Kabenda	U.S.S. Marion	8- 2-46	Mass.	D	HED 104, 35-2, pp. 2, 32
Titi	Brig	New Orleans		8- 3-46	E. La.	C [f]	4 *Op. Atty. Gen.* 567–575
Chancellor	Bark	Off Cape Palmas	U.S.S. Dolphin	4-10-47	S. N.Y.	D	HED 104, 35-2, p. 32; NA 89–103, #101

Ship	Rig	Place of arrest	Arresting authority	Date of arrest	Court	Results	Source
Mary Ann	Schr.	New York		12-11-47	S. N.Y.	D *	Fed. Cas. #9,194
Laurens	Bark	Off Rio de Janeiro	U.S.S. *Onkahye*	1-23-48	S. N.Y.	C	HED 7, 36-2, p. 628; SED 6, 31-2, p. 8
A. D. Richard-son	Bark	Off Rio de Janeiro	U.S.S. *Perry*	12-11-48	S. N.Y.	NT	HED 7, 36-2, pp. 628-629
Independ-ence	Brig	Off Rio de Janeiro	U.S.S. *Perry*	12-13-48	E. Va.	C	HED 7, 36-2, p. 630
Susan	Brig	Off Rio de Janeiro	U.S.S. *Perry*	2- 6-49	S. N.Y.	D	HED 7, 36-2, p. 629
Ohio	Bark	New Orleans		1849	E. La.	D *	Fed. Cas. #15,914
Excellent	Brig	Ambriz	U.S.S. *John Adams*	4-50	E. Va.	C	HED 104, 35-2, p. 32; Hendren to S., 1-31-51, S.L., Box 147
Martha	Ship	Off Ambriz	U.S.S. *Perry*	6- 6-50	S. N.Y.	C	HED 104, 35-2, p. 32
Chatsworth	Brig	Ambriz	U.S.S. *Perry*	9-11-50	Md.	C	HED 104, 35-2, p. 32
Advance	Schr.	Off Porto Praia	U.S.S. *German-town*	11- 3-52	E. Va.	C	HED 104, 35-2, p. 32; HED 7, 36-2, p. 630
R. P. Brown	Schr.	Off Porto Praia	U.S.S. *German-town*	1-23-53	E. Va.	C	HED 104, 35-2, p. 32; HED 7, 36-2, p. 630

Name	Type	Port	Vessel	Date	Location		Reference
H. N. Gambrill	Schr.	Off Congo R.	U.S.S. *Constitution*	11- 3-53	S.N.Y.	C	HED 104, 35-2, p. 32; HED 7, 36-2, p. 629
Glamorgan	Brig	Off Congo R.	U.S.S. *Perry*	3-10-54	Mass.	C	HED 104, 35-2, p. 32; HED 7, 36-2, p. 629
Jasper	Bark	New York		9-28-54	S.N.Y.	D	HED 7, 36-2, p. 629
G. H. Townsend	Schr.	New York		12-54	S.N.Y.	D	SED 53, 37-2, p. 2
Falmouth	Schr.	New York		3-18-56	S.N.Y.	C	SED 53, 37-2, p. 2
C. F. A. Cole	Schr.	Maryland		5-15-56	Md.	C[h]	HED 7, 36-2, p. 627; *NYDT*, 10-15-56
Braman	Brig	New York		6- 9-56	S.N.Y.	C	A.D., XIII, 383
William Lewis	Schr.	Newport, R.I.		8-11-56	R.I.	C[h]	HED 7, 36-2, p. 630; *NYDT*, 7-21-56
Panchita	Bark	New York		10- 8-56	S.N.Y.	D	*NYDT*, 12-18-56
J. P. Glover	Schr.	New York		1-31-57	S.N.Y.	C	HED 7, 36-2, p. 629
William Clark	Brig	New Orleans		2-20-57	E. La.	D	HED 7, 36-2, p. 627
Merchant	Schr.	New York		4-23-57	S.N.Y.	D	4 Blatchford 105
John Birkbeck	Tug	New York		4-23-57	S.N.Y.	D	A.D., XIV, 164

Ship	Rig	Place of arrest	Arresting authority	Date of arrest	Court	Re-sults	Source
Ellen	Brig	New York		4-30-57	S. N.Y.	D	NYDT, 7-18-57
Lewis McLain	Schr.	New Orleans		5- 5-57	E. La.	D	HED 7, 36-2, p. 627
Panchita	Bark	Congo R.	H.M.S. Sappho	5- 9-57	S. N.Y.	NT	SED 2, 35-2, p. 190; NYDT, 7-8-57
Flora	Brig	New York		7-20-57	S. N.Y.	NT[a]	SED 2, 35-2, p. 191; NYDT, 7-22-57
W. G. Lewis	Bark	New York		8-13-57	S. N.Y.	NT	SED 2, 35-2, p. 191
W. G. Lewis	Bark	Congo R.	U.S.S. Dale	11- 6-57	E. Va.	D	HED 7, 36-2, p. 630
Henry	Brig	New York		1-22-58	S. N.Y.	D[i]	Fed. Cas. #15,352
J. W. Reed	Bark	New Orleans		5-13-58	E. La.	D	HED 7, 36-2, p. 627
Huntress	Brig	Key West		5-22-58	S. Fla.	C	HED 7, 36-2, p. 630
Lyra	Bark	Key West		7- 8-58	S. Fla.	C	HED 7, 36-2, pp. 165–166, 631
Putnam	Brig	Off Cuba	U.S.S. Dolphin	8-21-58	S. Car.	C[j]	HED 7, 36-2, pp. 516–517, 628
Brothers	Ketch	Off Mayumba	U.S.S. Marion	9- 8-58	S. Car.	D	HED 7, 36-2, pp. 547, 628
Mystic Valley	Schr.	Key West		9-24-58	S. Fla.	U[k]	SED 3, 36-1, p. 204; NYDT, 11-18-58

Isla de Cuba	Bark	Boston		10-20-58	Mass.	C[1]	Fed. Cas. #15,447
Ardennes	Bark	Jacksonville		12- 8-58	N. Fla.	D	*NYDT*, 7-28-59
Wanderer	Schr.	Brunswick, Ga.		12-11-58	Ga.	C[t]	HED 7, 36-2, p. 631
Julia Dean	Bark	Cape Coast Castle	U.S.S. *Vincennes*	12-28-58	E. Va.	D	HED 7, 36-2, pp. 516, 630
Angelita	Bark	Savannah		Late 1858	Ga.	D	HED 7, 36-2, pp. 631, 638
Laurens	Bark	New London		1-20-59	Conn.	D	Shipman to Hillyer, Feb.–March, 1859, S.L., Box 14
Tyrant	Brig	Key West		3-10-59	S. Fla.	C	*New Orleans Daily Picayune*, March 16, 18, April 14, 1859
Rebecca	Ship	New Orleans		4- 7-59	E. La.	D	HED 7, 36-2, p. 627
Orion	Bark	Congo R.	U.S.S. *Marion*	4-21-59	S.N.Y.	C	HED 7, 36-2, pp. 516, 629
Ardennes	Bark	Congo R.	U.S.S. *Marion*	4-27-59	S.N.Y.	D	HED 7, 36-2, p. 516; A.D., XV, 412–413
Atlantic	Ship	New Bedford		7-21-59	Mass.	NT	HED 2, 36-2, p. 263
Emily	Bark	Loango	U.S.S. *Portsmouth*	9-21-59	S.N.Y.	D	HED 7, 36-2, p. 516; A.D., XV, 525

Ship	Rig	Place of arrest	Arresting authority	Date of arrest	Court	Re-sults	Source
J. P. Hooper	Brig	New York		11- 2-59	S. N.Y.	D	SED 53, 37-2, p. 2; HED 7, 36-2, p. 629
Cygnet	Brig	Off Cuba	U.S.S. Mohawk	11-18-59	S. Fla.	C	HED 7, 36-2, pp. 517, 631
Delicia	Brig	Off Kabenda	U.S.S. Constellation	12-21-59	S. Car.	NT [m]	HED 7, 36-2, p. 516; State Papers, LI, 1094
Wanderer	Schr.	Boston		12-24-59	Mass.	C [n]	Fed. Cas. #17,139
Virginian	Brig	Congo R.	U.S.S. Portsmouth	2- 6-60	E. Va.	U	HED 7, 36-2, p. 516; HED 2, 36-2, p. 273
Alice Rogers	Schr.	Virginia		4-10-60	E. Va.	C [o]	HED 7, 36-2, p. 273
C. E. Tay	Bark	New York		4-24-60	S. N.Y.	D	A.D., XVI, 60
Wildfire	Bark	Off Cuba	U.S.S. Mohawk	4-26-60	S. Fla.	C [p]	HED 7, 36-2, p. 517; HED 2, 36-2, p. 274
Falmouth	Brig	Off Porto Praia	U.S.S. Portsmouth	5- 6-60	S. N.Y.	C	HED 7, 36-2, p. 516; A.D., XVI, 91
William	Bark	Off Cuba	U.S.S. Wyandotte	5- 9-60	S. Fla.	C [q]	HED 7, 36-2, p. 517; HED 2, 36-2, p. 275
Cora	Bark	New York		5-19-60	S. N.Y.	C [r]	SED 53, 37-2, p. 2
Bogota	Bark	Off Cuba	U.S.S. Crusader	5-23-60	S. Fla.	C [s]	HED 7, 36-2, p. 517; HED 2, 36-

Josephine	Schr.	New York		5-28-60	**S.N.Y.**	**D**	A.D., XVI, 82
Mariquita	Schr.	New York		6-16-60	**S.N.Y.**	**NT**	A.D., XVI, 90
Thomas Achorn	Brig	Kabenda	U.S.S. *Mystic*	6-29-60	**S.N.Y.**	**D**	HED 7, 36-2, p. 516; **A.D., XVI, 126**
Triton	Brig	Loango	U.S.S. *Mystic*	7-16-60	E. Va.	C	HED 7, 36-2, p. 516; **Francis to Secy. of Treas., 2-12-61, S.L., Box 148**
Kate	Bark	New York		7- 3-60	**S.N.Y.**	C	69 U.S. 350
W. R. Kibby	Brig	Off Cuba	U.S.S. *Crusader*	7-23-60	**S.N.Y.**	C [t]	SED 53, 37-2, p. 2; HED 7, 36-2, p. 517
Erie	Ship	Off Congo R.	U.S.S. *Mohican*	8- 8-60	**S.N.Y.**	C [u]	SED 53, 37-2, p. 2; HED 7, 36-2, p. 516
Storm King	Brig	Off Congo R.	U.S.S. *San Jacinto*	8- 8-60	E. Va.	C [v]	HED 7, 36-2, p. 516; **Francis to Secy. of Treas., 2-12-61, S.L., Box 148**
Joven Antonio	Brig	Off Cuba	U.S.S. *Crusader*	8-14-60	S. Fla.	D [w]	HED 7, 36-2, p. 517; **A.D., S. Fla. Dist., 1857–1863, pp. 606–616**
Cora	Bark	Off Congo R.	U.S.S. *Constellation*	9-26-60	**S.N.Y.**	C [x]	SED 53, **37-2, p. 2**; SED 1, 37-1, p. 97

Ship	Rig	Place of arrest	Arresting authority	Date of arrest	Court	Re-sults	Source
Bonito	Brig	Off Congo R.	U.S.S. San Jacinto	10-10-60		U[v]	SED 1, 37-1, p. 97; HED 11, 36-2, p. 2
Weather Gage	Bark	New York		10-23-60	S. N.Y.	C	69 U.S. 375
W. L. Cogs-well	Schr.	New York		11-28-60	S. N.Y.	D	SED 53, 37-2, p. 2
Toccoa	Brig	Off Havana	U.S.S. Mohawk	12-20-60	S. Fla.	C	SED 1, 37-1, p. 97; Tatum to S., 2-25-61, S.L., Box 19
Mary J. Kimball	Bark	Off Havana	U.S.S. Mohawk	12-21-60	S. Fla.	C	Same as for *Toccoa*
Express	Schr.	African coast	U.S.S. Saratoga	2-25-61	S. N.Y.	U	NA 89-112, #145
Sarah	Bark	New York		4- 6-61	S. N.Y.	C	69 U.S. 366
Nightingale	Ship	Kabenda	U.S.S. Saratoga	4-21-61	S. N.Y.	C[a]	SED 1, 37-1, p. 97; SED 53, 37-2, p. 3
Triton	Brig	Congo R.	U.S.S. Constel-lation	5-20-61	S. N.Y.	C	SED 1, 37-2, pp. 21, 111; A.D., XVI, 368
Augusta	Bark	Greenport, N.Y.		6-23-61	S. N.Y.	C	Fed. Cas. #14,477
Falmouth	Brig	Congo R.	U.S.S. Sumpter	6-14-61	S. N.Y.	D	NA 89-112, #314; A.D., XVI, 379
Reindeer	Bark	Newport, R.I.		8- 7-61	R.I.	C	69 U.S. 383

Margaret Scott	Bark	New Bedford	9- 9-61	Mass.	C	Keys to S., Marshals' Letters; Sands to S., 2-62, Dept. of Interior, Misc. Ltrs. Recd.
Reindeer	Bark	New York	6-62	S.N.Y.	NT	NYDT, 6-10-62, p. 7

[a] Libeled for bringing foreign slaves into the United States.
[b] Confiscated under Section 16, act of December 31, 1792, for unreported sale to a foreigner.
[c] The Uncas was assisted home by a heavy guard, but was not made a formal prize.
[d] First seized by Brazilian officials upon the request of the United States consul.
[e] About 900 Africans were aboard at the time of seizure; 756 were delivered to the United States agent at Monrovia, Liberia.
[f] Confiscated for bringing foreign slaves into the United States.
[g] Surrendered by her own crew, who mutinied at Gallinas.
[h] Found as a derelict, and subsequently libeled.
[i] Not actually seized; see case reference.
[j] There were 318 Africans aboard, of whom 306 were landed at Charleston. This vessel was commonly known as the Echo, from a false name painted on her.
[k] Libeled for having an unmanifested slave aboard, in violation of the act of 1807.
[l] Surrendered to the authorities by her own captain.
[m] This was a Spanish vessel, and the Spanish consul filed a claim for her.
[n] Surrendered by her own crew, who mutinied off the African coast.
[o] Confiscated for having unmanifested slaves aboard, in violation of the act of 1807.
[p] There were 530 Africans aboard, of whom 507 were landed at Key West.
[q] There were 570 Africans aboard, of whom 513 were landed at Key West.
[r] The Cora was confiscated in absentia after her capture on September 26, 1860.
[s] The Bogota landed 411 Africans at Key West.
[t] The three African boys aboard were landed at New York.
[u] There were 897 Africans aboard, of whom 867 were landed at Monrovia.
[v] There were 619 Africans aboard, of whom 616 were landed at Monrovia.
[w] Proven to be a Spanish vessel outside United States jurisdiction.
[x] There were 705 Africans aboard, of whom 694 were landed at Monrovia.
[y] There were 750 Africans aboard, of whom 734 were landed at Monrovia.
[z] There were 961 Africans aboard, of whom 801 were landed at Monrovia.

APPENDIX B

CRIMINAL PROSECUTIONS UNDER THE SLAVE-TRADE ACTS, 1837–1862

The following abbreviations have been used in this appendix:

C: captain	SM: seamen	schr.: schooner
M: mate	O: owner	arr.: arrested
S: supercargo	conn.: connected with	ind.: indicted

1839

Isaac Morris
: C/O schr. *Butterfly*. Ind. act of 1800, Nov., 1839, S. N.Y. dist.; tried Nov. 30, 1839, and case sent to Supreme Court (39 U.S. 464); trial completed Aug., 1840, and Morris sentenced to $2,000 fine and 2 years' imprisonment. Prisoner escaped while free on bail.

Frederick A. Peterson
: C schr. *Catharine*. Ind. act of 1800, Nov., 1839, S. N.Y. dist.; released on bail, which he forfeited.

Joshua W. Littig
: C/O brig *Eagle*. Ind. act of 1800, Aug., 1839, S. N.Y. dist.; released on bail, which he forfeited.

Robert W. Allen
: O schr. *Catharine*. Ind. act of 1818, Nov., 1839, Md. dist.; tried and jury deadlocked, Dec., 1839; retried April, 1840, and acquitted.

(Sources for all the preceding cases are noted in chapter 2)

John Henderson
: Co-owner schr. *Catharine*. Ind. act of 1818, Nov., 1839, Md. dist.; case nol-prossed April, 1840, after acquittal of R. W. Allen.

(*Baltimore Sun,* April 27, 1840)

Francis T. Montell
: O schr. *Elvira*. Ind. act of 1818, Nov., 1839, Md. dist.; tried and acquitted April 27–29, 1840.

(*Baltimore Sun,* April 28, 30, 1840)

1840

Albert Sleter | M schr. *Sarah Anne.* Ind. act of 1800, S. N.Y. dist.; tried and convicted Aug. 5–6, 1840; sentenced to 2 years and $2,000 fine.

(*New York Morning Herald,* Aug. 6, 7, 13, 1840)

1844

Jason S. Pendleton | C brig *Montevideo.* Arr. at Rio de Janeiro; ind. act of 1800, Md. dist.; tried and convicted June, 1845; sentenced to 1 year and $1,000. Full pardon granted July, 1846.

Robert Baker | M brig *Montevideo.* Arr., indicted, and tried as Pendleton was; sentenced to 6 months and $500. Full pardon granted March, 1846.

(Pardons, V, 346, 375)

Cornelius Driscoll | C brig *Hope.* Arr. at N.Y.C.; ind. act of 1820; released on bail which he forfeited.

(See chap. 11)

1845

Hiram Gray | C brig *Agnes.* Arr. and examined Delaware dist., but charges dismissed by U.S. commissioner.

(SED 28, 30-1, pp. 20–21)

Thomas Duling | C brig *Washington's Barge.* Arr. at Bahia; ind. act of 1818, E. Penn. dist.; tried and acquitted Oct. 21–30, 1845.

(*Philadelphia Public Ledger,* Oct. 22, 31, 1845)

Joshua Clapp | C ship *Panther.* Arr. at sea; ind. act of 1800, S. Carolina dist.; tried and acquitted, June, 1846.

(*Niles' National Register,* 5th ser., XVIII, 272)

Cyrus Libby | C brig *Porpoise.* Ind. act of 1820, Aug., 1845, Me. dist.; tried and acquitted, July 7–16, 1846.

(Fed. Cas. #15,597)

Peter Flowery | C/O schr. *Spitfire.* Arr. in Pongas R.; ind. act of 1818, Mass. dist.; tried and convicted June, 1845; sentenced to 5 years and $2,000 fine. Full pardon granted May, 1847.

(See chap. 12)

J. M. Rush, J. Hamilton, J. P. Morris, and | SM Brazilian steam slaver *Cacique,* captured by H.M.S. *Penelope* in 1845. Turned over to African

A. J. Shute

squadron and sent into Charleston; further proceedings unknown.

(*NYDT,* March 16, 1846)

4 *Pons* seamen

SM bark *Pons.* Arr. at sea; discharged E. Penn. dist. after being proven Portuguese subjects.

(*Philadelphia Public Ledger,* April 9, 1846)

1846

Nathaniel T. Davis

C schr. *Patuxent.* Arr. at sea; ind. act of 1800, S. N.Y. dist.; tried and acquitted.

(*NYDT,* Feb. 15, 1847)

William Von Pfister

C schr. *Robert Wilson.* Arr. at sea; ind. act of 1818, S. Carolina dist.; tried and convicted March, 1846; sentenced to 3 years and $1,000 fine. Full pardon granted April, 1847.

Lorin Larkin

C schr. *Merchant.* Same circumstances as Von Pfister.

(Pardons, VI, 1–2)

1847

James A. Freeman

C bark *Chancellor.* Arr. at sea; ind. act of 1800, S. N.Y. dist.; tried and acquitted Dec., 1847.

Charles D. Matthews

O bark *Chancellor.* Arr. at N.Y.C. June, 1847; indictment nol-prossed.

John T. Gibson

M bark *Chancellor.* Arr. at sea; ind. act of 1800; indictment nol-prossed.

Theodore Canot

Charterer bark *Chancellor.* Arr. at sea; ind. act of 1818, S. N.Y. dist.; discharged by Judges Betts and Nelson because of technical defect in indictment.

(*NYDT,* June 11, 22, Dec. 9, 18, 1847; Jan. 6, April 19, 20, 1848)

1848

William Brown

M bark *Fame.* Arr. at sea; ind. act of 1820, E. Penn. dist.; tried and acquitted.

(Fed. Cas. #14,656; HED 61, 30-2, pp. 19–20, 29–30)

Theodore Littlefield

C ship *Laurens.* Arr. at sea; indictment under act of 1800 refused by grand jury of S. N.Y. dist., April 13, 1848.

(Criminal Case Records, U.S. Circuit Court, S. N.Y. dist., 1790–1853)

1849

Edward C. Walford

C brig *Susan.* Ind. act of 1800, May, 1849, S. N.Y. dist.; further proceedings unknown.

Thomas Brentnall   M brig *Susan*. Same circumstances as Walford.

(*NYDT*, May 28, 1849)

1850

Henry M. Merrill   C ship *Martha*. Arr. at sea; released at New York on $3,000 bail, which he forfeited. The bondsmen also fled.

Henry Johnson   M ship *Martha*. Arr. at sea; ind. act of 1800, S. N.Y. dist., tried and convicted Feb. 13–14, 1851; sentenced to 2 years and $50 fine. Full pardon granted July, 1852.

(Pardons, VI, 336; *NYDT*, Feb. 15, 19, 1851)

1851

William Tyson   C brig *R. de Zaldo*. Arr. Jan., 1851, at N.Y.C.; released on bail; further proceedings unknown.

(*NYDT*, Feb. 1, 1851)

1854

Charles Kehrman   C brig *Glamorgan*. Arr. at sea; ind. act of 1818 June 20, 1854, Mass. dist.; tried and convicted July 3; sentenced to 3 years and $1,000 fine. Full pardon, April, 1856.

John McCormick   M brig *Glamorgan*. Arr. at sea; ind. act of 1800 June 20, 1854, Mass. dist.; tried and convicted July 3; sentenced to 6 months and $500. Full pardon (i.e., remission of fine and citizenship rights), March, 1855.

(Pardons, VI, 473, 510; *Boston Post*, June 21, 30, July 4, 1854)

William C. Valentine   Conn. brig *Julia Moulton*. Arr. Sept., 1854; ind. act of 1818, June, 1855, S. N.Y. dist.; tried and acquitted May, 1856.

(Criminal Docket, I, 55; *NYDT*, May 15, 16, 1856)

James Smith   C/O brig *Julia Moulton*. Arr. at N.Y.C., Sept., 1854; ind. act of 1820; tried and convicted, but new trial ordered; ind. and pleaded guilty to act of 1800, May, 1855; sentenced to 2 years and $1,000. Fine remitted May, 1857.

(See chap. 13)

1855

James G. Darnaud   C brig *Grey Eagle*. Ind. act of 1820, E. Penn. dist.; tried and acquitted October Term, 1855.

(Fed. Cas. #14,918)

Rudolph E. Lasala O brig *Horatio*. Arr. May, 1855; ind. act of 1818 Nov., 1855, S. N.Y. dist.; tried and acquitted, June 16–18, 1856.

(See chap. 10)

William F. Martin C brig *Horatio*. Arr. May, 1855; ind. S. N.Y. dist.; turned state's evidence at Lasala's trial, and nolle prosequi entered.

(SED 53, 37-2, p. 3; *NYDT*, Nov. 6, 1855; June 17, 1856)

Manuel Echeverria Conn. *Mary Jane Peck*. Ind. act of 1818, S. N.Y. dist., Sept., 1855; tried and acquitted.

(SED 53, 37-2, p. 3; *NYDT*, Sept. 26, 1855)

1856

José Lopez, Joachim Antonio, Casper M. Cunha, and 9 others Supposed O, C, S, and crew schr. *Falmouth*. Civil suit begun, act of 1794, S. N.Y. dist.; Lopez and Antonio paid fines of $2,000; the others demanded a jury trial and were acquitted June 25, 1856.

(*NYDT*, June 25, 26, 1856)

Henrico da Costa Charterer brig *Braman*. Arr. June, 1856; ind. July 12, act of 1818, S. N.Y. dist.; escaped from custody before trial.

(SED 53, 37-2, p. 3; *NYDT*, July 14, 1856)

Josefi Pedro da Cunha Supposed S *Braman*. Arr. and ind. as Da Costa; tried and acquitted, July 14–17, 1856.

(*NYDT*, July 15, 16, 17, 18, 1856)

Placido de Castro Conn. *Braman*. Arr. and ind. as Da Costa; tried and acquitted, Sept. 12–16, 1856.

(*NYDT*, Sept. 13, 17, 1856)

Benjamin B. Naylor C bark *Panchita*. Arr. S. N.Y. dist., Oct., 1856; suit begun under act of 1794; jumped bail.

(Fed. Cas. #15,858; *NYDT*, Nov. 27, 1856)

Augustine C. de Mesquita S bark *Panchita*. *Arr.*, ind. Nov., 1856, act of 1818, S. N.Y. dist.; tried and acquitted Dec., 1856.

John P. Weeks and Benjamin F. Wenburg Owners bark *Panchita*. Arr. and tried as Mesquita was.

(*NYDT*, Dec. 5, 8, 1856)

8 seamen SM bark *Panchita*. Ind. act of 1800, S. N.Y. dist.; tried and acquitted Dec. 8, 1856.

(*NYDT*, Dec. 9, 1856)

M. B. da Cunha Reis   Conn. schr. *Onward,* alias *Altiva.* Arr. June, 1856;
                         ind. act of 1818, S. N.Y. dist.; tried and acquitted
                         Sept. 23–25, 1856.

                         (*NYDT,* Sept. 24, 26, 1856)

William Pent (or Pinto) M brig *Braman.* Ind. act of 1800 July 12, 1856,
                         S. N.Y. dist.; tried and convicted July 19; sen-
                         tenced to 2 years and $50 fine; escaped from
                         prison within two weeks.

                         (*NYDT,* July 14, 22, Sept. 13, 1856)

M. B. da Cunha Reis   Ind. at Boston for outfitting schr. *Mary E. Smith,*
                         but was repeatedly released on bail and never
                         tried.

                         (See chap. 11)

Antonio Silva   M schr. *C. F. A. Cole.* Arr. Oct., 1856, at N.Y.C.;
                         removed to Baltimore for trial under act of 1820;
                         further proceedings unknown.

                         (*NYDT,* Oct. 15, 1856)

Louis Brown   SM schr. *Onward,* alias *Altiva.* Ind. act of 1800,
                         S. N.Y. dist.; tried and acquitted Sept. 10–11,
                         1856.

                         (*NYDT,* Sept. 11, 12, 1856)

1857

Thomas Carlin,   Owner, charterer, and otherwise connected with
Vincent Beiro,   schr. *Merchant;* ind. act of 1818, S. N.Y. dist.,
Gasper M. da Cunha,   May, 1857; nolle prosequi entered 1858.
and Joseph Santos

                (SED 53, 37-2, p. 3; Criminal Docket, I, 119)

Philip S. Van Vechten,   C and S brig *Ellen.* Arr. May, 1857; ind. S. N.Y.
José de Aranga   dist.; complaint dismissed by U.S. commissioner.

                         (SED 53, 37-2, p. 3)

Lima Viana,   Charterer and otherwise connected with bark *W. G.*
Juan M. Smith,   *Lewis.* Arr. Oct., 1857; ind. act of 1818, S. N.Y.
Benjamin F. Wen-   dist.; nolle prosequi entered 1858.
burg, and William
Dewwis

                         (Criminal Docket, I, 125)

J. H. Hinckley and   C/O and S schr. *Lewis McLain.* Ind. act of 1818,
Juan B. Larrusca   May, 1857, E. La. dist.; tried and acquitted
                         June 8, 1857.

(*New Orleans Daily Picayune,* May 22, June 10, 1857)

John Freddell   C bark *William G. Lewis.* Arr. at sea; ind. E. Va.
                      dist. for violation of slave-trade acts; tried and
                      acquitted June, 1858. An indictment against his
                      mate was then nol-prossed.

(Gregory to Hillyer, Dec. 26, 1857, Aug. 14, 1858, Solicitor's Letters, Box 148)

1858

Richard T. Bates,   SM brig *Putnam.* Arr. at sea; ind. act of 1820, S.
Alex. Rodgers,   Carolina dist.; tried and acquitted April, 1859.
Antonio de Almeyda,
José Francisco, *et al.*
(total 16)

(*NYDT,* Dec. 4, 10, 1859; *New Orleans Weekly Picayune,* April 27, 1859)

Edward C. Townsend   C/O brig *Putnam.* Arr. at sea; ind. act of 1820, S.
                      Florida dist.; tried and acquitted May 21, 1859.

(*New Orleans Daily Picayune,* May 29, 1859)

Nicholas A. Brown,   SM schr. *Wanderer.* Arr. Dec., 1858; ind. act of
Miguel Arguin, and   1820, Ga. dist.; Brown tried and acquitted Nov.,
Juan de Bajesta   1859, and the other two indictments were then
                      nol-prossed.

(See chap. 13)

Jonathan T. Dobson   C/O bark *Isla de Cuba.* Arr. Nov., 1858, Mass.
                      dist., but complaint dismissed by U.S. commis-
                      sioner.

(*NYDT,* Nov. 9, Dec. 1, 1858)

James Gage, A. Blanco, C and crew ketch *Brothers.* Arr. at sea; grand jury
et al. (total 7)   of S. Carolina dist. refused to indict, 1859.

(Allan Nevins, *Emergence of Lincoln* [New York, 1950], I, 437;
NYDT, Nov. 16, 1858)

John B. Macomber   M ship *Haidee.* Arr. at New Bedford; ind. Oct.,
                      1858, S. N.Y. dist. under acts of 1800 and 1820;
                      escaped from jail.

José Francisco, Oliver SM ship *Haidee.* Arr. at New York and Boston;
Jacobson, Maurice   ind. Oct., 1858, acts of 1800 and 1820; tried
Rodriguez, John   and acquitted under both indictments, Nov. 24,
Battiste   1858, and Jan. 4, 1859.

(Chap. 13; Criminal Docket, I, 159, 165)

1859

Antonio Pelletier and
15 seamen

C/O and SM bark *Ardennes*. Arr. at sea; examined June 28, 1859, S. N.Y. dist.; complaint dismissed by U.S. commissioner.

(*NYDT,* June 28, 1859)

Tristas P. Canhao,
Thomas Morgan,
and 11 seamen

Charterer, M, and SM bark *Orion*. Arr. at sea; examined June, 1859, S. N.Y. dist.; complaint dismissed.

(SED 53, 37-2, p. 3; *NYDT,* June 18, 1859)

H. W. Allen

Alleged holder of African slaves. Ind. act of 1818, May, 1859, E. La. dist.; further proceedings unknown.

(*New Orleans Daily Picayune,* May 15, 1859)

T. V. Brodnax, Horatio
N. Gould, John H.
Haun

Alleged holders of African slaves. Ind. act of 1818, Alabama dist.; outcome of cases unknown.

(Fed. Cas. #15,239; Fed. Cas. #15,329; *American Law Register,* VIII, 525–526)

C. A. L. Lamar (2
counts), Richard F.
Aken, John F.
Tucker, William
Brailsford, Randolph
L. Mott, Nelson C.
Trowbridge, John
Dubignon, Henry
Dubignon

Alleged holders of African slaves. Ind. act of 1818, April–May, 1859, Ga. dist.; cases of Lamar, Aken, Mott, Tucker, and the Dubignons were nol-prossed May, 1860; outcome of remaining cases unknown.

(*New Orleans Daily Picayune,* April 22, 28, May 10, 1859; *NYDT,* May 29, 1860)

William C. Corrie

C/O schr. *Wanderer*. Ind. act of 1820, May, 1859, S. Carolina dist., and acts of 1818 and 1820, Ga. dist. Efforts to have him transferred to Georgia were defeated; disposition of S. Carolina indictment unknown.

(Fed. Cas. #14,869)

Matthew Lind

C/O brig *Tyrant*. Arr. April, 1859, and placed in prison at Key West to await further proceedings; results unknown.

(*New Orleans Daily Picayune,* April 14, 1859)

William Lindsey

C bark *Emily*. Arr. at sea; released on bail S. N.Y. dist.; forfeited his bail.

(*NYDT,* Nov. 14, 1859; June 1, 1860)

1860

Thomas Morgan, Byron J. Chamberlain, William Dunham
C/O and mates bark *Orion*. Arr. at St. Helena, Jan., 1860, upon formal request by Flag Officer Inman for their surrender; ind. act of 1800 (Morgan, act of 1818 also), Mass. dist.; Morgan pleaded guilty to violating act of 1800, Oct. 2, 1860, and was sentenced to $2,000 fine and 2 years. Chamberlain and Dunham were tried and convicted, and sentenced to 24 and 21 months and nominal fines of $1 each.

(*Boston Post*, April 3, May 15, Oct. 4, 1860; *Boston Evening Transcript*, Oct. 2, 3, 5, 1860)

J. Egbert Farnham
S schr. *Wanderer*. Arr. at New York; ind. act of 1820, Ga. dist.; tried with deadlocked jury, May, 1860.

(*NYDT*, May 30, 1860; Peyton to Thompson, April 24, 1860, Marshals' Letters)

Nathaniel Currier *et al.* (several others)
Crew brig *Bonito*. Arr. at sea; ind. acts of 1800 and 1820, Jan., 1861, S. N.Y. dist.; cases nol-prossed Nov., 1861.

(*NYDT*, Jan. 12, 1861; Criminal Docket, I, 245)

John Latham, Morgan Fredericks, John Wilson, Hans Olsen, and 4 seamen
C/O, mates, and SM bark *Cora*. Arr. at sea; ind. acts of 1800 and 1820, Jan., 1861, S. N.Y. dist. Latham was still in custody in May, 1861, but subsequently escaped; Fredericks also escaped before his trial; Wilson and Olsen pleaded guilty to violating act of 1800 in Nov., 1861, and were sentenced to 10 months each and $500 fine; cases against seamen nol-prossed.

(Chap. 13; Criminal Docket, I, 235; *NYDT*, Jan. 12, May 31, Nov. 26, 1861)

Nathaniel Gordon, William Warren, David Hale
C and mates ship *Erie*. Arr. at sea; ind. acts of 1800 and 1820, Oct., 1860, S. N.Y. dist.; Gordon convicted Nov., 1861, after a deadlocked jury in June, and was executed in Feb., 1862. The mates pleaded guilty to violating act of 1800, Feb., 1862, and were sentenced to 8 months and $1 (Warren), and 9 months and $1 (Hale).

(See chap. 13)

Philip Stanhope
C bark *Wildfire*. Arr. at sea; indictment under acts

of 1800 and 1818 requested of Key West grand jury, but no bill was found.

William Weston
C bark *William.* Arr. at sea; ind. act of 1820, S. Fla. dist.; tried and acquitted Jan., 1861.

(Tatum to Thompson, Jan. 13, 1861, Attorneys' Letters)

John Lockhart
C/O brig *Storm King.* Arr. at sea; ind. acts of 1800, 1818, 1820, E. Va. dist., 1860; result of prosecution unknown.

(Aylett to Hillyer, Oct. 2, 1860, Jan. 21, 27, 1861, Solicitor's Letters, Box 148)

William C. Carter
C schr. *Josephine.* Arr. May, 1860; released on $3,000 bond; ind. act of 1818, S. N.Y. dist., but could not be found.

(*NYDT,* June 1, 1860; Criminal Docket, I, 226)

Thomas Nelson,
Thomas Savage,
Samuel Sleeper,
John McCafferty
SM ship *Erie.* Arr. at sea; examined in New Hampshire dist., Nov., 1860; further proceedings unknown.

(*N.Y. Weekly Tribune,* Nov. 10, 1860)

Pierre L. Pearce
O bark *Wildfire.* Arr. N.Y.C.; ind. act of 1818; this indictment nol-prossed Dec., 1861, in favor of a Mass. indictment for fitting out the ship *Brutus.* He appeared at Boston, unsuccessfully applied for reduction of his $10,000 bail, and apparently forfeited his bond thereafter.

(*NYDT,* Dec. 6, 13, 27, 1861; *Boston Post,* Jan. 11, 1862)

Henrico da Costa,
Frederick Otto
Charterer and C bark *Kate.* Arr. July, 1860; released on bond in S. N.Y. dist. (da Costa, $5,000; Otto, $1,500), and forfeited their bonds.

(SED 53, 37-2, p. 4)

1861

Erastus H. Booth
C bark *Buckeye.* Arr. Oct., 1861; ind. acts of 1800 and 1820, Feb., 1862, S. N.Y. dist.; tried and acquitted Oct. 30, 1862.

(See chap. 13)

Henry C. Crawford
C steamer *City of Norfolk.* Arr. and ind. May, 1861, act of 1820, S. N.Y. dist.; nolle prosequi entered after Crawford testified against Albert Horn.

(*NYDT,* May 2, 1861; Nov. 17, 1862)

Albert Horn
O *City of Norfolk.* Arr. May, 1861; ind. act of

1818, Nov., 1861, S. N.Y. dist.; tried and convicted Oct. 23–29, 1862; sentenced to 5 years and no fine. Pardon May, 1863.

(See chap. 12)

John A. Machado   O bark *Mary Francis.* Arr. Oct., 1861, but discharged from custody by U.S. commissioner; rearrested Sept., 1862, after additional evidence was obtained; ind. Jan. 30, 1863, act of 1818, S. N.Y. dist. Released on bail Feb. 21, 1863; no further proceedings were had.

(*NYDT,* Oct. 19, 28, 1861; Sept. 22, 1862; Criminal Docket, I, 296)

Appleton Oaksmith   Arr. Nov., 1861, at N.Y.C. for complicity in fitting out the *Margaret Scott;* ind. 1862, Mass. dist.; tried and convicted June, 1862. Escaped from prison Sept., 1862. Also ind. Feb., 1862, S. N.Y. dist., for fitting out the schooner *Wells,* but no proceedings were had in that case.

(Chap. 12; *Boston Post,* Jan. 6, May 27, June 10, 16, 1862; Criminal Docket, I, 274)

Joseph (or José)   Ind. Aug., 1861, act of 1818, S. N.Y. dist., for
Santos   complicity in fitting out the bark *Cora;* brought to trial Oct. 31, 1862; fled under bail in the midst of the trial, but was nonetheless acquitted.

(Criminal Docket, I, 267; *NYDT,* Nov. 1, 6, 7, 1862)

Samuel B. Haynes   M ship *Nightingale.* Arr. at sea; ind. act of 1820, June, 1861, S. N.Y. dist.; tried with deadlocked juries May and Oct., 1862; released on bail and case abandoned.

Bradly Winslow   M ship *Nightingale.* Arr. and ind. as Haynes was; released on bail Nov., 1862; case abandoned.

Minthorne Westervelt   M ship *Nightingale.* Arr. and ind. as Haynes was; tried with deadlocked jury Nov., 1861; released on bail and case abandoned.

(See chap. 13)

Samuel P. Skinner   C bark *Margaret Scott.* Ind. act of 1818, Mass. dist.; tried and convicted Nov., 1861; sentenced to 5 years.

(Lousada to Russell, Dec. 2, 1861, House of Commons, *Slave Trade Papers, 1862,* Class B, p. 172)

1862

Antonio Rose   Conn. brig *Falmouth.* Ind. Feb., 1862, S. N.Y. dist., act of 1818; no further proceedings had, and indictment was formally nol-prossed May 31, 1879.

(Criminal Docket, I, 273)

John C. Cook   Ind. acts of 1800 and 1818, Mass. dist., for connection with ship *Tahmaroo;* pleaded guilty June 4, 1863, to lesser charge; sentenced to 2 years and $5 fine.

(*Boston Post,* June 5, 10, 1863)

Zeno Kelly   Ind. act of 1818, Mass. dist., for connection with ship *Tahmaroo;* first trial was begun June 26, 1862, and continued; case resumed April, 1863. Convicted, but sentencing deferred owing to defects in indictment.

(See chap. 12; *Boston Post,* June 26, 28, 1862; April 8–16, 1863)

James L. Chase   Arraigned May 26, 1862, U.S. Circuit Court, Mass. dist., for violation of slave-trade acts; no further details known.

(*Boston Post,* May 27, 1862)

APPENDIX C

PROFITS IN THE CUBAN SLAVE TRADE, 1857–1861

In February, 1861, Consul General Crawford figured the balance sheet of a slaving expedition as follows:

Cost of vessel and stores	$25,000
Cost of 500 negroes @ $50	25,000
Loss of 10 per cent of the slaves at sea	2,500
Wages to crew	30,000
"Blood money" (bribes to Spanish officials) @ $120 per slave landed	54,000
	$136,500
Twelve months' interest on capital invested @ 10 per cent	13,650
Total cost of expedition	$150,150
Sale of 450 slaves @ $1,200	540,000
Profit	$389,850

Crawford calculated that the loss to the slave traders was only $27,500 if a vessel was captured empty, because the crew's high wages were contingent upon a successful voyage. The loss of a laden slaver cost the owners only $55,000. Thus one successful slaving voyage would pay for the loss of ten empty or five laden slavers (Crawford to Russell, Feb. 5, 1861, House of Commons, *Slave Trade Papers, 1862*, Class A, p. 7).

The cost of each slave, delivered in Cuba, came to $300 in the above computation. But it is not clear why Crawford added $2,500 for mortality at sea, as that loss was covered by the smaller number of slaves sold and did not represent an out-of-pocket expense above the initial cost of the slaves. His computations took no account of the losses suffered by capture. Before finding Crawford's estimate, I made my own computations based on a variety of reports—some reliable, some highly unreliable—concerning expenses connected with the trade:

Cost of purchasing and fitting out a 300-ton vessel	$12,000
Cost of port clearance (bribes to officials)	3,000
Cost of crew (advance wages)	1,500
Miscellaneous costs and services	3,500
Total cost of putting a slaver to sea	$20,000
Because half of the slavers would be captured before embarking slaves, the average cost of each slaver actually shipping slaves would be	$40,000
Cost of 600 slaves @ $50	30,000
Cost of a laden slaver	$70,000
Add 30 per cent for slavers captured full of slaves	21,000
Cost of a shipload of slaves delivered to Cuba	$91,000
Cost of permits to land 500 surviving slaves, identification cards, etc., @ $85	42,500
Cost of paying off crew (captain @ $4,000, seamen @ $800)	16,000
Total cost, delivered to slave vendor	$149,500
Miscellaneous expenses	10,000
Total cost of expedition	$159,500
Cost per delivered slave	320
Proceeds from sale of 500 slaves @ $500	$250,000
Profit	$90,500

A profit of $90,500 on an outlay of $159,500 meant a return of 56 per cent. The principal conflict between my estimate and Crawford's is in the price for which smuggled slaves could be sold. I believe that Crawford's estimate of $1,200 was more than twice the price actually obtainable. But it is plain that a trade in which an investor could make 56 per cent on his outlay, allowing for all hazards, could easily attract abundant risk capital.

APPENDIX D

MORTALITIES ABOARD SLAVERS

The following reports are of varying reliability, but taken together they give a fair picture of both the over-all mortality and the wide variations in losses.

Name—rig	Date	Trade	Shipped	Died	Landed *
Huntress—brig	1864	Cuban	750	250	500
John Bell—brig	1861	"	482	82	400
Haidee—ship	1858	"	1,100	200	900
W. D. Miller—brig	1857	"	470	58	412
Julia Moulton—brig	1854	"	665	165	500
Paez—bark	1857	"	570	170	400
P. Soule—brig	1855	"	479	12	467
Unknown slaver	1860	"	400	40	360
Herald—ship	1848	Brazilian	1,150	40	1,100
Senator—brig	1847	"	900	300	600
Fame—bark	1847	"	530	3	527
Bogota—bark	1860	Cuban	418	7	411
Wildfire—bark	1860	"	650	100	550
William—bark	1860	"	744	174	570
Putnam—brig	1858	"	450	130	320
Spitfire—schr.	1844	"	346	7	339
Brutus—ship	1860	"	640	140	500
			10,744	1,879	8,865

Percentage of deaths: 17.5

* Number alive when captured by a warship in the West Indies, when applicable.
Sources: *NYDT*, Jan. 26, 1855; June 9, Aug. 3, 1860; May 2, 1861; SED 6, 31-2, pp. 3–5, 22–23; HED 61, 30-2, pp. 15–16; HED 7, 36-2, pp. 69–71, 76–79, 245–247, 616–618; SED 56, 38-1, pp. 19–21; Keys to Whiting, July 8, 1861, Marshals' Letters; A. H. Foote, *Africa and the American Flag* (New York, 1854), pp. 240–241; *New Orleans Daily Picayune*, April 19, 1859; Appendix B.

APPENDIX E

THE AFRICAN SQUADRON

Listed below are the warships assigned to each commander upon the date of his orders to take command (HED 104, 35-2, *passim*). The dispositions of warships given in SED 4, 36-2, and the annual reports of the secretary of the navy, tend to inflate the squadron by including vessels not yet on station and vessels soon to return from African duty. HED 73, 31-1, gives precise assignments of vessels down to 1850. The letter "F" denotes the flagship.

COMMODORE MATTHEW C. PERRY   (May, 1843)
Macedonian (F) – frigate   *Decatur* – 3d-class sloop
Saratoga – 1st-class sloop   *Porpoise* – brig

COMMODORE CHARLES W. SKINNER   (Dec., 1844)
Jamestown (F) – 1st-class sloop   *Yorktown* – 3d-class sloop
Decatur – 3d-class sloop   *Truxtun* – brig

COMMODORE GEORGE C. READ   (Dec., 1845)
United States (F) – frigate   *Marion* – 3d-class sloop
Boxer – brig   *Dolphin* – brig

COMMODORE WILLIAM C. BOLTON   (Sept., 1847)
Jamestown (F)–1st-class sloop   *Dolphin*–brig
                      Boxer – brig

COMMODORE BENJAMIN COOPER   (Nov., 1848)
Portsmouth (F) – 1st-class sloop   *Yorktown* – 3d-class sloop
Porpoise – brig   *Decatur* – 3d-class sloop
                      Bainbridge – brig

COMMODORE FRANCIS H. GREGORY   (Aug., 1849)
Portsmouth (F) – 1st-class sloop   *John Adams* – 2d-class sloop

Yorktown – 3d-class sloop   *Bainbridge* – brig
Porpoise – brig   *Perry* – brig

COMMODORE ELIE A. F. LAVALLETTE (May, 1851)

Germantown (F) – 1st-class sloop   *John Adams* – 2d-class sloop
Dale – 3d-class sloop   *Bainbridge* – brig
    Perry – brig

COMMODORE ISAAC MAYO (Dec., 1852)

Constitution (F) – frigate   *John Adams* – 2d-class sloop
Dale – 3d-class sloop   *Bainbridge* – brig
    Perry – brig

COMMODORE THOMAS CRABBE (April, 1855)

Jamestown (F) – 1st-class sloop   *St. Louis* – 1st-class sloop
Dale – 3d-class sloop   *Dolphin* – brig

FLAG OFFICER THOMAS A. CONOVER (June, 1857)

Cumberland (F) – 1st-class sloop   *St. Louis* – 1st-class sloop
    Dale – 3d-class sloop

FLAG OFFICER WILLIAM INMAN (May, 1859)

Constellation (F) – 1st-class sloop   *Portsmouth* – 1st-class sloop
Vincennes – 2d-class sloop   *Marion* – 3d-class sloop
San Jacinto – 1st-class steam sloop   *Mohican* – 2d-class steam sloop
Mystic – 3d-class steamer   *Sumpter* – 3d-class steamer

APPENDIX F

SOME AMERICAN SLAVERS IN THE CUBAN TRADE, 1837–1840

Washington – schooner. Cleared Havana 10-3-37; landed slaves 4-38.

Eagle – brig. Cleared Havana 5-9-38; suspected of carrying slaves to Brazil. Cleared Bahia 2-39; captured by H.M.S. *Buzzard* 3-12-39; condemned at Sierra Leone as Spanish property.

Mary Cushing – schooner. Cleared Havana 5-21-38; suspected of carrying slaves to Brazil. Cleared Bahia 1-26-39; captured by H.M.S. *Waterwitch* 9-27-39 with 427 slaves.

Ontario – schooner. Cleared Havana 6-38; captured by H.M.S. *Pelican* 12-18-38 with 220 slaves.

Dolphin – schooner. Cleared Havana 8-18-38; captured by H.M.S. *Waterwitch* 7-8-39 with 344 slaves.

Venus – ship. Cleared Havana 8-23-38; landed 860 slaves 1-39.

Euphrates – schooner. Cleared Havana 12-7-38; captured by H.M.S. *Harlequin* 7-39; sent to Philadelphia by U.S. consul at Monrovia.

Clara – schooner. Cleared Havana 11-7-38; captured by H.M.S. *Buzzard* 3-18-39; condemned at Sierra Leone as Spanish property.

Rebecca – schooner. Cleared Havana 1-23-39; captured by H.M.S. *Forester* 3-22-39; condemned at Sierra Leone.

Wyoming – brig. Cleared Havana 3-6-39; captured by H.M.S. *Buzzard* 5-17-39; condemned at New York.

George Crooks – schooner. Reported to have escaped from Africa with slaves, 7-39.

Hound – schooner. Cleared Havana 6-17-39; reported to have escaped with slaves.

Catharine – schooner. Cleared Havana 6-25-39; captured by H.M.S. *Dolphin* 8-13-39; condemned at New York.

Elvira – schooner. Cleared Havana 6-26-39; landed slaves in Cuba.

Butterfly – schooner. Cleared Havana 7-2-39; captured by H.M.S. *Dolphin* 8-26-39; condemned at New York.

Lark – schooner. Cleared Havana 9-10-39; captured by H.M.S. *Wolverine* 1-16-40; condemned at Sierra Leone as Spanish property.

Campbell – schooner. Cleared Havana 9-24-39; captured by a British cruiser 12-1-39. Notable as the former revenue cutter of Baltimore, sold out of federal service during 1839.

Laura – schooner. Cleared Havana and Matanzas 10-39; captured by H.M.S. *Viper* 1-7-40; condemned at Sierra Leone as Spanish property.

Asp – schooner. Cleared Havana 11-14-39; captured by H.M.S. *Wolverine* 1-16-40; condemned at Sierra Leone as Spanish property.

Sarah Anne – schooner. Captured by H.M.S. *Bonetta* 3-3-40; delivered by agreement to U.S.S. *Grampus;* condemned at New York.

SOURCES: H. Rep. 283, 27-3, pp. 497, 505, 519–521, 540, 649–654, 667–668, 687, 693–694, 707–709; *Baltimore Sun,* April 8, 30, 1840; and text references.

APPENDIX G

SOME AMERICAN SLAVERS IN THE BRAZILIAN TRADE, 1840–1850

Sophia – brig. Cleared Rio de Janeiro 2-21-41; transferred to Brazilians; landed slaves in Brazil.

Illinois – schooner. Cleared Bahia in 1842; destroyed by British cruisers 9-21-42 near Whydah.

Yankee – brig. Cleared Bahia in 1843; landed slaves in Brazil.

Leda – schooner. Cleared Bahia in 1843; landed slaves in Brazil.

Duan – brig. Cleared Rio 7-9-43; landed slaves.

Hope – brig. Cleared Rio 8-4-43; fitted out at Victoria, Brazil; shipped 600 slaves.

Ganneclifft – brig. Shipped slaves 3-44; landed them in Brazil.

Montevideo – brig. Cleared Rio 2-11-44; fitted out at Victoria; landed the survivors of 800 slaves in Brazil.

Agnes – brig. Cleared Rio in 1844; landed 500 slaves.

Kentucky – brig. Cleared Rio 3-31-44; landed 500 slaves.

Sooy – brig. Cleared Bahia 4-26-44; landed slaves.

Washington's Barge – brig. Cleared Bahia 12-44; landed slaves.

Calhoun – ship. Cleared Bahia 5-21-45; wrecked on African coast.

Pons – bark. Cleared Rio 7-21-45; captured by U.S.S. *Yorktown* 12-45.

Panther – ship. Cleared Rio 8-7-45; captured by U.S.S. *Yorktown* 12-45.

Enterprise – schooner. Cleared Rio 10-12-45; landed slaves. Notable as being a former United States naval vessel sold out of federal service in 1845.

Fame – bark. Cleared Rio 12-31-46 as a "whaler"; landed 527 slaves.

Senator – brig. Cleared Rio 1-2-47; landed 600 slaves.

Henry Clay – schooner. Cleared Bahia 1847; reportedly escaped from Africa with slaves.

Martin Van Buren – schooner. Cleared Bahia 1-47; captured by a British cruiser after her transfer to Brazilians.

Malaga – brig. Cleared Rio in 1847; captured with 830 slaves aboard by a British cruiser.

Brazil – brig. Cleared Rio 1-21-48; reportedly landed slaves.

Laurens – bark. Cleared Rio 1-23-48; captured by U.S.S. *On-ka-hy-e* and condemned.

California – bark. Cleared Rio 3-3-48; reportedly landed 400 slaves; later captured by a British cruiser.

M. L. Smith – schooner. Cleared Rio 3-23-48; captured by a British cruiser after her transfer to Brazilians.

Frederica – brig. Cleared Rio 4-1-48 and Pernambuco 5-16-48; reportedly landed slaves.

C. H. Rogers – brig. Cleared Rio 4-12-48; landed slaves.

Herald – ship. Cleared Rio 5-10-48 as a "whaler"; landed 1,100 slaves.

Juliet – schooner. Cleared Rio 6-8-48; reportedly landed slaves.

Globe – bark. Cleared Rio 8-29-48; reportedly landed slaves.

Marion – schooner. Cleared Rio 9-25-48; reportedly landed slaves.

Harriet – brig. Cleared Bahia 11-5-48; captured with 800 slaves by a British cruiser.

Caveira – bark. Cleared Rio in 1848 as a "whaler"; reportedly landed 1,250 slaves.

Mary Chilton – bark. Cleared Rio in 1848; reportedly landed 600 Africans.

Independence – brig. Cleared Rio 12-13-48; captured by U.S.S. *Perry* and condemned.

Zenobia – schooner. Cleared Rio 1-16-49; captured with 550 slaves by a British cruiser.

Quincy – bark. Cleared Rio 3-49; reportedly escaped from Africa with slaves.

Rowana – brig. Cleared Rio 6-11-49; captured by a British cruiser.

R. de Zaldo – brig. Cleared Rio 8-3-49; landed slaves.

Chester – bark. Cleared Rio 8-25-49; outfitted at Victoria; reportedly escaped with slaves.

Snow – brig. Cleared Rio 9-1-49; reportedly escaped with slaves.

Casco – brig. Cleared Rio 9-30-49; captured with a full cargo of slaves by a British cruiser.

Chatsworth – brig. Cleared Bahia in 1849; landed slaves.

Lucy Ann – brig. Cleared Rio in 1849; captured with 540 slaves by a British cruiser.

J. W. Huntington – brig. Cleared Rio 1849; captured by a British cruiser.

Imogene – brig. Cleared Rio in 1849; reportedly escaped with slaves.

Louisa – bark. Cleared Paranagua in 1849; captured with slaves aboard by a British cruiser.

Meteor – brig. Cleared Rio in 1849; reportedly escaped with slaves.

Coronation – brig. Cleared Rio in 1850; captured with 750 slaves by a British cruiser.

Bridgeton – schooner. Cleared Bahia in 1850; reportedly landed 300 Africans.

Navarre – bark. Captured 3-19-50 by a British cruiser.

Excellent – brig. Captured 4-50 by U.S.S. *John Adams* and condemned.

Chatsworth – brig. Cleared Pernambuco 6-27-50; captured by U.S.S. *Perry* and condemned.

Martha – ship. Cleared Rio in 1850; captured by U.S.S. *Perry* and condemned.

SOURCES: SED 217, 28-1, HED 148, 28-2, HED 43, 29-1, SED 28, 30-1, HED 61, 30-2, SED 6, 31-2, *passim; Lords Report,* pp. 439, 450, 455, 513, 516; NA 89–105, # # 22, 76, 78, 82; A. H. Foote, *Africa and the American Flag* (New York, 1854), p. 348; *NYDT,* June 16, 1849; Feb. 1, 1851; *Philadelphia Public Ledger,* March 3, July 14, 1848.

APPENDIX H

SOME AMERICAN SLAVERS FROM CUBAN PORTS, 1857–1860

William D. Miller – brig (175 tons). Cleared 3-3-57; landed 412 slaves at Sierra Morena, Cuba, and was afterward destroyed.

Minnetonka – bark (283). Cleared 4-3-57 under sea letter; carried Africans from Mozambique to Cuba; refitted in Yucatan; captured by H.M.S. *Heron* 4-15-58 while on second slaving voyage.

Joseph H. Record – schooner (110). Cleared 5-6-57 under sea letter; captured by H.M.S. *Antelope* 9-4-57 with 191 slaves.

Abbot Devereux – schooner (114). Cleared 5-9-57 under sea letter; captured by H.M.S. *Teazer* 8-1-57 with 226 slaves.

R. B. Lawton – brig (199). Cleared 5-16-57 under sea letter; reportedly landed 450 slaves on the north coast of Cuba, and afterward was destroyed.

Clara B. Williams – bark (331). Cleared 6-3-57; captured by H.M.S. *Alecto* 10-20-57.

James Buchanan – schooner (142). Cleared 6-23-57; escaped Africa with 300 slaves and landed the survivors in Cuba.

Windward – brig (177). Cleared 7-13-57; captured by H.M.S. *Alecto* 11-23-57 under the name *Lucia* with 603 slaves.

Telegraph – brig (186). Cleared 7-27-57 under sea letter; landed slaves on the south coast of Cuba.

Braman – brig (185). Cleared 8-18-57 under sea letter; captured by H.M.S. *Vesuvius* 10-10-57.

Niagara – schooner (174). Cleared 9-57; captured by H.M.S. *Hecate* 12-6-57.

C. Perkins – brig (176). Cleared 11-27-57; transferred the survivors of 533 slaves to smaller craft at Cayo Sal, Cuba, 4-58.

Wintermoyeh – schooner (96). Cleared 12-18-57 under sea letter; captured by H.M.S. *Conflict* 2-27-58.

R. M. Charleton – brig (140). Cleared 1-5-58 under sea letter; captured by H.M.S. *Medusa* 3-22-58.

General Scott – schooner (125). Cleared 1-25-58; captured by H.M.S. *Teazer* 5-5-58.

Almeida – bark (225). Cleared 2-58 from Santiago; captured by H.M.S. *Conflict* 4-26-58.

Angeline – schooner. Cleared 2-14-58 under sea letter; reported to have landed slaves near Matanzas 6-58.

Governor Parris – bark (210). Cleared 2-25-58 under sea letter; captured by H.M.S. *Heron* 7-2-58.

Lydia Gibbs – schooner (114). Cleared 3-9-58; captured by H.M.S. *Trident* 5-29-58.

St. Andrew – brig (104). Cleared 3-29-58; captured by H.M.S. *Viper* 6-20-58.

Venus – bark (246). Cleared 4-6-58; reportedly escaped from Africa with slaves.

Cortez – schooner (176). Cleared 4-16-58; captured by H.M.S. *Forward* 4-16-58.

Mary Elizabeth – schooner (118). Cleared 4-19-58; captured by H.M.S. *Heron* 7-9-58.

Huntress – brig. Cleared 5-58 from Matanzas; seized at Key West and condemned.

Brothers – ketch. Cleared 7-3-58; seized by U.S.S. *Marion* 9-8-58 but libel dismissed.

C. Perkins – brig (176). Seized at Havana 7-58; libel dismissed.

Lyra – bark (217). Cleared 7-7-58 under sea letter; seized at Key West and condemned.

Rufus Soule – brig (179). Cleared 7-10-58 from Matanzas; captured by H.M.S. *Viper* 10-10-58.

Nancy – brig (219). Seized at Havana 7-58, but libel dismissed.

J. W. Reed – bark (350). Cleared 7-19-58 from Santiago; reported to have escaped from Africa with slaves.

Ardennes – bark (231). Cleared 11-58 under sea letter; seized at Jacksonville but libel dismissed.

J. J. Cobb – bark (308). Cleared 12-58; landed slaves near Matanzas 5-59.

E. A. Rawlins – bark (274). Cleared 3-59; seized near Apalachicola, Florida.

Lillie Mills – brig (199). Cleared 4-20-59 under sea letter; captured by H.M.S. *Archer* 9-20-59.

Tavernier – brig (151). Cleared 7-27-59 from Cardenas; captured by H.M.S. *Viper* 11-4-59 with 518 slaves.

Pamphylia – bark (252). Cleared 9-21-59; outfitted at San Anguilla; captured by H.M.S. *Triton* 1-9-60 with 594 slaves.

William – bark (264). Cleared 11-10-59; captured by U.S.S. *Wyandotte* 5-9-60 with 570 slaves.

Erie – ship (500). Cleared 4-60; captured by U.S.S. *Mohican* 8-8-60 with 897 slaves.

Clara Windsor – bark (206). Cleared 8-22-60; captured by H.M.S. *Espoir* 12-14-60 with 677 slaves.

Nancy – brig (219). Cleared 10-30-60; landed 690 slaves at Guenaja, Cuba, 4-61, and was then destroyed.

Lyra – bark (217). Cleared 11-24-60; captured by H.M.S. *Ranger* 10-29-61 with 890 slaves.

Ardennes – bark (231). Cleared 11-28-60; captured by H.M.S. *Wrangler* 4-24-61 with 488 slaves.

Falmouth – brig (208). Cleared 12-4-60; captured by U.S.S. *Sumpter* 6-14-61 but libel dismissed.

Mexina – bark (246). Cleared 12-4-60; reportedly landed slaves in Cuba.

Express – schooner (90). Cleared 12-7-60; captured by U.S.S. *Saratoga* 1-27-61.

Toccoa – brig (227). Cleared 12-20-60; captured by U.S.S. *Mohawk* 12-20-60 and condemned.

Mary J. Kimball – bark (398). Cleared 12-20-60; captured by U.S.S. *Mohawk* 12-21-60 and condemned.

Note: Where no port of departure is specified, Havana is understood.

Sources: HED 7, 36-2, *passim;* SED 49, 35-1, *passim;* appendixes I and J; House of Commons, *Papers, 1861,* LXIV, 360–361; *1865,* LVI, 529.

APPENDIX I

SLAVERS PURCHASED AT NEW YORK, 1857–1860

J. J. Cobb – bark (308 tons.) Purchased 2-28-57 by José A. Mora; outfitted at Havana (see App. H).

Putnam – brig (188). Purchased 3-7-57 by Jonathan Dobson (M); escaped from Africa with slaves 5-57; later sold at New Orleans (see App. J).

Paez – bark (236). Purchased 3-20-57 by Frances M. Chase; cleared 3-22-57; captured by Spanish cruiser *Christina* 9-14-57 with 385 slaves aboard.

Ellen – brig (144). Purchased 4-1-57 by John P. Weeks; seized by federal officers but libel dismissed.

Clara B. Williams – bark (331). Purchased 4-3-57 by Nicholas Danese; outfitted at Havana (see App. H).

Charlotte – brig (231). Purchased 4-9-57 by Guilheme F. de la Figaniere; sold in the Congo River 7-58; escaped with 500 slaves.

Merchant – schooner (199). Purchased 4-13-57 by Thomas Carlin; seized by federal officers but libel dismissed.

Jamestown – schooner (136). Purchased 4-13-57 by Emilio Sanchez y Dolz; believed to have escaped from Africa with slaves in 1857.

Petrel – bark (381). Purchased 5-13-57 by John P. Weeks; captured by Spanish cruiser *Neptuno* 10-57 with 537 slaves.

Eliza Jane – brig (222). Purchased 6-4-57 by James Chaplin; captured by H.M.S. *Alecto* 8-24-57.

Braman – brig (185). Purchased 6-8-57 by John P. Weeks; sold and outfitted at Havana (see App. H).

E. A. Rawlins – bark (273). Purchased 6-11-57 by Alexander Grant; outfitted at Mobile 7-57 and at New Orleans 2-58; reportedly landed slaves on the second voyage.

William G. Lewis – bark (264). Purchased 7-8-57 by Benjamin F. Wenburg; seized at New York but libel abandoned; seized by U.S.S. *Dale* 11-6-57 but libel dismissed.

C. Perkins – brig (176). Purchased 9-28-57 by George Brown (M); outfitted at Havana (see App. H).

Haidee – ship (385). Purchased 1-4-58 by Emilio Sanchez y Dolz; outfitted at Cadiz; landed 903 Africans near Cárdenas, Cuba, 9-58.
General Scott – schooner (140). Purchased 1-6-58 by Adam A. Smalley (M); outfitted at Havana (see App. H).
Cortez – schooner (176). Purchased 3-5-58 by Adam A. Smalley (M); outfitted at Havana (see App. H).
Lyra – bark (217). Purchased 5-4-58 by George Wiggin (M); outfitted at Havana (see App. H).
Wanderer – schooner (235). Purchased 6-7-58 by William C. Corrie (M); partially outfitted at Charleston; landed slaves in Georgia 11-58.
Ellen – brig (143). Purchased 2-27-58 by Joseph Santos, and 6-22-58 by Augiolo Dello Astrologo; escaped from Africa with slaves.
Isla de Cuba – bark (215). Purchased 8-7-58 by Jonathan Dobson (M); taken into Boston by her own crew and condemned.
Panchita – bark (234). Purchased 8-7-58 by Jonathan Dobson; reported to have escaped from Africa with slaves, 1858.
Tavernier – brig (151). Purchased 9-21-58 by William B. Scranton; outfitted at Cárdenas (see App. H).
Tyrant – brig (211). Purchased 11-15-58 by Matthias Lind (M); cleared for Fernando Po, Africa, 11-15-58; landed slaves in Cuba 2-59; seized and condemned at Key West.

Orion – bark (449). Purchased 1-20-59 by Harrison S. Vining; captured by U.S.S. *Marion* 4-21-59 and condemned.
Memphis – ship (798). Purchased 1-19-59 by John B. Moody (M); reportedly escaped from Africa with slaves in 1859.
Star of the East – bark (317). Purchased 2-14-59 by Pierre L. Pearce; cleared for Loando 3-31-59; believed to be a slaver.
Isla de Cuba – bark (215). Purchased 3-17-59 by George M. Rea; believed to have escaped from Africa with slaves, 9-59.
J. Harris – brig (249). Purchased 5-11-59 by Samuel J. Curry; captured by H.M.S. *Spitfire* 9-20-59 with 500 slaves.
Cygnet – brig (199). Purchased 5-21-59 by Henry Gottell (M); cleared for Canary Islands 5-30-59; landed slaves in Cuba and then seized by U.S.S. *Mohawk* 11-18-59; condemned.
Triton – brig (208). Purchased 6-24-59 by Oneseme Buijson; outfitted at New Orleans (see App. J).
Emily – bark (302). Purchased 6-25-59 by William Richardson; seized by U.S.S. *Portsmouth* 9-21-59 but libel dismissed; cleared again for Congo River on 2-4-60, with unknown results.

Atlantic – ship (699). Purchased 6-27-59 by Francis J. Silva; seized at New London 7-59 but libel abandoned.

Orion – bark (449). Purchased 8-19-59 by Thomas Morgan (M); captured by H.M.S. *Pluto* 11-30-59 with 888 slaves.

Lyra – bark (217). Purchased 11-4-59 by William Thompson (M); outfitted at Havana (see App. H).

Wildfire – bark (338). Purchased 12-13-59 by Pierre L. Pearce; cleared for St. Thomas, Danish West Indies, and partially outfitted there; captured by U.S.S. *Mohawk* 4-26-60 with 530 slaves.

William G. Lewis – bark (264). Purchased 12-27-59 by Lima Viana (register #670) and immediately afterward by Francis Rivery (#671); cleared for Congo River 1-21-60; captured off Cuba by a Spanish cruiser on 6-27-60 with 300 Africans aboard.

Sultana – bark (452). Purchased 1-11-60 by Francis Braggiati and James T. Wood; cleared for Congo River 1-26-60; reportedly landed slaves in Cuba 6-60.

William R. Kibby – brig (190). Purchased 1-12-60 by Charles H. Smith; cleared for Congo River 1-28-60; landed slaves in Cuba and seized by U.S.S. *Crusader* with 3 Africans on 7-23-60.

White Cloud – bark (285). Purchased 3-15-60 by Pierre L. Pearce; sold into Montevidean registry at Havana 4-60, and renamed *Constantia;* captured by H.M.S. *Alecto* 8-15-60.

City of Norfolk – steamer (572). Purchased 3-20-60 by Albert Horn; captured by Spanish cruiser *Isabel Francesca* 10-3-60 with 560 slaves aboard.

Falmouth – brig (208). Purchased 3-28-60 by Francis Rivery; cleared for Congo River same date; captured by U.S.S. *Portsmouth* 5-6-60 and condemned.

Montauk – ship (505). Purchased 3-28-60 by William Sharpe ($\frac{1}{4}$), John D. Wilson ($\frac{1}{2}$), and John T. Pringle ($\frac{1}{4}$); cleared as a whaler on 4-28-60; captured 12-21-60 by Spanish cruiser *Neptuno* with 916 slaves, while under the assumed name *Lesbia*.

Atlantic – ship (699). Purchased 4-6-60 by Robert McCormick; cleared as a whaler 4-7-60; landed slaves in Cuba 12-60.

Storm King – brig (220). Purchased 5-1-60 by John Lockhart (M); cleared for Congo River 5-2-60; captured 8-8-60 by U.S.S. *San Jacinto* with 619 slaves.

Cora – bark (403). Purchased 5-4-60 by John Latham (M); captured by U.S.S. *Constellation* 9-26-60 with 705 slaves.

Buckeye – bark (328). Purchased 5-18-60 by James G. Baker; landed 500 slaves in Cuba, 1860.

Kate – bark (267). Purchased 5-30-60 by Charles N. Lake; seized at New York 7-3-60 and condemned.

Thomas Watson – ship (349). Purchased 6-13-60 by Mary Jane Watson; cleared as a whaler; reportedly landed slaves in Cuba.

Mariquita – schooner (145). Purchased 6-16-16 by Lima Viana; seized at New York but libel abandoned.

Clara Windsor – bark (206). Purchased 6-30-60 by William H. Powers (M); outfitted at Havana (see App. H).

Bonito – brig (277). Purchased 7-9-60 by Joseph W. Purdy; captured by U.S.S. *San Jacinto* 10-10-60 with 750 slaves.

Nightingale – ship (1,066). Purchased 8-30-60 by Francis Bowen (M), John N. Hall, and E. P. Stephens; outfitted at Liverpool; captured by U.S.S. *Saratoga* 4-21-61 with 961 slaves.

Ardennes – bark (231). Purchased 8-30-60 by George T. Pluma; outfitted at Havana (see App. H).

Weather Gage – bark (365). Purchased 9-11-60 by John Morris; seized at New York 10-60 and condemned.

Falmouth – brig (208). Purchased 10-12-60 by George H. Seinas (M); outfitted at Havana (see App. H).

NOTE: The letter "M" denotes an owner-master.

SOURCES: New York Registers Sail, vols. 114–130 *passim;* New York Registers Steam, vol. 1 *passim;* HED 7, 36-2, *passim;* SED 49, 35-1, *passim;* House of Commons, *Papers, 1861,* LXIV, 360–361; *1865,* LVI, 529; *NYDT,* June 5, 1860 (p. 4), and daily shipping columns, *passim.*

APPENDIX J

SLAVERS PURCHASED AT NEW ORLEANS, 1856–1860

W. D. Miller – brig (175 tons). Purchased 3-13-56 by Joseph Villarubia, Jr.; outfitted at Havana (see App. H).

Ardennes – bark (231). Purchased 11-14-56 by Benjamin F. Tisdale; sold and outfitted at Havana (see App. H).

Mary Elizabeth – brig (150). Purchased 12-23-56 by James B. McConnell (M); outfitted at Havana (see App. H).

Adams Gray – brig (152). Purchased 1-31-57 by John Henry (M); cleared for Cárdenas 2-5-57; captured by H.M.S. *Prometheus* 4-16-57.

Jupiter – schooner (167). Purchased 2-57 by John Gilbert (M); cleared for Teneriffe 2-26-57; captured by H.M.S. *Antelope* 6-29-57 with 70 slaves.

William Clark – brig (180). Purchased 2-12-57 by Francis Ranger (M); cleared for Teneriffe 2-26-57; captured by H.M.S. *Firefly* 8-22-57.

Splendid – bark (270). Purchased 2-12-57 by Joseph A. Barbosa; cleared for Nuevitas 2-12-57; captured by Portuguese cruiser *Cabo Verde* 7-17-57 under the assumed name *Velha Anita*.

Nancy – brig (219). Purchased 2-23-57 by Marcus N. Radovich (M); cleared for Ambriz 3-7-57; landed slaves in Cuba, late 1857.

Wizard – brig (191). Purchased 3-20-57 by John J. Miller (M); cleared for Ambriz 3-26-57; reportedly escaped from Africa with slaves.

Charles – ship (381). Purchased 3-27-57 by John S. Vent (M); cleared for Ambriz 3-28-57; driven ashore by H.M.S. *Sappho* 9-18-57, 358 of the Africans aboard being rescued.

Vesta – bark (259). Purchased 4-26-57 by William Smith (M); cleared for Ambriz 4-26-57; captured by Spanish cruiser *Isabel Segunda* 10-5-57 with 169 slaves.

Lewis McLain – schooner (176). Purchased 4-29-57 by John H. Hinckley (M); cleared for Annobon 5-1-57; captured by H.M.S. *Alecto* 10-15-57.

Windward – brig (177). Purchased 6-18-57 by Charles Rauch (M); outfitted at Havana (see App. H).

Putnam – brig (188). Purchased 11-27-57 by Edward C. Townsend (M); captured by U.S.S. *Dolphin* 8-21-58 with 318 Africans.

J. W. Reed – bark (350). Purchased 5-5-58 by Frederick B. Sladden (M); outfitted at Santiago (see App. H).

Toccoa – brig (227). Purchased 11-2-58 by Anthony Horta; outfitted at Havana (see App. H).

William H. Stewart – brig (207). Purchased 12-7-58 by Salvador Prats; sold into Chilean registry at Havana 9-59; captured by H.M.S. *Archer* 1-30-60.

Brownsville – brig (148). Purchased 2-9-59 by Salvador Prats; cleared for Congo River 2-14-59; reportedly landed slaves in Cuba.

Rebecca – ship (534). Purchased 3-29-59 by Salvador Prats; cleared for Monrovia 4-27-59; reportedly landed slaves in Cuba.

Stephen H. Townsend – schooner (182). Purchased 4-15-59 by Thomas A. Myers (M); cleared for St. Thomas 4-16-59; captured by H.M.S. *Archer* 7-23-59.

Mary J. Kimball – bark (398). Purchased 5-24-59 by five owners; outfitted at Havana (see App. H).

Triton – brig (208). Purchased 8-22-59 by John O. Dupeire from Onesime Buijson, who remained as master; captured by U.S.S. *Mystic* 7-16-60 and condemned.

William R. Kibby – brig (191). Purchased 11-21-59 by Ignacio de Ayala; sold and outfitted at New York (see App. I).

Peter Mowell – schooner (119). Purchased 2-6-60 by Salvador Prats; cleared for Monrovia 2-9-60; believed to be a slaver.

Nancy – brig (219). Purchased 6-9-60 by P. Oscar Aleix; outfitted at Havana (see App. H).

Mexina – bark (208). Purchased 11-12-60 by Salvador Prats; outfitted at Havana (see App. H).

NOTE: The letter "M" denotes an owner-master. There was some uncertainty as to whether or not the vessel destroyed by the *Sappho* was the *Charles* (see Napier to Cass, Jan. 7, 1858, with encs., SED 49, 35-1, pp. 30–34). There was, however, no ship *James Titers* registered at New Orleans.

SOURCES: *New Orleans Daily Picayune*, shipping columns; Work Projects Administration, *Ship Registers and Enrollments of New Orleans, Louisiana* (6 vols.; Baton Rouge: Louisiana State University Press, 1942), V, *passim;* HED 7, 36-2, *passim;* SED 49, 35-1, *passim;* House of Commons, *Papers, 1861,* LXIV, 360–361; *1865,* LVI, 529.

APPENDIX K

SIZE OF THE AFRICAN SLAVE TRADE, 1857–1860

As official estimates of the size of the slave trade are erratic and are based upon uncertain materials, another possible method of calculation is to consider the number of known slavers and to draw conclusions from it.

One of the striking facts about the late years of the trade was the large number of vessels captured. Between 1857 and 1860 the British took about seventy prizes, nearly all of which were confiscated (House of Commons, *Papers, 1861,* LXIV, 360–361; *1865,* LVI, 529–530). The American squadron and officers in American ports seized many vessels, though some were released by the courts. The Spanish navy made a number of captures (see, e.g., *State Papers,* LII, 698, 713), and even the tiny Portuguese squadron had some slight effect on the trade. Disregarding vessels that were released because of insufficient evidence or that landed slaves before being captured, there were more than a hundred slavers captured by the law before they had succeeded in landing their living freight.

Roughly seven of every ten of the slavers listed in Appendixes H, I, and J were captured. These, of course, do not comprise all slavers, but only those whose ports of origin are known. These appendixes exaggerate the risks of the trade. When a vessel was captured its guilt became a matter of record, and doubtless some successful slaving voyages were sufficiently well concealed so that the vessel never became suspicious enough to be included on a list of slave vessels. But really suspicious vessels are far less numerous than known slavers, so that a fair figure on a slaver's chances of success might be two out of five. If these odds held up, 65 slavers should have been successful while 100 others were being captured. The figure of 65 in the four-year period would take care of all known successful slavers, and leave a comfortable allowance for merely suspicious vessels—some of which were slavers and some of which were not. The number of slavers was apparently about the same each year; American and Spanish cruisers made more captures in 1860, but British captures declined.

Sixty-five slavers could not have landed nearly enough Africans to satisfy the more extreme estimates. The slavers of 1857–1858 seem to have averaged about 200 tons; the New York and New Orleans slavers were somewhat larger, and the Havana-based slavers were smaller. In 1859–1860 the size of slavers increased sharply. In 1857 the 381-ton *Charles* and *Petrel* and 331-ton *Clara B. Williams* were unusually large, but by 1860 vessels engaged in the trade included the 572-ton *City of Norfolk* and the largest of all slavers, the 1,066-ton *Nightingale*. The average tonnage of the 1859–1860 slavers listed in the appendixes is nearly 100 tons more than the average of 1857–1858 slavers. The successful slavers of 1857–1858 might have reached an aggregate of 6,000 tons, and those of 1859–1860, 11,000 tons.

We know far too little about the carrying capacity of slavers. Most of those captured had no Africans aboard, and the reports of landings are seldom very reliable about the exact number. But there are a score of cases in which the number of Africans captured, reported carried off, or landed is accurately known, and also the tonnage of the vessel. The average is about two Africans per ton, a generous figure considering that the majority of the reports give the number of slaves who left Africa, not the number who survived to be landed. Allowing two Africans landed alive for each ton of successful slaver, the total imports into the United States and Cuba in 1857 and 1858 could have been little more than 6,000 each year, and, in 1859–1860, 11,000 a year.

How many of these Africans were destined for Cuban plantations, and how many for American, remains an enigma. It is a fact that when the place of landing is definitely known, it was almost always Cuba. Of course this does not mean that slaves put ashore in Cuba proper or on offshore cays remained there. Cuba could have been used as a smugglers' rendezvous, taking in the large-scale landings and sending on the Africans to the United States in smaller, more easily concealed groups. The historian of Cuban slavery, puzzled by the fact that the number of slaves seemed to increase very slowly despite British reports of numerous landings, was forced to conclude that nearly all the Africans were later taken to the United States (Hubert H. S. Aimes, *A History of Slavery in Cuba, 1511 to 1868* [New York: Putnam, 1907], pp. 247–248). But the smuggled slave was as elusive in the United States as he was in Cuba, and it may be asked why the Cuban coast was more inviting than the American for landings, as the Florida coast line was, if anything, less well patrolled than the Cuban. The most reasonable conclusion seems to be that most of the Africans remained in Cuba, and that they were far fewer than the British claimed.

APPENDIX L

THE DEPARTMENT OF THE INTERIOR AND THE SLAVE TRADE

It is sometimes said that one of the reforms introduced by the Lincoln administration into the enforcement of the slave-trade acts was the centralization of all law enforcement activities under the Department of the Interior. Previously the State, Navy, and Treasury departments, the attorney general, and the various semiautonomous marshals and district attorneys had shared authority in this field; but, as Lincoln stated in his first annual message, "the execution of the laws for the suppression of the African slave trade has been confided to the Department of the Interior" (SED 1, 37-2, p. 13). Within that department there was established the Office for the Suppression of the African Slave Trade.

There is reason to believe, however, that this administrative reorganization was undertaken primarily for political purposes; that it was intended to give the appearance that the administration was implementing Republican promises to accomplish what the Democrats had allegedly not wanted to do. The executive order making the change was dated May 2, 1861, and it read: "The Secretary of the Interior is hereby charged with the execution of the Act approved March 3, 1819, and all subsequent Acts for the suppression of the African Slave Trade" (National Archives Microfilm Publications, "Records of the Office of the Secretary of the Interior relating to the Suppression of the African Slave Trade," Letters Received from the President, the Executive Departments, and Congress, 1858–1872).

The only Act for suppression of the African slave trade "subsequent" to the act of 1819 was the piracy act of May 15, 1820. Apparently the secretary of the interior was to supervise piracy prosecutions. But what of prosecutions under the act of May 10, 1800, for serving aboard vessels that had not yet shipped slaves, and the act of April 20, 1818, for fitting out slavers in American ports? What of suits for forfeiture of vessels under either of those acts, or under the act of March 22, 1794? These were all vital parts of slave-trade suppression, yet they were apparently not "confided" to the secretary of the interior and his new office. And the inclusion of the act of March 3, 1819, within his jurisdiction raised new problems. One part of that act dealt with the resettlement of liberated Africans in Liberia, but another part authorized the president to employ naval vessels and revenue cutters to "seize, take, and bring into any port" American slavers (3 *U.S. Stat. at L.* 532–533). Was the secretary of the interior supposed to give orders to the Navy and Treasury departments about the employment of their vessels?

During the following months it became clear to anyone privy to the secrets of the Department of the Interior that the reorganization was mostly buncombe. The office specializing in the punishment of law violators consisted of three men: George C. Whiting, a Virginia Unionist, and two clerks (*Register of Officers and Agents . . . of the United States, on the thirtieth September 1861* [Washington: Government Printing Office, 1862], p. 73). Neither Whiting nor Secretary of the Interior Caleb B. Smith gave any orders to warships, or consuls, or ministers. They received no reports directly from these field officers. Their control over marshals and attorneys was very slight. They did assemble all the marshals at New York in the summer of 1861, and had them inspect real slavers so that they could keep a sharper lookout for future expeditions. But that was their principal positive action, if the records of the office give any indication of its work. Dozens of letters came to the Department of the Interior from marshals and attorneys, but these letters were not regular reports of what the local officers were doing to combat the slave trade. On the contrary, not even all the piracy prosecutions were reported to the department; references to the *Bonito* prisoners, Captain Booth, and Captain Horn, for example, are lacking. The district attorney at New York apparently did as he pleased with them without making reports. No reports of prosecutions, or intended prosecutions, against men or ships under the acts of 1800 and 1818 were furnished. In short, marshals and attorneys went about their work paying little attention to the new office, except when they wanted some extra money. Then they wrote in, and the office paid out money if it thought the expenses justified. At various dates subsequent to March 3, 1819, Congress had appropriated money for extraordinary expenses arising from slave-trade suppression activities. Whiting and Smith controlled the money, and that was their principal function.

If Lincoln did not in fact place the secretary of the interior in charge of slave-trade suppression, did his order make the suppression more efficient? By no means. Lincoln merely formalized what the secretary of the interior had been doing under Buchanan. Jacob Thompson had supervised the resettlement of liberated Africans in Liberia, and had handled the money disbursed on that account. He had obtained counsel to assist District Attorney Tatum in the Key West prosecutions of 1860, and he had paid for other slave-trade suppression activities. Thompson had been in fact more active than Smith, for he took partial charge of the actions to prevent slave imports. Occasionally he sent warnings of rumored landings to marshals and attorneys, and it was he who sent off detective Slocumb. The fact that Thompson had got involved in these activities more or less by chance did not make him any less effective. The tale that the Republicans set up a new administrative structure to crush the slave trade is mere partisan talk. (The Marshals' and Attorneys' Letters, cited frequently herein, are very revealing, but the best sources for study of this topic are National Archives Microfilm Publications, *Records . . . relating to the Suppression of the African Slave Trade,* Register of Letters Received, 1858–1872; Letters Sent, 1858–1872; and Miscellaneous Letters Received, 1858–1871.)

APPENDIX M

BALTIMORE-BUILT SLAVERS OF THE
1840's AND THE 1850's

Following is a list of slaving vessels built in Baltimore in the 1840's and the 1850's. The date of construction follows the name; in parentheses is the date of the vessel's known entry into the slave trade. A single asterisk indicates vessels built in Dorchester County; a double asterisk, those built in Talbot County.

Cortez, 1852 (1858); *General Scott*, 1850 * (1858); *Storm King*, 1854 ** (1860); *Kate*, 1853 (1860); *Thomas Watson*, 1848 (1860); *Clara Windsor*, 1851 (1860); *Falmouth*, 1847 (1860); *Cora*, 1851 (1860); *Lyra*, 1847 (1858); *Ellen*, 1846 (1857); *W. R. Kibby*, 1853 (1859); *Merchant*, 1849 (1857); *C. F. A. Cole*, 1851 * (1856); *Braman*, 1851 (1856); *C. B. Williams*, 1854 (1857); *Adams Gray*, 1848 (1857); *Mary Elizabeth*, 1848 (1858); *Nancy*, 1848 (1857); *Rebecca*, 1849 (1859); *W. H. Stewart*, 1851 * (1858); *Putnam*, 1845 (1857); *Glamorgan*, 1843 (1854); *Oregon*, 1845 * (1854).

Many slavers of this period were built in Maine, Massachusetts, and other shipbuilding centers outside Maryland: Hanover, Mass.: *Silenus*, 1840 (1852); Newburyport, Mass.: *Mariquita*, 1858 (1860); *Ardennes*, 1844 (1858); Cohasset, Mass.: *Panchita*, 1839 (1856); Amesbury, Mass.: *Wildfire*, 1853 (1859); Salem, Mass.: *Herald*, 1822 (1845); Kingston, Mass.: *Charles*, 1836 (1857); Boston, Mass.: *Sultana*, 1850 (1860); Salisbury, Mass.: *Cyrus*, 1836 (1842); Robbinston, Me.: *Horatio*, 1849 (1854); *J. J. Cobb*, 1850 (1858); Bath, Me.: *Brownsville*, 1851 (1859); Damariscotta, Me.: *J. W. Reed*, 1857 (1858);

Rockland, Me.: *Lewis McLain,* 1853 (1857); *Tyrant,* 1854 (1858); *M. J. Kimball,* 1853 (1860); Calais, Me.: *Cygnet,* 1856 (1859); Newcastle, Me.: *Orion,* 1846 (1859); Freeport, Me.: *Rufus Soule,* 1844 (1858); Belfast, Me.: *Mexina,* 1849 (1860); Camden, Me.: *Toccoa,* 1854 (1860); Prospect, Me.: *J. Harris,* 1853 (1859); Richmond, Me.: *Vesta,* 1847 (1857); Pembroke, Me.: *W. G. Lewis,* 1857 (1857); *Petrel,* 1851 (1857); Bristol, R.I.: *White Cloud,* 1849 (1860); Providence, R.I.: *Haidee,* 1854 (1858); Haddam, Conn.: *Uncas,* 1833 (1843); Syrene, Conn.: *J. P. Glover,* 1846 (1857); Portsmouth, N.H.: *Nightingale,* 1851 (1860); Brookhaven, N.Y.: *Wanderer,* 1857 (1858); Sag Harbor, N.Y.: *Charlotte,* 1850 (1857); *Weather Gage,* 1852 (1860); New York, N.Y.: *Bonito,* 1853 (1860); *Atlantic,* 1836 (1859); *Montauk,* 1844 (1860); *Memphis,* 1839 (1859); *Isla de Cuba,* 1849 (1858); Milwell, N.J.: *Eliza Jane,* 1847 (1857); Philadelphia, Pa.: *Paez,* 1846 (1857); *Emily,* 1848 (1859); Norfolk, Va.: *E. A. Rawlins,* 1854 (1857); Conwayboro, S.C.: *C. Perkins,* 1854 (1857); Covington, Ky.: *Buckeye,* 1852 (1860); French-built: *Tavernier,* date unknown.

SOURCES: Work Projects Administration, *Ship Registers and Enrollments of New Orleans, Louisiana* (6 vols.; Baton Rouge: Louisiana State University Press, 1942), IV, 67, 285; V, 2, 18, 35, 43, 147, 172, 173, 178, 185, 198, 214, 217, 227, 243, 256, 258, 264, 269, 273, 274, 278; register of the *Lewis McLain,* National Archives; SED 34, 27-1, p. 33; SED 28, 30-1, p. 105; New York Registers Sail, vol. 94, #429; vol. 103, #675; vol. 114, ## 116, 124; vol. 115, ## 166, 212, 225, 237; vol. 116, ## 317, 338, 359, 367, 368; vol. 117, #566; vol. 119, #10; vol. 120, #152; vol. 121, ## 315, 347, 363, 411; vol. 122, ## 483, 492, 494, 570; vol. 123, ## 713, 36, 37; vol. 125, ## 244, 260, 322; vol. 126, #493; vol. 127, ## 587, 670, 26, 63; vol. 128, ## 162, 195, 216, 220; vol. 129, ## 249, 275, 305, 316, 351, 366; vol. 130, ## 448, 465 (National Archives).

NOTES

ABBREVIATIONS

NYDT	*New York Daily Tribune*
Lords Report	*Report from the select committee of the House of Lords . . . for the final extinction of the African slave trade . . . 15 February 1850*
State Papers	*British and Foreign State Papers*

EXAMPLES OF CONGRESSIONAL DOCUMENTS

HED 7, 36-2	H. Exec. Doc. 7, 36th Cong., 2d sess.
H. Rep. 283, 27-3	H. Rep. 283, 27th Cong., 3d sess.
SED 6, 31-2	S. Exec. Doc. 6, 31st Cong., 2d sess.

DOCUMENTS IN THE NATIONAL ARCHIVES

Microfilm Publications

NA 89	Letters Received from Commanding Officers of Squadrons (reels 20, 102–107, 109–112)
Attorneys' Letters	Records of the Office of the Secretary of the Interior relating to the Suppression of the African Slave Trade, Letters Received from United States Attorneys, 1854–1869
Marshals' Letters	Records . . . relating to the Suppression of the African Slave Trade, Letters Received from United States Marshals, 1857–1869

Records Group 45: Letters Received by the Secretary of the Navy

Captains' Letters	Letters from Captains (by year, volume number, and item number)
Commanders' Letters	Letters from Commanders (by year, volume number, and item number)
Officers' Letters	Letters from Officers beneath the Rank of Commander (by volume for month and year, and item number)

Records Group 60: Letters Received by the Attorney General

Attorney General's Letters	Letters from U.S. Attorneys, Marshals, and Judges

Records Group 206: Letters Received by the Solicitor of the Treasury

Solicitor's Letters	Letters from U.S. Attorneys, Clerks of Court, and Marshals

NOTES

1. THE ILLEGAL SLAVE TRADE

[1] Craven to Toucey, June 8, 1860, HED 7, 36-2, p. 619.

[2] For mortalities aboard specific slavers, see Appendix D. An estimate of $16\frac{1}{2}$ per cent for the Cuban trade was given in Appleton to McKeon, June 9, 1857, HED 7, 36-2, p. 67. Mortality in the Brazilian trade may have been somewhat lower; some estimates ranged from 10 to 15 per cent (*Lords Report,* pp. 192, 257, 335).

[3] See, e.g., Dyer and Hibbard to Usher, Feb. 21, 1864, SED 56, 38-1, p. 24.

[4] In the Brazilian trade in the mid-'forties, British commissioners at Rio de Janeiro estimated prices at $150–$300 (Samo and Grigg to Aberdeen, Jan. 1, 1844, *State Papers,* XXXIII, 336–337) and $400 (Hesketh and Grigg to Aberdeen, March 21, 1845, *ibid.,* XXXIV, 528–530). American minister H. A. Wise asserted that slaves were bought in Africa for $40–$45 and sold in Brazil for $250–$400 (Wise to Buchanan, May 1, 1845, HED 61, 30-2, p. 150). The British commissioner at Loando estimated that they could be bought for $17.50 and sold at $300, which, after the $85 cost of transportation and all other expenses, meant a profit of 130 per cent on the investment. Gabriel estimated that a fair return—rate unspecified—could be obtained if only one of six slavers got through the blockade (Gabriel to Aberdeen, Dec. 31, 1845, *State Papers,* XXXV, 357). See also Appendix C.

[5] See, e.g., Upshur to Tyler, Dec. 29, 1842, H. Rep. 283, 27-3, pp. 775–776. In the years 1854–1858 British merchants shipped out £4,500,000 worth of goods, and got back African produce valued at £8,000,000 (*Annual Statement of the Trade and Navigation of the United Kingdom . . . in the year 1858* [London, 1859], pp. 341, 380–382).

[6] See *Documents Illustrative of the Formation of the Union,* H. Doc. 398, 69-1, pp. 588–594, 616–618, for the attempt of the Georgia and South Carolina delegates to the Constitutional Convention to force the United States to legalize the slave trade for twenty years.

[7] See, e.g., *Lords Report,* pp. 82, 266, 308–309, 439.

[8] On the movement of "liberated" Africans to the West Indies, see *ibid.,* p. 90. For British efforts to persuade the American government to turn over liberated Africans to their West Indian colonies, see Russell to Lyons, Sept. 22, 1860, *State Papers,* LI, 1100; Irvine to Russell, Oct. 23, 1860, *ibid.,* p. 1102; Russell to Lyons, April 17, 1861, *ibid.,* LII, 722–723. The British here used as a pretext the idea that it would be cheaper for the United States to dispose of liberated Africans in this way than to resettle them in Liberia.

[9] The *Lords Report* is full of statements to the effect that the slave trade hampered legitimate commerce. On the dumping of unneeded cargo, see *ibid.,* pp. 266–267; Willis (U.S. commercial agent at Loando) to Cass, Feb. 12, 1858, HED 7, 36-2, p. 80; July 29, 1859, *ibid.,* p. 352.

[10] This kind of treaty is discussed in chapter 2. A list of treaties between Great Britain and foreign powers relating to the slave trade appears in *Lords Report,* p. 370.

[11] Various incidents are described in the congressional documents listed in the bibliography. Sometimes it is rather difficult to decide whether or not the American vessel was as honest as its crew claimed. For an unquestioned example see the *Caroline* incident, HED 7, 36-2, pp. 320–326.

[12] Upshur to Tyler, Dec. 29, 1842, H. Rep. 283, 27-3, pp. 775–776; Mayo to Dobbin, Nov. 10, 1853, NA 89-107, #36.

[13] *Lords Report,* p. 371; for actual examples, see *ibid.,* pp. 390–404.

[14] See, e.g., the dispute with the Sherbro chiefs in 1857; after they imposed a trade embargo in retaliation for exploitation by British merchants, the governor of Sierra Leone threatened war, declaring that "nothing can be admitted as an excuse for such a violation of Treaty engagements as is involved in a stoppage of lawful trade." The British Public Records Office has microfilmed the correspondence relating to this affair in the reel designated F.O. 2-21; see, especially, item #202.

[15] *Lords Report,* pp. 372–373, and map facing p. 550.

[16] British and American official documents contain very few references to the east African slave trade. One of the few recorded cases in the 1840's was that of the *Kentucky,* in which a Portuguese official was bribed (see deposition of T. H. Boyle, SED 28, 30-1, pp. 71–77). One of the few cases of the 1850's involved the bark *Minnetonka* (see Howard to Marquis de Loule, Jan. 16, 1858, *State Papers,* XLVIII, 1173–1174).

[17] *Lords Report,* p. 373; for the treaty itself see *State Papers,* IV, 85.

[18] For the British interest in keeping Portuguese customhouses out, see, e.g., Gabriel and Jackson to Palmerston, March 9, 1847, *State Papers,*

XXXVI, 528; Brand to Wilmot, Feb. 19, 1853, *ibid.*, XLIV, 1260. The latter volume, pp. 1209–1214, 1257–1279, contains extensive correspondence relating to the dispute over Ambriz. For the case of the Brazilian slaver, see Palmerston to H.M. Commissioners, Oct. 12, 1846, *ibid.*, XXXV, 368.

[19] For favorable testimony about Portuguese activities see *Lords Report,* pp. 269–270, 292, 342, 419; Macaulay to Aberdeen, May 25, 1846, *State Papers,* XXXV, 310; Gabriel to Aberdeen, Dec. 31, 1845, *ibid.*, p. 361; Melville and Hook to Aberdeen, Dec. 31, 1845, *ibid.*, p. 381. For unfavorable reports of the Portuguese see Macaulay and Pettingal to Aberdeen, Oct. 22, 1845, *ibid.*, pp. 371–372; *Lords Report,* pp. 253, 256. For the assistance given by the British in stamping out the trade from Angola see *Lords Report,* p. 387. For Portuguese seizure of a supposed American slaver see the case of the brig *Boxer, Baltimore Sun,* April 4, 1840, p. 2. For the case of an American auxiliary seized at Benguela in 1856, and subsequent prosecutions of the Portuguese implicated, see Gabriel to Clarendon, Feb. 11, May 30, 1857, Feb. 25, 1858, House of Commons, *Slave Trade Papers, 1857–58,* Class A, pp. 69, 76–77, 105.

[20] It is unlikely that the correspondence printed in the British *State Papers* was ignored at Washington, but the facts revealed therein were plainly reported to the State Department in Willis to Cass, Jan. 26, 1859, HED 7, 36-2, p. 301.

[21] In 1845 a British merchant vessel was seized by a Portuguese warship and confiscated by a mixed court (Stanley to Horsfall, Nov. 3, 1846, *State Papers,* XXXV, 369–371); but this is the only such case I found. In 1848 the British squadron's commander registered a formal complaint against the permission given by the Lords Commissioners of the Treasury for a vessel to sail to Africa with a mixed cargo of plank, rice, boilers, and empty casks, but he did not seize the vessel (Hotham to Secy. of Admiralty, Aug. 4, 1848, *Lords Report,* pp. 419–420). In 1848 H.M.S. *Alert* did seize a small English steamer for supplying a slave depot with rice; the vice-admiralty court dismissed the charges (*Lords Report,* pp. 353, 367, 419).

[22] So a House of Commons committee decided in 1842 (H. Rep. 283, 27-3, p. 1053). The 1849 Lords committee heard much testimony about the use of British auxiliaries (*Lords Report,* pp. 74, 213, 217, 238, 240, 262–263, 265). British law forbade the sale of goods to aid the slave trade (5 George IV, c. 113, secs. 5–6), but in practice it proved impossible to obtain convictions. Evidence that the purchaser dealt in slaves was not sufficient unless it could be proved that he dealt only in slaves, and that the seller could not have avoided knowing this fact. For two instructive cases, see *Rex v. Pedro Zulueta the Younger* and *The Newport,* 14 Eng. Rep. 654–667; 174 Eng. Rep. 781–787.

[23] See, e.g., Trist's arguments in SED 125, 26-2, pp. 93–94, 99–110, 136–142.

24 The various American official documents listed in the bibliography are full of illustrations of these traits; it is particularly instructive to read both British and American accounts of any particular incident.

25 The annual volumes of the Treasury Department's *Report . . . on the Commerce and Navigation of the United States* contain a wealth of information on this subject. The reports for fiscal years 1858–1860, e.g., reveal imports valued at $4,900,000 during the three-year period. Although the figures as given do not make it possible to determine precisely the total value of African trade at each port, it appears that in the three items of palm oil, ivory, and gums, Salem led with more than $1 million, Boston had roughly $.5 million, and New York was about midway between them. Baltimore had a small-scale traffic in palm oil, and Providence a fairly brisk trade in ivory; no other ports had any substantial African trade (*Report . . . 1858*, pp. 410–411, 448–449, 476–477, 564–608; *Report . . . 1859*, pp. 408–409, 446–447, 474–475, 556–603; *Report . . . 1860*, pp. 412–413, 450–451, 478–479, 564–608). One set of tables gives the value of merchandise of each type imported into each district, without specifying origin; another set gives the total value of each type of merchandise imported into the entire nation, broken down by origin. Hence the origin of merchandise brought into separate districts can be determined only when there was substantially one source alone for a particular item. More than three-fourths of the palm oil, nearly as much of the ivory, and a large share of the gums came from Africa, so that most of these items imported into a particular district can be set down as African products. The tables do furnish the number of vessels entering each district from each foreign region.

26 See, e.g., A. H. Foote, *Africa and the American Flag* (New York: Appleton, 1854), p. 389; *Annual Report of the Secretary of the Navy, Nov. 1, 1853*, HED 1, 33-1, pp. 388–389; *Report of the Committee on Naval Affairs . . . Praying the Establishment of a Line of Steamers from the United States to the Coast of Africa*, Aug. 1, 1850, H. Rep. 438, 31-1, pp. 7–8.

27 Foote, *op. cit.*, p. 300.

28 Wise also disliked the trade for the support it gave to the abolitionist movement. See his warning to Marine Minister Cavalcanti, related in Wise to Calhoun, Feb. 18, 1845, HED 61, 30-2, pp. 70–86.

29 Wise to Hamilton, Dec. 1, 1844, HED 148, 28-2, p. 62.

30 Wise to Aberdeen, Aug. 31, 1846, SED 28, 30-1, pp. 7, 12–65. This is an elaboration of the charges made earlier and broadcast by President Tyler.

31 The message and correspondence are reprinted in HED 148, 28-2. Tyler's comment was that "it seems to me that the policy it [Great Britain] has adopted is calculated rather to perpetuate than to suppress the trade." He asked, as Wise had, for more stringent American laws.

32 *The Journal of an African Cruiser* was reviewed in the *Boston Post*,

June 24, 1845, p. 1. The review was published anonymously, but the views are plainly Bell's (see Bell to Paulding, July 28, 1840, H. Rep. 283, 27-3, pp. 534–536; Bell to Chester, April 3, 1840, *ibid.*, p. 829). Very few American naval officers had returned from cruises on the African coast by 1844.

[33] Trist to Forsyth, Jan. 12, 1839, HED 34, 27-1, pp. 25–26.

[34] See, e.g., the *Philadelphia Public Ledger* editorial ("The object of the British government in maintaining a fleet on the coast of Africa, is the supply of the British West Indies and British South America with laborers! Huzza for British philanthropy!"), March 15, 1848, p. 2; *New Orleans Daily Picayune*, July 3, 1860, p. 3; Jefferson Davis in *Congressional Globe*, 36th Cong., 1st sess., IV, 2304.

[35] There is a good account of this controversy in Hugh G. Soulsby, *The Right of Search and the Slave Trade in Anglo-American Relations, 1814–1862* (Baltimore: Johns Hopkins Press, 1933). American notes seemingly went so far as to deny that British warships had any right to stop and board vessels hoisting the American flag, to determine if they had American registration papers. This has led to the occasional charge that the United States government proposed to allow pirates of all nationalities to shelter under the American flag, as anyone could easily obtain such a flag and hoist it, but in fact the United States made no such claim. The official position was that British cruisers had no right to stop any vessel showing American colors, if that vessel was actually of American registry. If it was not, the United States was not concerned, and, as a practical matter, would excuse the trespass on an American-registered vessel if the visit aboard was conducted with courtesy and was not unduly prolonged. This explanation was incorporated in the instructions of every American cruiser that went to Africa. See HED 104, 35-2, *passim;* Cass to Napier, April 10, 1858, *State Papers,* L, 716.

[36] For reports of slave-trading companies, see correspondence in HED 148, 28-2, p. 47; H. Rep. 283, 27-3, pp. 678–679; SED 28, 30-1, pp. 19, 24, 26; *State Papers*, XXXIV, 528–530; XXXV, 344–345, 353–355; HED 61, 30-2, pp. 168–169; HED 7, 36-2, pp. 519–520.

[37] For losses in the late Cuban trade, see Appendix K. For losses in the Brazilian trade, see, e.g., *Lords Report*, pp. 352–355, 442–446, which indicates that about half of the slavers sent out from Bahia in 1848 were captured. There seems to be no reliable information on the attrition rate of slavers in the Cuban trade of the 1830's; from the incomplete data available, it would seem that half of the 1837–1862 slavers were captured, the proportion being somewhat lower in the earlier years and higher in the later years.

[38] The notorious Mrs. Mary Jane Watson was used as a "front" by John A. Machado in New York City about 1860. For some details about her career see *NYDT*, Sept. 22, 1862, p. 8; Murray to Seward, Nov. 11, 1861,

SED 56, 38-1, p. 5; Murray to Whiting, March 29, 1862, Marshals' Letters.

[39] The whalers *Herald* and *Fame* were literally stolen from their owners by unscrupulous captains who then put them into the slave trade (SED 6, 31-2, pp. 15–24, 33; HED 61, 30-2, p. 6). The captains of the *Haidee* and the *Governor Parris* were removed from command by criminal subordinates once at sea (HED 7, 36-2, pp. 245–246, 249). The second mate of the schooner *Robert Wilson* was kidnaped and forcibly taken out of Havana aboard that vessel when, discovering that she was a slaver, he attempted to leave (deposition of James Griffin, NA 89-102, #109). A seaman aboard the *Grey Eagle* who thought he was going on an honest voyage denounced the vessel to the authorities after he got ashore (SED 99, 34-1, pp. 61–63). The Rio de Janeiro mercantile firm of Maxwell, Wright, & Co. became an unwitting agent in the chartering of slavers and auxiliaries, and abandoned the business when this was pointed out to them (HED 148, 28-2, pp. 63–88; HED 61, 30-2, p. 24).

[40] In none of the sources was I able to find a single instance of violence offered to American officers by a slaver's crew. Occasionally the British met with violence (e.g., SED 150, 28-2, pp. 109–110, 112), but such instances were rare, perhaps because the British customarily released their prisoners, who thus had the best of reasons to avoid injury in a fight (see, e.g., *Lords Report,* pp. 211, 252, 312, 424). Very few slavers had enough weapons even to attempt resistance; cannon were very rare, and it was seldom that large quantities of muskets or other small arms were found aboard captured vessels.

[41] The only documented slave revolt in the period covered by this book was aboard the *Kentucky* in 1844 (see deposition of T. H. Boyle, SED 28, 30-1, pp. 71–77).

[42] Tonnages of many slave vessels are given in Appendixes H, I, and J. The dimensions of vessels of a particular tonnage were remarkably similar; any collection of ships' registers, such as the New York registers preserved in the National Archives or the New Orleans registers published by Louisiana State University Press in 1942, gives abundant information on the dimensions of vessels of any particular size.

[43] Christopher Lloyd, *The Navy and the Slave Trade* (London: Longmans, Green, 1949), pp. 279–284. See, for an example of a lucky slaver, the *Haidee,* HED 7, 36-2, pp. 245–249; *NYDT,* Oct. 9 (p. 3), 12 (p. 7), 14 (p. 7), 1858.

[44] Some idea of the relative size of the British, French, and Portuguese squadrons in 1846–1847 may be obtained from the fact that American warships cruising along the African coast sighted 113 English, 33 French, and only 3 Portuguese warships (NA 89-103, ## 6, 20–22, 31, 42, 44, 57, 69, 81–84, 91, 95, 106, 109). In 1850 the British squadron numbered 18 ves-

sels; the French, 11 (Gregory to Preston, March 26, Sept. 3, 1850, NA 89-105, ## 64, 244).

[45] See, e.g., McBlair to Toucey, Sept. 23, 1857, HED 7, 36-2, p. 521. Numerous examples of the various techniques are scattered throughout the source materials.

[46] The existence of relatively few slaver-whalers is well documented. Besides the *Herald* and the *Fame,* known examples include the *Atlantic,* the *Augusta,* the *Brutus,* the *Tahmaroo,* and the *Margaret Scott,* all of the latter group from the 1859–1861 period when the whaling industry was badly depressed.

[47] Act of Dec. 31, 1792, Secs. 4, 7, 16, 1 *U.S. Stat. at L.* 289–291, 295.

[48] Numerous examples are scattered through the sources; see, e.g., Ondor to Foote, March 26, 1850, NA 89-105, #86: "Being convinced that her papers were false, I informed the person calling himself master of her, that it was my duty to send him to the American squadron, or in the event of not falling in with them, to New York. He said, he hoped I would not do so. I told him I had no alternative. He immediately went upon deck and ordered the mate to haul the American ensign down, to throw it overboard, and to hoist the Brazilian ensign." But frequently no other flag was hoisted; British cruisers had authority, of course, to capture vessels claiming no nationality, and British vice-admiralty courts had authority to confiscate such vessels. A convenient group of examples from the later 'fifties may be found in HED 7, 36-2, pp. 100, 530–532; SED 49, 35-1, pp. 37–39. All the vessels involved in these affairs had been legitimately cleared, and possessed undoubtedly valid American papers (though held by perjury); the temporary register of the *Clara B. Williams,* though scorned by a British officer, was in fact quite valid. The word "temporary" merely meant that she had been registered in one port to a new owner whose permanent residence was in another port; the register was good until the vessel happened to touch at her new home port. The *Clara B. Williams* had been registered at New York to Nicholas Danese of New Orleans (see National Archives, New York Registers Sail, vol. 115, #212).

[49] Early in 1850 the brig *Lucy Ann* of Boston was intercepted by a British cruiser while she had 540 slaves aboard, but her crew drove all the Africans below and put a boat over the hatch. The American flag was kept flying. But the boarding officer, hearing a groan from below decks, discovered that the vessel was a slaver, whereupon the flag and the papers were quickly disposed of (Hastings to Foote, March 24, 1850, NA 89-105, #78). In September, 1858, the brig *Ellen* of New York was similarly intercepted, and her crew sealed the hatches and produced American papers to preclude inquiry. The boarding party could tell from the stench what kind of vessel the *Ellen* was, but they let her proceed rather than risk an international in-

cident by breaking open the hatches—an act that would probably have led to renunciation of nationality (Grey to Conover, March 21, 1859, NA 89-110, #50). I have found no other cases in which American papers were displayed, even briefly, by a laden slaver.

⁵⁰ See the British cases cited in n. 23, above, and the House of Commons committee opinion reprinted in H. Rep. 283, 27-3, pp. 1050–1053. For American opinions to this effect, see Nelson to Upshur, Aug. 29, 1843, 4 *Opinions of the Attorney General* 245–246; *United States v. Libby*, Fed. Cas. #15,597, vol. 26, pp. 928–936.

⁵¹ SED 6, 31-2, pp. 37–38, 40–41; *Lords Report*, pp. 453–454, 513; *Essex Institute Historical Collections*, XLI (1901), 164. That the bringing back of crews of captured slavers could be big business is suggested by the fact that in 1847–1848, at the peak of the illegal slave trade, there were more than 160 slavers captured by British cruisers, with some 2,600 men aboard. Although a substantial number of these castaways died of fever before they got passage away from the African coast (one estimate was one-fourth), and others came back aboard other slavers, there were still many hundreds to be brought back on auxiliaries (*Lords Report*, pp. 252, 343, 349–355).

⁵² SED 28, 30-1, pp. 126–127; SED 6, 31-2, pp. 37–39; NA 89-103, # # 22, 70; *Essex Institute Historical Collections*, XLII (1902), 98; LXXIII (1937), 366.

⁵³ HED 7, 36-2, pp. 324–326.

⁵⁴ Act of May 10, 1800, Secs. 2–3, 2 *U.S. Stat. at L.* 70–71. No minimum sentence is specified in the statute, but in an early case the judge, convinced that the crime had been committed in ignorance, decided that imprisonment as well as fine was mandatory upon conviction. He sentenced the prisoner to 24 hours in jail and a fine of $10 (*United States v. Vickery*, Fed. Cas. #16,619, vol. 28, p. 374). In later cases fines as small as 1 dollar were imposed (see, e.g., the case of Henry Johnson, *NYDT*, Feb. 19, 1851, p. 6).

⁵⁵ Act of March 22, 1794, Secs. 1–2, 1 *U.S. Stat. at L.* 347–349.

⁵⁶ Act of April 20, 1818, Secs. 2–3, 3 *U.S. Stat. at L.* 451.

⁵⁷ This was not explicitly written into the statute, but any reasonable interpretation of it would give that meaning. It was so interpreted in early Supreme Court decisions: *The Plattsburgh*, 23 U.S. (10 Wheaton) 133; *United States v. Gooding*, 25 U.S. (12 Wheaton) 460.

⁵⁸ Act of May 15, 1820, Secs. 4–5, 3 *U.S. Stat. at L.* 690–691.

⁵⁹ Act of 1818, Sec. 2; act of 1794, Sec. 1; act of 1800, Sec. 1. Note also that slavers could be confiscated under the act of Dec. 31, 1792 (1 *U.S. Stat. at L.* 289 ff.) for unreported sale to foreigners. The act of 1800 also provided (Sec. 1) that the owner could be fined twice the value of his interest in the vessel, but, so far as I have found, this provision remained a dead letter. Most "owners" really had no financial interest.

2. PIRATES AND THE GOVERNMENT

¹ *NYDT,* July 28, 1860, p. 7; *New Orleans Daily Picayune,* July 19 (p. 2), 22 (p. 3), 27 (p. 5), 1860; National Archives, New York Registers Sail, vol. 127 (Nov. 17, 1859, to Feb. 6, 1860), ## 26, 27.

² For a list of captures in 1820–1821 see H. Rep. 283, 27-3, pp. 361–362; for the disappearance of the American flag see *ibid.,* p. 359, and Fox to Forsyth, Oct. 30, 1839, SED 125, 26-2, p. 165. For prosecutions in the early 'twenties, see *United States v. Malebran,* Fed. Cas. #15,711; *United States v. Kennedy,* Fed. Cas. #15,525; *United States v. LaCoste,* Fed. Cas. #15,548; *United States v. Smith,* Fed. Cas. #16,338; *United States v. Andrews,* Fed. Cas. #14,454; *The Alexander,* Fed. Cas. #165; *The La Jeune Eugenie,* Fed. Cas. #15,551.

³ For the existence of this trade, see Trist to Forsyth, Feb. 18, 1841, HED 115, 26-2, pp. 556–557 (quoting an 1834 dispatch); McTavish to Palmerston, Jan. 30, 1840, *State Papers,* XXVIII, 947; and the testimony of Captain John Faunce, *NYDT,* July 15, 1856, p. 8. As to the legal question, at the trial of R. W. Allen, Justice Taney ruled (among other things) that "if a sale was actually made at Havana . . . he is not guilty, if the sale was bona fide," and "to find the defendant guilty he must have had a fixed intention when the vessel left Baltimore to employ her in procuring negroes; his intention must not have been conditional or contingent, depending on future arrangements" (*Baltimore Sun,* Dec. 7, 1839, p. 2). But Allen was indicted under the act of 1818, which was apparently more stringently worded than the act of 1794. Attorney General Nelson—Allen's defense attorney—later ruled that a bona fide sale to a slave trader was lawful, so long as the ex-owner did not then assist the slaving voyage in any manner; but his opinion (4 *Opinions of the Attorney General* 245–246) was only that. It seems to me that, under a reasonably broad interpretation of the act of 1794, an owner could have been fined and his vessel confiscated if he caused it to sail from an American port with the intent that it become a slaver. For further discussion of these two acts see chapter 10.

⁴ The treaty is reprinted in *State Papers,* XXIII, 343–374; see especially Art. X (pp. 352–353) for prohibited equipment. Between 1840 and 1848, inclusive, 152 vessels were brought before Anglo-Spanish, Anglo-Brazilian, and Anglo-Portuguese mixed commissions. Twenty-five had slaves aboard when captured; of the 127 arrested for incriminating equipment, 112 were confiscated (*Lords Report,* pp. 356–368).

⁵ See the report of the Commons committee, quoted in H. Rep. 283, 27-3, pp. 1050–1053, and the report of Inspector General William Irwin in *ibid.,* pp. 1076–1085.

⁶ For the commissioners' estimates, see Kennedy and Schenley to Palmerston, Jan. 1, 1838, *State Papers,* XXVI, 377; Kennedy and Dalrymple to Palmerston, Jan. 1, 1840, *ibid.,* XXVIII, 518. For their method of computation, see Everett to Forsyth, July 21, 1840, HED 115, 26-2, p. 473. Details on many vessels are given in Fox to Forsyth, Oct. 30, 1839, with encs., SED 125, 26-2, pp. 165 ff.

⁷ McTavish to Palmerston, Jan. 30, 1840, *State Papers,* XXVIII, 947. According to McTavish, if the register was not removed at Havana, the price was higher by $1,200–$2,000 or more, suggesting that the surcharge was chiefly a hedge against possible loss of the registry bond. Each owner had to post a bond of $800–$2,000, depending on the size of the vessel, to guarantee that the register would be removed if the vessel was sold to a foreigner (act of Dec. 31, 1792, Sec. 7, 1 *U.S. Stat. at L.* 290–291).

⁸ Fox to Forsyth, Oct. 30, 1839, with encs. (SED 125, 26-2, pp. 165 ff.), gives many well-documented examples of these practices. For the *Campbell,* see *Baltimore Sun,* April 8, 1840, p. 2. Shipbuilding statistics are conveniently collected in William A. Fairburn, *Merchant Sail* (6 vols.; Center Lovell, Maine: Fairburn Marine Educational Foundation, 1955), II, 938, 958. Certainly the notorious *Catharine* was flimsily built, as the detailed testimony at Allen's trial brought out; she was rigged as cheaply as possible and had fewer than normal iron fittings (*Baltimore Sun,* Dec. 7, 1839, pp. 1–2). The detailed testimony necessary to state that all the "boom" vessels were shoddy is unfortunately lacking.

⁹ J. F. Rippy, "Nicholas Philip Trist," *Dictionary of American Biography,* XVIII, 645–646, is pro-Trist; for a recent anti-Trist view, see Basil Rauch, *American Interest in Cuba: 1848–1855* (New York: Columbia University Press, 1948), pp. 32–33. Rauch draws his view of Trist from William L. Mathieson, *Great Britain and the Slave Trade, 1839–1865* (London: Longmans, Green, 1929). Rippy states that a House committee (H. Rep. 707, 26-1) exonerated Trist of wrongdoing; but this is incorrect. The committee was looking into Trist's treatment of American seamen, not his dealings with slavers, and admitted, moreover, that it had been unable adequately to investigate the charges.

¹⁰ The best compilation of accusations is in Fox to Forsyth, Oct. 30, 1839, with encs., SED 125, 26-2, pp. 165 ff. "A want of proper caution" or "habitual carelessness and want of vigilance" were ascribed to Trist in the note (pp. 172–173), but his alleged furnishing of "blank forms" is characterized (p. 178) as "willful and criminal connivance." The note was mild compared to some of the statements made by subordinate British officials; for samples of the invective of the British commissioners (with whom Trist carried on a running feud) see Kennedy and Dalrymple to Palmerston, Oct. 27, 1839, *ibid.,* pp. 150–153, and Kennedy and Dalrymple to Palmerston, Jan. 1, 1840, *State Papers,* XXVIII, 519. The "blank forms" Trist furnished

to slave vessels, and authenticated with his signature, "to be filled up at the pleasure of persons in command of these vessels," have been a major part of the Trist controversy. Actually, they should not have been, for the accusation concerning them was proved to be a fabrication of the British Foreign Office (Stevenson to Forsyth, Aug. 12, 1840, with encs., SED 125, 26-2, pp. 160–164). Trist was also unfairly accused of permitting a heavily armed pirate ship to put to sea (see the conflicting British reports on this vessel in SED 125, 26-2, pp. 151, 196). Trist's acid comments on these charges are worth reading (Trist to Forsyth, Feb. 13, 1841, HED 115, 26-2, pp. 496–502).

[11] Trist poured forth his views on slavery, the slave trade, and the British in a celebrated manifesto, almost a hundred pages long, addressed to the British commissioners (Trist to Kennedy and Dalrymple, July 2, 1839, SED 125, 26-2, pp. 49–144; for his views on Negroes and slavery, see pp. 62, 64, 93–94, 99–110, 135–143).

[12] *Ibid.*, pp. 59–65.

[13] Trist to Forsyth, Jan. 20, 1839, HED 34, 27-1, p. 27.

[14] The State Department discreetly withheld publication of Trist's dispatch on the subject of issuing papers to Portuguese slavers, but it is quoted by official investigator A. H. Everett in Everett to Forsyth, July 21, 1840, HED 115, 26-2, p. 483.

[15] Trist to Forsyth, Jan. 22, 1839, with encs., HED 115, 26-2, pp. 295–298; deleted portions may be found in HED 34, 27-1, pp. 29–31.

[16] Trist fully expressed his views of his powers when giving testimony at the second trial of R. W. Allen (*Baltimore Sun*, May 15, 1840, pp. 1–2; a shorter version appeared in *ibid.*, April 25, 1840, p. 1). The instructions under which he operated were published in *General Instructions to the Consuls and Commercial Agents of the United States, July 1, 1838* (Washington: Blair & Rives, 1838). Articles 26 and 30 (pp. 15, 17–18), following the act of Feb. 28, 1803, required consuls to return papers impounded in port and grant clearance to American vessels, so long as the local port authorities had cleared the vessel, dismissed crew members had been paid off properly, and the consul's own fees had been paid. No article in the instructions authorized consuls to block changes in the crews of vessels (so long as the dismissed men had been paid off), or to refuse to recognize changes in ownership—though no article authorized consuls to recognize such changes, either. The statutes were silent on this question, giving Trist some perplexity about the method of indicating changes in ownership. Sea letters—temporary registers issued by consuls to purchasers—were apparently introduced by departmental initiative in the early 'forties to solve the problem (for a specimen sea letter, see HED 7, 36-2, pp. 64–65).

[17] For Trist's views on testimony and assassination, see Trist to Forsyth, May 22, 1838, HED 34, 27-1, pp. 19–20; Jan. 20, 1839, *ibid.*, pp. 26–27.

His instructions to obtain evidence against lawbreakers are in Articles 35 and 44 of *General Instructions to the Consuls* . . . , pp. 20–21, 24. In Trist's defense it may be argued that the instructions applied literally only when the criminal and two witnesses could be secured and sent home for trial; he was not ordered to send home witnesses against criminals who had not been apprehended, or to send reports of crime when he had no sworn witnesses to the crime. But this is a very strict construction indeed; the spirit of the instructions plainly was that he was to do everything in his power to expose crimes against federal law.

[18] There were minor exceptions; see his actions in regard to the register of the schooner *Washington* (Trist to Forsyth, May 22, 1838, HED 115, 26-2, pp. 256–260; for deleted portions, HED 34, 27-1, pp. 18–22) and against the *Thomas* and other Spanish slavers attempting to pose as American vessels (Trist to Forsyth, Dec. 18, 1838, HED 115, 26-2, pp. 260–276; Jan. 25, 1839, with encs., *ibid.*, pp. 298–304). The *Thomas* was seized by the U.S. sloop of war *Ontario* at Trist's behest, but was eventually released (3 *Opinions of the Attorney General* 406–407).

[19] Everett, arriving at Havana while Trist was in the United States, had his ears filled by the British commissioners and wrote a report distinctly critical of Trist, though exonerating him of criminal connivance (Everett to Forsyth, July 21, 1840, HED 115, 26-2, pp. 471–495). Trist prepared a rambling, verbose rebuttal which, though filled with invective, struck telling blows at Everett's findings (Trist to Forsyth, Feb. 18, 1841, *ibid.*, pp. 503–766). The one point raised by Everett which Trist avoided was Trist's "spirit of defiance" in releasing papers to Portuguese slavers.

[20] Trist, a hard-money Democrat, had made "soft-money" as well as other sorts of enemies at home (H. Rep. 707, 26-1, esp. pp. 345–348, 459–460, 463–465).

[21] Webster to Trist, July 15, 1841, Library of Congress, Trist Papers, Vol. XVII.

[22] Trist to Tyler, Sept. 4, 1841, *ibid.* Among the Trist Papers in the Library of Congress are several indicating that he dabbled in Cuban agriculture as a side line to his work as consul; this may have given him still another motive for his stand in favor of the Cuban slave trade and for his dislike of the British, who were seeking, perhaps deliberately, to limit Cuban agriculture by cutting off the island's supply of African labor.

[23] Fox to Vail, June 18, 1839, H. Rep. 283, 27-3, p. 569; Beddoes to Fox, June 29, 1839, *ibid.*, p. 577; *Baltimore Sun*, Oct. 14 (p. 2), 29 (p. 2), 1839.

[24] Macaulay and Doherty to Palmerston, Jan. 31, 1839, H. Rep. 283, 27-3, pp. 618–620; *New York Morning Herald*, April 15, 1840, pp. 2–3.

[25] See, e.g., *New York Morning Herald*, July 1 (p. 1), Nov. 25 (p. 4), 1839.

[26] Vail to Fox, June 20, 1839, H. Rep. 283, 27-3, pp. 575–576.

²⁷ The legal problem, in brief, was that the act of 1800 confiscated American-owned vessels employed in the slave trade, not Spanish-owned vessels. The latter could be confiscated only upon evidence that they had been intended for the slave trade while still American property. They could be confiscated under the acts of 1794 and 1818, however, if they had sailed from American ports, and if their owners, masters, or factors had intended to enter them in the slave trade; but these acts did not apply if the intent so to use the vessels originated in a foreign port. The act of 1792 applied only when the owner knew of the secret sale of his vessel to a foreigner and failed to report it; the act did not apply if the captain or some other agent sold the vessel "behind the owner's back." Because the *Wyoming*'s owner admitted that he knew of her sale, the vessel was confiscated under the act of 1792. The *Catharine* and the *Butterfly* were confiscated under the act of 1800, the question of the nationality of their true owners apparently slipping into oblivion in the course of the proceedings. Ostensibly they were American-owned, and the courts accepted that as full evidence of their true nationality. This precedent was usually followed in later cases. (See Vail to Fox, Aug. 14, 1839, with enc., H. Rep. 283, 27-3, pp. 578–579; Fox to Forsyth, Aug. 16, 1840, with encs., *ibid.*, pp. 657–661; Fox to Palmerston, Sept. 25, 1839, *State Papers*, XXVIII, 921–922; Judge Betts's decision on the *Butterfly*, reprinted in *ibid.*, XXIX, 649–655; and *The Catharine*, Fed. Cas. #14,755, vol. 25, p. 337.) One of the prisoners died in jail, and the other three presumably jumped bail; as the surviving records of the Circuit Court for the Southern New York district (preserved in the National Archives) are practically useless, the latter fact is inferred from a variety of circumstances too lengthy to describe here (the necessary source materials are Butler to Vail, Aug. 9, 1839, H. Rep. 283, 27-3, pp. 579–580; *New York Morning Herald*, Oct. 30 [p. 2], Dec. 2 [p. 1], 1839, Aug. 13, 1840 [p. 1]). It is noteworthy that Betts, in passing judgment on the *Butterfly*, asked why her captain was not produced, and that there is no reference to any trials in the *Morning Herald*. Presumably Morris was tried *in absentia* in August, 1840, all the testimony in his case having been put in at his abortive trial in December, 1839; that trials could be completed despite the absence of the defendant is revealed by the case of José Santos, who fled in the midst of an 1862 trial at New York but whose case, nonetheless, went to the jury (*NYDT*, Nov. 6 [p. 3], 7 [p. 3], 27 [p. 3], 1862). For the Supreme Court ruling arising from Morris' first trial see 39 U.S. (14 Peters) 464.

²⁸ The various proceedings can be traced in the *Baltimore Sun*, Dec. 7 (pp. 1–2), 9 (p. 2), 10 (p. 1), 1839; April 25 (p. 1), 27 (p. 1), 30 (p. 1), May 20 (p. 1), 1840. The purely legal part of Taney's decision appears in *Strohm v. United States*, Fed. Cas. #13,539, vol. 23, p. 240. Allen lost his registry bond (see *Allen et al. v. United States*, Fed. Cas. #240, vol. 1, p. 518).

29 See Appendix M.

30 Doherty and Hook to Palmerston, Jan. 20, 1840, *State Papers,* XXVIII, 490–491.

31 For the mixed court's actions, see Palmerston to Doherty and Hook, Nov. 15, 1839, *ibid.,* XXVIII, 502; Jeremie and Lewis to Aberdeen, Dec. 31, 1840, *ibid.,* XXX, 700–701; Doherty and Hook to Palmerston, Jan. 31, March 12, 1840, H. Rep. 283, 27-3, pp. 687–691, 693–695. Altogether seven vessels which had sailed from Havana with American papers were confiscated by the mixed court in 1840, but it is not clear that all were still navigating under American papers when seized. For the sudden end of secret sales at Havana, see Kennedy to Everett, June 9, 1840, H. Rep. 283, 27-3, p. 704, and Kennedy and Dalrymple to Aberdeen, Jan. 1, 1842, *State Papers,* XXXI, 379–380.

32 The Anglo-American Treaty of Aug. 29, 1842, Arts. VIII, XI, 8 *U.S. Stat. at L.* 576–577. Article X of the treaty provided for the extradition of American pirates captured by British cruisers, but the British regularly released such men without notifying the United States government. This article was invoked only once, in 1859, when Flag Officer Inman of the African squadron learned of the arrest of three pirates before the British released them, and sent a warship to request their extradition (HED 7, 36-2, pp. 586–588).

33 For Buchanan's opposition to the treaty, see J. B. Moore, ed., *The Works of James Buchanan* (12 vols.; Philadelphia: J. B. Lippincott & Co., 1906–1911), V, 356–360. For his work as secretary of state in furthering criminal prosecutions, see *ibid.,* VI, 124–125, 170–171, 204–206, 229–230, 259–260. Note his comments (VI, 206) on the prosecution of Captain Gray of the *Agnes:* "The offence with which he is charged [violation of the act of 1800] is one of great aggravation, and the chief object of the Government in his prosecution is to punish him for his crime, if he be guilty. You [the district attorney] will be expected to use your utmost exertions to bring him to trial, and not suffer him to escape from justice. The expense of the witnesses, although considerable, is but a small matter when compared with the punishment of a man, if he be guilty, who has disgraced his country by violating the laws of the United States against the slave trade."

34 See the instructions to the squadron commanders in HED 104, 35-2, *passim;* HED 7, 36-2, pp. 575–576.

35 SED 4, 36-2, Jan. 30, 1861, "Report of the Secretary of the Navy . . . upon various subjects pertaining to the naval establishment"; see pp. 4–30 for detailed information on the fleet's disposition, 1840–1860. This material also appears, for each year, in the annual reports of the secretary of the navy. As to the number of American merchant vessels, there are no precise figures available. The published annual *Report . . . on the Commerce and Navigation of the United States* gives detailed statistics on the

tonnage of the merchant marine, but not on the number of vessels. The reports do, however, give both the tonnage and the number of vessels in particular categories each year: built, lost, condemned as unseaworthy, and sold to foreigners. For the fiscal years 1858–1860, I averaged the tonnage of vessels in each of these categories, and then averaged the four groups together; although the number of vessels in each group was different, this weighting probably gives the most accurate index to the whole merchant marine, because the figures tend to reflect the oldest as well as the newest vessels, and the average size of new vessels was increasing from year to year. The average tonnage of American merchant vessels obtained by this method was roughly 400 tons; hence, a merchant marine of 2.5 million tons (engaged in foreign commerce) would comprise 6,000 vessels (*Report . . . 1858*, p. 652; *Report . . . 1859*, p. 640; *Report . . . 1860*, p. 654). The number of vessels in the 'forties was undoubtedly much smaller.

[36] Various writers have claimed that the vessels of the African squadron were unduly large, so that the 80 guns were concentrated in too few hulls; but this is not true. As may be seen in Appendix E, the squadron was mainly composed of "third-class" sloops mounting 16 guns, and brigs mounting 8 to 12 guns. These were the smallest cruising warships in the fleet, and the African squadron drew disproportionately upon the small number of vessels of these types available; therefore the average size of its cruisers was the smallest among all six squadrons of the navy. Small cruisers were in short supply in the navy because first- and second-class sloops made the best compromise between economy and the needs of a service whose warships had to be fit for long cruises in any waters, isolated from other American warships in event of war. They had to be of fair size and well armed. Most British and French warships used on the African coast likewise carried substantial numbers of guns (see, e.g., Gregory to Preston, March 26, Sept. 3, 1850, NA 89-105, # # 64, 244). The American fleet put about as large a proportion of its smaller warships on the African coast as the British navy did; for figures on the British see Christopher Lloyd, *The Navy and the Slave Trade* (London: Longmans, Green, 1949), pp. 279–284. Finally, as the larger sloops were somewhat faster than the smaller sloops and brigs, though less handy for inshore work, they were probably at least as suitable for catching slavers. See *The Navy of the United States, 1775 to 1853 . . . compiled . . . under the authority of the Navy Department* (Washington: Gideon & Co., 1853). pp. 100, 102, 110, 112, 114.

[37] The sailors believed that tropical "night air" was the cause of fever. For fever in the British squadron, see Lloyd, *op. cit.*, pp. 130–136, 288; in the American, HED 73, 31-1, p. 3. For fear of fever among American naval officers, see A. H. Foote, *Africa and the American Flag* (New York: Appleton, 1854), p. 255; Macaulay to Aberdeen, June 10, 1846, *State Papers*, XXXV, 381–382.

[38] See the gloomy reports of Commodore Perry's fleet surgeon in DuBarry to Perry, Nov. 22, Dec. 21, 1843, June 14, 1844, SED 150, 28-2, pp. 21, 52–53; Glentworth to DuBarry, Dec. 9, 1843, *ibid.,* p. 126.

[39] For the length of a cruise to Madeira, see Read to Bancroft, Sept. 16, 1846, NA 89-103, #6, and Gregory to Preston, March 26, 1850, NA 89-105, #61. Read's dispatches show that there were no cruises to Madeira during the year he was in command. On the health of the squadron, see, e.g., the *Annual Report of the Secretary of the Navy, 1854* (HED 1, 33-2, pt. 2, p. 578); *Annual Report . . . 1856* (SED 5, 34-3, vol. 2, pp. 730–731); *Annual Report . . . 1860* (HED 1, 36-2, vol. 3, pp. 373–375). The 1854 and 1856 reports show that in 1853 and 1855 the African squadron had the lowest death rate of any squadron, but the second highest sickness rate, being exceeded only by the East India squadron. Men became ill rather readily on the African coast, but seldom died. According to the 1860 report, in 1859 the squadron had the lowest rate in both deaths and sickness, because of good luck (and care) aboard the *Marion* and the *Vincennes.* As to shipboard jollities, a brief glimpse is given in Albert Gleaves, *Life and Letters of Rear Admiral Stephen B. Luce* (New York: Putnam, 1925), p. 153. Another striking fact about the unpleasantness of the African coast is that the commanders of the squadron often begged to be relieved of duty ahead of time (see, e.g., Read to Mason, Dec. 10, 1846, NA 89-103, #41; Cooper to Mason, Sept. 3, 1849, NA 89-104, p. 82; Gregory to Graham, Oct. 14, 1850, NA 89-105, #279; Lavallette to Graham, Nov., 1851, NA 89-106, p. 125).

[40] Perry's views on the supply depot are reprinted in SED 150, 28-2, pp. 8, 67, 82–83, 92–94.

[41] See, e.g., the cruises of African squadron vessels in 1858. In four months of cruising the *Dale* spent less than a month off the active slave coast; in five months, the *Marion* accounted for only about thirty-five days of useful patrol; even a direct passage from Porto Praia to Loando (at the southern limits of the station), made far out at sea where no slavers were likely to be met, took the *Cumberland* thirty-two days (HED 7, 36-2, pp. 539–548).

[42] See Read to Mason, Sept. 16, Dec. 11, 1846, NA 89-103 ## 6, 42, for the lack of warships. A careful study of the dispatches of Commodores Cooper and Gregory (NA 89-104, 89-105) indicates that in 1849 there were, on the average, two vessels on patrol cruises at any one time; in 1850, three; and in the first third of 1851, only one and one-half. Checking the long lists of American vessels boarded by Commodore Read's squadron (NA 89-103, *passim*), against known American trade between Rio de Janeiro and Africa (SED 6, 31-2, pp. 37–39), we find that only on seven of fourteen voyages did American merchantmen meet an American cruiser, and not one of those seven was boarded more than once.

[43] The *Merchant,* the *Robert Wilson,* and the *Spitfire* (Appendix A) were Havana-based. The revival and the decline of the Cuban trade may be noted in the dispatches of commissioners Kennedy and Dalrymple, *State Papers,* XXXIII, 329–336; XXXV, 326–332; XXXVI, 500–501.

[44] The complacence or the connivance of the Brazilian authorities was alleged by many, and was very aptly stated by Minister David Tod in November, 1847: "Brazil will not dare to violate a treaty . . . with us to lend her aid to suppress the slave trade—she having the power to prevent the introduction of blacks at nearly, if not quite all, of her ports. . . . By many of the people of this country, the slave trade is considered bad only because it is illegal, and this prohibition has existed but a very few years. Viewing the crime in this light, the requisite vigilance cannot be expected on the part of those invested with the power of enforcing the law. The sympathies of public officers are aroused on the side of the accused, and in many instances, I fear, to such an extent as to prevent right and justice being done. Again, many, if not all, of those engaged in the traffic are men of great wealth. Their money is to be feared. . . . Consequently, it will not do to give the tribunals of this country the power of inquiring into the truth of the accusations when extradition is demanded" (Tod to Buchanan, Oct. 16, 1847, National Archives, Legation Dispatches, Brazil, Vol. XVII, #11). This passage was deleted from the dispatch as published in SED 6, 31-2, p. 3. There is voluminous published correspondence on the efforts of the American minister and consul at Rio de Janeiro to discourage the trade; the documents are listed in the bibliography. Wise to Buchanan, Feb. 18, 1845, with encs., HED 61, 30-2, pp. 70–147, recounts the striking *Porpoise* episode; for the administration's disapproval of Wise's policy of seizing American pirates within Brazilian territory by force, see Buchanan to Wise, Sept. 27, 1845, in *The Works of James Buchanan,* VI, 267–271. Wise was told rather "to urge upon the authorities of Brazil such representations and remonstrances as, without giving offence, will be best calculated to accomplish the humane and important object provided for by the Treaty [with Great Britain] and which the Government and people of the United States have so much at heart." Wise's successor Tod received similar orders (Buchanan to Tod, June 11, 1847, *ibid.,* VII, 332).

[45] On the "guesstimated" size of the Brazilian trade, see, e.g., Lloyd, *op. cit.,* pp. 275–277. The method by which these calculations were made was inaccurate (see, e.g., *State Papers,* XXX, 746–747; XXXIII, 336–337). On the increase of the Brazilian slave trade after 1845 (caused, ironically, by a lowering of British tariffs on sugar and an inflow of British investments to Brazil), see testimony of Consul Hesketh, *Lords Report,* p. 223. The exact size of the increased trade was also in dispute; in 1848 the British consuls in Brazil estimated that 30,000 slaves had been landed, whereas the Foreign Office computed the total at twice that figure (for the consular re-

ports, see *Lords Report,* pp. 442–454). The consular reports reveal that no more than one-fifth of the slaves came in American vessels sold "on the coast"; Brazilian slavers, clearing for Africa under Brazilian colors, were both numerous and efficient. American vessels seem to have been used mainly as auxiliaries. *Lords Report,* pp. 442–446, 449–450, 453–455, and the annual reports of British commissioners at Rio de Janeiro (*State Papers, passim*), indicate that the proportion of American vessels apparently becoming slavers (i.e., sailing from Rio and never returning there under American colors) rose from 15½ per cent in 1843 and 19 per cent in 1845 to 28½ per cent in 1847 and 35 per cent in 1848. On the orders to the consulate to issue temporary registers, despite Wise's and Parks's protests, see Parks to Tod, Jan. 29, 1850, SED 6, 31-2, p. 35.

[46] On Clapp's trial, see Appendix B. Parks's reports on his activities in issuing sea letters, and specimen copies of the examinations he gave to prospective purchasers, may be found in HED 61, 30-2, pp. 20–44; SED 6, 31-2, p. 41.

[47] On the seizures, see Appendix A. Tod's wish to ban all African trade (Tod to Clayton, Jan. 8, 1850, SED 6, 31-2, pp. 25–30) echoed that of Consul Slacum in the early 'forties (Slacum to Webster, May 1, 1842, HED 43, 29-1, pp. 16–17). On the proportion of slaves carried in formerly American vessels in 1848, see note 45, above; for the estimate of a British naval commander, that by 1850 half the successful slavers were ex-American, see Cumming to Fanshawe, Feb. 22, 1850, NA 89-105, #122.

[48] A movement among Brazilian citizens to end the illegal slave trade was noted as early as 1848 (Westwood to Palmerston, Feb. 28, 1849, *Lords Report,* p. 510). *State Papers,* XLI, 317–377 *passim,* and later volumes of this series, contain many references to the suppressed condition of the Brazilian slave trade (see, e.g., Christie to Russell, June 2, 1860, *ibid.,* LI, 1013–1015).

[49] Schenck to Webster, April 20, 1852, and Schenck to Everett, Feb. 5, 1853, with encs., SED 47, 33-1, pp. 2–11.

[50] Gillmer to Marcy, Feb. 1, 12, 1856, HED 7, 36-2, pp. 32–34; Marcy to Hallett, Jan. 7, 1857, *ibid.,* pp. 49–50.

[51] Lloyd, *op. cit.,* pp. 279–284.

[52] Lavallette to Graham, Nov. 13, 1851, with encs., NA 89-106, pp. 108–111. Commodores Read and Perry had asked for steamers (SED 150, 28-2, pp. 82–83; NA 89-103, #42); on the need for a more southerly supply depot, see Read to Bancroft, Sept. 11, 1846, NA 89-103, #6; Cooper to Mason, May 4, 1849, NA 89-104, #8 (p. 38); Gregory to Preston, Feb. 12, March 25, June 8, Sept. 3, 1850, NA 89-105, ## 21, 61, 92, 244.

[53] There was a second printing of Foote's book in 1852. For the department's views, see *Annual Report of the Secretary of the Navy* for 1851 (SED

1, 32-1, pp. 4–5); for 1852 (SED 1, 32-2, p. 293); and for 1853 (HED 1, 33-1, pp. 298–299).

[54] For information on the Portuguese Company, gained when Portuguese authorities in Angola seized papers aboard one of the company's vessels, see enclosures in Crabbe to Dobbin, NA 89-108, pp. 191–197; for the breakup of the trade north of the equator, see Lavallette to Graham, May 20, 1851, NA 89-106, pp. 33–34; for an unsuccessful attempt to reopen the trade in the Sierra Leone area in 1853–54, see Kennedy to Clarendon, Jan. 12, 1854, *State Papers*, XLIV, 1169–1170. But until the fall of 1860 there was still some trade from the Bight of Benin, as was demonstrated by various British captures and by the escape of the *Buckeye* in September, 1860 (House of Commons, *Papers, 1861*, LXIV, 360–361; Lyons to Cass, Nov. 30, 1860, HED 7, 36-2, p. 513). Concerning the preference for New York as a base for slavers, note the harassment of Spanish slavers at Havana in 1852 (Crawford to Malmesbury, Jan. 1, 1853, *State Papers*, XLII, 285–287; Crampton to Marcy, Feb. 6, 1854, *ibid.*, XLIV, 1392). Between 1852 and 1861, inclusive, some 7,700 sailing ship registers and almost 300 steamship registers were issued at New York (National Archives, Record of Registers, XII, 161–162, 266, 346, 369; XIII, 115, 219–220, 318; XIV, 68, 165–166, 258, 354).

[55] The addresses of these attorneys may be readily obtained from the New York City directories of the period. Evidences of their complicity are numerous (see, e.g., Appendix B; *State Papers*, LIV, 373–374; SED 99, 34-1, pp. 59–60; HED 7, 36-2, pp. 83–85, 110–111, 262–263; *NYDT*, Nov. 10, 1854, p. 3, and July 16, 1857, p. 5; *United States v. Darnaud*, Feb. Cas. #14,918).

[56] See Appendix A; Lavallette to Kennedy, Nov. 21, 1852, and Feb. 8, 1853, with encs., NA 89-106, pp. 302–314, 319–348; Wilmot to Manning, Jan. 7, 1853, Bruce to Secy. of Admiralty, April 1, 1853, and Jackson and Goodrich to Malmesbury, Jan. 31, 1853, SED 99, 34-1, pp. 46–47, 49–51; National Archives, New York Registers Sail, vol. 94 (Sept. 27 to Dec. 4, 1852), #429.

[57] For reports of specific vessels see SED 99, 34-1, pp. 49–50, 53, 66–70, 114–117; *NYDT*, July 21 (p. 7), Oct. 15 (p. 7), 1856. For the *Tribune's* general estimates, see the issues of Nov. 11, 1854, p. 4; March 19, 1856, p. 5; July 10, 1857, p. 4. For the State Department figure, see Appleton to McKeon, June 9, 1857, HED 7, 36-2, p. 67. For the 1853 British estimates, see Backhouse to Clarendon, Jan. 2, 1854, *State Papers*, XLIV, 1169–1170; Kennedy to Clarendon, Jan. 12, 1854, *ibid.*, pp. 1174–1175.

[58] For estimates of profits in the late Cuban trade, see Appendix C. For reported slave prices in Africa, see Gabriel to Clarendon, Feb. 25, 1858, House of Commons, *Slave Trade Papers, 1857–58*, Class A, p. 104; enc.

in Wilmot to Walker, Oct. 3, 1863, *State Papers,* LIV, 374; and report of the *Herald*'s Key West correspondent, HED 7, 36-2, p. 451. For a reported sale of smuggled Africans at an average price of $630 in Cuba in 1860, see *NYDT,* Aug. 3, 1860, p. 5; for a report that the average price was $800–$1,000, see Russell to Lyons, July 29, 1859, *State Papers,* L, 972. For the increase in prices of domestic slaves in the United States (by 1860 many were selling for nearly $2,000, or twice as much as a decade earlier), see A. H. Conrad and J. R. Meyer, "The Economics of Slavery in the Ante Bellum South," *Journal of Political Economy,* LXVI (1958), 100, 117, 125–130.

[59] Available information does not make it possible to determine just what proportion of slavers were "American" vessels during the 'fifties, but the mass of reports suggests that it was very large. There were, however, a few openly Spanish vessels, and a few of other nationalities (see, e.g., *NYDT,* March 16 (p. 6), May 14 (p. 5), 1857; Buchanan to Collantes, Nov., 1859, *State Papers,* L, 952).

[60] Burgess to Wise, Aug. 12, 1857, SED 49, 35-1, pp. 35–36; Buchanan to Collantes, Nov., 1859, *State Papers,* L, 955; Crawford to Russell, May 14, 1860, *ibid.,* LI, 1058–1059.

[61] See Appendix K on the size and carrying capacity of slavers of this period.

[62] On Abranches' move into New York, see Joachimssen to Hillyer, Jan. 26, 1858, Solicitor's Letters, Box 80 (Southern New York district, 1856–1860). Pearce was in business as a ship chandler as early as 1854; his name is given as "Pierce" and "Peirce" in various accounts.

[63] Skelton to Clarendon, July 20, 1857, and Hope to Adams, April 20, 1857, House of Commons, *Slave Trade Papers, 1857–58,* Class A, 5, pp. 116–117; Crawford to Clarendon, Jan. 26, 1858, *ibid.,* p. 44; Campbell to Clarendon, May 11, 1857, SED 49, 35-1, p. 4; House of Commons, *Papers, 1861,* LXIV, 360–361.

[64] See Appendixes H, I, and J for examples.

[65] On the *Nancy*'s registered owners, see Work Projects Administration, *Ship Registers and Enrollments of New Orleans, Louisiana* (6 vols.; Baton Rouge: Louisiana State University Press, 1942), V, 185–186. On her varied career, see *State Papers,* XLVIII, 1248; HED 7, 36-2, pp. 145–165, 171–191, 194–202, 205–235, 308–314, 508–511, 526; *New Orleans Daily Picayune,* June 2, 1858, p. 8, and June 3, 1859, p. 8; House of Commons, *Slave Trade Papers, 1862,* Class A, pp. 16–18, 73.

[66] Fairburn, *op. cit.,* II, 1563–1564; *New Orleans Daily Picayune,* April 10, 1859, p. 6; U.S. Bureau of the Census, *Historical Statistics of the United States, 1789–1945* (Washington: Government Printing Office, 1949), p. 211.

[67] On the east African trade, see, e.g., *State Papers,* XLVIII, 1173–1174; L, 942; LI, 1034, 1036.

[68] Crawford to Clarendon, Jan. 26, 1858, *Slave Trade Papers, 1857–58,* Class A, p. 43; Lloyd, *op. cit.,* pp. 275–277; Buchanan to Collantes, Nov., 1859, and Jan. 12, 1860, *State Papers,* L, 953, 958; Russell to Cowley, Lyons, *et al.,* July 11, 1860, *ibid.,* LI, 1024; Buchanan to Collantes, Oct. 17, 1860, *ibid.,* p. 1054; Crampton to Russell, Aug. 25, 1861, *ibid.,* LII, 710.

[69] See chapter 9 for further discussion of this subject.

[70] E.g., the *Haidee,* arriving on the African coast in the summer of 1858, landed her supercargo and then went to sea for forty days while her cargo was being collected and taken to the rendezvous (testimony of William Kins, *NYDT,* Oct. 9, 1858, p. 3). The *Glamorgan* reached Africa in January, 1854, but was not to pick up her Africans until early March (SED 99, 34-1, pp. 59–60). During the summer of 1859 there seems to have been a glut of slavers off the Congo (see chap. 8).

[71] See Appendixes A and B for information on arrests and prosecutions of vessels and men.

[72] The Spanish act is reprinted in HED 7, 36-2, p. 191; for this peculiar interpretation of it, see Buchanan to Collantes, Nov., 1859, *State Papers,* L, 952, 954.

[73] John A. Machado's bark *Mary Francis* was outfitted at Wilmington (see testimony of Captain John A. Perkins, *NYDT,* Sept. 22, 1862, p. 8). The extent to which the whaling ports were used is unknown; the *Brutus* (Keys to Whiting, July 8, 1861, Marshals' Letters) is the only known successful whaler-slaver outfitted outside New York after the spring of 1860. But other attempts were made; see the cases of the *Margaret Scott,* the *Tahmaroo,* and the *Augusta* in Appendixes A and B. On the consular action, see chapter 7.

[74] The strength of the British west African squadron, 1855–1859, was as follows: 1855, 7 sail, 5 steam; 1856, 3 sail, 10 steam; 1857, 2 sail, 13 steam; 1858, 2 sail, 16 steam; 1859, no sail, 13 steam (House of Commons, *Papers, 1861,* LXIV, 348–350). For the American naval dispositions see, e.g., *Annual Report of the Secretary of the Navy, 1859,* SED 2, 36-1, pp. 1138–1139.

[75] British Commodore Edmonstone believed that only five slavers, carrying 3,100 Africans, had escaped from west Africa in the last six months of 1860, while ten slavers and 4,100 Africans had been captured by Anglo-American cruisers in the same period. Spanish cruisers seized three laden slavers off Cuba in the same period (Edmonstone to Keppel, March 24, 1861, House of Commons, *Slave Trade Papers, 1862,* Class A, p. 18; Crawford to Russell, Sept. 30, 1861, with enc., *ibid.,* p. 76).

[76] The orders to the African squadron were sent on May 14, but were not received until August 7; the *Saratoga* alone was left behind (Inman to Welles, Aug. 11, 1861, NA 89-112, #462).

[77] On the situation off Africa, see Edmonstone to Walker, Nov. 7, 1861, House of Commons, *Slave Trade Papers, 1863*, Class A, pp. 108–109. On Havana, see Shufeldt to Seward, July 5, 1861, Savage to Seward, Sept. 6, 1861, and Shufeldt to Seward, Feb. 22, 1862, SED 56, 38-1, pp. 3, 8. On New York, see Murray to Seward, Nov. 11, 1861, *ibid.*, p. 5; Murray to Smith, Jan. 15, 1862, Murray to Seward, April 23, 1862, and Murray to Whiting, May 16, June 2, 1862, Marshals' Letters. The later letters of course had no effect upon the initiation of treaty negotiations. Murray may have been overly pessimistic (see, e.g., *NYDT*, June 10, 1862, p. 7, and Deacon to Whiting, June 12, 1862, Marshals' Letters); but the slave trade undoubtedly took an upturn in the spring of 1862. The British squadron captured sixteen slavers from March through October, as against ten in the entire year of 1861 (House of Commons, *Papers, 1865*, LVI, 529–530).

[78] See *State Papers*, LIII, 1424–1433, for the most complete published file of correspondence on this treaty. Note especially Russell to Lyons, Feb. 28, 1862, and Seward to Lyons, April 24, 1862, pp. 1424, 1430. Lincoln's message and the text of the treaty appear in SED 57, 37-2, and the treaty also in 12 *U.S. Stat. at L.* On congressional action on the appropriations bill, see *Congressional Globe*, 37th Cong., 2d sess., IV, 2941, 3155, 3245. The *Journal of the Executive Proceedings of the Senate . . . Dec. 2, 1861, to July 17, 1862* (Washington: Government Printing Office, 1887), briefly mentions the treaty on pp. 230–231, 240, 254, 256.

[79] Articles VI and VII deal with arrests and prohibited equipment.

[80] On the New York court, see Smith to Fish, Oct. 11, 1870, National Archives, Records of the Office of the Secretary of the Interior relating to the Suppression of the African Slave Trade, Letters Received Relating to Judges and Arbitrators of Mixed Courts at New York, Cape Town, and Sierra Leone, 1862–1870 (microfilm). The story of the court at Capetown may be traced in *ibid.*, groups 1 and 7.

[81] See *ibid.* for Hibbard to Usher, Feb. 10, March 16, 1863; March 21, Aug. 21, 1864; Hibbard to Whiting, March 10, 1863, with enc.; Hibbard to Harlan, Sept. 20, 1865; Palmer to Secy. of Interior, June 30, 1869. Groups 3 and 6 reveal the withdrawal of Dyer and Hibbard. See also House of Commons, *Papers, 1865*, LVI, 530.

[82] Walker to Didelot, June 2, 1863, *State Papers*, LIV, 368.

[83] Wilmot to Walker, Oct. 3, 1863, with encs., *ibid.*, pp. 373–374.

[84] Bunch to Russell, Nov. 28, 1864, Crampton to Russell, Jan. 20, 1865, Puig to Bunch, July 14, 1865, Russell to Bunch, Aug. 25, 1865, Vredenberg to Russell, Sept. 30, 1865, *ibid.*, LVI, 1194, 1202–1203, 1307, 1331–1334, 1336.

[85] See, e.g., the *Tribune* editorial of March 18, 1846: "The fact that these infernal slavers deem themselves peculiarly safe under the American flag should clothe our nation with blushes! So much for having a 'peculiar institution' with its hosts of Argus-eyed defenders to control and shape our legislation at their will! If there were an honest determination on our part to detect and punish such villainy, who believes that these slavers would dream of finding protection under our flag? And how can such a determination exist in a nation which hugs to its bosom the institution of which this traffic is one of the natural fruits? Freemen of America, will you not consider these things?" On Republican use of the issue, see chapter 9; *NYDT*, Aug. 1, 1860, p. 6; Nov. 4, 1862, p. 4. The historical work is W. E. B. Du Bois, *The Suppression of the African Slave Trade to the United States of America* (New York: Longmans, Green, 1896).

[86] See chapter 9 for discussion of this problem. Note also the indictments and convictions of men and confiscations of vessels in Southern courts, Appendixes A and B.

[87] See Appendix L.

3. HOW TO CATCH A SLAVER

[1] National Archives, Log of U.S. Steamer *San Jacinto,* July 20, 1860–August 3, 1861, entries for Aug. 8, 9, Oct. 2–10, 1860; Dornin to Toucey, Oct. 11, 1860, with encs., Captains' Letters, 1860, IV, #16. The voluminous correspondence on the bearings and the removal from command is in NA 89-110, ## 30, 51–52, 92–101, 169.

[2] For the grand jury action see *Boston Post,* June 30, 1854, p. 1. The acts of 1800 and of March 3, 1819 (3 *U.S. Stat. at L.* 532–534) give authority for the seizure of slavers and their crews. For data on the two vessels see Howard I. Chapelle, *The History of the American Sailing Navy* (New York: Norton, 1949), pp. 450, 549; Work Projects Administration, *Ship Registers and Enrollments of New Orleans, Louisiana* (6 vols.; Baton Rouge: Louisiana State University Press, 1942), V, 278. For the capture itself see Jackson and Gabriel to Clarendon, March 28, 1854, SED 99, 34-1, pp. 59–60. For Kehrman's past see Wilmot to Manning, Jan. 7, 1853, *ibid.,* pp. 50–51. For examples of the use of English colors by American cruisers when approaching suspicious vessels, see SED 28, 30-1, pp. 36, 111; *NYDT,* June 9, 1860, p. 9; *New Orleans Daily Picayune,* April 19, 1859, p. 2; SED 49, 35-1, p. 27.

[3] Taylor to Welles, April 21, 1861, and Guthrie to Welles, June 15, 1861, with encs., *Official Records of the Union and Confederate Navies,* Series I, vol. 1, pp. 11–14; Wilmot to Walker, Dec. 31, 1863, *State Papers,* LV, 1046.

[4] For the capture see *Boston Post,* May 15, 1860, p. 3. On the amount of

boarding necessary on this patrol see HED 7, 36–2, p. 452; *New Orleans Daily Picayune,* July 19, 1860, p. 2.

⁵ For examples of breakdowns see HED 7, 36-2, pp. 452, 614. See *NYDT,* June 20, 1859, p. 6, for an allegation that the Paraguayan expedition steamers purchased by the navy were in bad condition when acquired from Secretary of the Navy Toucey's former business partner under suspicious circumstances. For a report on the poor condition of the *Sumpter* and the *Mystic,* see Inman to Toucey, April 4, 1861, NA 89-112, #157. But good new steamers—like the *Mohican,* whose first cruise was to Africa—also had trouble; see Inman to Toucey, Jan. 1, 1861, with encs., *ibid.,* ## 124–128, on a severe case of boiler rust aboard that vessel. For Maffitt's letter see Emma N. Maffitt, *The Life and Services of John Newland Maffitt* (New York: Neale Publishing Co., 1906), p. 210; and see *ibid.,* pp. 206–208, 212–214, on the capture of the *Bogota.*

⁶ For the affair of the *Crusader* see *NYDT,* Aug. 10 (p. 8), 16 (p. 5), 1860. Reports on the number of Negroes landed ranged from 413 to 650. On Stanly's being outwitted, see Stanly to Toucey, July 20, 1860, Officers' Letters, July, 1860, II, #34. The governor with whom Stanly spoke was rumored to have received $30,000 for his connivance (see *NYDT,* Aug. 3, 1860, p. 5).

⁷ *NYDT,* March 19, 1856, p. 5.

⁸ Deposition of George W. Palmer, HED 7, 36-2, pp. 76–77.

⁹ For the *Braman* see *NYDT,* July 3, 1856, p. 7. The affairs of the *Merchant* may be traced in SED 53, 37–2, p. 3; *NYDT,* April 25 (p. 11), May 1 (p. 8), 2 (p. 7), 7 (p. 5), 9 (p. 8), 12 (p. 8), 15 (p. 8), 22 (p. 7), June 6 (p. 8), 19 (p. 7), 1857; National Archives, Admiralty Docket (U.S. District Court, Southern New York district), XIV, 164; *The Merchant,* Fed. Cas. #9, 436, vol. 17, pp. 36–37.

¹⁰ *NYDT,* Nov. 20 (p. 3), 22 (pp. 6–7), 1860; SED 53, 37-2, p. 4; Roosevelt to Hillyer, July 18, 1860, with encs., Solicitor's Letters, Box 80. On the decline of the trade from New York, see *New York Weekly Tribune,* Aug. 11, 1860, p. 4; *Report . . . on the Commerce and Navigation of the United States . . . 1860,* p. 572; *Report . . . 1861,* p. 461.

4. HOW TO RECOGNIZE A SLAVER

¹ Tod to Buchanan, April 29, 1848, SED 6, 31-2, p. 9.

² Deposition of Joseph Souder, April 18, 1848, HED 61, 30-2, p. 33.

³ *NYDT,* March 31 (pp. 2, 4), April 1 (p. 3), 1848. For the ultimate confiscation of the *Laurens,* see Appendix A.

⁴ Hunter's instructions are in NA 89-20, pp. 214–216; the general instructions are reprinted in HED 104, 35-2, pp. 5–6, 10, 19.

⁵ The story of the *Alleghany*'s searches is fully related in Storer to Mason, June 10, 1848, NA 89-20, pp. 200–218; June 14, 1848, with encs., *ibid.*, pp. 228–237. For additional information on cargoes and sailings see reports of Consul Westwood in *Lords Report,* pp. 454–455, 514–516, and lists in SED 6, 31-2, pp. 38, 40–41. Material on the *Alleghany* may be found in *The Navy of the United States, 1775 to 1853 . . . compiled . . . under the authority of the Navy Department* (Washington: Gideon & Co., 1853), pp. 30–31; *NYDT,* Aug. 4, 1849, p. 4; Storer to Mason, June 30, 1848, NA 89-20, p. 266.

5. CONFUSION ON THE BENCH

¹ There was no circuit court for Florida, and cases tried in district court would go on appeal directly to the Supreme Court. Normally district courts had no authority to try capital cases, but those in Florida had special authority (4 *U.S. Stat. at L.* 78). On the captures and confiscations see Craven to Toucey, Dec. 24, 1860, Officers' Letters, Dec., 1860, #221; Tatum to Hillyer, Feb. 25, 1861, Solicitor's Letters, Box 19 (Florida, 1846–1863).

² Work Projects Administration, *Ship Registers and Enrollments of New Orleans, Louisiana* (6 vols.; Baton Rouge: Louisiana State University Press, 1942), V, 256.

³ Or so it would seem. Horta also purchased the brig *Tallulah* on March 25, 1857, and sold her into Mexican registry at Havana in September, 1859; it was suspected that she was destined for the slave trade, but there is no proof (*Ship Registers . . . of New Orleans,* V, 250; Buchanan to Collantes, Nov., 1859, *State Papers,* L, 955).

⁴ A certified copy of the decision is enclosed in Boynton to Attorney General, Nov. 21, 1861, Attorney General's Letters, Florida. On the *Toccoa*'s capture while free on bond, see enclosure in Crawford to Russell, Sept. 30, 1861, House of Commons, *Slave Trade Papers, 1862,* Class A, p. 18.

⁵ Magrath's opinion is in Federal Records Center, East Point, Georgia, Admiralty Journal, 1857–1861 (U.S. District Court, South Carolina district). See also Brent to Conover, Oct. 8, 1858, HED 7, 36-2, p. 547; *NYDT,* Nov. 15 (p. 6), Dec. 1 (pp. 4–5), 1858.

⁶ *The Laura,* 13 L.T.R. (n.s.) 133.

⁷ Act of March 3, 1819, Sec. 5, 3 *U.S. Stat. at L.* 534. Only if the port to which a seized vessel "belonged" could not be determined, was it to be sent into whatever port might be most convenient. Perhaps this gave some leverage for sending vessels into Norfolk, Key West, or other ports where convictions were frequently obtained, because the true ownership of a captured slaver was often in doubt.

⁸ As usual, these cases were never reported in the legal press. Judge Gil-

crist's opinion may be found on pages 59–65 of the printed brief prepared when the case of the *Panther* was sent to the Supreme Court (National Archives, Supreme Court case record #3,150). Evidence about the *Chancellor* may be obtained from Pope to Betts, April 10, 1847, NA 89-103, #101; Pope to Read, July 30, 1847, *ibid.*, #104; List of vessels boarded . . . by the "Dolphin," *ibid.*, #106.

⁹ Shipman's decision against the *Augusta* was published (*The Augusta*, Fed. Cas. #14,477, vol. 24, pp. 892–896). The correspondence between Shipman and Solicitor Hillyer about the *Laurens*, and a detailed newspaper account of the trial and decision, are in Solicitor's Letters, Box 14 (Conn., 1859–1895).

¹⁰ In the *Butterfly* case; see chap. 10.

¹¹ In the *Orion* case; see chap. 11.

¹² For the Supreme Court decisions, all sustaining the verdicts of lower courts, see 69 U.S. (2 Wallace), 350–408. On the *Brothers*, see Conner to Hillyer, Oct. 25, 1859, Solicitor's Letters, Box 136 (S.C., 1844–1896).

¹³ The attorney general was given power to control district attorneys only in August, 1861 (12 *U.S. Stat. at L.* 285–286); the Department of Justice was created even later. Before 1861 the attorney general was merely the chief legal adviser of the government, with powers as established by 1 *U.S. Stat. at L.* 92–93. He did occasionally correspond with district attorneys, as revealed by the correspondence preserved in the National Archives; so did other cabinet officers. Some interesting examples of the relationships of district attorneys to various departments, and of departments with one another, in slave-trade cases may readily be found in HED 7, 36-2, pp. 12–24, 67, 135–136, 284–285, 417, 423, 435, 624. The act of May 29, 1830 (4 *U.S. Stat. at L.* 414–416) came closest in the ante-bellum period to providing a chief for the various district attorneys. This act required attorneys to inform the newly created solicitor of the treasury of all suits in which the United States was a party, and to accept his instructions on these cases. But the statute is not clear as to whether criminal cases were to be reported, or merely suits in which the United States had a financial interest; in practice only suits for fines and forfeitures were reported, as is revealed by the solicitor's files in the National Archives and was so stated by him in HED 7, 36-2, p. 626. It need hardly be added that there was no Federal Bureau of Investigation, no Secret Service, and no staff of any consequence in the solicitor's office; there was no central file of violators, suspects, or fiugitives from justice.

6. BURNED FINGERS

[1] Bispham to Read, April 15, 1846, with encs., NA 89-103, ## 9, 11. On Fonseca, see, e.g., Minister Wise in SED 28, 30-1, pp. 19, 24, 26.

[2] Bispham to Read, Dec. 23, 1846, NA 89-103, #70. The *Boxer* was very foul; vessels accumulated marine growth uncommonly fast on the African coast (Read to Mason, Dec. 11, 1846, *ibid.*, #42).

[3] *United States v. Libby,* Fed. Cas. #15,597, vol. 26, pp. 928–936. This is the only case reported in the lawbooks, but apparently Woodbury made an unreported charge to the Boston grand jury in similar vein about the same time (Parks to Buchanan, Aug. 20, 1847, HED 61, 30-2, p. 7).

[4] *The Porpoise,* Fed. Cas. #11,284, vol. 19, pp. 1064–1067. Curtis ruled that vessels used to further the slave trade were in fact "engaged in the transportation of slaves." This was a new doctrine; Curtis' citations of *United States v. Morris* and *The Alexander* were not really precedents, because they related only to the question of whether or not a vessel actually intended as a slaver was "engaged" before the slaves were taken aboard. But the *Porpoise* was no mere auxiliary; she was a tender that actively assisted in the preparation of specific slavers. Judge Curtis' policy on confiscation of ordinary auxiliaries is unknown, for none were involved in later cases.

[5] On the *Casket*'s arrest see Simonds to Read, Sept. 15, 1846, NA 89-103, #7. For other details of her voyage, see *ibid.*, #22; SED 28, 30-1, p. 127. On the dismissal of the libel see HED 7, 36-2, p. 629. For Secretary Mason's warning, see Hugh G. Soulsby, *The Right of Search and the Slave Trade in Anglo-American Relations, 1814–1862* (Baltimore: John Hopkins Press, 1933), pp. 134–135.

[6] For the voyage of the *Senator* see HED 61, 31-2, pp. 8–14 (or the same depositions in SED 6, 31-2, pp. 3–6). For Bispham's release of the *Senator,* see Bispham to Read, April 16, 1847, NA 89-103, #80; for the *Boxer*'s boarding report, *ibid.*, #84.

[7] For the suit against Bispham, see *Philadelphia Public Ledger,* July 13, 1848, p. 1. For the suit against Simonds, see HED 104, 35-2, p. 2. According to this, Congress did not repay Simonds' expenses in defending himself until several years had passed. See also 5 *Opinions of the Attorney General* 397–398 on the Navy Department's aid to Simonds.

[8] Read to Mason, Dec. 11, 1846, NA 89-103, #42.

[9] Read to Mason, Aug. 6, 1847, *ibid.*, #95.

[10] The dispatches of Commodore Bolton are missing from the National Archives, but those of Commodore Cooper (NA 89-104) clearly reveal that none of his cruisers went south of the line. See also Foote to Preston, March 20, 1850, NA 89-105, #77. Whether or not the Navy Department was in-

formed of this shirking is unclear; Cooper's dispatches offer no explanation as to why his cruisers were patrolling where they were. Cooper to Mason, May 4, 1849 (NA 89-104, #8) suggests that the department was not informed. On the general movement of the trade southward see, e.g., *Lords Report,* p. 373; *State Papers,* XXX, 700–701; XXXV, 310–311, 376.

[11] British Commodore Hotham knew of their fear (see *Lords Report,* p. 145).

[12] Parks to Buchanan, Aug. 25, 1848, HED 61, 30-2, p. 29.

[13] *The Malaga,* Fed. Cas. #8,985, vol. 16, pp. 535–540. The case is mistitled; it should read *Lovett et al. v. Bispham.* For the outcome of the suit against Simonds, which was not reported in the legal press, see HED 104, 35-2, p. 2.

[14] Also figuring in the resumption of patrolling (though to what extent cannot be stated) were the advent of a vigorous new commander, Francis H. Gregory, and a visit to him soon after he arrived on the station by the British commodore, who had decided to make a personal appeal for American patrols south of the equator (see Gregory to Preston, Feb. 12, 1850, with encs., NA 89-105, pp. 21–24).

[15] Mayo to Dobbin, March 10, 1854, NA 89-107, #43. Note the departmental notation on the back of the letter. Mayo was also interested in prize money, as he clearly revealed in Mayo to Dobbin, Nov. 10, 1853, *ibid.,* #34.

[16] *NYDT,* Aug. 16, 1860, p. 5. For the ultimate dismissal of the libel see National Archives, Admiralty Docket (U.S. District Court, Southern New York district), XVI, 126. For LeRoy's release of the *Triton*'s crew see LeRoy to Toucey, July 16, 1860, Officers' Letters, July, 1860, II, #44. LeRoy did not tell Toucey why he released the *Triton*'s crew.

[17] For Wilson's bill see *Congressional Globe,* 36th Cong., 1st sess., III, 2207–2211. That no legislation was passed can be determined from any digest of bills of that period.

[18] An account of this case is in Federal Records Center, East Point, Georgia, Admiralty Docket, 1857–1863 (U.S. District Court, South Florida district), pp. 606–616. See also Maffitt to Toucey, Aug. 14, 1860, HED 7, 36-2, p. 623.

7. UNSUNG HERO

[1] Kennedy and Dalrymple to Aberdeen, Jan. 1, 1841, *State Papers,* XXX, 722–727; Jan. 1, 1842, *ibid.,* XXXI, 379–382.

[2] Trist to Kennedy and Dalrymple, July 2, 1839, SED 125, 26-2, pp. 59–65.

[3] Stanly to Toucey, July 10, 1860, Officers' Letters, July, 1860, I, #116.

4 Russell to Seward, Oct. 15, 1862, SED 56, 38-1, pp. 9–10.

5 See, e.g., the case of the *Cortez;* her manifested cargo and her actual cargo are described in HED 7, 36-2, pp. 100–101, 253–254.

6 There are no records in the National Archives on Savage. What seems to be his family genealogy is in Lawrence Park, "Old Boston Families, Number Three: The Savage Family," *New England Historical and Genealogical Register,* LXVIII (1914), 24. This article states that the elder Thomas Savage, born in Boston in 1786, migrated to Havana before 1814 and spent the remainder of his life there, serving as United States consul for many years. His wife was Lydia V. de Forcade, formerly of Charleston. The younger Thomas Savage, apparently our vice-consul, was born on August 27, 1823, and married Mary Dolores Lucena, a Castilian, at Havana in 1850. As she died in the early 1860's at Havana, her husband was then obviously a resident of the city. But Park's article gives no information on the younger Thomas Savage's occupation. It is also wrong in saying that the elder Thomas Savage served as United States consul at Havana; he may have been confused with his son. That Vice-Consul Savage had lived a long time in Havana, and that he is therefore probably the Thomas Savage, Jr., mentioned by Park, is revealed not only by his knowledge of affairs in the city but also by a letter from Echevarria to Savage, July 27, 1858: ". . . you, from your great experience and long residence in this country, may have been convinced . . ." (HED 7, 36-2, p. 159). Further evidence is that two of Savage's dispatches, written at a time of great personal stress, are signed "Thomas Savage Jr.," as if he had unconsciously fallen back into a former habit (*ibid.,* pp. 269, 274). On his salary see Helm to Cass, Nov. 29, 1858, National Archives, Consular Dispatches, Havana, XXXIX.

7 Savage to Appleton, Oct. 14, 1858 (HED 7, 36-2, p. 267): "The trade, as it is carried on, is iniquitous, and the least circumstance against it is the fact of bringing negroes, if they contented themselves with bringing no more than the vessel can safely bring." To an abolitionist the enslavement of men was one of the most heinous parts of the crime.

8 See, e.g., Savage to Cass, Aug. 7, 1857, HED 7, 36-2, pp. 69–71. For the dissemination of his reports, see Streeter to Van Dyke *et al.,* Nov. 7, 1857, Attorneys' Letters, Sec. 3 (Correspondence of J. C. Van Dyke).

9 Blythe to Cass, April 24, 1857, HED 7, 36-2, pp. 63–65; March 9, 1858, *ibid.,* pp. 80–81. For Blythe's complaints to the British consul about his lack of authority, see Crawford to Napier, May 22, 1858, *ibid.,* pp. 109–110.

10 See Appendix H for a list of known slavers. For the *Cortez* affair and the harassment of American shipping, see Hugh G. Soulsby, *The Right of Search and the Slave Trade in Anglo-American Relations, 1814–1862* (Baltimore: Johns Hopkins Press, 1933), pp. 171–172; HED 7, 36-2, *passim.* See

also *Annual Report of the Secretary of the Navy, 1858,* HED 2, 35-2, p. 3.

[11] Quoted in Helm to Cass, Nov. 29, 1858, Consular Dispatches, Havana, XXXIX.

[12] Savage was also willing to refuse to change ships' captains. For examples of his determination, in addition to those noted in the text, see Savage to McIntosh, July 20, 1858, HED 7, 36-2, p. 153; Savage to Cass, Aug. 29, 1858, *ibid.,* p. 200.

[13] State Department correspondence is arranged chronologically in HED 7, 36-2. The sheer volume of papers for July through October, 1858, is in itself an eloquent testimony to Savage's activity. For the neglect of his routine work, see Helm to Cass, Nov. 29, 1858, Consular Dispatches, Havana, XXXIX.

[14] This was the *W. D. Miller,* secretly purchased in March, 1857. See Savage to Cass, Aug. 7, 1857, HED 7, 36-2, pp. 69–71; Aug. 9, 1858, with encs., *ibid.,* p. 172.

[15] Baldwin and Randolph to Tatum, July 14, 1858, Solicitor's Letters, Box 19 (Florida, 1846–1863); HED 7, 36-2, p. 631; Baldwin to Savage, July 17, 1858, Savage to Baldwin, July 19, 1858, Savage to Echevarria, July 23, 1858, and Savage to Cass, Aug. 9, 1858, *ibid.,* pp. 165–168, 172.

[16] The voluminous correspondence on this affair is reprinted in HED 7, 36-2, pp. 114–123, 126–129, 256, 374–375.

[17] Savage to Appleton, July 25, 1858, *ibid.,* pp. 146–147.

[18] Savage to Cass, Aug. 9, 1858, *ibid.,* p. 171.

[19] The truly formidable mass of correspondence on the *Nancy* is in *ibid.,* pp. 145–165, 171–191, 194–202, 205–235, 308–314, 526.

[20] Savage to Cass, Aug. 29, 1858, *ibid.,* p. 196.

[21] Savage to Appleton, Sept. 14, 1858, *ibid.,* p. 207.

[22] Judge McCaleb had lately dismissed libels against two undoubted slavers, the *William Clark* and the *Lewis McLain;* both were afterward captured by British cruisers (HED 7, 36-2, p. 627; House of Commons, *Papers, 1861,* LXIV, 360). On the other hand, Marvin had only recently confiscated the *Huntress* (HED 7, 36-2, p. 630). Pelletier frankly told Savage, in the presence of witnesses, that if the *Ardennes* went to Key West, Savage would send evidence causing her confiscation (encs. in Savage to Appleton, Oct. 24, 1858, HED 7, 36-2, pp. 274–275). Savage said he was "merely consulting their own convenience, as well as that of the United States steamer," in insisting on Key West; of New Orleans he wrote: "Of course, I could have no objection to the latter port" (Savage to Appleton, Oct. 14, 1858, *ibid.,* p. 267). No doubt this was true, in the main, but plainly Pelletier's convenience was no reason for Savage to insist upon Key West, for Pelletier strongly desired to avoid going there. And a prize crew could have come back from New Orleans, if less conveniently than from Key West. Savage also objected to Marsh and Pelletier's proposition to post bonds to

go to New Orleans, on the ground that the bonds would be unenforceable, but he never offered to send the *Ardennes* under prize crew to New Orleans; he always coupled his request for a prize crew with the demand that they go to Key West (Savage to Marsh, Oct. 16, 1858, *ibid.*, p. 274). Pelletier would probably have gone to New Orleans, just as he later went to Jacksonville; it was Key West that he was afraid of. Flemming to Cass, Dec. 9, 1858 (*ibid.*, p. 284), notes that it was rumored at Jacksonville that the *Ardennes* had come there to obtain a new register because a slaver had recently been condemned at Key West.

[23] Savage to Appleton, Oct. 24, 1858, *ibid.*, p. 269.

[24] For the story of the *Ardennes* and the *Enterprise,* see Savage to Appleton, Oct. 14, 24 (with encs.), 1858, HED 7, 36-2, pp. 265–275; Parrott to Toucey, Oct. 16, 1858, with encs., Officers' Letters, Oct., 1858, #171.

[25] H. D. Jordan, "Charles John Helm," *Dictionary of American Biography,* VIII, 512–513.

[26] Helm to Cass, April 11, 1860, HED 7, 36-2, pp. 417–420.

[27] Helm to Cass, Nov. 15, 1858, with enc., *ibid.*, pp. 279–281; Flemming to Cass, Dec. 9, 1858, *ibid.*, pp. 284–285; *NYDT,* June 28, 1859, p. 7.

[28] Helm to Cass, Dec. 27, 1858, with encs., HED 7, 36-2, pp. 292–299.

[29] Helm to Cass, April 11, 1860, *ibid.*, pp. 417–420.

[30] See Buchanan's annual message in James D. Richardson, *A Compilation of the Messages and Papers of the Presidents* (Washington, 1897), IV, 3041.

[31] See Black to Cass, May 3, 1860, HED 7, 36-2, pp. 422–423; Helm to Cass, May 30, 1860, *ibid.*, p. 436.

[32] Savage to Seward, Sept. 6, 1861, Seward to Savage, Sept. 30, 1861, Shufeldt to Seward, Dec. 11, 1862, Seward to Welles, Dec. 29, 1862, and Welles to Seward, Jan. 3, 1863, SED 56, 38-1, pp. 3–4, 12–14.

8. MEN WITH CLAY FEET

[1] *Boston Post,* Aug. 29, 30, 31, Sept. 1, 25, 26, 27, 28, 29, Oct. 1, 1855 (all p. 2); Marcy to Hallett, Jan. 7, 1857, HED 7, 36-2, pp. 49–50; Gillmer to Marcy, Feb. 1, 12, 1856, *ibid.*, pp. 32–34. For marshals' fees see act of February 26, 1853, 10 *U.S. Stat. at L.* 161–165.

[2] The correspondence relating to the *Horatio*'s career is in HED 7, 36-2, pp. 12–24. Ingraham remained on as registry clerk until at least 1858; see, e.g., his testimony in *NYDT,* Oct. 9, 1858, p. 3.

[3] *NYDT,* May 7 (p. 7), 21 (p. 3), 28 (p. 3), June 15 (p. 3), 16 (p. 11), Aug. 9 (p. 7), 1860. A copy of the testimony against the deputies may also be found in the Marshals' Letters. For the abandonment of prosecutions, see National Archives, Criminal Docket (U.S. Circuit Court, Southern New York district), I (1853–1864), 217. The indictments were not formally

nol-prossed, but simply abandoned. The act under which the deputies were finally indicted was that of March 2, 1831, 4 *U.S. Stat. at L.* 488.

⁴ *New York Leader,* May 26, 1860, quoted in *NYDT,* May 30, 1860, p. 8.

⁵ The findings of the investigation are reprinted in SED 40, 37-2, "Letter of the Secretary of the Interior . . . in relation to the slave vessel the 'Bark Augusta,' " April 4, 1862 (note particularly pp. 3–6, 15–22, 24–25, 28, 35–37, 60). All these papers may also be found in the Attorneys' Letters. Marshal Murray, who instigated the investigation, did not agree with the findings (see Murray to Smith, Jan. 10, 1862, Marshals' Letters).

⁶ Tyler, a clerk in the office of John S. Gillmer and only a part-time consul, certainly was not quick to denounce the use of American vessels as auxiliaries, nor their sale on the coast to Brazilian slave traders. His knowledge that no vessels actually carried slaves while still American-owned, and the fact that his employer Gillmer was deeply implicated in the slave trade, may well have curbed his tongue. Learning of Tyler's uncoöperativeness, Minister Wise urged his dismissal, and wrote him so denunciatory a letter that Tyler had an American tender seized, which cost him his job with Gillmer. Wise thereupon recommended that Tyler be allowed to remain on as consul. For the voluminous correspondence on Tyler, see HED 61, 30-2, pp. 148–151, 161–169, 181–209. According to John P. Harrison (*The Archives of United States Diplomatic and Consular Posts in Latin America* [Washington: National Archives, 1953], p. 12), the personal business papers of Tyler among the Bahia consulate records in the National Archives reveal that "Tyler, while working for Gillmer, was engaged in the slave trade on his own initiative." No further details are offered. The published correspondence suggests that Gillmer, who was consul from 1850 to 1862, was the slave trader, not Tyler. I found no papers incriminating Tyler among the business records in the National Archives; many of these papers, however, are in Portuguese, which I cannot read.

⁷ Eggleston, upon the orders of the State Department, withheld return of the American register of the suspected slaver *Clarissa,* but the *Clarissa* nonetheless left Cadiz. According to Eggleston, she went out without papers. But British Commodore Edmonstone personally boarded her off the Congo, and was shown a certificate from the American consul at Cadiz, certifying her American registry. If Edmonstone was not deceived by a forgery, Eggleston had plainly been turning a dishonest penny on the side. But the *Clarissa*'s crew afterward voluntarily renounced the protection of their papers, which suggests that they may have been forged (Seward to Eggleston *et al.,* Nov. 12, 1861, SED 56, 38-1, pp. 5–6; Marin to Welles, March 28, April 14, 1862, *Official Records of the Union and Confederate Navies,* Series I, vol. 1, pp. 366–367, 374–378; Edmonstone to Secy. of Admiralty, June 22, 1862, House of Commons, *Slave Trade Papers, 1863,* Class A, p. 140; House of

Commons, *Papers, 1865,* LVI, 530). In a second suspicious case, the captain of the American slaver *Huntress* testified, after his arrest in Cuba, that Eggleston had actually recruited him for the voyage after the original American captain of the *Huntress* had died at Cadiz. The captain claimed that Eggleston had promised him several thousand dollars to serve as the *Huntress'* captain on a voyage to South America, if the voyage was "successful." The American protested that he did not know navigation, but Eggleston replied that this did not matter, and installed him as captain. This was plainly connivance, if true—but the testimony came from a pirate (deposition of John McCarthy, SED 56, 38-1, pp. 19–21).

[8] In general, the statutes provided that half of the proceeds of vessels confiscated and of the fines levied should go to the informer or to the officers making the arrest. Exactly how prize money should be divided when several persons had a claim to it was not specified, except when the ordinary naval prize laws governed distribution. For an interesting case regarding the disposition of prize money, see *The Josefa Segunda,* 23 U.S. (10 Wheaton) 312. The crew of a naval vessel or a revenue cutter seizing Africans from a laden slaver was entitled to a bounty of $25 for each African delivered alive to a United States marshal, or to the federal agent at Monrovia, Liberia. The law (act of 1819) did not specify how the money was to be distributed, but in practice the ordinary prize law was applied (see, e.g., *NYDT,* Oct. 12, 1858, p. 6).

An interesting calculation can be made in the case of the *William.* Lieutenant Stanly had been offered $25,000 to let the vessel go on the ground that she was in Cuban territorial waters (Stanly to Toucey, July 10, 1860, Officers' Letters, July, 1860, I, #116). The *Wyandotte's* crew shared a little more than half of this amount—$12,825 bounty on 513 Africans who were landed at Key West—and $879.13 prize money from the *William* herself; the smallness of the latter sum reflects the poor condition of the slaver. Thus, if all the *Wyandotte's* men had agreed on a fraud, they would only have doubled their income, with a fair likelihood that "the truth would out." If Stanly, however, had been willing to sell out his own men, he could have done much better, for the $25,000 was about twelve times the prize money he received.

Bribes were likely to be most attractive, however, not in the realm of ships and Africans, but of men. Officers responsible for the arrest and imprisonment of slave traders normally received little or no prize money; and, of course, to the slave-trading organization the freedom of its men was more important than the liberation of its property. But it is very hard to prove that the officers concentrated on seizing ships, and ignored men; for slave traders, armed as they were with legal defenses (such as bail and the rigid requirements of evidence) that were unavailable to seized property, were certain to be much more difficult to arrest and hold.

9 The official *Register of Commissioned Officers*, published annually, makes it possible to calculate how long it took officers to reach various posts. The figures I have cited are based on a broad selection of officers who served against the slave trade at various times. See Leonard D. White, *The Jacksonians: A Study in Administrative History, 1829–1861* (New York: Macmillan, 1954), pp. 233–250, for a good account of the navy's personnel problems in this period.

10 For Conover's cruising see NA 89-109, ## 1, 8.5, 13, 17, 38, 41, 52, 55, 64, 66, 67, 96, 111, 116, 120, 134, 140, 143, 163, 166, 169, 174. For his allusion to newspaper reports see Conover to Toucey, Feb. 27, 1858, *ibid.*, #64. The various naval registers contain ample data on Conover's career. Data on his flagship and the *Constellation* may be found in *Official Records of the Union and Confederate Navies*, Series II, vol. 1, p. 69, and in Howard I. Chapelle, *The History of the American Sailing Navy* (New York: Norton, 1949), pp. 464, 466–469, 534.

11 A copy of Inman's pamphlet, entitled "Objections to the Finding of Naval Court of Inquiry No. 3, in the Case of Captain William Inman," is in the Henry E. Huntington Memorial Library, San Marino, California.

12 Inman to Toucey, Aug. 20, Sept. 18, Sept. 22, Oct. 1, 26, 1859, Jan. 14, 1860, NA 89-110, ## 22, 28, 32, 33, 49, 194; April 20, 1860, NA 89-111, #4.

13 Toucey to Inman, March 27, 1860, HED 7, 36-2, p. 595; Inman to Toucey, May 2, 1860, NA 89-111, ## 12, 13. An interesting side light on Toucey's awakened interest is his strict supervision of the movements of the Cuban steamers (see, e.g., HED 7, 36-2, pp. 610–611).

14 General Orders, Feb. 1, 1860, enc. in Inman to Toucey, March 28, 1860, NA 89-111.

15 Inman to Toucey, Jan. 13, 1860, with encs., NA 89-110, ## 197–266. These documents give abundant evidence on the capture of the *Orion*, but no explanation about her escape. See also "Vessels boarded by . . . the U.S. Squadron," *ibid.*, #177, and Armstrong to Inman, Nov. 22, 1859, *ibid.*, #99. Another case involved the *William Taylor Hall*, which Inman allowed to slip out of Loando harbor even though she was under suspicion; the vessel was afterward found a derelict in the Bahamas, having evidently carried slaves (Inman to Amaral, Feb. 7, 1860, NA 89-111, #346; *NYDT*, May 18, 1860, p. 5).

16 Inman to Toucey, Aug. 14, 1860, HED 7, 36-2, pp. 601–602.

17 National Archives, Log of the U.S. Steamer Mohican, I (Nov. 29, 1859 to Nov. 25, 1860), entries for Aug. 1–8, 1860; Log of U.S. Steamer San Jacinto, July 20, 1860–Aug. 3, 1861, entries for Aug. 1–8, 1860.

18 Inman to Toucey, Sept. 26, 1860, with encs., NA 89-111, #62.

19 Edmonstone to Walker, Nov. 7, 1861, House of Commons, *Slave Trade Papers, 1863*, Class A, pp. 108–109.

[20] Conover to Toucey, June 27, 1858, with encs., NA 89-109, # # 84–86; Inman to Toucey, Jan. 21, 23, 24, 1860, with encs., NA 89-110, # # 284–291, 293–304, 307–317.

[21] For the British complaint, see Lyons to Cass, Dec. 5, 1859, with enc., HED 7, 36-2, pp. 379–380; Gabriel to Russell, Sept. 20, 1859, with enc., *State Papers,* L, 866–869. On Totten's lateness to his rendezvous at Porto Praia, see Inman to Toucey, Sept. 18, Oct. 26, 1859, NA 89-110, # # 28, 49. Totten had previously shown skill in chasing the *Wanderer* (chap. 9), and had arrested the suspicious *Julia Dean*. Totten, unlike Conover and Inman, was given duty during the Civil War, but in a shore billet.

[22] Gabriel to Russell, Sept. 20, 1859, *State Papers,* L, 866–868; Wise to Brent, Sept. 6, 1858, HED 7, 36-2, p. 559; Lyons to Cass, May 23, 1859, with enc., *ibid.,* pp. 337–338.

9. THE ELUSIVE SMUGGLED SLAVE

[1] *NYDT,* Aug. 4, 1858, p. 4; Sedgwick to Hillyer, Aug. 4, 1858, Solicitor's Letters, Box 80; Savage to Cass, Aug. 29, 1858, HED 7, 36-2, p. 201; Cobb to Hatch, March 2, 1858, *ibid.,* p. 632; Parrott to Toucey, Aug. 10, 1858, Officers' Letters, Aug., 1858, #88; Sept. 8, 1858, *ibid.,* Sept., 1858, #101; Harvey Wish, "The Revival of the African Slave Trade in the United States, 1856–1860," *Mississippi Valley Historical Review,* XXVIII (1941), 583. On Lamar's advocacy of the slave trade see *New Orleans Daily Picayune,* June 12, 1858, p. 2; Cobb to Cobock, May 22, 1858, HED 7, 36-2, pp. 632–636.

[2] Blackburn to Thompson, Dec. 25, 1858, Marshals' Letters.

[3] Blackburn to Thompson, Sept. 1, 1858, National Archives, Records of the Office of the Secretary of the Interior relating to the Suppression of the African Slave Trade, Register of Letters Received, 1858–1872 (microfilm).

[4] Hatch to Thompson, Nov. 21, 1859, National Archives, *ibid.,* Miscellaneous Letters Received, 1858–1871 (microfilm).

[5] Thompson to Blackburn, Aug. 5, 27, 1859, National Archives, *ibid.,* Letters Sent, 1858–1872 (microfilm), # # 14–16; Zehnbauer to Thompson, Oct. 1, 1859, Marshals' Letters; *NYDT,* Aug. 1, 1859, p. 7.

[6] Hatch to Cass, March 18, 1858, SED 49, 35-1, p. 41.

[7] Flemming to Cass, Dec. 9, 1858, HED 7, 36-2, p. 285.

[8] Ganahl to Black, Dec. 25, 1858, Attorney General's Letters, Georgia; Conner to Black, Feb. 9, March 28, 1859, *ibid.,* South Carolina.

[9] Turnley to Black, June 22, 1859, *ibid.,* Alabama.

[10] *NYDT,* Dec. 1 (p. 5), 2 (p. 4), 3 (p. 4), 4 (p. 5), 6 (p. 4), 8 (p. 6), 9 (p. 5), 10 (p. 5), 1858; *New Orleans Weekly Picayune,* April 27, 1859, p. 5; *New Orleans Daily Picayune,* April 30, 1859, p. 1.

[11] *New Orleans Daily Picayune,* May 29, 1859, p. 10. No court record of this trial has survived, and the *Picayune*'s correspondent is the most reliable reporter available. His account reads in part: "The Court rejected this evidence [a copy of the register] on the ground that a copy certified under the seal of the Collector was not admissable, and also on the ground of its irrelevancy to the issue, the point to be proved not being the nationality of the vessel, but the ownership or title in a citizen of the United States; and that the register did not prove ownership. The District Attorney then offered in evidence an original bill of sale of the brig Putnam from a former owner to Townsend which had been left on file in the Custom House at New Orleans, but failed to prove its execution. The District Attorney rested here. Without argument or summing up, the Court directed the jury to find the prisoner not guilty, inasmuch as there was no proof before the jury that the Echo or Putnam was owned in whole or in part by a citizen of the United States, or navigated in behalf of a citizen of the United States, which was material to be proved in order to maintain the indictment, nor was there any proof that the vessel was a foreign vessel. The jury brought in a verdict of 'not guilty.' " Apparently the technicality was that Townsend had been indicted under counts charging him with committing piracy as an American in a foreign vessel, as a foreigner in an American vessel, and so forth. Plainly he was guilty of one of these charges—but of which one? He could not be guilty of all, nor could he be found guilty of any one of them on the evidence submitted. This is another example of how law can defeat justice, and suggests that Judge Marvin did not like the severe penalty of the piracy act. In *United States v. Gordon,* Fed. Cas. #15,231, vol. 25, pp. 1365–1366, Justice Nelson ruled that so long as Gordon was an American citizen, the ownership of the vessel was immaterial; Townsend also was an American citizen. Marvin's ruling made it virtually impossible to convict pirates in his court, because the true ownership of slave vessels was almost always obscure unless the defense chose to reveal the truth.

[12] Wish, *op. cit.,* pp. 569–588, gives the best account of this agitation, and of its failure. The Southern opponents of the slave trade have unfortunately received little attention from historians; but see, e.g., the *New Orleans Daily Picayune* editorials of July 8, 1858; April 30, May 5, 14, 17, 29, 1859; July 15, 1860.

[13] HED 7, 36-2, p. 631; *New Orleans Daily Picayune,* March 8 (p. 3), 16 (p. 6), 18 (p. 3), April 30 (p. 8), 1859.

[14] Duer to Toucey, March 30, 1859, HED 7, 36-2, p. 574; Wish, *op. cit.,* p. 583; *New Orleans Daily Picayune,* March 29, 1859, p. 3.

[15] No full, accurate account of the *Wanderer*'s voyage and of the subsequent prosecutions has ever been written. The most valuable single source is a collection of papers concerning the prosecutions at Savannah, evidently purloined from the circuit court records and ultimately finding its way into

the Manuscripts Division, Library of Congress. Among the collection are numerous transcripts of testimony and court orders. Other useful sources include: National Archives, Log of U.S. Ship Vincennes, entry for Oct. 12, 1858; Missroon to Conover, Dec. 8, 1858, HED 7, 36-2, p. 540; Conover to Toucey, March 12, 1859, *ibid.*, p. 550; *NYDT*, June 8 (p. 8), 11 (p. 7), Dec. 25 (pp. 6–7), 1858; Ganahl to Black, Dec. 13, 27, 28, 1858, with encs., Stewart to Cobb, Dec. 27, 1858, Couper to Black, Oct. 2, 1860, Attorney General's Letters, Georgia; *New Orleans Daily Picayune*, March 11 (p. 4), 15 (p. 4), April 21 (p. 1), 22 (p. 3), 28 (p. 3), May 4 (p. 2), 10 (p. 3), 15 (p. 3), 1859; Thompson to Spullock, May 3, 1859, Records . . . of the African Slave Trade, Letters Sent, # # 10–11.

[16] Republican Association of Washington, *The Slave Trade* (Washington: Buell & Blanchard, 1859, p. 7.

[17] See, e.g., "Report of the Superintendent of the Coast Survey, . . . 1858," HED 33, 35-2, pp. 121–123; "Letter . . . transmitting estimates of appropriations," HED 1, 35-2, pp. 125–128; "Report of the Secretary of War, 1858," HED 2, 35-2, vol. 2, pt. 3, pp. 761–785.

[18] See *United States v. Corrie*, Fed. Cas. #14,869, vol. 25, pp. 658 ff. Magrath's ruling gives a peculiar judicial interpretation. It is doubtful that there would have been much point in moving the case because of the outcome of the trials of crew members of the *Wanderer* in Georgia (see *NYDT*, Dec. 2, 1859, p. 5; May 30, 1860, p. 4).

[19] *NYDT*, April 20, 1860, p. 5; Cobb to Shell, Oct. 26, Nov. 2, 1859, Cobb to Faunce, Nov. 2, 1859; HED 7, 36-2, pp. 641–643. For an example of vain cruising see National Archives, Monthly Transcript of the Journal of the U.S. Revenue Steamer "Harriet Lane," From the 1st to the 29th of February [1860] Inclusive. This document shows how thin the patrol was; because of foul weather, the need to coal, and so forth, the *Lane* was at sea only fifteen days, steaming and sailing about 1,000 miles, and meeting only fifteen vessels. Obviously, her chances of meeting a slaver coming inshore were small on so long a patrol sector.

[20] For Slocumb's report of his conversation with Newman, see Slocumb to Thompson, Sept. 30, 1859, Marshals' Letters. By some quirk his over-all report was filed with the miscellaneous letters (Slocumb to Thompson, Nov. 21, 1859, Records . . . of the African Slave Trade, Miscellaneous Letters Received). Hatch to Thompson, Nov. 21, 1859, *ibid.*, also reports adverse Southern sentiment to slave imports.

[21] Peyton to Thomson, April 24, 1860, Marshals' Letters. Peyton's implication that slave vessels were built in Maine for the slave trade has no foundation in fact (see Appendix M). For additional rumors of landings see, e.g., *NYDT*, April 21 (p. 9), Aug. 8 (p. 6), 1860; the former report was found upon investigation to be another hoax perpetrated upon Northerners. A rumored landing from the *Clotilde* in Mobile Bay in July, 1860, has

been accepted by several historians as true, but no good evidence of it has ever been found. Moreover, three authors give three different versions of the affair, and not one offers a sound source for his assertions. Wish, *op. cit.*, p. 585, states that the *Clotilde* landed 116 Negroes in July, 1859, the survivors of an initial cargo of 175, and that the owner, Captain Timothy Meagher, a plantation magnate of Alabama, was arrested but, thanks to a costly defense involving bribery and perjury, managed to be released. Wish's sources are S. H. M. Byers, "The Last Slave Ship," *Harper's Monthly Magazine,* CXIII (1906), 742–746; *27th and 28th Annual Reports of American Anti-Slavery Society,* 1859–1860, p. 127. The American Anti-Slavery Society is thoroughly unreliable on such matters, and Byers' article seems to be no better. Byers, though claiming to have obtained his information from some of the Africans who were landed, gives numerous details about the business side of the voyage which must have been unknown to them; furthermore, he cites no authority for these details. He is vague about Captain Meagher's trial. The general tenor of the article is so emotional and antigovernment that it is worthy of little credence on that ground alone. John R. Spears, in *The American Slave Trade* (New York: Scribner, 1900), p. 208, states that the *Clotilde* brought over 175 Negroes, and lost not a single one. He puts her down as a 327-ton vessel, remarkably large for a schooner, and states that only twenty-five Negroes could be sold because of the rush of officials for prize money. He contends that Meagher lost $100,000 on the venture, even though the slaves cost only $8,460 in gold plus ninety casks of rum and eight cases of cloths. Spears says nothing about the trial of Meagher, nor does he give any indication as to where he obtained his detailed information. Frederic Bancroft, *Slave-Trading in the Old South* (Baltimore: J. H. Furst, 1931), p. 359n., states that 103 Africans were transferred to a steamer in July, 1860, in line with the contemporary rumors. Then he adds: "The main facts about the *Clotilde* were quickly made known to the Department of Justice; but, presumably on account of the presidential campaign then raging, prosecution was delayed, and secession soon intervened." Bancroft, normally a careful scholar, gave no source for this information. There was, of course, no Department of Justice at the time, and the letters received by the Attorney General from officers in Alabama contain nothing relating to the *Clotilde* landing. Bancroft's claim that there were no prosecutions conflicts with the reports of Wish and Byers; however, it is not clear why secession would necessarily have interrupted them, because Southern courts took over pending federal cases and because importation of slaves was prohibited by Alabama law. For contemporary rumors, and the opinion of the *Picayune* and the *Mobile Mercury* that the whole business was a hoax, see *New Orleans Daily Picayune,* July 12 (p. 2), 21 (p. 5), 29 (p. 3), 1860.

[22] Department of Interior, *The Statistics of the Population of the United States . . . compiled, from the original returns of the Ninth Census* (Wash-

ington: Government Printing Office, 1872), p. 336, states that a total of 1,984 Negroes, natives of Africa, were found in the United States. The largest concentration was in the lower South: 414 in Louisiana, 318 in Texas, 314 in Georgia, 237 in Alabama, 231 in South Carolina, 122 in Mississippi, and 86 in Florida. Forty-seven African-born Negroes were found in Tennessee, and 32 in North Carolina; no other state had any appreciable number, and the "slave-breeding" states of Kentucky and Virginia had only six and three, respectively. Unfortunately the published statistics do not break down these African-born Negroes by age; some of them could have been smuggled in before 1820, when smuggling was unquestionably carried on to a considerable extent, and a few might have been survivors of the legal slave trade which ended in 1808. There is evidently an opportunity for research in the original returns of the Ninth Census, but in any event there could not have been much smuggling in the late 'fifties, unless there were a conspiracy of silence among African Negroes to conceal their origin. A possible motive for silence was that the Fourteenth Amendment gives federally protected citizenship rights to "all persons born or naturalized in the United States," but not to illegal immigrants smuggled in by stealth. The number of African Negroes found, however, suggests that there was never a large-scale African slave trade after 1820, and that the *Wanderer* landing was probably not unique except in the fact that the crime was judicially established.

²³ See Buchanan's third and fourth annual messages in James D. Richardson, *A Compilation of the Messages and Papers of the Presidents* (Washington, 1897), V, 555, 649. See also Seward to Lyons, March 22, 1862, *State Papers,* LIII, 1425.

10. LASALA, MORRIS, AND JUDGE BETTS

¹ *NYDT,* June 17 (p. 3), 18 (p. 8), 19 (p. 3), 1856.

² E.g., *United States v. Valentine,* reported in *ibid.,* May 15 (p. 7), 16 (p. 8), 1856.

³ *United States v. Cunha et al.,* reported in *ibid.,* June 25 (p. 8), 26 (p. 7), 1856; McKeon to Streeter, March 29, 1856, Solicitor's Letters, Box 80 (Southern New York district, 1856–1860).

⁴ *NYDT,* June 26, 1856, p. 7. In this case Betts was charging the jury under the act of 1794, but the language of the acts of 1794 and 1818 is identical on this point. None of these rulings was ever published in the legal press; *United States v. Naylor,* Fed. Cas. #15,858, vol. 27, p. 78, deals only in a small measure with these questions.

⁵ *NYDT,* June 19, 1856, p. 3. For the act of 1807 see 2 *U.S. Stat. at L.* 426–430.

[6] That is, it repealed the sections prohibiting the outfitting of slavers; Secs. 7–10 remained in force. The first of these allowed the seizure of laden slavers of any nationality, found in or near American territorial waters; the other three set up rigid safeguards so that the trade in domestic slaves carried on coastwise could not be used as a screen for the smuggling of African slaves.

[7] *United States v. Gooding*, 23 U.S. (12 Wheaton) 478, states in part: "There is a clear distinction between causing a vessel to sail, or to be sent away, with intent to employ her in the slave trade, and with intent that she should be employed in that trade. The former applies to an intent of the party causing the act, the latter to the employment of the vessel, whether by himself or a stranger. The evidence may fully support these counts, and yet may not constitute an offence within the act of Congress; for the employment by a mere stranger would not justify the conviction of the party charged with causing her to sail, or to be sent away, with intent to employ her in the slave trade, as owner." At first glance, this seems to support Betts, but there is good reason to believe that it did not do so. Some of its language is ambiguous; and in any event Gooding was the owner, and had control of the voyage. This fact seemed well established at the trial, and the only question was whether or not the indictment (ineptly framed on the wording of the act of 1794) was properly suited to his conviction under the act of 1818. The Supreme Court held that the grand jury had indeed used the wrong language in describing Gooding's crime, but it did not consider the question of someone like Lasala who, while acting in the capacity of owner, aided and abetted the person who actually had control of the vessel.

[8] Alexander C. Flick, "Samuel Rossiter Betts," *Dictionary of American Biography*, II, 231.

[9] *The Alexander*, Fed. Cas. #165, vol. 1, p. 362.

[10] *The Emily and Caroline*, 22 U.S. (9 Wheaton) 381; *The Plattsburgh*, 23 U.S. (10 Wheaton) 133; *United States v. Gooding*, 25 U.S. (12 Wheaton) 460.

[11] For the absconding of Morris and Peterson see chapter 2. For Betts's pretrial statement see *New York Morning Herald*, Nov. 2, 1839, p. 2, and, for the trial, *ibid.*, Dec. 2, 1839, p. 1. Thompson implied in his public statement that he and Betts differed from Story, rather than he and Betts from each other; he explained that he did not want a conflict between the two circuit courts. But he must have been trying to gloss over the clash between himself and his colleague, for the case was sent to the Supreme Court on a certificate that Betts and Thompson could not agree. For this certificate see National Archives, Criminal Records, 1790–1853, Box 2 (U.S. Circuit Court, Southern New York district). For the Supreme Court's ruling see *United States v. Morris*, 39 U.S. (14 Peters) 464.

[12] Betts's decision is reprinted in full in *State Papers*, XXIX, 649–655.

[13] The papers found on board the *Catharine* are printed in H. Rep. 283, 27-3, pp. 217–221. See also *The Catharine*, Fed. Cas. #14,755, vol. 25, p. 337; Buchanan to Palmerston, Aug. 14, 1840, *State Papers*, XXIX, 655–656.

[14] *The Catharine*, Fed. Cas. #14,755, vol. 25, pp. 332 ff.

[15] The *Emily's* inventory is in *NYDT*, Nov. 12, 1859, p. 8. For similar cargoes see *The Orion*, Fed. Cas. #10,575, vol. 18, p. 817, and *The Isla de Cuba*, Fed. Cas. ## 15,447 and 15,449, vol. 26, pp. 548–549, 554. Both these vessels were confiscated—one at Boston, the other by Judge Nathan Hall who was temporarily filling in at New York. For the dismissal of the libel against the *Emily*, see National Archives, Admiralty Docket (U.S. District Court, Southern New York district), XV, 521, 525. For Commodore Wise see Wise to Secy. of Admiralty, July 11, 1859, HED 7, 36-2, p. 349.

[16] The cases of the *Kate* and the *Weather Gage* ultimately reached the Supreme Court; see 69 U.S. (2 Wallace) 350, 375. For Betts's ruling on them see *NYDT*, Feb. 2, 1861, p. 3. Betts confiscated the *Kate* on grounds that, although her cargo could have been used in lawful trade, her owner's inability to prove that he was really her owner and really an established merchant, to produce the captain or the supercargo (the former having departed while out on bail), and to explain Da Costa's connection with her made the case against him a damning one. Betts confiscated the *Weather Gage* on the ground that her cargo was unsuited for a voyage to China, her announced destination; he also remarked that the case against her was not so strong as the case against the *Kate*. At the same time Betts dismissed the libel against the schooner *William L. Cogswell;* this case is unreported, but the district court records in the National Archives (file A-16-209) show that the cargo included 49 barrels of rice, 80 barrels of bread, 6 cases of "clarifying" boilers, 2 cases of medicines, 50 packages of wooden pails, 2 crates of crockery, some lumber, and a large quantity of cotton goods and muskets. The principal incriminating item lacking was water casks.

[17] *NYDT,* July 18, 1857; McKeon to Streeter, Nov. 18, 1857, with encs., McKeon to Hillyer, Dec. 14, 1857, Joachimssen to Hillyer, Jan. 15, 1858, Sedgwick to Hillyer, Feb. 22, 1858, Joachimssen to Hillyer, April 6, 1858, Solicitor's Letters, Box 80. The Supreme Court dockets reveal that the case was never docketed. For the *Ellen's* subsequent career see National Archives, New York Registers Sail, vol. 119 (Dec. 28, 1857, to March 3, 1858), #143; vol. 121 (April 27 to July 16, 1858), #411; Grey to Conover, March 21, 1859, NA 89-110, #50. For additional information on the prosecution see *NYDT*, May 1 (p. 5), June 12 (p. 8), 13 (p. 8), 16 (p. 8), 1857; SED 53, 37-2, p. 3.

[18] This was the *Panchita* case; see *NYDT*, Oct. 9 (p. 5), 10 (p. 5), 11 (p. 8), 15 (p. 7), 16 (p. 3), 20 (p. 8), 21 (p. 8), 22 (p. 8), 25 (p. 7), Nov. 11 (p. 8), 19 (p. 8), 21 (p. 8), 22 (p. 8), 25 (p. 7), 27 (p. 7), 28 (p. 3), Dec. 5 (p. 7), 8 (p. 7), 9 (p. 8), 18 (p. 7), 1856.

[19] This was the case of J. P. da Cunha; see *NYDT,* July 16, 1856, p. 8.

[20] See election editorial, *ibid.,* Nov. 4, 1862, p. 4.

[21] *Ibid.,* July 10, 1857, p. 4.

[22] *Ibid.,* Oct. 10, 1856, p. 4.

[23] See, e.g., the vain efforts of Marshal Murray to have Congress pass a stringent bill specifically penalizing shipping agents, pilots, and others who knowingly aided the outfitting of slavers (Smith to Murray, Jan. 16, 1862, Marshals' Letters; Murray to Smith, Jan. 25, 1862, with enc., *ibid.;* *Journal of the Senate,* 37th Cong., 2d sess., p. 143; 37th Cong., 3d sess., pp. 231–232).

11. THE VANISHING SLAVERS

[1] This was the decision in the *Butterfly* case, April, 1840, reprinted in *State Papers,* XXIX, 649–655.

[2] For the *Orion's* double deck, see National Archives, New York Registers Sail, vol. 123 (Nov. 8, 1858, to Jan. 29, 1859), #37. For Vining's lawful trade with the West Indies see, e.g., *NYDT,* Jan. 28 (p. 8), Feb. 1 (p. 8), March 19 (p. 7), 1859. It was Vining who dispatched the *Lyra* to Havana for her prearranged sale (*ibid.,* May 10, 1858, p. 8), and shipped the *Ellen's* cargo on her 1858 slaving voyage (*ibid.,* June 25, 1858, p. 8). Most of the facts about the *Orion's* first slaving voyage are presented in Judge Hall's verdict (*The Orion,* Fed. Cas. #10,575, vol. 18, pp. 817–819). For the international dispute see the extensive correspondence in HED 7, 36-2, pp. 358–372; for release of the prisoners, SED 53, 37-2, p. 3, and *NYDT,* June 18, 1859, p. 7. Morgan's letter to Cass appears in HED 7, 36-2, p. 353; the *Orion's* bonding, in SED 53, 37-2, p. 2; Morgan's purchase, in New York Registers Sail, vol. 125 (May 11 to Aug. 17, 1859), #395. Inman to Toucey, Dec. 15, 1859, Jan. 30, 1860, with encs., HED 7, 36-2, pp. 585–588, describe affairs on the African coast on the *Orion's* second voyage; Blumenberg's trials are recounted in *NYDT,* Nov. 17 (p. 8), 1860; March 8 (p. 3), 9 (p. 8), May 15 (p. 3), 16 (p. 3), 29 (p. 3), 1861; his pardon, in National Archives, Pardons, VII (1857–1865), 470–471.

[3] The *Isla de Cuba* was bonded and sold, and when last seen was headed for Black Point full of slaving equipment; her bond was not confiscated until five years later. See *The Isla de Cuba,* Fed. Cas. ## 15,447 and 15,449; New York Registers Sail, vol. 124 (Jan. 31 to May 11, 1859), #147; enc. in Lyons to Cass, Dec. 5, 1859, HED 7, 36-2, pp. 380–381; Buchanan to Collantes, Nov., 1859, *State Papers,* L, 952. The *Cora* was bonded (with a worthless bond) and captured full of slaves; for her bond, see SED 53, 37-2, p. 2. The *Ardennes* was bonded, and after sundry changes of ownership was sent to Africa and captured full of slaves; the libel upon which

she was bonded was ultimately dismissed. See SED 53, 37-2, p. 2; National Archives, Admiralty Docket (U.S. District Court, Southern New York district), XV, 412–413; New York Registers Sail, vol. 126, ## 493–495; vol. 127, #592; vol. 130, #452; House of Commons, *Papers, 1865,* LVI, 529. The *Lewis McLain* and the *William Clark* were released on bond at New Orleans in 1857 and were captured by British cruisers; the original libels against them were dismissed (see, e.g., HED 7, 36-2, p. 627; House of Commons, *Papers, 1861,* LXIV, 360). For the case of the *Augusta* see chap. 8, n. 5. Other suspected vessels, such as the *Wanderer,* the *Emily,* the *Triton,* and the *Falmouth,* were bonded and went back to sea, but proof that they went on slaving voyages while free under bond is not available.

⁴ Wise to Buchanan, May 8, 1845, HED 61, 30-2, pp. 178–180; Tyler to Wise, June 12, 1845, *ibid.,* pp. 205–206; Wise to Buchanan, Nov. 24, 1845, *ibid.,* p. 210; *NYDT,* Aug. 1 (p. 3), 5 (p. 2), 6 (p. 2), 7 (p. 2), Sept. 14 (p. 2), 1844.

⁵ *NYDT,* Oct. 4 (p. 8), 6 (p. 8), 1858; Sprague to Hillyer, May 3, 1860, Solicitor's Letters, Box 51 (Mass., 1860–1867). An interesting question raised by the above letter is why no action had been taken by May, 1860, to collect any of the bonds declared forfeit when Reis failed to appear.

⁶ Appendix B records various known cases. For the statutory requirement that prisoners be bailed, except in capital cases, see act of Sept. 24, 1789, Sec. 33, 1 *U.S. Stat. at L.* 91.

12. "EVERYTHING I DID WAS LAWFUL"

¹ The *Pilgrim* was only an auxiliary, and her name therefore does not appear in the appendix (Slacum to Webster, Sept. 14, 1841, HED 43, 29-1, pp. 10–11).

² This is reminiscent of the device exposed by Nicholas Trist in December, 1838 (see Trist to Forsyth, Dec. 18, 1838, HED 115, 26-2, pp. 260–276; Jan. 25, 1839, with encs., *ibid.,* pp. 298–304).

³ A detailed report of the proceedings against Flowery appears in the *Boston Post,* June 4–7, 9–10, 13, July 14, Aug. 2, 1845 (all p. 2).

⁴ For Flowery's release see National Archives, Pardons, VI, 8–9. For his death at sea see *NYDT,* Dec. 11, 1847, p. 1. For the case of the *Mary Ann's* crew, see *The Mary Ann,* Fed. Cas. #9,194, vol. 16, pp. 949–952.

⁵ *NYDT,* Oct. 24 (p. 3), 27 (p. 3), 30 (p. 3), Nov. 17 (p. 2), 1862; Pardons, VII, 450–451.

⁶ A few facts about the prosecution may be found in the *Boston Post,* Jan. 6, May 27, June 10–14, 16, 30, 1862 (all p. 4). For Oaksmith's escape see Keys to Smith, Sept. 13, Nov. 18, 1862, with encs., Marshals' Letters. In 1863 Zeno Kelly was convicted under the act of 1818, but the conviction

was quashed, ostensibly because of a defective indictment (*United States v. Kelly*, Fed. Cas. #15,515, vol. 26, pp. 697–700). As the court records of this case are held incommunicado by the Federal Records Center in Massachusetts, I have been unable to ascertain what eventually became of Kelly.

7 The following table, compiled from Pardons, VII, 35–39, reveals this clearly:

Pardons Granted
(November 4, 1858, to August 10, 1859)

Initials of prisoner	Offense	Sentence	Pardon
C. B.	Murder	Death	Commuted to life imprisonment
S. M.	Post-office robbery	Five years from January, 1854	Citizenship rights restored, January, 1859
J. B. S.	Mail robbery	Ten years from March, 1855	Full pardon, January, 1859
C. W.	Counterfeiting	Eight years from October, 1854	Full pardon, February, 1859
S. C., Jr.	Passing counterfeit coin	Six months from June, 1858	Citizenship rights restored, February, 1859
P. K.	Manslaughter	Three years from November, 1855, and court costs	Costs remitted, February, 1859
J. C.	Assault	Six months from December, 1858, and court costs	Costs remitted, April, 1859
J. F.	Stealing a letter	Ten years from December, 1858	Full pardon, May, 1859
A. E.	Assault and battery	Three years from March, 1858	Full pardon, May, 1859
T. L.	Counterfeiting	Five years from June, 1854, and $500 fine	Fine remitted, May, 1859
H. T. L. W.	Aiding prisoner to escape	Two years from June, 1856, $20 fine, and costs	Fine and costs remitted, June, 1859

C. W. P.	Murder	Death	Commuted to life imprisonment at hard labor
J. M.	Petty larceny	Eight months from December, 1858	Citizenship rights restored, July, 1859
P. H.	Counterfeiting	Ten years from November, 1853, and $2,500 fine	Full pardon, August, 1859

13. PIRATES WHO WERE NOT HANGED

[1] Act of May 15, 1820, Secs. 4–5, 3 *U.S. Stat. at L.* 690–691.

[2] For Smith's arrest, trial, and sentence see *NYDT*, Sept. 21 (p. 6), Oct. 2 (p. 7), Nov. 6 (p. 3), 7 (p. 3), 9 (p. 6), 10 (p. 3), 21 (p. 7), 1854; Jan. 26 (p. 5), May 17 (p. 7), 18 (p. 8), 21 (p. 6), 1855; July 17 (p. 7), 1856; June 9 (p. 4), 1857. For his pardon see National Archives, Pardons, VI (1847–1857), 545–546. Nelson's ruling about a new trial was reported in the legal press (see *United States v. Smith*, Fed. Cas. #16,320, vol. 27, pp. 1138–1139). On Story's ruling about the act of 1818, see *United States v. La Coste*, Fed. Cas. #15,548, vol. 26, pp. 829 ff. On the fact that the slave trade was not piracy under international law, see, e.g., *The Antelope*, 23 U.S. (10 Wheaton) 114.

[3] For Macomber's arrest, arraignment, and escape see *NYDT*, Oct. 5 (p. 5), 12 (p. 7), 18 (p. 8), Nov. 2 (p. 7), 1858. For the jailer's lack of pay see *ibid.*, Dec. 9, 1856, p. 7. For the lack of action on the indictment see National Archives, Criminal Docket (U.S. Circuit Court, Southern New York district), I (1853–1864), 168, 173. Note that William Pent, the *Braman*'s second mate, also escaped from the same jail (*NYDT*, Sept. 13, 1856, p. 7).

[4] Among them were Captain Bowen of the *Nightingale* (chap. 3), and Captain Latham and mate Morgan Fredericks of the *Cora* (see *NYDT*, Nov. 26, 1861, p. 3). The paper incorrectly attributes their escape to Democrats; in fact they escaped from Republican marshal Robert Murray (*ibid.*, May 31, 1861, p. 8; Criminal Docket, I, 235, 239–240).

[5] Senator Wilson of Massachusetts, deeming the act of 1820 too severe, proposed to lessen its penalty to life imprisonment, although extending it at the same time to owners (*Congressional Globe*, 36th Cong., 1st sess., III, 2207–2211). It is significant that the Georgia secession convention, while keeping the slave-trade laws in force, reduced the penalty from death to a maximum of 25 years and a minimum of 5 years in prison (*NYDT*, Jan.

29, 1861, p. 5). Judge Magrath, presumably mirroring South Carolina sentiment, argued that it was not piracy to hold a Negro in bondage aboard ship,
if he was already a slave when brought aboard; this would remove the stigma
from Southern slaveowners, all of whom held Negroes who were already
slaves (*United States v. Corrie*, Fed. Cas. #14,869, vol. 25, pp. 658 ff.).
His view was of course absurd, for a reason long before expounded by
Justice Story in *United States v. Battiste*, Fed. Cas. #14,545, vol. 24, pp.
1042 ff. The attorneys for J. E. Farnham, the *Wanderer*'s supercargo, used
this argument in their successful defense of him at Savannah in May, 1860
(*NYDT*, May 30, 1860, p. 4). On the unsuccessful Georgia prosecutions of
three *Wanderer* seamen, see *NYDT*, Nov. 18 (p. 5), 23 (p. 5), Dec. 2
(p. 5), 1859; Molyneux to Russell, Nov. 28, 30, 1859, House of Commons,
Slave Trade Papers, 1860, Class B, p. 263. On Weston's acquittal see Tatum
to Thompson, Jan 13, 1861, with encs., Attorneys' Letters. For other material on that prosecution see HED 7, 36-2, pp. 460–463.

⁶ For other piracy prosecutions that failed because of the nationality
claim see *United States v. Brown*, Fed. Cas. #14,656, vol. 24, p. 1245;
United States v. Darnaud, Fed. Cas. #14,918, vol. 25, pp. 755–765; and
the cases of four *Haidee* seamen, *NYDT*, Nov. 30, 1858, p. 7. For a prosecution under the act of 1800 frustrated by lack of citizenship, see *NYDT*,
Sept. 12, 1856, p. 7. For testimony that foreign-born captains were preferred, see enc. in McBlair to Conover, Oct. 9, 1857, HED 7, 36-2, pp.
523–525.

⁷ For examples of such pleas see the depositions of James McGuire and
George W. Palmer, HED 7, 36-2, pp. 17–20, 76–79; the testimony of
Henry Fling at Smith's trial, *NYDT*, Nov. 9, 1854, p. 6; and the testimony
of the *Senator*'s crew members, SED 6, 31-2, pp. 3–6.

⁸ For the proceedings against Morgan and his mates see HED 7, 36-2,
pp. 423–424, 436–438, 440; *Boston Post*, April 3 (p. 4), May 15 (p. 4), Oct.
4 (p. 1), 1860; *Boston Evening Transcript*, Oct. 2 (p. 4), 3 (p. 4), 5 (p. 2),
1860. These pirates were the only ones ever turned over by the British, who
did so only upon the request of Flag Officer Inman after he had heard that
they had been landed at St. Helena.

⁹ In E. D. Smith to C. B. Smith, Nov. 22, 1861 (Attorneys' Letters), the
district attorney wrote that Roosevelt had made no preparations to try Gordon, and had publicly declared that he did not think public opinion would
justify a capital conviction. It is true that when Roosevelt announced he
would not promise to accept a conviction under the act of 1800, he left it
unclear what he would do, stating that "in the present excited condition of
the public mind on the African question, and the consequent liability to
misconstruction of official acts, he had come to the conclusion to leave the
prisoners to plead . . . without any understanding or commitment on the
part of the authorities" (*New York Weekly Tribune*, Nov. 10, 1860, p. 1).

This does not sound like the language of a man about to press for a capital conviction. On the other hand, in April, 1861, he announced that he was preparing the case for his successor to carry on, and adverted to the absence of needed witnesses (*NYDT*, April 2, 1861, p. 8). One of his witnesses had previously been ill (*NYDT*, Jan. 30, 1861, p. 3). Smith himself had some delays (see, e.g., *NYDT*, April 25 [p. 7], May 14 [p. 3], 1861). It is therefore not clear that Roosevelt was undercutting the case.

[10] On Smith, see *NYDT*, April 5 (p. 4), 11 (p. 8), 1861; for the trial, *ibid.*, June 21 (p. 8), 22 (p. 3), 1861.

[11] Smith to Whiting, Oct. 17, 1861, Attorneys' Letters; Smith to Smith, Oct. 18, Nov. 22, 1861, *ibid.*; *NYDT*, Nov. 7 (p. 7), 8 (p. 7), 9 (p. 8), Dec. 2 (p. 7), 1861; Feb. 24 (p. 3), 1862; *United States v. Gordon,* Fed. Cas. #15,231, vol. 25, pp. 1364–1368.

[12] For the *Bonito* prisoners see Criminal Docket, I, 245; *NYDT*, Nov. 8, 1861, p. 7 (quoting a remark by Smith that he was not going to prosecute one of the *Bonito*'s crew members because he was a foreigner); Smith to Smith, Nov. 22, 1861, Attorneys' Letters, in which he remarks that three of the *Bonito* prisoners had previously been aboard the *Erie,* and had been released by the *Mohican* because they were Spaniards. For the escape of the *Cora*'s mate see *NYDT*, Nov. 26, 1861, p. 3. Crawford's part in the prosecution of Albert Horn may be seen in the account of that trial (chap. 12); for the sentences of the *Erie* and *Cora* mates see Criminal Docket, I, 228–230, 239–240.

[13] Smith to Smith, Feb. 4, 1862, Attorneys' Letters; *United States v. Westervelt,* Fed. Cas. #16,668, vol. 28, pp. 529–531; *NYDT*, Nov. 12 (p. 3), 13 (p. 8), 15 (p. 3), 25 (p. 3), 1861.

[14] *NYDT*, May 7 (p. 3), 9 (p. 5), 10 (p. 3), 12 (p. 5), Oct. 14 (p. 3), 18 (p. 5), 20 (p. 3), Nov. 10 (p. 3), 1862; Criminal Docket, I, 260.

[15] *NYDT*, Oct. 19, 1861, p. 8; Oct. 31, 1862, p. 3; Criminal Docket, I, 278. It is not clear whether the jury found him "not guilty" of both indictments, or only of the indictment under the act of 1800, but no further proceedings were had in his case.

[16] U.S. Code, Title 18, Sec. 1585. The crime of confining, and so forth, with intent to make Negroes slaves, is also no longer described as "piracy."

BIBLIOGRAPHY

BIBLIOGRAPHY

SOURCE MATERIALS

The illegal slave trade is one of the best-documented criminal enterprises on record, and those who wish to find answers to the numerous unsolved questions surrounding it will have no difficulty obtaining an abundance of information beyond that presented in this volume.

A century ago all records were kept, and all letters were written, by hand. Many of the writers could not boast of good penmanship, and even good penmen made numerous errors. Their manuscripts contain many ambiguously shaped letters, and printed sources are full of wrong choices made by typesetters when translating manuscript into print. The letters *e* and *o* and *a* often were scarcely distinguishable, an *n* with sharp points looked like a *u,* and many other slips occurred. These cause little confusion in ordinary words of standard spelling, for it is obvious what the semilegible letter was meant to be. But proper names have no standardized spelling, and errors are legion. Thomas Morgan's last name was once spelled "Moreau" in an official document, the *J. W. Reed* is persistently called the *J. W. Reid* in British reports, Lima Viana's first name was frequently spelled "Lenia," Pierre Pearce's last name was often written as "Peirce," and so on. Further confusion is created by the lack of standardized place names. The Congo was often called the "Rio Zaire," its Spanish name; Santiago, "St. Jago"; Snake's Head, "Cabeca de Cobra." Kabenda appears also as Kabinda, Cabenda, and Cabinda. Punta da Lenha, the notorious slave-trading depot in the Congo, appears as "Punta Lena," "Punta da Linha," "Puenta da Lehne," "Ponta de Lehna," "Porto de Lena," "Ponte de Lenhoo," "Puente da Lenhe," and even "Port de Sehna."

Students of American lawbreaking will find that the most valuable source of information is the occasional reports furnished by the executive to the House or the Senate, and published by them. They consist almost entirely of official correspondence between the State Department and the British Foreign Office, the State Department and American ministers and consuls, and the Navy Department and naval officers. Some reports are quite voluminous, and collectively they offer a wealth of details, frankly presented. They were not "edited" to make the administration look better. On the contrary, they make American law enforcement look worse than it was. The British notes were seldom complimentary, but rather complained of inadequate law enforcement. The consular correspondence is one long tale of lawbreaking. There was relatively little naval correspondence, and it did not do justice to the work of the cruisers. As almost no correspondence from marshals, attorneys, and collectors was published, the documents contain little information on arrests in American ports or judicial proceedings against ships and men. Whatever the reason for these omissions, they made it look as though the government made no serious attempt to prosecute offenders. Another shortcoming of the reports is their arrangement. They are not indexed, and the correspondence is usually presented chronologically, rather than by subject. Within these limits the reports are very useful.

For study of the slave trade in general, and for additional details of American participation in it, British official correspondence is invaluable. Each year a broad selection of reports from naval officers, commissioners, and diplomats, and of correspondence with foreign governments, was furnished to the House of Commons. These were published as part of its sessional papers, under the title *Slave Trade Papers.* More convenient for general use is the slave-trade correspondence included in the annual volumes of *British and Foreign State Papers,* published under the auspices of the Foreign Office. Generally speaking, the *State Papers* reprint the more important pieces of correspondence appearing in the *Slave Trade Papers.* In both series the correspondence is grouped first by originating officer and then chronologically, but brief abstracts of each letter appear at the front of each group, making use relatively easy. Little needs to be added to what has been said earlier about the unreliability of British reports on the slave trade. Plainly a great many "facts" set forth in these letters were no more than gossip, and the student will be wise to use them with reserve and to cross-check whenever possible. A remark made by Justice Leigh in the *Newport* case is pertinent: "Though Lieutenant De Robeck swore thus positively to these facts, he did not state how he had acquired a knowledge of them, and from his subsequent examination it appears that he did not know them at all, that he never saw nor was acquainted with either Garrido or Flores, nor ever saw anything of any slave establishments of theirs, and that he knew nothing of them except from the information of others."

Another useful British publication is the *Report from the select committee of the House of Lords, appointed to consider the best means which Great Britain can adopt for the final extinction of the African slave trade . . . ordered to be printed by the House of Commons, 15 February 1850* (n.p., n.d.). It reprints much correspondence, includes extensive testimony, and gives a more unvarnished account of British activities in slave-trade suppression than the documents furnished to Parliament by the Crown.

Although published American naval correspondence concerning the slave trade is scanty, large quantities are readily available in National Archives microfilm publications. The series, Letters Received by the Secretary of the Navy from Commanding Officers of Squadrons (NA 89), includes many reels of letters from the Brazilian and African squadrons. Usually one reel is devoted to the dispatches of each commander, and there are fairly useful indexes at the front. The dispatches, interspersed among correspondence dealing with administrative or other matters unconnected with the slave trade, contain considerable information of value. The general movements of warships can usually be traced, either in the squadron commander's reports or in the reports of his subordinates appearing as enclosures. Reports describing captures are included, as well as information on American slavers that escaped the squadron. But much is lacking. Absentee commodores like Skinner and Conover did not furnish detailed accounts of their cruisers' operations, precisely because they did not know what the vessels were doing. Though other commanders kept a closer check, their correspondence is weak on the American slavers that escaped, either because they did not know about them, or because, like Inman, they did not wish to admit their existence.

Much information not appearing in the squadron commanders' dispatches may be recovered from other series of letters received by the

Navy Department. Frequently naval officers having news to report wrote directly to the secretary of the navy. These letters were bound chronologically in three series, by rank of the writers: captains, commanders, and lower-ranking officers (Officers' Letters). The student must know the name of the officer whose report he is seeking, and the approximate date of his report, in order to locate it. So little of this correspondence pertains to the slave trade that general screening of it is impracticable. Each volume of letters has an alphabetical index, giving locations of each officer's letters throughout the volume. The National Archives has already microfilmed a large part of this correspondence, and is working on the rest.

A final source for the operations of naval vessels and of revenue cutters is ships' logs. The National Archives holds a vast collection of logbooks which give a complete record of the vessels' movements, weather conditions, vessels met at sea, and other events of interest. As narrative reports of cruises, even when extant, are often not specific, the logbooks provide the only record of many events.

There is no satisfactory record of operations in American ports against the slave trade. As marshals and attorneys did not make regular reports on their activities, many details are lost forever. Their routine efforts to watch out for possible slave vessels and known criminals cannot be learned, and even arrests were not often reported to Washington. If a vessel was libeled after investigation, the solicitor of the treasury would probably hear about it, but there were no regular reports of criminal prosecutions. The Letters received by the Solicitor of the Treasury from U.S. Attorneys, Clerks of Courts, and Marshals (National Archives, RG 206), as well as the Letters received by the Attorney General from U.S. Attorneys, Marshals, and Judges (National Archives, RG 60), are useful, but altogether they are a meager and incomplete source. These records have not yet been microfilmed, but the National Archives has microfilmed several reels covering the Records of the Office of the Secretary of the Interior relating to the Suppression of the African Slave Trade and Negro Colonization. They are of considerable value, though the Department of the Interior had so little control over slave-trade suppression activities that its records are incomplete.

Even when official reports can be found, they are likely to give few details. Therefore the contemporary newspaper becomes very valuable. Much of the material in this study has come from the legal columns of the *New York Herald* or the *New York Tribune,* the *Baltimore Sun,* the

Boston Post, and the *New Orleans Picayune.* Newspapers were usually interested in arrests, examinations, and trials, and their coverage ranged from highly detailed transcripts to brief accounts, or sometimes to none at all. Whether good or bad, their reports in many instances offer the only surviving information. Court records of criminal cases were skimpy, judged by the Southern New York district records in the National Archives, and few slave-trade cases have found their way into lawbooks. *The Federal Cases* (30 vols.; St. Paul: West Publishing Co., 1894–1897), and *Reports of Cases Argued and Adjudged in the Supreme Court of the United States* (various reporters, publishers, and dates) include only a small number of the prosecutions. Few cases went to the Supreme Court. and the legal profession was very erratic in sponsoring reports of decisions in the lower federal courts. These lawbooks boast fine indexes, but the student working in newspaper sources and manuscript court records has no sure way of tracking down cases. As certain congressional documents give information on libels against vessels, the student is given a key to the most likely newspaper files and court records to search. But the records are incomplete, cases were sometimes dropped without notice, and long delays ensued in prosecution.

Various other sources may be used with profit, such as the consular and legatine correspondence preserved in the National Archives. So much of this correspondence has been published that for ordinary purposes no reference to the complete files is necessary, but students working on limited periods might find the manuscript material of distinct value.

The National Archives contain other useful material, such as the record of pardons. Here, oddly enough, are the only references preserved in the archives to certain criminal prosecutions. Three volumes cover the period 1837–1862; one is indexed by name and offense, the second has only a name index, and the third is unindexed. There are also the triplicate copies of ships' registers; of particular value is a complete set of New York registers. As slavers almost invariably changed registry, I found it possible to trace New York slaving operations simply by leafing through the volumes looking for familiar names. A prerequisite to such a search is a list of slavers of a particular period compiled from other sources, but the registers add helpful information to such a list. Reports of suspicious vessels seldom specify tonnage (and hence slave-carrying capacity), ownership, or port of origin. The Works Projects Administration publication, *Ship Registers and Enrollments of New Orleans,*

Louisiana (6 vols.; Baton Rouge: Louisiana State University Press, 1942), does the same service as the New York manuscript registers, though a few registers are missing. A great advantage of the WPA publication is that it has an index of owners' and masters' names. A great deal of criminality can be uncovered by using ships' registers in conjunction with other sources. The Record of Registers, a series of manuscript volumes preserved in the National Archives, records every register granted in the United States; the material is arranged chronologically by ports. Unfortunately it was kept in a very illegible hand.

Also useful are the shipping clearance columns in newspapers, particularly the one in the *New Orleans Picayune.* Having learned that a particular slaver was registered at New Orleans on a particular day, one may surmise that it sailed within a few days, and find without undue searching who was the shipper of the cargo. The *Picayune* also published manifests. The *New York Tribune* unfortunately did not, nor did it always publish the departures of slavers. Whether this was because a clearance clerk deliberately kept this information out of the paper (as was once alleged), or for other reasons, the *Tribune* leaves much to be desired in supplying such news.

The unwary researcher, seeking information about ships' clearances, should be cautioned that there were two islands named St. Thomas; one was a Danish possession in the West Indies, and the other was a Portuguese island in the Bight of Biafra.

Caution is also needed in other matters connected with sources. One of them relates to spurious "inside" accounts of the slave trade. Apparently there was enough interest in the trade to make production of such accounts a worthwhile enterprise. G. F. Dow, *Slave Ships and Slaving* (Salem: Marine Research Society, 1927), reprints excerpts from Captain Drake's "Revelations of a Slave Smuggler," almost certainly spurious, and from two other accounts of unproven authenticity: "Six Months on a Slaver" and "The Last Voyage of an American Slaver." *Adventures of an African Slaver,* the supposed memoirs of Captain Theodore Canot, is likewise of dubious validity despite its publication in many editions. But these works, whether authentic or not, have little to say about American lawbreaking in general or about the government's efforts to suppress the slave trade.

Of more importance is "A Slave-Trader's Letter Book," published in the *North American Review* for October, 1886. The letter book is supposed to be that of C. A. L. Lamar, and is full of details of his schemes to introduce Africans into the United States, legally or otherwise. It has been accepted as authentic and quoted by later writers, yet there is good reason to doubt its genuineness. The *North American Review* claimed that the letter book was saved at the last moment from being turned into pulp in a New England paper mill, but this explanation seems flimsy. It does not say where the book was between 1864 and 1886, or how it found its way north, or who rescued it from the paper mill. Neither does it offer satisfaction regarding the reasons for Lamar's keeping such highly incriminating correspondence in his possession. The letter book came to light only when a kinsman of Lamar's, L. Q. C. Lamar, had been appointed secretary of the interior by the *Review*'s political enemies, and the magazine carefully linked the two Lamars together in its comments. It is also curious that the letter book was published just before the election of 1886, in which the Republicans once more attempted to "wave the bloody shirt" and denounce the Democrats as a party of slavery and secession. Furthermore, the *Review* was noted for publishing literary hoaxes.

The letters themselves raise further suspicions. They contain nothing about the *E. A. Rawlins* and the *Wanderer* which had not appeared in newspaper accounts. None of the letters solves the mystery of the *E. A. Rawlins'* first voyage to Africa. Lamar, a shrewd criminal, could hardly have seriously contemplated arming a steamer and sending it off to fight American and British cruisers. If nothing else, it would have been difficult for him to obtain the cannon. Many of the individuals named in the letters were unquestionably engaged in the slave trade, but anyone well acquainted with the history of the trade could have written up any of the actions described for the *Review*. If the letters are a hoax, they are a well-done hoax, but this does not increase their reliability. This questionable document adds nothing of value to other source materials.

OTHER PRINTED WORKS

Official Opinions of the Attorneys General of the United States. Vols. III–V. Washington: Robert Farnham, 1852.
United States Statutes at Large. Vols. I–III, XII. Boston: Little, Brown, 1845–1866.

DuBois, W. E. B. *The Suppression of the African Slave Trade to the United States of America.* New York: Longmans, Green, 1896.

Lloyd, Christopher. *The Navy and the Slave Trade.* London: Longmans, Green, 1949.

Mathieson, William L. *Great Britain and the Slave Trade, 1839–1865.* London: Longmans, Green, 1929.

Soulsby, Hugh G. *The Right of Search and the Slave Trade in Anglo-American Relations, 1814–1862.* Baltimore: Johns Hopkins Press, 1933.

Wish, Harvey. "The Revival of the African Slave Trade in the United States, 1856–1860," *Mississippi Valley Historical Review,* XXVII (1940–41), 569–588.

CONGRESSIONAL DOCUMENTS

Malpractices Imputed to the American Consul at Havana. 26th Cong., 2d sess., Jan. 20, 1841, S. Exec. Doc. 125. Valuable correspondence received from the British government dealing both with Trist and with abuse of the American flag.

Message . . . in Relation to Seizures or Search of American Vessels, &c. 26th Cong., 2d sess., March 3, 1841, H. Exec. Doc. 115. Includes material exchanged between the British and American governments, Trist's correspondence with the State Department, and Everett's report.

Message . . . in Relation to the Seizure of American Vessels . . . and Also Correspondence with Consul Trist. 27th Cong., 1st sess., July 14, 1841, H. Exec. Doc. 34. Includes parts of Trist's dispatches deleted from preceding document.

Report of . . . the Committee on Commerce . . . on the Subject of African Colonization, and the Commerce, etc., of Western Africa, Together with All the Diplomatic Correspondence . . . on the Subject of the African Slave Trade. 27th Cong., 3d sess., Feb. 28, 1843, H. Rep. 283. A vast collection of source materials, including much duplication of earlier documents.

Message . . . in Relation to the Abuse of the Flag of the United States. . . . 28th Cong., 1st sess., March 21, 1844, S. Exec. Doc. 217. A brief document including British reports on American slavers in 1842–1843, and some of Consul Slacum's dispatches.

Message . . . Transmitting Copies of Dispatches from the American Minister at the Court of Brazil, Relative to the Slave-Trade, &c. 28th Cong., 2d sess., Feb. 20, 1845, H. Exec. Doc. 148. This is the celebrated document giving Wise's findings on American and British participation in the trade.

Message . . . Communicating Information Relative to . . . the United States Squadron on the West Coast of Africa. . . . 28th Cong., 2d sess., Feb. 28, 1845, S. Exec. Doc. 150. Includes Commodore Perry's dispatches, and a great mass of information on Liberia.

Message . . . Transmitting So Much of George W. Slacum's Correspondence, As Was Not Published by the Senate in March 1844. 29th Cong., 1st sess., Dec., 1845, H. Exec. Doc. 43. Despite its title, this document duplicates part of S. Exec. Doc. 217, 28th Cong., 1st sess.

Message . . . Communicating . . . the Correspondence of Mr. Wise . . . in Relation to the Slave Trade. 30th Cong., 1st sess., March 3, 1848, S. Exec. Doc. 28. Valuable continuation of H. Exec. Doc. 148, 28th Cong., 2d sess.

Message . . . Transmitting . . . the Correspondence of George W. Gordon and Gorham Parks . . . on the Subject of the African Slave Trade. 30th Cong., 2d sess., March 2, 1849, H. Exec. Doc. 61. This very valuable document contains no dispatches from Gordon, but several useful dispatches from Wise which were not previously printed.

Message . . . Transmitting Information in Reference to the African Squadron. 31st Cong., 1st sess., July 22, 1850, H. Exec. Doc. 73. A brief document listing vessels assigned to the squadron, the deaths that occurred, and, incompletely, the prizes taken by it.

Message . . . Communicating . . . Documents Relating to the African Slave Trade. 31st Cong., 2d sess., Dec. 18, 1850, S. Exec. Doc. 6. Includes the valuable dispatches of Minister Tod, and lists American vessels trading between Rio and Africa, 1844–1849. The statement that all but five of these vessels became slavers should not be accepted, for many were only auxiliaries.

Message . . . Communicating . . . the Correspondence between Mr. Schenck . . . and the Secretary of State, in Relation to the African Slave Trade. 33d Cong., 1st sess., March 14, 1854, S. Exec. Doc. 47. This relates chiefly to the *Camargo.*

Report . . . in Compliance with a Resolution . . . Calling for Information Relative to the Coolie Trade. 34th Cong., 1st sess., Aug.

5, 1856, S. Exec. Doc. 99. Reprints (pp. 27 ff.) information supplied in May, 1856, to the House on the Cuban slave and coolie trades. Contains much useful information.

Message . . . in Relation to the African Slave Trade. 35th Cong., 1st sess., April 23, 1858, S. Exec. Doc. 49. Reprints naval and diplomatic correspondence covering the Cuban trade of 1856–1857.

Message . . . in Answer to a Resolution . . . Calling for a Copy of All Instructions Given to . . . Our African Squadron. . . . . 35th Cong., 2d sess., March 1, 1859, H. Exec. Doc. 104. This includes instructions to all commanders from Perry through Conover, and a list of captures made by the squadron.

Report . . . on the Number of Persons Belonging to the African Squadron Who Have Died. 36th Cong., 1st sess., April 24, 1860, H. Exec. Doc. 73. This very brief statement makes no comparisons with other squadrons. The *Annual Report of the Secretary of the Navy* included statements by the fleet surgeon each year on the health of all squadrons; these reveal the squadron to have had good health.

Message . . . in Reference to the African Slave Trade. 36th Cong., 2d sess., Dec. 6, 1860, H. Exec. Doc. 7. This bulky and very valuable mass of correspondence covers the period 1855–1860, and in part duplicates S. Exec. Doc. 49, 35th Cong., 1st sess. Note particularly (pp. 625–631) the only official attempt at a complete listing of vessels libeled. The list is incomplete.

Letter . . . in Relation to the Slave Vessel the "Bark Augusta." 37th Cong., 2d sess., April 4, 1862, S. Exec. Doc. 40. Reprints the investigation of the escape of the *Augusta.*

Letter . . . in Answer to Resolutions . . . Calling for Information in Relation to Persons Who Have Been Arrested in the Southern District of New York. . . . . 37th Cong., 2d sess., May 30, 1862, S. Exec. Doc. 53. Contains lists of persons arrested and vessels bonded, and describes the disposition of their cases Although the lists are cryptic, incomplete, and inaccurate, they are an invaluable aid in tracking down newspaper accounts of prosecutions.

Message . . . Communicating . . . Information in Regard to the African Slave Trade. 38th Cong., 1st sess., July 2, 1864, S. Exec. Doc. 56. Reprints some correspondence, chiefly diplomatic, for 1861–1864. Seriously incomplete.

INDEX

INDEX

Abbot Devereux, 246

Abranches, Innocencio A. de, 53–54

Act of April 20, 1818: provisions of, 26–27; rulings on, 155–161, 185, 273 n. 3; criminal prosecutions under, 224–235 *passim;* Supreme Court on, 272 n. 57. See also *United States v. Gooding*

Act of December 31, 1792, and foreign ownership of American-registered vessels, 20. See also *Wyoming*

Act of March 2, 1807, 3; repealed in part by act of 1818, 160; sections of, remaining in force, 304 n. 6. See also *Alice Rogers; Mystic Valley*

Act of March 3, 1819, provisions of, 98, 289 n. 7

Act of March 3, 1847: provisions of, 172–173; used by slave traders, 173–176

Act of March 22, 1794: provisions of, 25, 27; ruling on, 158; prosecutions under, 158–159, 228

Act of May 10, 1800: provisions of, 25, 27; rulings on, 161–164; and foreigners in foreign vessels, 199; criminal prosecutions under, 224–235 *passim;* and American regis-try, 277 n. 27; and Spanish-owned slavers, 277 n. 27; and tenders, 291 n. 4

Act of May 15, 1820: provisions of, 26, 192–193; declared constitutional, 144; prosecutions under, 192–205, 224–235 *passim;* rulings on, 200, 203, 300 n. 11, 310 n. 5; viewed as too severe, 309 n. 5

Adams, Charles Francis, 60

Adams Gray, 54, 253, 261

Advance, 51, 73, 216

Africa and the American Flag, 10, 48–49

African squadron: purpose of, 41; size of, 41; dislike of duty in, 41–42, 133, 280 n. 39; supply depot for, 42, 48, 59; ineffectiveness of, 43; proposal to abolish, 48–49; discontinued, 59; captures slavers, 70–72, 135, 137–138; uses British colors, 74; and fear of damage suits, 105–108; cruises of, 130–131, 135; and Flag Officers Conover and Inman, 131–138; vessels arrested by, 214–222 *passim;* types of warships in, 239–240, 279 n. 36; health of, 280 n. 39; condition of vessels in, 291 n. 2

Agnes, 243